THE WIND IN
MY HAIR

THE WIND IN MY HAIR

✤

My Fight for Freedom in Modern Iran

✤

MASIH ALINEJAD
WITH KAMBIZ FOROOHAR

Little, Brown and Company

New York Boston London

Little, Brown and Company
Hachette Book Group
1290 Avenue of the Americas, New York, NY 10104
littlebrown.com

First Edition: May 2018

Little, Brown and Company is a division of Hachette Book Group, Inc. The Little, Brown name and logo are trademarks of Hachette Book Group, Inc.

The publisher is not responsible for websites (or their content) that are not owned by the publisher.

The Hachette Speakers Bureau provides a wide range of authors for speaking events. To find out more, go to hachettespeakersbureau.com or call (866) 376-6591.

ISBN 978-0-316-54891-5
LCCN 2017959142

10 9 8 7 6 5 4 3 2 1

LSC-C

Printed in the United States of America

*To the brave women of the My Stealthy Freedom
and White Wednesdays campaigns*

CHAPTER ONE

It was pitch-black. Actually, blacker than black, if such a thing is possible. A blackness that extended forever and pulsed like a living being that could reach out and swallow you whole. On this warm summer night, it seemed as if even the moon and the stars had abandoned me. I stared into the night and the darkness stared back. If you let your fear win, the darkness can devour you, I told myself. "Don't be afraid," I said quietly, over and over, like a mantra.

From behind me a faint sound of scraping and shuffling got louder and louder.

"Wait. . . . Wait for me," my brother Ali whispered as he caught up with me. "I lost one of my slippers." His voice trailed off. "Look, I've brought the lantern."

I was tempted to say that I didn't need it. But the dim glow was comforting. I reached back and grabbed the lantern from Ali and lifted it high above my head so that there was a globe of light around us. Though Ali was two years older than me, right now I was in charge, because he was afraid of the dark. We started walking. The end of the backyard was still about fifty yards away.

Ten minutes earlier, I was with the rest of my family—Mother and Father, my three brothers, and my sister—blissfully sleeping on the floor in the big room. Hard to believe but I was in the backyard because of Ali's weak bladder. At thirteen, he'd started wetting his bed. "It's just a phase," I had overheard Mother explain to our father, or, as we called him, AghaJan, which means "dear sir" in Persian. AghaJan merely grunted, but I could see that he was troubled.

Sometimes Ali wet the bed in his sleep. Other times, he'd wake up in the middle of the night with a great urge to pee, but we didn't have an indoor toilet, so he faced the long trek in the dark to the outhouse at the end of the backyard. He tried to steel himself to hang on till dawn, when there was enough light for him to feel brave. But no matter how much he tossed and turned, no matter how much he prayed to all the saints to give him endurance, he couldn't hold on. Ali was too old to be scared of the dark, AghaJan used to say, without too much sympathy. I was never afraid of the dark, and you can imagine how humiliating it was for Ali to wake me up so that I could walk with him to the outhouse. He didn't have to worry about waking our parents with his tossing and turning; AghaJan snored—the noise was like the sound of the tractor that he used to till the land.

"Wake up.... I need to go.... Wake up.... Wake up...."

I shrugged and rolled over, but he wasn't to be deterred.

"Get up.... I need to pee," Ali said with greater urgency, shaking my shoulder.

"Okay... okay... I'm awake," I said eventually.

A few weeks earlier, when he first started going through this phase, Ali was too embarrassed to wake me, and in the morning, there were the telltale signs. He'd rush outside as soon as he woke, but Mother discovered the wet stains when she rolled the bed up. She'd pretend that the wet patch and the stains were due to some household accident; often she blamed a leaking tea thermos, to save him from embarrassment.

"Someone must have knocked over the thermos," she'd say loudly, with a smile.

"Who drinks tea in bed at night?" I'd ask mischievously. "Isn't it strange how all the tea spills happen on his futon," I'd say with a laugh.

Maybe he wanted to pay me back, because tonight Ali was determined to get me up.

"Please, I need to go," he begged. "I'm getting desperate."

"Okay...okay, just hurry up," I mumbled as I rolled out of bed. "I am having a good dream and want to get back to it."

In the backyard, even with a lantern in my hand, the distance to the outhouse looked pretty daunting. The warm air was dense with the summery whiff of crushed grass and a hint of burnt charcoal. Under the veranda, dozens of chickens were huddled, fast asleep. I wished I was back in my warm bed, but Ali's eyes were fixed on the structure at the far end of the yard.

"Let's go," I said wearily. I wanted to get back to my beautiful dream.

We shuffled forward sleepily.

During the daylight hours, Ali was like other teenagers—fearless, boastful, and rebellious, part of a gang of boys who, when they tired of wrestling each other to the ground, took turns riding their rickety bicycles and then went for a swim in the Kolahrood (Kolah River). I used to think Ali was different. He read constantly, and he liked to recount stories in a colorful and dramatic style. But during the hot summer months I hardly saw him. From breakfast till dinner he was out and about, roaming the narrow dirt roads of our village. He'd come back dirty and stinking of sweat, his face red from hours of playing in the sun. Mother would drag him to the barn, where we kept our two cows, and would hose him down roughly with cold water before he was allowed inside the house. It was the same hose that she used to wash the cows.

Ali never took me with him no matter how much I begged him. I desperately wanted to run around the fields and ride a bicycle and jump in the river.

This was not possible, he said.

"No girls are allowed. The other boys would laugh at me." He looked sheepish when he said this. "Be reasonable. Even if I wanted to, AghaJan wouldn't allow it."

"It's not allowed."

"It's not permissible."

"Girls can't do that."

I wasn't asking for much, but every time I wanted to do something that the boys were already doing, I heard the same refrain. I was eleven and I was tired of hearing it: "You can't do that." Even now, the phrase "You can't do that" is like waving a red rag at a bull. It gets my blood boiling.

AghaJan expected girls to stay indoors and out of sight. He wasn't alone in his thinking. No other girls were allowed to run around and play outside the house. Boys had freedom and girls were kept indoors. It seemed so unfair.

"Go on inside. I'll count to twenty and then I'm heading back," I whispered to Ali as I yawned. "If we don't hurry back I'll forget my dream."

"Don't go," Ali said meekly. He took the lantern and gingerly opened the door to the outhouse, a narrow stand-alone room, as if half expecting a mouse or a snake to dart out. It was not unusual to find a grass snake inside, but as they were not poisonous I didn't mind them. Ali waved the lantern inside a few times before stepping in.

Inside, it was a typical Iranian-style toilet—basically a large hole in the ground. Even in the daytime, going to that toilet was a scary experience. I used to worry that one day I would fall in and sink deep into the fetid muck.

Once a year, AghaJan would spend half a day digging a hole twice his own height. Climbing out, he was always coated in sludge and grime. He'd cover the opening with wood and stone, leaving only a hole. Months later, when the hole was almost full, AghaJan would tie a scarf around his nose and mouth and spend a day emptying the foul-smelling contents to use later for fertilizer. The stench was stomach-churning.

Without the lantern, I was once again enveloped in darkness. The yips and howls of coyotes, the croaks of frogs, the strumming of beetles, the clicking of cicadas, and the ever-present rustling sounds from the undergrowth were like a symphony providing the background music of my early life. I once spent an afternoon sitting in the fields to record the chirps and clicks of insects. When I told Ali, he cracked up as if this was the funniest thing he'd ever heard. But some of *his* ideas were so outlandish that they made me laugh out loud. Like when he said he was going to be so rich he'd build himself a house with the toilet inside it.

"You mean a toilet right next to your bedroom?" This truly *was* the funniest thing I had ever heard. "You don't mean you want a toilet inside the house? Next to where you eat?" I laughed so much that tears flowed down my cheeks.

I wasn't afraid of the dark, but I was petrified of falling into that pit.

My mother used to say that the darkness is a monster, a shapeless black demon that feeds on your fear. If you are scared of it, then the shadow grows bigger and it will envelop you and swallow you whole.

"Open your eyes wide, as wide as possible," she'd urge me when I was a young girl. "Stare into the darkness and the shadows will disappear. Never be afraid of the darkness, but stare it down."

So, from early on, whenever I faced something scary, instead of running away or turning my back to it, I'd force my eyes wide-open and meet it head-on.

"Are you done yet? Still in there?" I kicked the door gently. I was getting tired of keeping my eyes wide-open and wanted to go back to bed.

Ali came out fidgeting with his trousers and handed me the lantern.

"Let's go back now." He sounded relieved. Once again, I led the way.

This was my chance to ask for a favor in return. I wanted to run around with the boys and learn how to ride a bicycle.

"In the morning, can you take me with you? It's not fair that I've got to stay indoors while you get to run around."

"I can't. AghaJan won't like it."

"Then stay home and play with me. We can build a house together or...you can teach me to ride. AghaJan's old bicycle is in the barn."

"Okay. I promise," he said breezily as we entered the house.

The next morning, after breakfast, Ali rushed out to meet his gang and left me behind by myself.

I'm the proud daughter of Ghomikola, the capital of the world. That's how I introduced myself whenever someone asked about my origins. I'd wait a beat or two before breaking into a big grin to let them know that I was joking. Ghomikola is the capital of my world, but it's not even a dot on a map of Iran. I was born and raised, like the rest of my family, in Ghomikola, a lush village in the province of Mazandaran, in northern Iran. I couldn't imagine a better place anywhere else in the world. It was only after I became a teenager that I realized how tiny Ghomikola really was.

Mazandaranis, or Mazanis, as the people are affectionately called, are proud of their long history of independence, which predates Islam. We have our own dialect, Mazani or Tabari, and nothing gives me more pleasure, now that I live in the West, than to find a fellow Mazani and speak in my local tongue. The sandy beaches of the Caspian Sea, the world's largest inland sea, form our northern borders. To the south, the rugged, snowcapped Alborz range and Mount Damavand, the highest peak in Iran, a sight known to all Iranian children, stretch to reach the sky. There may be as many as two hundred rivers, streams, and brooks in the province.

The region's roots go back at least three thousand years, and it was only in the early twentieth century that major roads were constructed linking Mazandaran and the neighboring Gilan Province to the southern regions. These two provinces are known as the Shomal, meaning "the north" in Persian, and for most Iranians it's the same as what the Riviera means to the French or what the Hamptons signify to New Yorkers. Thousands of Iranians flock to the mountains or the shores of the Caspian for vacation and to get away from the polluted air of Tehran.

In between the mountains and the sea, forests, orchards, and farm-lands make the area one of the greenest spots in Iran. For me, this was as close to paradise as you could get. I guess that's where my love of trees comes from. As a young girl, I used to sneak into our neighbor's garden and climb their trees to pick pears and walnuts; in our garden we grew oranges and green plums and had a lone pome-granate tree. Climbing trees was one of my favorite pastimes, always going higher and higher, leaving my brothers and friends behind, much to the chagrin of my mother, who complained that clambering up trees was not for girls. But I couldn't help it. Even today, when-ever I see a fruit tree my first impulse is to scramble to the very top branches. I've climbed a plum tree outside the Vatican (it was a dark night) and inched my way up a pear tree in London in cowboy boots, as my husband, Kambiz, nervously kept watch on each occasion.

There is more to the north than just trees. Even in Iran, a land with three millennia of history, the Shomal is a magical place of legends. Mazandaran resisted the Arab invasion that brought Islam to Iran around the 640s and maintained a Zoroastrian majority for nearly five hundred years—thanks to its independent-minded population—until around the twelfth century.

In the Shahnameh, or Book of Kings, the Persian national epic poem, which describes Iran's long pre-Islamic history, Mazandaran is an area mostly inhabited by Divs, or demons. In the book, Rostam, the legendary hero of Iran, brawny and powerful just like Hercules, has to make the arduous journey to the region to battle and kill the White Div, the biggest and meanest of the mythical monsters.

All the demons were gone by the time I was born.

About 100 families or so live in Ghomikola, and it hasn't changed much over the years—it is a small and intimate place of 650 people where everyone knows everyone else and there are no secrets. When I was growing up, it seemed as if half the village was made up of my aunts, uncles, and cousins.

The unpaved lanes crisscrossing Ghomikola are narrow and

filled with tall trees that have thick branches and provide cool shade in the summer. Houses have gabled roofs, typical of the north, and high walls to provide privacy. Historically, our village was made up of two neighborhoods—Upper Ghomikola, where the wealthier families lived, and the humbler Lower Ghomikola, where the rest of us lived, in unpretentious homes made out of clay and mud mixed with straw, and with unvarnished wooden pillars. Our house had a wooden terrace all the way around, with a courtyard in front and a backyard where my mother grew vegetables, in a garden set behind a brick wall. Like most families, we had a small barn in the courtyard, where we kept our cows.

Up until the 1960s, Ghomikola was owned by an absentee landlord and most folks were either sharecroppers or day laborers. In fact, in those days, most villagers were like serfs, working for the big landlord. Only a few had their own plot of land.

One sign of wealth and social mobility was the metal gate—if you had one, it meant you had money. Life was simple in the village, and whenever a family replaced their wooden gate with a metal one they handed out sweets and local delicacies—cooked broad beans dusted with a spice called golpar—as the men labored. The women would chant: "Let there be blessings on this house, / Let this gate be a token of better things to come."

Until I became a teenager, we had a wooden gate. In fact, we were one of the last families to upgrade. I like to think it was because I kept badgering AghaJan to get a red gate, since that is my favorite color. But AghaJan remained firm in resisting the tide.

"I don't have money to waste," he'd say gruffly whenever I approached him on the topic. "Our door is good enough to keep the wolves at bay."

There were hardly any stray dogs in Ghomikola, let alone wolves, but AghaJan used to say he worked too hard for his money to waste it on what he considered to be frivolous matters. Then, one day, I returned from middle school and saw a brand-new gate. It was blue.

"I paid for it, I get to pick the color," AghaJan said.

Upper and Lower Ghomikola came together around the ceme- tery and the village's two stores across from it. The grocery store, run by Mamadali Dekondar, sold everything from eggs, milk, and fruit to pencils, notepads, and shampoos. We grew our own food, including grains to bake bread, and the animals we kept gave us eggs and milk. We bartered with other families for the food we couldn't produce ourselves. The other store was the village Cooper- ative, which had everything from bolts of cloth to color TVs and gas cookers.

I remember, one year, all everyone was talking about was the new technological marvel that the Coop was offering: a ceiling fan. We had one table fan, with its distinctive white blades that whirred mightily to fight off the humidity and heat of the summer. At night, as the humidity levels climbed higher and higher, my brothers and I would always squabble to see who got to sit closest to the fan. Now, a fan that was attached to the ceiling changed everything and of- fered a chance to end all our bickering. The whole family trooped off to the Coop one afternoon and gawked at the blades going around and around above our heads. AghaJan stared for a long time, watching them rotate, before declaring that the contraption was too dangerous—if the fan ever came loose the blades could decapitate the whole family.

"Imagine if it fell during the night. With one blow, it'd chop off our heads," he said.

I don't think safety was his main concern. As usual, we didn't have enough money to afford such luxuries. We left the Coop empty-handed, but for weeks Ali and I would plead with Mother to take us back so we could stand under the fan and dream of owning it one day.

Money was always tight.

It's fair to say that I grew up as far away from the country's elites as possible. Both my grandfathers were poor sharecroppers who became destitute and died young. One fell ill and died, and the other was killed by a wild animal. I only learned their stories from my grandmothers. AghaJan's father, Hassan, lost his job as a day laborer and had to beg for food to feed his family. He'd look for work, but at the end of the day, he'd be forced to knock on doors and collect leftovers such as pieces of stale bread and day-old rice. After a short illness, Hassan died, leaving a wife and three children. My father at age fourteen became the breadwinner of the family. He didn't want to be a sharecropper, so to make money he became a street peddler and sold fruit and vegetables on street corners. AghaJan never forgot what it was like to be destitute. Whenever a beggar knocked on our door, AghaJan welcomed him with a warm smile and filled his basket with the same food that we ourselves ate. "Always be kind to the less fortunate," AghaJan used to say.

I grew up with two wonderful storytellers, AghaJan's mother, Naneh, and my own mother, Zarrin, which means "golden." My mother never had any formal education, but she had the gift of poetry and composed poems and sonnets in the Mazani dialect about life in the village and working in the rice fields. She was famous in the village for her poems. She and Naneh spun stories that sent my imagination wandering off beyond the green fields and orchards surrounding our home.

I like to think we are all, to some degree, reflections of our parents and grandparents, and for this reason, I believe my penchant for writing and public advocacy is a gift from my mother. As for my stubborn nature and quick temper, well, that's all on me.

From Naneh, I learned how to cope with hardship and to beware of the fickleness of fortune. Naneh had already moved in with us when I was born. Of course, Naneh wasn't her real name, but it was what I called her as a toddler, and for me the name stuck. She was frail but tough in spirit. She had become a widow in her twenties, with three children to look after. I often wondered why she never remarried. A light had gone out in her heart.

"You live once, you marry once, and you die once. You go to your husband's house in a white dress and leave in a white shroud," she told me as her spindly hands held my arm. She had lost her eyesight by then and relied on me to guide her on her walks around the garden. "A good mother stays with her kids and raises them."

That barb was aimed at my other grandmother, Beebee. Like Naneh, Beebee also came from a poor family. She married a sharecropper, who was allotted a small piece of land far in the wilderness in return for clearing the area of brush and weeds to make it suitable for farming. He was all alone when he was attacked and killed by a wild boar. Today, people brought up in the cities don't really have an understanding of the abject poverty that existed in the Iranian countryside at the time.

The lesson for Beebee was that life was brutish and short. She was in her twenties but already had become a widow, with two small children, my mother, Zarrin, then only nine, and her brother, Hassan, who was four. Beebee wanted to remarry, but found no suitor willing to raise another man's children. So Beebee abandoned her children to the care of her aunt and found a new husband. My mother's childhood was anything but golden—even when her father was alive, they barely could make ends meet. But Zarrin's life took a turn for the worse when her mother left her with her great-aunt Ameh Geda ("Pauper Auntie" in Persian). It was a nickname but there was truth to it—Ameh Geda lived in a decrepit shack, where everything was old and dirty. She sometimes went to Babol, the nearest city, to be a housecleaner, but more often she begged for food and money on the street.

Zarrin loved Ameh Geda as if she were her real mother, but she never forgave Beebee for abandoning her.

I often wonder about the choices I'd have made if I had found myself in my grandmothers' shoes. Would I have sought my own happiness, or sacrificed myself for my kids? Beebee and Naneh were like the two angels said to sit on each person's shoulders, the first urging me to take a chance and fly and the latter urging me to keep my feet on the ground.

When AghaJan was twenty-four, his family went to see Ameh Geda and asked for Zarrin's hand. She was only fourteen and had no say in the matter. Her dowry was the tiny plot of land that her father had left her, and they got married. The land alone wasn't large enough for them to grow rice or other crops to make a living, and both my parents had to find other ways to supplement their income. Having experienced a tough life, AghaJan was determined that all his children would receive an education and never go hungry at night.

Unlike the other men in the village, AghaJan was quite tall and had an athletic build, with strong, broad shoulders. Even now, in his seventies, he is in far better shape than his friends. That's probably because he always had to work hard. He planted trees and grew rice, and sold eggs and chickens and geese on the streets of Babol. He is still an expert tree grafter, often called to graft orange and lemon trees.

When he was younger, AghaJan would tie a boxful of chickens and eggs to the back of his bicycle and pedal ten miles on dirt roads and back alleys to Babol. When it rained, the dirt roads turned to mud and were unusable. That didn't deter AghaJan. He carried the bicycle, with the boxful of chickens still attached, on his shoulders along muddy roads until he reached the main highway, an asphalt road. Years later, he bought a moped to get around faster and sell more chickens and eggs.

For a long time, I associated AghaJan with the smell of chickens, sweat, and fertilizer. He had a fierce temper, and when he became angry, it was like a volcano exploding. But he was always sweet with my mother.

She had soft, cream-colored skin; gentle, plump hands; and kind, smiling eyes. She never applied any moisturizer or wore makeup, not even lipstick. Her piercing brown eyes could see right through me, especially when I was up to some mischief, which was quite often. My tricks and evasions never worked with her. She had long, light-brown hair, soft as silk, but we rarely saw it, as it was mostly covered up. Her head scarf was a part of her identity and she never took it off, not even for sleeping. I never thought that was unusual, since everyone in my family did the same.

Mother raised all of her children on her back. After each of us was a few weeks old, she'd wrap us in swaths of cloth, put us on her back, and head to our plot of land to work alongside AghaJan. In the village, everyone had to work. Mother wasn't the type to sit back and relax; she was always up and about, never hesitating to roll up her trousers and get involved with rice planting and harvesting. She had her own vegetable patch, where she planted mint, basil, and parsley alongside tomatoes and cucumbers. She made regular treks to Babol to sell her herbs and vegetables in the market. We churned our own butter and made yogurt. Mother was great at making vats of tomato paste and pomegranate puree, both of which she used for cooking special dishes.

She almost always wore a flowery patterned tunic and baggy trousers, with a woolen cardigan and flowery head scarf. When she was going to Babol she put on a black chador, a large piece of cloth worn wrapped around the head and the body. It even covered the ankles, though it left the face exposed. It had no zippers or buttons or hooks. You gripped it tight with your hand under the chin.

She was twenty-eight when she had me, the last of her six children.

I was born at home on a hot September afternoon with just a village midwife and my sister Mina helping my mother to bring me into this world. Having a doctor come to our house cost almost the same as going to the hospital, and it was money that we didn't have. All my brothers and sisters were born at home with the same midwife. I joined Mina and, along with Ali, two other brothers, Mohsen and Hamid. My other sister, Mehri, died when she was a year or so old.

I truly think the earliest years of my life were spent in paradise. My father was severe but kind, my mother cooked delicious meals and doted on me, and we all spoke Mazani. I ran around the yard, picked apples and pears for my mother, and sometimes tended our cows. I didn't learn to speak Persian until I went to school.

My parents named me Masoumeh (meaning "innocent"), after Fatima Masoumeh, the sister of Ali ibn Musa al-Rida, better known as

Imam Reza. The eighth saint of Shia Islam, she was poisoned on her way to Mashhad, in northeast Iran. Most Iranians belong to Shia Islam. Legend has it that Fatima was traveling to Mashhad to visit her brother when her caravan was attacked by bandits. The details are sketchy, but she was killed and buried in the tiny village of Qom, on the edge of the desert. Eventually a shrine was built, dedicated to Fatima, which helped Qom to prosper and become the intellectual capital of Shiism in Iran, attracting thousands of seminarians. Even today, hundreds of thousands of pilgrims travel to Qom to honor Fatima Masoumeh. Perhaps my parents hoped I would be religious, endowed with some of her attributes, when they picked my name.

Truth be told, I didn't look like the rest of my family. I was thin and dark-featured, as if I had been left in the sun for too long, and as for my hair...coils of thick, snarling curls. The rest of the family had light skin and soft, straight hair. I was constantly teased by other children, who said that I had been adopted. I would stare at my reflection in the mirror and look at Ali and Mother to see if I could detect any resemblance.

I plucked up my courage one day and asked Mother, "Why don't I look like you? I have curly hair. I look darker than you."

It was a serious question. I wanted reassurance. I feared that maybe the other children were right and my real parents had abandoned me. I looked at Mother expectantly.

"Your real parents are dead. They were killed in the war," she said calmly as she stirred the boiling pot of rice. She was referring to the war following Iraq's invasion of Iran in 1980. "We were going to tell you the truth when you got older. You are really from the South."

"I knew it," I said. "My real parents wouldn't abandon me."

In my mind, everything made sense. But this meant that Ali was no longer my brother and Mina was not my sister. I felt very lonely and sad. I started crying.

"What were my real parents like? Did they love me?" I said between sobs.

I continued asking serious questions about my parents, but

Mother couldn't keep a straight face and laughed quite a lot, even though she tried hard to show concern. Eventually I ran away from her in tears. That night, I refused to eat and kept sobbing. Finally, she came and held me tight.

"I was only joking," she said. "You are my very own Masoumeh."

I was so relieved my parents were alive that I forgot that she had played a trick on me.

My eldest brother, Mohsen, was fifteen years older than me, and he was like a second father to Ali and me. He was tall and thin and his head was always in a book, usually one about history. He was the first person in our family to go to high school in Babol and the first to obtain a university degree. Mohsen joined the army to fight in the war between Iran and Iraq, which lasted eight horrible, miserable years, until 1988. He made friends easily, and they all played with me when he brought them around. One of his friends, Omid, was from Babol and spoke proper Persian, whereas the rest of us spoke a dialect of Mazani and Persian. I liked Omid—he would turn me upside down and swing me around by my legs.

Mohsen, Omid, and three other friends, Ramzoon, Abbas, and Eissa, all went to the front to fight the Iraqis together. Ramzoon, who later married my sister Mina, was wounded by shrapnel. Mohsen was also injured after eighteen months at the front. Abbas lost his legs. Eissa was captured by the Iraqis. His family gave him up for dead and held a funeral service. But in the 1990s, released in a prisoner exchange, he returned to Babol, looking gaunt and acting a bit strange. His mind was damaged by the years of captivity. As for Omid, who used to tickle me and play with me, he was killed. More than 250,000 men didn't return home from the battlefield and another half million returned shattered.

My sister Mina was the real beauty in the family, with gorgeous hair and delicate features. She was devout and always wore a hijab (a veil or head scarf), even indoors with the family. Whenever she left the house, she wore her head scarf and a chador. I rarely saw Mina's hair, which reached down to her waist. She was always praying and fasting during the holy month of Ramadan, and going to the mosque for special Quran study programs. Both my parents loved Mina's religious fervor. Every weekend, Mina walked forty-five minutes to the next village, Noushiravankola, and took a bus to Babol so she could attend the special Friday prayers.

My middle brother, Hamid, the shortest of the boys in the family, was always trying to be the bridge builder. He was the brainiest of the lot and was accepted at Sharif University, considered the Harvard of Iran, where he studied chemistry. Mohsen studied history at Ferdowsi University of Mashhad.

"The country needs engineers and historians," AghaJan told anyone who'd listen. He was proud of his sons. "My sons are at the best colleges in the country, not bad for a poor peasant who can't read or write."

After graduation, Hamid also enlisted to fight in the war. From basic training, he was sent straight to the front, where his unit was shelled with mustard gas and sarin. He spent months in the hospital and returned listed as partially disabled. The war continued. Even AghaJan volunteered to go to the front, at age forty-seven. It was 1988, and after suffering a massive military setback, the Iranian government called for more volunteers. It was his religious duty, AghaJan said as he packed his bag. Mohsen also reenlisted. Mother looked after the farm, milked our cow, and made sure nothing was amiss, even as she worried that her son and husband could be killed. The war ended soon after, and both returned unharmed.

The villagers called me Zari Khayat Kija, which in Mazani means "daughter of Zari the tailor." My mother was the only tailor in the village, and women from Ghomikola and neighboring villages would trek to our house carrying bolts of cloth for her to turn into dresses, shirts, and jackets. I would sneak in sometimes to watch Mother talk to her customers in her soft Mazani dialect to put them at ease as she measured their waists, arms, and chests. Sometimes she'd call out the measurements to me to jot down on a notepad.

Mother also offered sewing classes once in a while, and when she did, women and teenage girls flocked to our house. We slept in one room, which left our other room free for Mother's class. It would fill with women's voices and then the whirring sound of sewing machines, and all the while my mother issued instructions. I'd watch in awe as all these women treated my mother with so much respect. For Mother, this was not a hobby. We needed the extra income, since the plot of land didn't generate enough cash for us. My parents in their own ways were entrepreneurial—not that they knew what that meant. AghaJan sold chickens, ducks, geese, and their eggs on street corners, and Mother sewed and gave sewing lessons. Mother was unique in one other way: She earned her own money rather than relying on AghaJan. Every time they called me Zari Khayat Kija it made me proud.

One of the earliest photos of myself that I can find was taken when I had just turned seven. I have the biggest and goofiest smile in the world, because I'm wearing new clothes that Mother had made for me. For me, owning and wearing a new skirt or dress was better than living in a palace.

Our house was modest and made out of mud. The wealthy families had brick houses. Mud houses make sense in warm countries, but in the north of Iran it rains a lot, and every year at the end of winter we had to repair our house. AghaJan would make a special paste using cow dung, which we also used for fuel. Mixing it with mud, straw, and rice husks, we used it to coat the cracked walls and roof. It was smelly work. After it had dried, AghaJan and my brothers would paint the walls, but that didn't kill the smell. For weeks, there was a smell of cow manure around the house, and to this day, I associate the smell of cow dung with the smell of home. I went to a farm outside New York City when I first arrived in 2014 and the animal smells there transported me back to my childhood. I looked around half expecting to see AghaJan and Mother, even though I knew it was a ridiculous expectation. I became so emotional that we left soon after we arrived.

Until I was in middle school, our house had only two rooms. In the room where we all slept, we'd roll up our futons in one corner next to a neat stack of folded blankets, sheets, and pillows. Every night, we rolled out the futons and made our beds on the floor. In the morning, I helped Mother fold the bedding and stacked it in layers in one corner. That was our main room—we spent our leisure time there, we ate our meals there, on a *sofreh* (a sheet of plastic or fabric spread on the floor like a tablecloth), and we did our homework there. The other room was for entertaining guests. Much later, AghaJan built an extension to create a third room.

We didn't have an indoor kitchen. AghaJan had built a *tash dar khaneh* ("fire house," in Mazani) in the courtyard, which was an open-air kitchen, an enclosure with three walls made from cinder blocks and a corrugated metal roof that provided only partial protection against the rain and snow. Almost every day, Mother would send us to collect bits of wood and charcoal to start a fire in a blackened shallow pit filled with ash. As we worked on the fire, she would coat the pots and pans with a protective mixture of mud and rice husks to stop them from burning. Breakfasts were simple affairs: eggs, bread, and cheese with hot tea. Eventually, AghaJan saved enough money to buy a gas stove.

Our water came from a deep well that Father had dug on the other side of the house. We'd throw a bucket into the well, and by rocking the bucket in a special way, we'd fill it with water to be used for both drinking and washing. When I was in high school, AghaJan installed a water pump and a water tank and we stopped hurling the bucket into the well.

There was no place to bathe or shower in the house. During the summer months, until I was six or seven, Mother would fill a large cast-iron cauldron with warm water and scrub me down with loofahs and a rough soap, the same kind that she used to wash our clothes. Ali suffered the same fate till he got too old.

I dreaded the shampoo that mother used, a thick yellowy goo that smelled of fresh egg yolk. Everyone in the village used the same brand of shampoo because that was the only one available.

When the weather got cooler, she'd move the cauldron to the barn, which had a cement floor—so overflowing water would not make everything muddier. As I grew older, I used the hose in the barn as a makeshift shower. It was very uncomfortable washing myself under the huge watchful eyes of our cows.

During the winter months and especially later, when I got too big to fit into the cauldron, we'd go to the public baths at the far end of the village. They were segregated—mornings, open only to the women; in the afternoon, it was the men's turn. There was also a smaller bathhouse next door where, for a higher fee, you could have your own room for an hour. I liked the private setting better because I felt shy about being naked in front of other women.

As for our furniture, there was little of it to get in our way—we had no tables or chairs or sofas. One luxury was the small television, which showed news and religious programs. Children's programs were cartoons imported from eastern Europe and Japan. During the summer months, we'd sit on the terrace and eat watermelon, drink tea, and talk, and friends would drop by and sit with us for hours till after sunset.

Winters could be brutally cold. We relied on a vintage Aladdin paraffin heater, which smelled really bad. And of course, every afternoon mother would start up the *korsi*—a heater made up of a low table with a brazier underneath and blankets thrown over it. The whole family would gather around the *korsi* with our feet under the blankets, and the kids would even sleep there.

I remember one winter it was so cold that every evening AghaJan walked the little calf that had recently been born up the steps and into the house. Looking back, it seems bizarre, but at the time, I thought it was pretty cool to have a little cow under our roof, sleeping with us.

Even as a kid I was always an optimist and thought we were special. Perhaps one reason was that since AghaJan regularly went to Babol, he'd buy us treats that were not available in Ghomikola, like fruit-flavored chewing gum or cheese puffs.

One lunchtime AghaJan returned from Babol looking especially pleased with himself. "I have something special for you all," he said as he washed for noon prayers. "A special treat that has come from Tehran."

Tehran! In my mind, Tehran, the capital, was so far away that there was an almost exotic quality about anything associated with it. I don't remember what we had for lunch that day, but we raced through the meal and cleared the plates and waited. Mother came back carrying a long, thick yellow stick on a plate. In her other hand, she had a big knife, the same one that she used to decapitate chickens.

"What is it?" I asked impatiently. I couldn't have been more than eight or nine years old, and I was sure we were all witnessing something historic.

"It's called a *moze*," AghaJan said authoritatively—a banana. "Not many people in Babol have seen a *moze*. This is from *farang*," he added: the West.

Farang! This was even better than Tehran, I thought. A mysterious treat from the West. I knew I had to remember every detail so I could brag about it at school the next day.

"Did you buy just one?" I asked. "Will that be enough?"

"Count your blessings," Mother said. She hated boastfulness and used every opportunity to instill a sense of gratitude in us. "Be thankful you have a kind father who loves you."

She poked the banana with the knife and was surprised by its softness. We held our breath.

"It's too soft," Mother said.

"Just cut it," AghaJan said in a reassuring voice. "Go ahead, don't worry."

Mother held one end of the banana firmly and solemnly cut it into six pieces and placed the plate in front of us. No one made a move. Mother hesitatingly picked up a piece and took a tiny bite, skin and all. She made a face and spat out the skin.

"This part is bitter and makes my mouth all sticky," she said. Slowly, she pulled the fleshy part away from the skin and put it in her mouth.

"It's sweet." Her face lit up with pleasure.

That settled it. We all grabbed a piece, peeled the skin off, and put the fleshy part in our mouths. I chewed mine very slowly and then opened my mouth and stuck my tongue out with the half-chewed banana on it to show Ali that I still had mine.

Before Mother could clear the plate, I grabbed a piece of the skin to take to school and show off.

"Masoumeh is keeping a piece of the *moze*," Hamid said. He sold me out. "She is going to show our *farangi* fruit to her friends."

Mother just gave me a disappointed look. She didn't have to say anything. I knew I was going to get a lecture later that day about the sin of showing off.

Until high school, I don't think I ever wore anything that wasn't a hand-me-down, made by my mother, or bought from a secondhand store. I liked to be different, and begged Mother to use different patterns and cloth to make my dresses and skirts rather than the same flowery patterns that other girls wore. I wanted to be unique.

As we got older, Ali and I headed off to middle school, which was in another village. Mother couldn't make the anoraks and waterproof winter coats that we needed. One evening, AghaJan came from Babol and handed me a red winter coat that I instantly fell in love with. It had a hood with faux white fur to keep me warm and snug. Ali received a yellow anorak with lots of pockets that could be zipped and unzipped and a removable inner layer, which meant he could wear it in both winter and spring. Immediately, Ali shoved his books and notepads into different pockets and announced to everyone that he no longer was going to carry a schoolbag.

There was only one problem with the coats: Both gave off a chemical odor that was rather off-putting.

"This is the smell of new clothes—they came straight from the shop," AghaJan said.

It was only half true. Ali and I found out later that the clothes came from a charity shop that sold used clothing at a huge discount. As for the "new clothes" aroma, it was the smell of disinfectant.

That winter, I also craved a new pair of boots. I complained incessantly about how my feet were always wet because my cheap shoes let in water. I hankered after a pair of red knee-high plastic boots with fake fur inside. I had seen them in a store in Babol, but Mother shook her head when I pleaded with her.

As the first snowflakes arrived, Mother found a solution. She and my aunt bought a pair to be shared between my cousin and myself.

I was not happy with the sharing arrangement. "Is it too much to have a pair of boots all to myself?"

"You either share or you get nothing," Mother retorted.

So I had the boots for one week before handing them over to my cousin, who kept them for a week before handing them back. This was the arrangement that had been made by the grown-ups, but I hated the idea of parting with the boots.

One night, a month or so later, AghaJan came home holding a brown paper bag, out of which he took a pair of red boots exactly like the ones I had been sharing with my cousin.

"These are yours. You don't have to share anymore," he said.

I jumped with joy. I kissed his hand repeatedly. I had a brand-new pair of boots all to myself and no more sharing with my cousin. I unwrapped the plastic coverings and tried the boots on. Almost immediately something felt wrong.

"They don't feel right," I said. "They're too loose."

AghaJan looked away. I was struck with a dreadful thought.

"Did you give these to my cousin first?" I cried. The ones I had been sharing with my cousin felt tight and snug. These felt worn-in.

AghaJan folded the brown paper bag that had contained the boots.

"The boots are a gift from a family that doesn't need them anymore," he said, without looking me in the eye. "We'll stuff some newspaper inside to make them fit better."

That night I told Ali about my not-so-new pair of boots.

"I think all our new clothes are donated," Ali said. "What if we bump into the previous owners on the street and they demand we hand the things back?"

It didn't happen, but in our minds there was always that fear of being confronted with the person whose discarded clothes we were now wearing.

CHAPTER TWO

I was born on September 11, 1976, and was just a babbling two-year-old toddler when the Islamic Revolution overthrew Shah Mohammad Reza Pahlavi, ending more than two millennia of rule by Persian kings.

The cataclysmic events are the most dramatic in the history of modern Iran. I am a child of that Islamic Revolution and have lived nearly all my life under its shadow. My story is the story of modern Iran, the tension between the secular tendencies of its population and the forced Islamification of the society, and the struggle of women, especially young women, for their rights against the introduction of Sharia law, against violations of human rights and civil liberties.

The revolution changed much, but for women it was many steps backward. In the Islamic Republic, being born a woman is like having a disability.

Even to this day, almost forty years after the revolution, there are debates within many Iranian families about whether my father's generation made a mistake in overthrowing the Shah and his Western-inspired ideas to modernize the country to bring in a regime that looked to the seventh century for moral and legal guidance. Of course, the picture is not black-and-white, and although many conservative and religious families favored the new regime, many others were not so favorably disposed.

Growing up, we talked about politics all the time in my family. As a teenager, I had loud arguments with AghaJan over politics. When the whole family got together during the weekends, Mohsen and Ali would be on my side against AghaJan, who had Hamid and Mina supporting him. Often, AghaJan would end the discussion with a rueful shake of his head and say: "You still don't know what you don't know."

The revolution was supposed to benefit families like ours, the downtrodden, the meek, and the poor. I'm a product of that revolution, which my parents supported, but I and many millions of Iranians have rebelled against the Islamic Republic.

One day many years later, hunting through family photographs, I discovered a batch of old pictures of my parents. It's always jarring seeing younger versions of your mother and father, but these photographs made a big impression on me for a different reason. In one, which must have been taken soon after their marriage, Mother is wearing a colorful scarf and a fashionable coat. Next to her is Agha-Jan, with a fierce black mustache; he's wearing a suit and a tie. Before seeing that photograph, I had never seen him in a tie. He never wore a tie after the revolution.

In another photograph, which must have been taken a decade later, the family is standing dolefully in a field. My mother, beautiful as ever, holds my brother Hamid in her arms as Mina and Mohsen stare sullenly at the camera. The children look as if they've missed their afternoon nap. AghaJan sports the same mustache as in the earlier photograph but is otherwise clean-shaven; he's wearing a dapper jacket and a pair of brogues totally unsuitable for walking around the countryside. I was in shock when I found those photographs—the only ones of my father without a beard. I rubbed my fingertips over the photographs as if I could touch his unblemished face.

There was something else that was out of place. In that photograph, we appear to be thriving: Everyone is wearing store-bought clothes rather than those sewn or patched by Mother. We don't look like farmers living in a tiny village. We look like city folks.

What happened to us? I wondered. How could the relative prosperity of my family in these photographs be explained?

I was too young to follow the nuances of the political upheaval in the country, but the transformation was obvious in our little patch of Iran. Even in the first decade after the revolution, there were divided loyalties in many families, including my own. AghaJan was all in favor of the Islamic government, whereas my uncle Valiollah was a Shah supporter, and every time we had a family gathering the two of them would bicker and snipe at each other. My father called him Shah Doost (Shah supporter), and Valiollah reciprocated by calling my father Khomeini Doost.

I remember one particular row clearly. It was a hot summer weekend and all the family sat on the *sofreh* together on the terrace. As dishes of rice and kebabs were being passed around, one of my cousins cleared his throat and addressed my father.

"Uncle, was life better during the Shah's time?" he asked. He tried his best to look innocent, but I could see that he was just trying to rile up AghaJan. "Uncle Valiollah says we had bigger harvests and more money back then."

My father always said he was willing to give his life for the revolution. He wasn't going to let that comment go unchallenged.

"No. No and no. We had more money, but we didn't have God's government. The Shah"—he made a face as if he'd just eaten a rancid piece of meat—"the Shah spent all the wealth on himself and his family. He was corrupt. We have an Islamic government and we follow the Quran."

AghaJan looked pleased with himself. Until he saw Valiollah walk over to him. Valiollah bent down and slowly scooped up a fistful of rice from the serving plate and started eating it from his cupped hand. Grains of rice fell through his fingers.

"If you say the Shah was corrupt, I guess you know better than the rest of us," Valiollah said sarcastically. "But at least when he ate he let the crumbs fall down to the people. Your *akhonds*"—an old-fashioned and derogatory term for clerics—"are just as corrupt." He now clenched his fist tight.

"But they eat with their hands closed, and still they take and take from us. The Shah never did me any harm."

Valiollah was a simple farmer, didn't take life too seriously, and always had a stick of gum or a piece of candy to hand out when he visited. Maybe that's why I liked him.

AghaJan craned his neck to address Mother. "I told you not to invite this Shah Doost." Then, addressing Valiollah, he said, "One day, you'll get it through your thick head that you still don't know anything. The Shah was giving our oil to the Americans."

"Who do you think is buying our oil now? American companies," Valiollah said triumphantly.

Usually it was up to the women in the family to bring peace to these gatherings. This time, Mother had had enough. "Why do you have to fight all the time?" she asked. "We had the Shah, now we have Khomeini. Who knows what tomorrow will bring."

AghaJan was willing to give his life for the Islamic Revolution, but even he couldn't deny that the Shah's father, who founded the Pahlavi regime, saved Iran from total collapse.

In 1921, with Iran under the thumb of superpowers Britain and Russia, Reza Mirpanj, the powerfully built commander of the Persian Cossack Brigade, marched with his four thousand men to Tehran to impose order. Eventually he ousted the previous king and proclaimed himself Shah, as the first Pahlavi king. Though illiterate, Reza Shah planned to modernize Iran, and as part of that, he built railroads and highways, established schools and a health care system, and sent thousands of Iranian students to study abroad. He dragged Iran into the twentieth century, even promoting the idea of men wearing modern Western clothing and calling for women to remove their hijab. With his urging, in 1936, came Kashf-e hijab (the unveiling), a law making it obligatory for women to remove their veil or head scarf in public.

More than eighty years ago, there was a law that banned the wearing of the hijab. If I had been alive then, I'd have opposed that law not because I believe in the hijab but because I believe in freedom of choice. Women should have the right to choose what they wear.

Reza Shah's reign came to an end after Soviet and British forces occupied the country in August 1941 to ease the shipment of weapons to Russia, then fighting Nazi Germany. Reza Shah had hired hundreds of German technicians to help on various projects, and the British demanded their expulsion. The presence of these technicians was the justification that Britain needed to invade Iran. Reza Shah abdicated in favor of his twenty-two-year-old son, Mohammad Reza Pahlavi. The new king pursued his father's program of modernization and introduced secular education and a legal system, imported Western technology and industry, and spent heavily on his armed forces. Thanks to the Pahlavis, Iran became a modern country.

This was the peak of women's rights. Under the Pahlavis, women made substantial gains, especially in matters of family law and divorce. They drove cars, worked outside the home, voted in elections, ran for political office, and were appointed to cabinet positions.

Until then, the hijab was not a contentious issue, at least not in the cities. In urban centers, you could find women without hijab working and living alongside religious women who wore the full hijab.

In 1978, the Shah was hit by the perfect storm of protests when liberal opponents who wanted more political freedom joined forces with the clerics, who complained about lax morals, and the radical left, which wanted a worker's paradise. The combined opposition under the leadership of Khomeini proved too much, and Mohammad Reza Pahlavi left Iran in January 1979, never to return.

He was the third king in a row to be forced into exile. A more democratic freedom beckoned, but instead Iran turned toward religious authoritarianism. Ayatollah Ruhollah Khomeini, exiled for more than fifteen years, mostly in Iraq and then in France, returned to a hero's welcome, greeted by millions of Iranians as if he were the Messiah. The unsmiling Khomeini, then in his late seventies, didn't look heroic at all. Even on the day of his triumphant return, Khomeini had the look of a coldhearted man: There was no sign of elation or joy. He promised harsh justice. Within ten days, the regime left behind by the Shah collapsed and the Islamic militants took over.

As the revolution took on a more Islamic hue, the question of the hijab and women's rights came up more and more. The trouble was that at the dawn of revolutionary Iran, women's concerns were an afterthought. In the beginning, Khomeini had spoken of his respect for democracy, human rights, and freedom of religion. It was only after the triumph of the revolution that many women realized that they had willingly ceded their rights and brought about a regime that demanded their subjugation.

On March 8, 1979, one hundred thousand women turned up for International Women's Day to protest laws to introduce compulsory hijab and other Islamic restrictions. Until then, Women's Day had passed unnoticed in Iran. Shadowing the demonstration were mobs of zealots and paramilitary forces armed with knives, broken glass, bricks, and stones. They attacked and injured many women while security forces watched passively.

The huge demonstration certainly had some results—one leading cleric, Ayatollah Mahmoud Taleghani, declared that "women cannot be forced to wear the hijab." His was a minority voice.

The Islamists were undeterred. In 1979, Hassan Rouhani, a junior cleric who in 2013 became Iran's seventh president, oversaw the reorganization of the armed forces. He was the first to order the women who worked for him to wear the hijab or be fired. In ministry after ministry, women were given a choice: Wear the hijab or don't come to work. Soon after, even those entering a government building had to wear the hijab. By 1983, compulsory hijab was the law.

Over a number of years, the Islamic government made life worse for women. The law in the Islamic Republic put the value of a woman's life and the value of her testimony at half of a man's. Women were barred from becoming judges, in accordance with Islamic tradition. Beaches were segregated, as were cinemas and many public spaces, including sports stadiums. Under the Shah, family law was based on Sharia law but was reformed to allow women the right to divorce and retain custody of children. After the revolution, those reforms were reversed. The changes didn't happen overnight, and the women resisted and put up a fight, especially over the issue of compulsory hijab, which set the tone for how women's rights would shape up.

Iran's first revolutionary decade was traumatic and bloody. First came revolutionary terror, as the new regime executed hundreds of former political leaders and military commanders, often without trial. Iraqi dictator Saddam Hussein took advantage of the turmoil to invade Iran. The war started days after my fourth birthday.

Even as the bombs were falling, the regime went about eliminating all internal opposition, from Islamic Marxist groups like the Mojahedin-e Khalq to the Fedayin and the communist party, the Tudeh. Executions, forced confessions, and torture were common.

But the Islamic Revolution had also brought about changes in village life. In the fields, men and women worked together and the women, including my mother, aunts, cousins, and nieces, would roll their trousers up to their knees and wade into the rice paddies. They'd put on a loose head scarf, and if it slipped off, no one complained.

The new regime tried to ban laughter and fun. For a while, chess and pop music were banned. Women singers were particularly hated and most of the stars, among them Haydeh, Mahasti, and Sousan, left the country or were forced to stay hidden from view—a fate that befell the country's biggest pop star, Googoosh, before she too left Iran, in 2000. Wedding parties were segregated, with men and women sitting in different rooms or in the same room but separated by a rope and blankets so no one could see the other side.

My father was more than just committed to the Islamic Republic. He enlisted in the Basij, a paramilitary group used as an auxiliary security force, and part of the Islamic Revolutionary Guards, created to protect the regime. In the early days of the revolution, he and other basijis would set up roadblocks at night stopping cars coming from Babol to search for music tapes and alcohol, both of which were forbidden.

He'd delight in smashing cassette tapes, stomping on them or even breaking them with his hands. With his short temper and angry manner, he was known as the "cranky basiji" who lectured the young men he caught. AghaJan was famed for his zeal in lecturing young men about attending the Friday prayers.

As far back as I can remember, all the women in my family slept with our head scarves on. Everyone including Mother, my sister, my grandmother, even cousins and nieces. It sounded strange years later when I tried to explain it to my friends in Tehran, or even later, in London and New York. But the truth of it is that we kept our head scarves on all the time, indoors and outdoors. After sleeping with my head scarf on, every morning before getting up I had to make sure it had not slipped off during the night, as it would upset AghaJan and he'd complain.

My hair was part of my identity, but you couldn't see it. When I was growing up, my hair was no longer part of my body. It had been hijacked and replaced with a head scarf.

CHAPTER THREE

School was all wrong. For the first three years, the classes were set up so that boys sat on one side of the room, girls on the other. After fourth grade, boys and girls were taught in different classrooms. Before going to school, I had the freedom to run around and play with other boys and girls, but that stopped when I turned seven.

When the recess bell rang, we'd race out of the classroom to the school yard, screaming with pent-up energy and happiness at being let loose. We were as one, boys and girls together. Our freedom lasted for a few fleeting minutes before the supervisor caught up with us with a ruler in his hand and shouted his daily instruction: "Girls...girls...run to the back of the yard now."

I, too, would retreat, along with the other girls, and could only envy the boys their freedom to run, wrestle, fight, kick a football.

Going to school brought another change to my outfit. I had to wear—over a tunic and baggy pants—a maghnaeh: a combination hooded neck and head scarf that resembled a habit, tightly covering my forehead, chin, and neck and part of my chest as well. Until then, I used to run around with just a head scarf tied tightly with a knot under my chin to keep all my hair in check. Later, in middle school, I wore the manteau—a drab, loose-fitting longish coat—over a long skirt or pants.

How I envied the boys, who could wear almost anything they liked.

At school, the teachers rewarded us with stickers of cartoon characters for good behavior, or for getting good grades on tests. The TV cartoon characters chosen were popular in Iran at the time: a girl called Nell, Hannah in the field (or Katri of the meadows, as she is called in the West), and Alice in Wonderland. I looked at the pictures with great envy. The three heroines were girls with long blond hair loosely brushed or tied in a ponytail. Their hair was not captive inside a piece of cloth. These girls were full of energy—they ran around, met people, made friends, and were active and happy. And they didn't have a hijab. They had freedoms that I didn't.

If I wanted to be free like the cartoon girls I would have to start my own revolution.

Our teachers were all men, except for Zahra Moaalem (Zahra the teacher). She was different from all the women I had met until then. Zahra was from the city of Kerman, in the southeast of Iran. She was very exotic. She looked different from other women I had met until then—she had darker features, wore colorful scarves, and took off her chador inside the classroom, folding it neatly over her chair. She was friendly to children in ways that the male teachers couldn't be. They relied more on giving us a beating with the back of the ruler or the rod. I was entranced by her and soon daydreamed about being Masoumeh Moaalem, Masoumeh the teacher, when I grew up.

During the month of Ramadan, when Muslims worldwide fasted from dawn till dusk, the local mosque offered Quran classes in the evening, and AghaJan made sure to take me and Ali with him. I learned not only to read the Quran but to recite it aloud in a melodic way. My parents encouraged me to develop this gift and hoped that I might become a professional Quran reciter.

At an early age, all children are taught to chant "Death to Amrika" (the way "America" is pronounced in Iran), and I was not immune. On special occasions, like the anniversary of the occupation of the U.S. embassy or the anniversary of the revolution, we would assemble in the school yard and chant, under the watchful eye of the principal and other teachers, "Death to Amrika, death to Israel, death to Ingilis"—England.

To attend middle school, I had to commute to Noushiravankola, a bigger village, where I met girls from different hamlets. The middle school was a single-sex institution; the boys went to school a block away.

In the summer of 1989, as I approached teenagehood, I thought my world was going to end. On Saturday, June 3, Khomeini, the founder of the Islamic Revolution and the Supreme Leader of Iran, died. He was eighty-nine, but his death was still a big shock to the nation. People said Khomeini had been sent directly by God to save Iran and that he was divinely blessed, for how else could he overthrow the monarchy and stand up to the Americans? Some even claimed to have seen his image on the moon. Khomeini was the only leader of Iran that I had ever known, a stern father figure who was always around. When I heard the news at school tears streamed out of my eyes as we were let out early. Teachers and students—we were all in shock. I cried all the way home and burst in to tell my mother, who had already heard the news on the radio. I remember distinctly that everyone I knew thought the United States was going to attack and take over the country.

"The Americans are coming to steal Iran away. They'll kill us all."

I really thought we'd face another war immediately. It was not rational, but, like millions of Iranians, I had been brainwashed by the daily propaganda on the national television and radio stations. I thought it was only Khomeini who was strong enough to stand up to the greedy U.S. capitalists. Many years later, I discovered that Khomeini was a coldhearted dictator who ordered the execution of thousands of Iranians.

But at middle school I had different, and more personal, concerns—that was when my body started changing. I developed curves where there had been none before. I was becoming more feminine, and I was confused and embarrassed by these developments.

Many girls felt the same way—we were taught to hide our bodies, to hide our feminine shape.

At high school, I named my breasts my "two orbs of sin." I felt guilty about my new body. I was taught that women's bodies encouraged men to commit sin, so it was up to us to hide our curves under the hijab. I'd stoop as I walked, and cross my arms to cover and hide my chest. I certainly didn't talk about such matters at class or at home. The first time I got my period, I was almost fourteen. I was hanging out with friends and had to run home to tell Mother. I was frightened and kept apologizing to her and wishing the bleeding would stop. She kept smiling, as if this was something to be happy about.

Maybe she thought I was ready to be married off.

Mother and AghaJan did not have much of an education, but they were determined that their children would not end up like them. There were no suitors for me, and in any case, they both insisted that I get my high school diploma. At fourteen I had to leave home for high school in Babol, then a small city of fifty thousand or so but to me the biggest and most exciting place to be.

During winters, I used to wake up to the stink of shoes. AghaJan would bring our shoes in from the veranda before dawn every day. He didn't want us to wear freezing cold shoes. But Ali and I each had only one pair, and we wore them all the time. They were smelly. My father's daily act of kindness meant that the room would fill up with the rancid smell of shoes that retained the sweaty odor of the day and night before.

At around six o'clock Mother would shake me gently to get me up.

"C'mon, my sweet girl, time to get ready for school. The day has started and you're going to be left behind," she'd say in a singsong voice. "Hurry, my child."

But the smell of shoes would already have woken me up. I've always been hyper in the mornings, bouncing with energy. I'd stumble outside, carrying my stinky shoes to the veranda before racing to the toilet to beat Ali. In early autumn, this was not a problem. As the rains came, stumbling around on the muddy path to the outhouse as a torrent pelted us was a challenge. Even when it was raining, I'd still want to race Ali, but now the risks were much greater. If I fell, I had to go back and change, and Mother would not be happy. But that never stopped me.

Mother didn't like scolding me. AghaJan usually left before we were up and about, but he'd tell Mother to make sure we said our morning prayers. Ali and I were not terribly keen on praying. Mother prayed but didn't have the heart to force us. Some days AghaJan would not leave for the fields and instead did chores around the house. On those days, as soon as I opened my eyes I could just tell if Father was around. Maybe all children have that extrasensory power, being able to detect how the electric charge in the air changes when a parent is away. When AghaJan was gone, there was more noise, more silliness, more life—Ali would spread the *sofreh* on the floor as I helped make the tea and warm up the bread. He and I would mock-fight and try to trip each other up even as we rushed around doing our morning chores. When AghaJan was there, we were more careful—stealthy in our movements and quiet in our speech.

At around 6:20, we packed our schoolbags and rushed to catch the bus that traversed the other villages—Noushiravankola, Esbukola, and Hajikola—to the central bus station in Babol. From there it was a short walk to Azarm High School, which dated back to the 1930s. The school had survived a world war, two revolutions, and three heads of state and was still going strong. Ali went to the boys' school not too far away.

For the return journey, all the children, boys and girls, would gather in two separate groups at a square near our school and wait together for the buses home. Ali hung out with the boys, who talked and laughed loudly and sometimes staged mock fights. The girls all turned their backs on the road and the boys, and instead faced a wall. It made for a strange sight: girls of all sizes and shapes wearing black chadors that completely covered their bodies, revealing only their faces, turned to the wall so as not to have any contact with the boys. Sometimes as I was waiting I'd catch sight of AghaJan on his moped heading home. But he never once looked in my direction. The geese and chickens he hadn't managed to sell stuck their heads out of air holes in the cardboard box he had tied to the rack on the back of his moped. I guess it was funny seeing AghaJan zipping by with a bunch of scrawny birds swaying precariously on the back. The boys would laugh and jeer at him. Ali didn't want to lose face in front of his friends, so he kept quiet. But once I realized they were laughing at AghaJan, I was steaming mad. The next time I saw him coming toward us, I turned away from the wall and glowered at the boys, daring them to laugh at my father.

No one laughed that day. Or ever again, whenever I was around.

That evening, AghaJan called me over to him. I thought he was going to thank me for standing up for him and the family honor. I should have known better.

"Why can't you be chaste and virtuous like other girls?" he said with real displeasure. "All the other girls were facing away from the boys, but you were the only one who was flirting."

"Flirting?" I asked incredulously. "I didn't want them to laugh at you."

He wasn't convinced. "If you mix with boys, you bring shame to the family."

The daily commute to Babol sapped my strength and I was sick a lot. I was so skinny that my mother was convinced I had worms and kept taking me to the doctor to be checked.

My sister Mina had married Mohsen's wartime buddy Ramzoon, who was in the Revolutionary Guards, and they lived in a small one-bedroom apartment in Babol. To save on my daily commute, it was decided that I should move in with them and only return to Ghomikola for the weekends. Ramzoon and Mina would sleep in the bedroom, while their two children and I would sleep on the floor in the living room. This was the first time I was going to be away from home, and I was very excited. I felt I was on the cusp of being a grown-up.

Ali and I were both avid readers—addicted to books, really. In high school, I had an insatiable urge to read. I read everything from the science fiction tales of Jules Verne to the novels of Victor Hugo and Charles Dickens—Miss Havisham gave me the creeps, but I read *Great Expectations* again and again. And I wasn't just hooked on translations of Western novels; I read Persian classics and modern masterpieces: Ahmad Mahmoud's *Hamsayeha* (*The Neighbors*), Nader Ebrahimi's seven-volume *Atash Bedoon Dood* (*Fire Without Smoke*), and the poetry of the immensely influential Ahmad Shamlou, whose vivid imagery of everyday life often left me breathless.

AghaJan didn't pay a penny toward the cost of my books. I had no choice but to "liberate" books—I sneaked them out of the public library and even raided the school library but soon ran out of choices. Of course, "liberate" is a fancy word for "steal." I saw myself as a female Robin Hood. After I finished reading the books, I always passed them on to other kids in my circle. I'd convinced myself that I wasn't actually stealing but finding new readers for books that were gathering dust on shelves. I didn't keep any of these books for myself.

I also visited the bookstores of Islamic centers, where I could get my hands on Ali Shariati's interpretations of Shia Islam. Shariati, a sociologist with a PhD from the Sorbonne, encouraged revolutionary ideas in Islam and was very popular with the teenage crowd.

When I wasn't reading, I was getting into trouble. I have always had a beautiful voice, and if you don't believe me I'd be happy to sing for you to prove it. I was singled out at school to recite Quran, which is a great honor. Every year there are nationwide competitions to choose the best Quran reciter. And not just in Iran. There are international competitions in which reciters from across the Muslim world turn up to compete.

At Azarm, I was hailed as one of the school's top reciters, which of course made my father very proud. My voice was a gift from God, he said. As usual, Ali teased me, because he knew I wasn't religious at all. "One day you're reading Marx, the next you are reciting Quran," he joked. "You're going back and forth between heaven and hell."

On the day of the competition, I sat cross-legged on a futon on the stage, opened the Quran that rested on the little table in front of me, and very deliberately adjusted the microphone stand. I closed my eyes and started intoning a verse from the Quran in Arabic, and then I switched to reciting an epic poem by Shamlou in Persian.

Instead of the Quranic verse, I recited:

"They smell your mouth
Lest you have said: I love you!
They smell your heart!
These are strange times, my dear."

As my voice reverberated through the hall, the effect was electric. Students started shouting, whooping, clapping, and whistling in delight. I was shaking my fist in the air to punctuate the poem. One of the teachers in charge of the program turned off the microphone to shut me down. Undeterred, I stood up and continued to shout out the rest of the poem.

"We must hide our emotions in dark closets!"

Two teachers rushed the stage, and each grabbed me by one arm and began dragging me away. Even then, I continued to shout out the poem as thunderous cheering erupted all around me. I screamed the last line really loudly:

"We must hide our God in dark closets."

I was reprimanded for my unannounced and unappreciated poetry recital. That was the end of any plans to push me to become a Quran reciter.

I was living in Babol with my sister for a year or so before I decided that I didn't want to wear the chador. Women from the village wore it, but the young girls in the city, although still adhering to compulsory hijab rules, were not so conservative. I wanted to be modern, but it took me some time to get my courage up. It was around my sixteenth birthday that I abandoned the chador. I'd leave Mina's house wearing it, but once I turned the corner, I'd take it off and stuff it in my backpack. I was still covered head to toe—I had a maghnaeh and a head scarf; a roopoosh, or long-sleeved dress, over my shirt and trousers; and a manteau. I'd put the chador on again on my way back as I neared Mina's. I still feared that Mina and Ramzoon would not tolerate me without my chador. Most girls in Azarm wore a chador, but that's because the school catered to very traditional families. My teenage freedom was stealthy! I spent the weekends in Ghomikola and wore my chador whenever I left the house.

Of course, as luck would have it, I was found out in the worst possible manner. One afternoon on the way back to Mina's, I bumped into AghaJan, the last person on earth I expected. As usual, I was daydreaming and not paying much attention to my surroundings. I had thought of myself as safe, since AghaJan never ventured near my high school, preferring to set up his stall on street corners near the central bus station, but there he was, bent over his moped, patiently tying a cord around his cardboard box, from which several geese peered out curiously. I practically tripped over my own feet as I saw him. Just then, AghaJan turned and our eyes locked. Actually, his eyes widened so much that I thought they would pop out of his head. In just two strides, he was by my side. He towered over me.

"Where is your chador?"

"It's in my backpack."

"Put it on," he said urgently. "Why are you bringing shame on me, on your family?"

"I'm not going to wear the chador anymore," I said, marveling at my own bravery. Over the years, one thing I have realized about myself is that when someone shouts at me and tries to bully me, I always fight back. "There is nothing about me that is shameful. I'm completely covered up. I just don't want to wear the chador."

"Shame on you," AghaJan sputtered, at a loss for words. "Your sinning ways would make the devil blush with shame." That was his favorite insult. He turned and sat on his moped. "You have brought shame on me, brought shame on your mother. You have ruined our reputation."

With a mighty kick, he started his moped and joined the flow of traffic. I was surprised and hurt by his response. I looked at the chador as something that my mother's generation wore, and I wanted to be a modern city girl. I walked in tears to Mina's. I didn't expect much support there, but I had nowhere else to go. I didn't even bother to put the chador back on again. I sat in the kitchen and bawled my eyes out.

"I don't want to be like other girls in Ghomikola; I don't even like wearing this head scarf," I said, pulling it off my head. "Girls just can't have any fun. Can't go swimming, can't go running, and can't do anything because boys might get excited."

Mina always wore a chador, but she could see I was different from her. That night, when Ramzoon came home, she told him about what had happened. Surprisingly, he was sympathetic to my views.

"Masoumeh is chaste and she'll come around when the time is right," he said. "I'll talk to AghaJan."

From then on, when I was in Babol I didn't have to wear a chador if I didn't want to. I didn't go to Ghomikola for more than two months. Finally, AghaJan sent a message that he was ready to see me again. But he never forgave me. I had betrayed Islam. Mother's faith was more flexible.

"A chador isn't going to turn Masoumeh into a saint. It's what's inside that matters, and our Masoumeh is a good girl," Mother said in my defense the first time I visited, expecting another big row. "She goes to Babol, and in the city they do things differently from here.

Masoumeh wants to act and dress like them. When she's married and has a home of her own, then she'll put on a chador because she'll respect her husband."

I was never big on religion. Every week at Azarm, a cleric came at noon to lead the special Friday prayers. I remember having my own gang by the time I was sixteen, a group of other troublemakers who always got detention. Our parents were often summoned to school to meet the principal or the religious adviser. One of our tricks was to place plastic bowls of water on a windowsill above the school entrance, and as the cleric arrived, we would push the bowls over, hoping that one would land on him. We would run away as fast as we could from the window and down the stairs, giggling uncontrollably. From the floor below would come sounds of bowls crashing and water splattering. After a few weeks, the cleric refused to come to school and for some time we were relieved of performing Friday prayers.

The school authorities always found out that I was behind such antics and would summon my poor mother, who had to sit in the principal's office and listen to a litany of my crimes. The subtext of it all was that she was a bad mother who was failing to correctly nurture me. Mother was always apologizing for my antics. At the end of these meetings, I'd promise not to misbehave, and usually I kept my promise. For a short time, at least.

Azarm had a huge yard, and another of my little acts of rebellion was to write political slogans calling for freedom and democracy on the school walls. Again, Mother was called in and had to apologize on my behalf. If I wasn't breaking things or writing political graffiti on the walls, I was disruptive in class. I called it asking questions, but my teachers had another view. I was particularly upset by the different standards applied to boys and girls.

"Why are girls expected to be so subservient?" I asked one day. "Why do we need to wear the hijab? Why don't men cover themselves up, too?"

"An obedient woman brings peace and prosperity to the home and allows the man to be productive," my religious teacher said. It was the standard response and did nothing to appease me. I didn't like the compulsory hijab rules, and it seemed to me the rules were designed to benefit men.

"If hijab is a good thing, then men should wear it also," I shot back. "Some men are so ugly that they do need to be covered up to protect us women."

For my witticism, I was sent to the principal's office.

I liked challenging my religious teachers best. In Islam, there is great emphasis on the unity of God. There is no god but Allah, all Muslims say during prayers. One time in class I argued that if one God is good, surely two would be better, because there would be less chance for God to make errors like sending an earthquake or flood to kill the poorest people on earth. As you can imagine, I didn't endear myself to my teachers.

Another time, when a new religious studies teacher joined the school, I raised my hand innocently toward the end of class.

"Don't you agree that there is a certain order in the universe?" I asked.

She agreed.

"Then, by the same logic, our class and our school must have a certain order, too," I continued.

"Exactly," she said, encouraging me to continue. The rest of the class knew me better than the teacher did. They all became quiet, waiting for me to cause some mischief.

"If there is order, then there must be a creator, just like there is an architect who planned this school and these classes."

"Exactly, exactly, there must be a creator." She was nodding appreciatively. "There is a creator. Look around you and you'll see the signs everywhere."

"The earth, this planet, and all the people, animals, plants—everything must have a creator, too."

"That's right. That's God who has created everything."

"Well, then, who created God? Who creates the creator?"

Some of the girls snickered.

The teacher belatedly realized that perhaps I wasn't so innocent.

"What? You stupid blockhead. Nobody creates God."

I was in my element. "It is you who is wrong. We humans created God. We had no choice but to create God."

"The human brain cannot fathom the greatness of God," she said angrily. "Just because you've read some books from America or Germany or France or Russia that say God doesn't exist, that doesn't make you smart. You know nothing."

I knew that I was headed to another detention and that the school was going to call Mother again. Looking back, I still get upset at the memory of that day.

The school principal finally ran out of patience with me. Although I had only one year left of high school, the teachers had had enough of me. The final straw came after a bookstore owner complained that I had stolen from him. Admittedly, it was at this time that I had begun reading Ebrahimi's *Atash Bedoon Dood*. And I had liberated the first volume from the store. When I went back for the second, the owner was waiting for me. It was quite an embarrassing scene, and he complained to the school principal. I got a reprimand. I didn't like stealing, but we had no money, I reasoned with myself.

At the end of the summer that year, when I went to register for my final-year classes, I was sent to the principal's office. A secretary handed me an envelope addressed to my parents. Naturally, I opened it. The letter said that I was being expelled and that my parents had to report to Babol's Board of Education the next day to discuss my situation.

I read and reread the letter, but my prospects still looked bleak no matter how many times I went through it. All my bravado left me and I burst into tears in the office in front of the secretary. I saw the principal and begged her to give me just one more chance. I hadn't thought that my teenage antics would produce such a terrible end. Torrents of tears flowed from my eyes, but nothing moved the principal. I was out. I had no idea how I was going to break the news to my parents. I knew AghaJan would be angry, but I was more nervous about how my mother would take it.

She was in the kitchen baking bread over the open oven. One look at my teary eyes, puffy face, and runny nose and she knew something was up.

"Did you fail the finals?" she asked. "You can still take makeup exams."

"They expelled me." I blurted it out. "And we have to see the Board of Education. I got expelled for being poor."

Between sobs, I promised never to steal books again, and to behave myself for my final year. Mother was always on my side. No matter how many times I got into trouble or let her down, which was quite often, she'd forgive me in the end. She didn't like the idea of talking to the Board of Education bureaucrats. She thought she could persuade the principal to give me a final chance.

The next day, we took the bus to Babol and headed straight to Azarm.

"They've seen me enough these past years, and for my sake I'm sure they'll give you another chance," she said, wrapped in a black chador, with large plastic-frame glasses that hid half her face. In the village, no one wants to create bad blood, and people learn to forgive and forget for the sake of harmony. Mother felt the same mentality prevailed in Babol.

The principal didn't budge. In fact, it was a very quick meeting. We were barely in the room where I'd spent many hours getting lectures about my shortcomings before the principal explained that my file had already been sent to the Board of Education and that the matter was out of her hands. She was very sorry, she said. But she didn't look sorry. It was up to the board to determine my future.

We were ushered out without ceremony. I was a constant source of trouble, the principal said as we left, and now I was going to be someone else's headache. I felt bad for Mother. She was a simple woman who had come in good faith for a simple favor and had been sent packing.

"I promise to behave better," I told her. There was a chance I would not be allowed to enroll in any school and that I would miss getting my diploma the next year. I'd be labeled a failure. Mother was deep in thought, perhaps dreading the confrontation with the Board of Education officials. She'd had no schooling herself and barely spoke Persian. With every step, I felt more sorry for myself, and I secretly hoped that some of my friends had also been expelled so I wouldn't be alone in my ordeal.

The Board of Education occupied a squat, tan-colored building on a busy street in downtown Babol. Cars and motorbikes zipped past with their horns blaring. We didn't have to wait long in the reception area before we were brought in to meet the official in charge of my file. He was in his thirties and fleshy, wearing round metal-frame glasses with a trim black beard. As we walked in he stood up from behind his desk, stiffly bowed his head, and pointed to a pair of hard-backed wooden chairs placed directly in front of him before returning to an open file he had been flipping through on his desk. The room was airy and light; street sounds drifted through the half-open window. There was a hint of body odor and tobacco in the room.

Before long, there was a quick tap on the door and a short, old man entered, carrying a tray with three glasses of tea and a bowl of sugar cubes. With a flourish, he placed the tea in front of us and quietly limped away. Only then did the official snap the file shut. He took out a pen and made some notes on a pad in front of him before looking up, as if noticing us for the first time.

He smiled at my mother, who had her chador tightly wrapped around her. I glared at the man, wondering what new humiliation awaited me.

"I can see you are a good person, a pious person," he said to Mother, bowing his head in a sign of respect. "I'm at your service."

"We are a revolutionary family, we are pious, and we are a family that has shed blood in the war. We have defended the revolution," Mother said. "Why did you expel my daughter?"

"She must be a source of shame for a devout and revolutionary family like yours." He glanced at me disapprovingly. "Her file is full of misdeeds that should have been corrected long ago."

The implication was clear: My parents had failed to raise me properly. He had no time for or appreciation of the finer points of my bad behavior. But if he thought he could intimidate Mother, he was quite mistaken.

"I'm a simple farmer, and in our orchard, I tend to the apple trees," Mother said quietly. "When a tree is full of apples and I see that those apples are juicy and tasty, then I'm not worried about that tree." She spoke so quietly that the official had to lean forward to catch her words.

"But sometimes a tree is hit by blight or the apples have worms," she continued, sitting up straighter. "That's the tree that needs nurturing and love. I don't cut sick trees down, but I spend more time to restore them back to health."

"Now, you are a gardener, too." She fixed him with a stare. "These kids are your responsibility. The ones who do their homework and never cause you any trouble, they are the ones who are easy to teach. They don't need any special attention, and in the eyes of God, you don't get any rewards for teaching those kids."

The official and I were both surprised by Mother's robust defense.

"Now you have my Masoumeh," she said, nodding to me, as if introducing me. "This one is like a tree that's been infested by blight. I have two sons who are devout and fought in the war. They've both graduated from university." She put three sugar cubes into her tea and stirred it. "They don't need me to tell them to stay on the righteous path. The real challenge is in raising Masoumeh and making sure she stays on the right path."

She sat back to catch her breath. I had never seen her speak like this. I stared at her as if I were meeting a new woman. I was mesmerized.

"Right now, her faith is weak; she is questioning everything. Yes, she doubts God and the Quran and she does not pray or fast, but that's why she needs help."

Mother stopped, pausing to take a sip of her tea.

The official made a weak attempt to regain control.

"Esteemed mother..."

But my mother was not to be denied.

"Instead of nurturing her, you have abandoned my daughter." She was chiding him. "Instead of expelling my Masoumeh, you need to help her find answers. You have failed her and ME."

The official sat back in his chair as if he'd been slapped in the face. He had lost his superior air and was looking at Mother with real respect. He tapped the notepad in front of him with his pen.

"I've met hundreds of people more educated than you, but they don't have one ounce of your common sense. You've really put your finger on it." He sounded contrite. "What you said cannot be taught. You see with your heart." He looked down at his notes. "We must help Masoumeh. We must nurture the young generation. That's why we had a revolution."

He seemed infused with new energy. "Your daughter is a...a challenge, and I have the full file here." He grinned and patted the folder in front of him. "But our job is to help her overcome her doubts."

As we waited, he wrote a letter directing me to register at Horiyat, the top high school in Babol. It was funny how my world had turned upside down. A day ago, I'd thought the expulsion would bring shame to my family, but now I was on top of the world, heading to one of the best schools in Babol. Even then, I had a mischievous thought: If I knew I was going to be treated so well, maybe I should have gotten expelled much earlier. The day belonged to Mother. It was her triumph.

CHAPTER FOUR

Mother was treated like a hero on our return. And deservedly so. Mother, who barely reached five feet and could not read or write, had outsmarted the government busybodies and bureaucrats from the big city. Soon enough, neighbors, friends, and family all came around to drink sweetened tea, crack sunflower seeds, and hear how she had bested the system—managed to get me not only back into the education system but into Horiyat, in a posh part of town, in Bagh-e Ferdos, no less. Even in Ghomikola, people had heard of Bagh-e Ferdos, a fancy plaza with a fountain in the center surrounded by a beautiful flower garden.

Our visitors shook their heads in amazement as Mother and I competed to tell the tale; it was as if Mother had performed a minor miracle. I guess that's when I realized what a terrible reputation I had. As some of the guests were on their way out, they offered words of wisdom, something along the lines of *Now that you have a second chance to prove yourself…* And: *I hope you won't be climbing trees in Bagh-e Ferdos,* or *Ladies don't carry box cutters under their chadors.*

It's amazing how some people kept reminding me of my bad deeds. One time I did carry a box cutter, but it was for protection against boys who said lewd things. And it is true that, one time, I threatened a boy with my cutter. But I never actually touched him. I was so proud of Mother that day that I vowed to myself that I would be on my best behavior thereafter. My box-cutting days were behind me.

The truth is that as the last days of the summer sped past, I became more and more nervous. It was as if a bear was in my stomach, clawing at my insides. The notion that I had to curb my mischief-making habits was alien to me. One minute, I'd be telling myself that I'd still be able to climb trees and no one could stop me, but the next minute I'd be having an anxiety attack, wondering what my new friends would think of me. Just to make a point, I climbed the trees in our orchard every day, often taking a book with me to read as I perched precariously on the tallest branch, but it was joyless. For the first time, as the first day of school arrived, I was nervous.

The day before school started, I moved back in with my sister Mina. I tossed and turned all night, and with the first hints of dawn, as the sky was turning pink, I was up and about. The first order of the day was to have a shower—that was the only way I could tame my wild hair, today of all days uncontrollably frizzy. With a towel wrapped around my head, I put on a pair of loose black pants; a light shirt; a roopoosh, which reached past my knees; and then a magh-naeh. I could barely move wearing so much clothing. But no chador.

I squeezed myself onto the bus, packed more than usual with all the students going to different schools. The first day of school is always the worst, for some reason. The children are all chatty and loud and wild, while the regular folks are grumpy. At least that's how it seemed to me. I was hyper, as usual, and I wanted to sing out loud and scream wildly, but if I did, I was sure someone would report me to the morality police and I'd be in trouble again. You saw them on street corners, telling women to fix their hijab or asking couples if they were related or married. Ali and I were often stopped in Babol and had to prove that we were actually brother and sister. To be fair, we didn't look as if we were related. Ali was light-skinned, with straight hair, and I was dark-skinned, with curly hair. One time we were separated and grilled about our relationship.

"You think I want to be married to her?" Ali asked mockingly. "I wouldn't choose her, but I don't have a choice. She's my sister." Even so, we had to answer questions about AghaJan and other relatives before the morality police finally relented and released us.

The bus crawled along the road, which was jammed with cars and bicycles and even an old horse carriage. Everywhere you looked, dozens of students were moving, zigzagging past each other. As the bus inched forward and cars honked nonstop, I could barely contain my excitement about going to a new school. I jumped off the bus well before my stop and started up the hill to Horiyat.

Even though it was early, the day was quite hot already, and even the crowded sidewalk was radiating heat. I had to walk really fast, and by the time I got to school, I was panting and wheezing. My face was beet red and I was swimming in sweat. The compulsory hijab laws were a major discomfort for me and all the women. It seemed so unfair to see boys and men walk around in tee shirts or short-sleeved shirts.

I stood to one side and observed my new environment as more and more girls arrived. I felt lost and small, but I remembered how proud my mother was to have won me this chance. I rallied and marched to the gate.

Horiyat was a compact modern building, just two floors, with the name of the school in big white letters on the front entrance. A tall wall circled the school, with just an opening for a metal door. Behind the wall, the school yard was only a third the size of Azarm's. Even though I had promised to behave, I was still disappointed that the yard offered few places to hide and cause mischief.

Something was missing. It took me a while to notice as I surveyed my new surroundings. Then it hit me. The smell of poverty. Azarm was full of kids like me, children of poor farmers or workers, mostly wearing hand-me-downs or used clothing. We all wore similar outfits because that's what we could afford. At Azarm, the school was always undergoing construction and repairs, and because of it, there was always dust and dirt and the smell of cement. Now I saw a different crowd of teenagers, nearly all arriving without chadors, wearing their long manteaux over trousers. At the gate, one of the teachers was doing guard duty, making a cursory check for makeup and jewelry. This was so unlike Azarm, where most students wore a chador and we were patted down and checked for any signs of nail polish and lipstick.

I didn't know it at the time, but Horiyat liberated me from my teenage anger. I was taken out of the little pond of Azarm, where I felt stifled, and thrown into a bigger pond. Not in terms of size but in terms of expectations. The atmosphere was freer; you could let a few strands of hair escape from under your head scarf without getting punished. I could have political discussions with my classmates and with their families, who seemed to be much better read than the people in Ghomikola. When one of my new friends invited me to her house, I was shocked to see a pack of playing cards on the dining room table. I was raised to think that playing cards meant gambling and were *haram*—forbidden under Islam. I experienced a different lifestyle visiting the homes of my new friends.

At Horiyat I also found that there was so much more to discover outside the covers of books. For starters, not all my new friends were interested in reading and discussing ideas. They were more involved in making secret arrangements to see their boyfriends, and in making marriage plans.

That first week, I became friends with Missa, a petite and very pretty girl whose easy laughter and honey-colored eyes had suitors lining up for her. She had been promised to a distant cousin or nephew, but she had a secret boyfriend, Majid, who was a few years older than her and halfway through the local university.

At Azarm, I had waged a campaign against boys, even forming my own gang—the Gadfly—which you could only join by swearing off boys. Here it was different. All the girls were interested in getting engaged and married. There was so much for me to learn. So when Missa asked me to go shopping after school, I readily agreed. I didn't have any money, but I wanted to see how the other half shopped. There was a mall near the plaza at Bagh-e Ferdos and it was only a short walk.

Missa wasn't after something for herself. "I want to buy him after-shave," she said coyly. It was a present for Majid. "It's for his birthday."

"You give presents? To your boyfriend? For his birthday?" I was incredulous. It was almost a sin for someone as beautiful as Missa to buy a present for a boy. And just what was an aftershave? I had never bought anyone any presents, ever.

"I want to get him something," she said, giggling.

"But why?" I persisted.

"It's his birthday," she repeated, looking at me with a raised eye-brow to indicate that the conversation on this topic was over.

In our family, we rarely remembered birthdays, let alone cele-brated them or gave presents to each other. To this day, I always forget my brothers' birthdays and even my husband's. What's so spe-cial about congratulating someone for being born? They didn't do anything. The praise should go to the mother who did all the hard work and pushed them out.

"I want to get him aftershave so he smells good for me. I've seen all the ads on satellite television," Missa said knowingly. "I want Ma-jid to smell nice and sexy for me."

Satellite television, men who shaved everyday and wore aftershave. This was all unknown territory to me.

Missa dragged me to a store in the mall and made me smell every brand on offer as she flirted with the salesman before eventually settling on a hideously sweet-smelling concoction. I developed a massive headache, which did not improve my mood.

"Buying presents for a boy is very silly," I protested one last time as she was counting her money. "Buy yourself something instead."

She counted off a few more bills from her purse.

"This is how much the aftershave costs. If I give you this money, will you try and be nice? I'm buying this for Majid. You can buy something nice for yourself." She sauntered off to pay for her pre-cious present.

I didn't have a boyfriend, and even if I did I wouldn't waste good money on him. Instead, I bought myself all seven volumes of *Atash*

Bedoon Dood. The irony was that this was the same set of novels that had indirectly led to my expulsion, and here I was buying the books for myself.

I had the better deal because two months later, Majid dumped Missa.

Books were my life. I was an avid reader, but I stopped pinching books from bookstores and the libraries of the local Islamic centers.

Another friend, Ayda, who had a pretty smile and big brown eyes, didn't study and rarely spoke in class. Ayda planned to get married soon after graduation and have lots of children, but she liked me because I was always asking our teachers provocative questions. After a few weeks, she invited me to come over to her house after school one day. Everything about Ayda's house and family looked magical to me—her mother worked in an office; she had dyed her hair and wore makeup. Ayda's mother wore perfume and smelled nice. When I told her how nice she looked, she took off her head scarf and invited me to do the same until Ayda's father came home.

Their house was huge compared to my sister's little apartment. It was spacious, modern, and clean; handwoven Persian carpets were strewn on the floor in the living room, which had a sofa and comfy chairs. In our family, we always sat on the floor.

Ayda's parents liked me because I was always reading and talking about poetry and literature, and they wanted me to influence their daughter. They wanted Ayda and me to be best friends. Not long after meeting me, Ayda's mother called me aside and gave me one thousand tomans, then about six dollars.

"My Ayda is more interested in goofing off and playing," she said, handing me the money. I was not in the least embarrassed to take a handout. They were paying me to be myself. "This is for ice cream or sweets. I like you, Massy," she said, using my nickname. "Be her friend, read to her, *make* her read." All my friends called me Massy rather than Masoumeh. It sounded modern and new.

One thousand tomans! That was a small fortune to me. No one had ever given me that much money before. Once again, I immediately headed to a bookstore and bought books: *Salhai Abri* (*The Cloudy Years*), by Ali Ashraf Darvishian, and Romain Rolland's *Jean-Christophe,* which had a big influence on me.

The new school had not dulled my sense of rebellion, but now I aimed for something higher and bigger.

Maryam was tall, with long, black hair, and skinny, just like me. She liked reading and debating. The two of us started a book club, with the twist that we would focus on political books, and we invited select friends to join. We started reading leftist literature and books about the United States to counter the constant anti-American propaganda churned out daily on Iranian TV. Like many teenagers living under political and social restrictions, we grappled with themes such as freedom and human rights, and the meaning of democracy. We were full of youthful energy and enthusiasm.

It was a secret club but we needed members, and Maryam brought in her friend Reza, a year older than me and studying at a teachers' training college. His sister Leila, seventeen, who planned on going to art school, also joined us. Ali had enrolled to study history at the University of Bojnord, in the northeast corner of Iran, but he was homesick and almost every weekend he returned to Babol. When he heard about the book club, he demanded to be allowed in—Ali was more than just my elder brother, he was my best friend, my confidant and mentor, and we often read the same books.

"They are teaching us lies," he complained about his new university. "All the history they are teaching—lies. They are twisting the truth, as if history only began twenty years ago." The Islamic government was whitewashing the past, diminishing the achievements of the pre–1979 revolution era. The Islamification of Iran was continuing at a rapid pace, and Iran's pre-Islamic history and culture were being swept away. Ali, always a romantic, was so frustrated that he was contemplating dropping out of college.

"We should write our own history," he said. In our earnestness, we wanted to educate the masses.

I was already in awe of Ali because he was so smart and well-read, and at our first meeting, others also looked up to him, since he was the only one studying at university. We should all read important books, Ali said, and not just Paine's *Common Sense* or the Declaration of Independence but also the history of the French Revolution and the history of the Tudeh.

We all agreed to each read a political text and discuss it at our next meeting. I don't know who came up with the idea, but after hours of discussion, by the end of that night we had formulated a plan to create a *shabnameh*—a secret publication, an underground pamphlet surreptitiously distributed. *Shabnamehs* had been used in Iran before, to protest against foreign occupation, or against the autocratic edicts of the Shah. It was a crazy idea for a bunch of kids to publish their own *shabnameh,* but also thrilling. We had to recruit more people, however, and Ali agreed to come back every other weekend to help us with the project. That was fair, since he was the one who had gotten us enthused.

Looking back, we were so innocent, our activities nothing more than what a high school political club might engage in, but in Iran this was almost sedition. Reza offered to hold meetings at his parents' house, where he still lived. Leila and I oversaw collecting weekly dues from the members. We thought we were rebels and intellectuals, but we were just teenagers with awkward manners and bad haircuts. We read books on history, especially the Russian Revolution, and discussed producing hundreds of leaflets to be secretly deposited throughout town, some in prominent locations and the rest in libraries and bookstores. For us, being members of a secret club was the best part.

All revolutionary groups need a name, and we chose Faryad-e Kaveh (Call of Kaveh). We had created a special logo—in the shape of a man's mouth open wide as if he's shouting—with the words "Faryad-e Kaveh" coming out of his mouth. It was not a random choice. Kaveh, a legendary blacksmith and one of the most famous figures in Iranian mythology, became the rebel who led a national uprising in Babol against the despotic and ruthless foreign tyrant Zahak, then ruling Iran. Zahak was of Arab origin and had a snake growing out of each shoulder. Kaveh is always invoked by Iranian nationalists, since the Islamic Republic promotes Arabic words and traditions.

We kept looking for new members to expand our group, and one of the latecomers was Ahmad. He was in his thirties, twice as old as some of us. A tailor who had his own shop in downtown Babol, he was an odd choice to join a group of teenagers. Ahmad had soulful eyes, a thick brush mustache drooping over his lips, and shoulder-length hair. He looked like Maxim Gorky, the Russian writer; there was always a glint in his eyes, as if he could see the humor in the world before any-one else did. Babol is a small city, and Ahmad had heard about our group and thought he could help. I was against him joining, because I thought he was too old, but in the end I was overruled and he came on board. It never occurred to us that if Ahmad had heard about our group, then we were not good at keeping secrets.

I particularly remember a visit to his shop one day. On a sideboard near the counter, he kept a vase of dried flowers, mostly roses. I asked him to tell me the story of the flowers.

"To remind me of long-gone friends," he said with a sad smile.

"Ah, but time is the nemesis of memory." I had recently bought a translation of Proust's *In Search of Lost Time* and was showing off how clever I was.

"I hope not. Otherwise I may end up joining my friends before my time."

"To truly remember you need a connection, a taste, a smell. Some-thing to jog your memory." I bent down to smell the flowers. "These flowers smell of nothing."

"That's right."

"But they all have thorns." I brushed the stem of one flower with my index finger. The thorns were still sharp.

"Don't complain that the rose has thorns; rejoice that the thorns bear roses."

"Did you just make that up?"

"No. The Prophet Muhammad said that. It's in the Quran."

I wasn't sure I'd ever come across that passage and later asked Ali about it. Ali said he'd never heard of it in the Quran or in any religious book he'd read. You just never knew with Ahmad. He made everything sound so believable. Ali was around more often and he was serious about dropping out of university. Our group was now thirteen strong, with Ahmad bringing in three new faces. Ali had stolen a printing machine, a "gift" from his university, to make our pamphlet.

"It was gathering dust in some corner," he said. "No one even knew how to use such a machine. We'll do more good with it."

When you have a group of boys and girls mixing, odd things are bound to happen. In the meetings, I would sometimes catch Reza staring at me, and he'd blush every time I caught him. I knew that I was no beauty, but I liked the attention, truth be told. I approached Leila, the only other female in our group.

"Why is your brother acting all strange? Don't tell me he's in love?"

"He's been in a mood for a while," Leila said. She was the youngest member of our group, but she wasn't at all shy like her brother.

Later, as everyone said their good-byes, Reza asked to speak to me privately.

"I've written some poems," he said, nervously twisting a notepad in his hands. He hadn't said much at the meeting, but now he looked feverish.

"You write poetry? I thought you were a teacher." I was teasing him and enjoying it, too. I had heard him read one of his poems in our first group meeting but now pretended that this was all new to me.

"I'm going be a teacher, but I really want to be a poet."

He wanted me to say something, but for once, I kept quiet. I felt funny. All warm and strange. There were all kinds of emotions running through me. He took a step closer.

"Your name, Massy, should really be Masih, as in Messiah, or Jesus, as the Westerners say."

"I'm not Christian," I said, confused. I hadn't expected him to lecture me about my name.

"You don't have to be Christian to be a Masih."

He handed me the notepad. "I've written something for you."

I returned home to Mina's and quietly read his poem about me. I could tell that my face was flushed and my heart beat wildly. This was the first time someone of the opposite sex had written me a poem. There had been boys who had whistled at me or made catcalls and lewd comments, but no poems. Till now. I inspected every line again and again, expecting a trick.

...But you, my Jesus,
when they place the Crown of Thorns on your head,
spring will have just begun.

Crown of thorns for Jesus. I had never felt comfortable with Masoumeh. Somehow, Masih was more my style.

Reza was thin and pale, with unkempt hair and a permanent four-day stubble. He looked as if he had fixed a car and forgotten to wash the oil off his face. He was a loner. A bookworm.

But I had no time for love. I showed the notepad to Ali.

"We are so messed up in this country that the moment we have a mixed group, everyone wants to fall in love and get married," I complained. "How can we strive to change society when he is sending me love poems?"

I tore the notepad in two and threw it on the floor in front of him. I didn't care for love.

"It's shameful," I said, borrowing one of AghaJan's favorite words. "I'm sure you'll agree if you read it."

I knew if I showed the slightest positive sign to Reza, he'd head straight to Ghomikola and ask AghaJan for my hand in marriage. All around me I had seen how my female relatives who had gotten married were confined to a life of cooking and cleaning and rearing children. I hated the idea of being a traditional woman, submerging my identity into that of my husband.

"Marriage is a prison," I said to Ali. I had been telling him about my feelings for a long time. "I don't want to get married and be trapped. I want more from life than cooking and cleaning."

I knew Ali was on my side, but I also knew that my parents were getting nervous. I was eighteen and still unmarried. Not one suitor had visited my parents and sought their permission to marry me. In Ghomikola this was a big deal for Mother. Girls were married off early and Mother didn't want to lose face. Her neighbors and friends liked to brag about the number of suitors who had come to ask to marry their daughters. The truth is that as I had matured and developed, my looks had not improved. I still had thick, coarse, curly hair; my skin was *sabzeh,* meaning I was olive-skinned; and I was skinny. I wore thick glasses with heavy frames and had a loud voice. My laughter was like a rumble that started deep down and erupted into a roar. My brothers were always telling me to act and behave like a lady, but I wanted to be a free spirit and be true to myself.

Ali visited me at Mina's house the next day. He had put the two halves back together and read the poem, and he liked it. I felt betrayed by my own brother.

"If you like the poem so much, why don't *you* marry him?"

"He's·the only suitor you've got," he said. "It's either that or you can return to Ghomikola after you finish high school and wait it out."

Reza was my only suitor, even if I refused to consider marriage. But I also realized that my alternative was a future of sitting at home in Ghomikola waiting for someone to knock on AghaJan's door. I hated to be so powerless. Ali saw the tears in my eyes and held me tightly by my shoulders.

"It's not as if you can go traveling anywhere if you are a single woman. AghaJan won't allow it. Reza is your ticket out of Ghomikola."

He was right, of course. I didn't want to return to the isolation of village life. For all I knew, AghaJan was already looking for a suitor. It would be better if I picked someone myself. If I wanted to be independent, I had to get married—but to the right man. And the chances of finding one in Ghomikoka were less than zero. Maybe Reza might do. At least he was interested in books and reading.

I met Reza at Niloofar lagoon, which was still full of pink-and-white water lilies even though fall was ending. I took a good look at him as he stood in line to buy us two dooghs—a salty, mint-flavored yogurt drink. His khaki shirt was neat, his jeans had been ironed, probably by his mother, and he carried his aviator sunglasses hooked to his back pocket. He looked like a low risk, the kind of man who'd stand by me and support me. We walked silently side by side along the waterway, sipping our drinks. I decided to cut out the small talk and deal with the main issue.

"I'll marry you, but on one condition: If I don't like married life, I want the right to divorce." I blurted it out. "I don't want to be chained to the kitchen sink."

"I haven't asked you yet," Reza said indignantly, looking around to see if anyone had overheard me, but other couples and families were lost in their own worlds, happily ignoring our awkward courtship. "It's not right."

"Of course you are going to ask me," I said, amused by his confusion. "But I will only say yes if I have the right to divorce."

Asking for the right to divorce was a huge demand for a woman in the Islamic Republic. The law gives men more rights to demand a divorce. Women have few rights in marriage, and if they divorce they can lose custody of their children.

"So you are saying yes." He grinned broadly, looking happy and relieved. "I'm confident that you'll never divorce me, so I'll gladly give you that right."

"I'm marrying you to get out of Ghomikola. Don't think I'm doing it for love. I want to move to Babol and, who knows, maybe Tehran." There was no stopping me. "I want to write, I want to be a photographer. I want to live."

"How romantic," he said, laughing. "Sounds like you have mistaken me for a travel agent."

"If I marry someone in Ghomikola, maybe it won't go so well. Marrying you will give me more freedom."

"Okay. When do we get married?"

He was eager to say the wedding vows right away, but I had to get my parents to agree. It all had to be done in the proper manner if AghaJan was to accept Reza. That night I told Mina and Ramzoon that I had a suitor who wanted to come and meet them to get pointers before heading to Ghomikola to ask AghaJan for permission to marry me. Ramzoon burst out laughing.

"Since when do brides go and find their own grooms? It's a new world."

"It's not as if I have other suitors waiting. It's him or nothing."

"Bring the poor chap," Ramzoon said. He liked how I was different. "Let's see if he's ready and willing for his fate to be sealed."

The following night, at the Kaveh group meeting, Reza and Ali brought two hundred *shabnamehs* that they had produced. Written partly by me, the leaflet was two pages long and the main theme was calling for greater freedom in Iranian society. We were going to distribute them discreetly. Ahmad and his friends agreed to daub political slogans on the walls outside the city hall and the police station. There was no better time to tell Reza that he needed to come and meet my family.

"You better not get arrested," I whispered half in jest to Reza in a quiet moment. Amazingly, having decided that I was going to marry him, I was unsure of my feelings toward him. "You need to come see Mina and her husband soon."

Reza was more excited about the marriage than I was. With a big grin he said, "I'll be there," and grabbed a pile of *shabnamehs,* which he stuffed into a plastic bag.

The next day in the town center, all the walls were covered with our political slogans. "Freedom of Speech for All" and "Free the Political Prisoners" appeared in big letters. Faryad-e Kaveh was everywhere.

I was giddy walking to school, especially as the first snowflakes of the year twirled around me. It was freezing, but I felt a warm glow inside about our political act of defiance. In the far corner of the school yard, one of my friends, Fatemeh, was reading excitedly to a small group of students from a piece of paper in her hand. When I got closer, I realized that she was reading my words that had appeared in the *shabnameh*.

"What's that? A love letter?" I feigned blissful ignorance. Deep inside I was dying to show off and tell everyone that they were reading my words.

"Shhhhh, I'm almost done," Fatemeh said, not allowing any interruptions. She continued reading, but I wasn't listening to her. I knew the words better than she did. Finally, she came to a stop.

"Where did you find it? Whose is it?"

"It was left outside my father's shop, by the metal barrier."

"Have you seen the graffiti in the town?" I asked innocently. "It's everywhere. I wonder if the two are connected."

Fortunately, the bell rang and we all headed inside. I thought everyone could tell just by looking at me, as if a sign were etched on my forehead that I was behind the *shabnameh* and the graffiti. Throughout the day, I was feverish with excitement and scared at the same time. One minute I was euphoric and the next I was panicking I'd be discovered.

I couldn't wait to get out of school and walk around the city to look at our handiwork. But in the afternoon, as I headed home, municipal workers were busy whitewashing our slogans.

There was little time to celebrate, as we had to prepare our next issue. Right away, there were signs of trouble. Now that we had published the first *shabnameh,* Ahmad and his three friends wanted to change the name of the group from Faryad-e Kaveh to Faryad-e Mojahed. The name change seemed a minor affair, but Ahmad insisted on it and we had a number of heated discussions.

"Why change the name now, just as we're starting?" Ali asked the question that was on all our minds.

"Kaveh is old-fashioned. Mojahedin are warriors, and we are engaged in a struggle," he said, pausing dramatically. "I thought you guys wanted to be more than just a high school publication and be real revolutionaries."

"It sounds too close to Mojahedin-e Khalq and I want nothing to do with them," Ali said forcefully, and most of us agreed with him. There was a dark history involved.

The Mojahedin-e Khalq had been crushed by the Shah, after taking up armed struggle in the 1970s. After the 1979 revolution, the Mojahedin were popular among the youth, but they lost a power struggle with Khomeini and ended up resorting to terrorism. They later made a pact with Saddam Hussein, the Iraqi dictator, whose forces had attacked Iran. In 1989, the Mojahedin even launched a military attack on the country but were soundly defeated.

The government was particularly brutal in how it dealt with the group. In 1988 thousands of Mojahedin supporters, and some members of other left-wing groups, were summarily executed. The exact numbers are unknown, but twenty thousand is what some human rights groups claim.

I wasn't alone in feeling we were heading for an implosion.

Was Ahmad a secret Mojahed? He denied it. But his insistence on changing the name made us suspicious of his every move. Finally, we put the name change to a vote, and Ahmad lost, 9–4. The name remained Kaveh.

I had my own worries. Reza kept postponing plans to meet Mina and Ramzoon. I wanted to make sure he passed his audition with Ramzoon so he could come to Ghomikola and ask AghaJan for my hand.

Reza didn't like the two-step setup and wanted to head straight to Ghomikola for a sit down with AghaJan.

"You get only one chance with AghaJan, and if he doesn't like you, there go our chances of getting married," I told him.

Finally, he agreed to come and meet Ramzoon on a Friday afternoon. Quite frankly, I didn't trust Reza to come, and met him beforehand. He wore a green shirt and a tight pair of jeans under a brown duffle coat. With his unkempt hair and stubble, he looked more like a college dropout than a man seeking a wife.

"Is this the best you could do?" I couldn't keep the disappointment out of my voice.

"You need to look the part of a man ready to take a wife to win over my parents. It'd make a big impression on Mina if you wore a jacket, and I don't mean a jean jacket."

He became grumpy after that. His mood didn't improve after I made him buy some flowers and a box of candy and some pastries to bring with him. He complained a lot but agreed.

I went ahead to Mina's home and waited for him to show up. Thankfully, he wasn't late, and Ramzoon and Mina greeted Reza warmly as if he were some rich prince from India. Mina was wearing her new black chador, which she saved for special occasions. It was shiny and shimmered as she walked. She took the men into the living room and then blocked me from following them in.

"You can't go in there," she said in hushed tones as she shut the door behind her.

"They're talking about me. I have every right to be there," I said, trying to wriggle free of Mina.

"This is the time for the men to get the measure of each other." Mina pushed me toward the kitchen. "It's for the men to have a private talk. Ramzoon is going to tell him about our family and what kind of wife he's getting."

"Reza already knows me, and I need to be in the room to make sure Ramzoon doesn't tell embarrassing stories and ruin my reputation."

There was no way past Mina.

"In a few minutes, I'll take in the tea and exchange a few pleasantries and then you can come in with some fruit." Mina wasn't budging.

This wasn't going how I had envisioned it. They were going to discuss me as if I were a piece of property.

"I'm not coming in, so you can talk behind my back all you like," I said petulantly, and retired to the bedroom to play with Mina's children. I stayed there until Reza had left.

Later, Ramzoon said he liked Reza and wanted to set up a time for Reza and his parents to visit Ghomikola to formally ask for my hand.

"Don't worry," Ramzoon said with a smile. "I didn't tell him that he was your only suitor."

Despite myself, I was excited about the fuss being made over me. I regarded the marriage as a contract between two equals and thought that if we agreed, getting parental permission was rather unnecessary.

That weekend, I went back to Ghomikola with Ramzoon to make sure he was handling AghaJan right. We needed to fix a date for Reza and his family to come over. Ali also came along, but he seemed particularly agitated.

The next day, after lunch, AghaJan and Mother went on an errand. I was sitting on the windowsill in the back room with my legs dangling outside when Ali came in, all excited. There was a crazy glint in his eyes. He tried to look calm, but it was obvious he was dying to tell me something. If he had had a tail he'd have thumped it on the floor like a cartoon dog.

"Are you strong enough to kill someone?" he asked.

"I haven't thought about it."

"What if you had a gun—would you kill the president or the Supreme Leader?"

We had played this game before. If you could kill a historical figure to change history for the better, would you do it? In our games, the list included Hitler, Stalin, Genghis Khan, Khomeini, and sometimes even the current Supreme Leader, Ayatollah Ali Khamenei.

"No, because...I don't have a gun."

With a dramatic flourish Ali pulled out a gun from his belt.

"Now we do. What would you do if you came face-to-face with the Supreme Leader? I don't want you to lose your nerve."

"I'm not going to lose my nerve," I said sharply. Ali always knew how to get me riled up.

"Have you ever held a gun in your hand? Here's your chance."

I hopped down from the windowsill and held the gun in both hands. It was heavier than it looked. I liked the sensation of the cold metal.

"Let's pretend-practice so when the time comes you won't mess up." Ali's voice brought me back.

I pointed the gun at a random leaf on a tree in our yard and quietly said, "Pow. Pow."

"That's not going to do it," Ali said as he put his arm around me. "When you fire it, there is a loud noise and the gun has a kick."

"I'm not going to mess it up. Pow...pow...pow," I shouted. The gun felt good in my hand. I closed one eye as if I were really aiming. "Pow...pow..."

"Now put your finger on the trigger." Ali gently adjusted my grip while still holding me firmly with his other hand across my back.

"Now aim at that big tree and press the trigger."

I held the gun with both hands, and, using both index fingers, I squeezed the trigger as hard as I could.

There was a very loud sound as the gun went off and I could swear that I felt the bullet speed away out of the barrel. My ears hurt from the loud noise. I yelled involuntarily and threw the gun out the window. Pulling free from Ali, I punched him in the chest a couple of times.

"What did you make me do?" I yelled.

Outside, our neighbor rushed to the wall, looking worried.

"What was that sound? What are you guys doing?"

"Did you hear that, too? Maybe it was a motorbike backfiring," Ali shouted, as he jumped down into the garden to retrieve the gun.

"What are you going to do with the gun now?" I was worried that AghaJan would find out about it. He would not be too thrilled with the idea of Ali having a gun.

"I'll return it to the guy who loaned it to me. I only had two bullets. I fired one and you fired the other one. A gun without a bullet is useless."

Of course, Ali couldn't keep his mouth shut. He told all our friends in Babol about Masih the gunslinger.

A week after that episode, Ali escorted Reza and his family to our house. Reza didn't need to be escorted, but Ali was returning to Ghomikola anyway. He had finished the semester at Bojnord and had decided to drop out.

Reza arrived with his parents, and this time he was wearing a suit. Of course, he had the sense not to put a tie on, because that would have set AghaJan off on a rant about West-toxification and how ties were a sign of enslavement to Western thinking. I thought Reza looked quite fetching alongside his parents, and he had remembered to bring flowers and candy with him.

I also wanted to look my best. I put on a nice black jacket and a skirt borrowed from a school friend. But the skirt was both long and too big for me. I had to fold the top over and fasten it with a safety pin so that it wouldn't fall down. I was in the middle of hitching the skirt up above my knees when Father walked in.

"Don't show your skinny legs—they might mistake you for a crane." He departed, laughing mightily.

AghaJan and Mother didn't know that Reza and I had already made plans. Traditionally, the groom's family first meets the girl's parents and agree on the terms of marriage. The bride-to-be enters a bit later, bringing in tea and refreshments. After the parents have approved of each other, and only then, will the young couple be left alone for a few minutes, to see if there is any attraction.

Iranian weddings are really a contractual agreement, pure and simple, where families negotiate how much should be paid and what should be included in the transfer. There are two different sums. First is the *jahaziyeh,* or dowry, which the bride brings with her. This is usually household goods: plates, sheets and towels, pots and pans, and modern stuff like cookers and juicers. The other payment to be negotiated is the *mehrieh,* the sum of money the husband agrees to pay the bride in case of divorce. A man can divorce his wife whenever he wishes to do so. A woman cannot divorce her husband unless there are special circumstances—such as if he turns out to be a drug addict or a murderer.

I hated the fuss made over the dowry and whether it was large enough, and grumbled loudly to Mother about it. I'm not a piece of meat or cattle to be valued this way, I told her. I grew so upset that when Ali told me to take in some tea, I said he could do it himself and stormed out to the backyard with a bucket of feed for the dozens of chickens we kept. Ali had no choice but to go in my place to serve the tea.

"So where is our beautiful bride?" Reza's mother, Banoo, asked. "We had hoped to see her by now."

Before Ali could answer, my cries of "Chickee, chickee, c'mon, chickee, chickee" came through the window.

"She has a loud, fine voice, I see," Banoo said.

AghaJan was very pleased with the arrangements, and three days later we all met in Babol's registry office for the *aghd*—the legal wedding ceremony—and signed the marriage contract, having agreed to a *mehrieh* of 20,000 tomans (about $120 in 1995), a copy of the Quran, and 12 gold coins. The *mehmooni,* or wedding reception, would wait till we finished our studies at the end of June.

My mother hugged me.

"*Dokhtar jan,* my lovely daughter, now you'll have to put childish things aside and settle down."

"And you can tell all the family that I have found a husband."

Meanwhile, tensions continued at the Kaveh group. A second *shabnameh* had been published, but Ahmad and his friends kept pushing for more radical language for the third issue. Our original idea was to educate our audience, not to call for an armed struggle. The rows over editorial control of the third issue sapped our energy. I was tired of the infighting, and I wasn't the only one. The final straw came when we discovered that without informing the rest of the group, Ahmad had crossed out our logo and replaced it with the words "Faryad-e Mojahed."

After a heated meeting, we disbanded the group. On Ali's advice, we destroyed our printing equipment; the paintbrushes and spray cans we dumped in a lagoon. Once it was done, I felt a great weight had been lifted off my shoulders. I wanted to finish my studies, and although at first I had started out loathing the idea of getting married, now I wanted to have my wedding reception so that I could be officially married and start a new phase of my life.

CHAPTER FIVE

It was a glorious afternoon in May when disaster struck.

By the middle of spring, Reza was a regular at my parents' house, arriving every weekend for lunch and staying on till after dinner before returning to his parents' place back in Babol.

We were married and not married. Sounds confusing, but we couldn't call ourselves husband and wife until our wedding party. We eagerly waited for the end of the school term, a month or so away.

That May weekend, Reza and I sat with AghaJan as he listed all the uncles and aunts and even a dozen army buddies he wanted to include as guests at the wedding. The more we talked, the more dispirited I became. It was an opportunity for AghaJan to pay back all the favors he owed. Of course, this was going to be a wedding party without any music. To have music we needed a special dispensation from the local cleric. And the party would be segregated.

Still, I was excited. My father and I often clashed over politics and my lifestyle, but that day over lunch we were both very happy. As a rebellious teenager, I was no different from thousands of other teenagers, but my father kept saying that after the wedding I wasn't going to be his problem anymore. And each time he laughed heartily at his own joke.

After lunch, everyone took a nap. That's the culture of village life. Get up early for work. Then lunch and a siesta, especially on weekends. The men slept in one room and my mother and I in another. I woke up early and quietly crept out of the room to sit outside on the porch, waiting for Reza to join me.

The long, hot summer was not far away. The trees, as usual, were filled with birds of all sizes and colors, most hidden among the branches and leaves, but their chirping was a pleasant soundtrack. Sitting all alone, I had a big goofy grin on my face as I waited for the others to get up as well. I don't know how long I sat there, but suddenly I had a feeling that I was not alone.

I detected movement from the corner of my eye. When I looked over, I saw a strange man casually walking through our front yard. We had high walls surrounding our house and orchard, like all the other houses in the village, but we never locked the front gate. Our neighbors came over to our house regularly for a chat over cups of tea.

I retied my head scarf under my chin and stood to get a better look at him. The stranger casually surveyed our house and garden without paying any attention to me, as if he was deliberately avoiding me. Instantly, I could tell he was not from our village, but there was something familiar about him. With his black pants, white shirt buttoned all the way up to his neck, and neat beard, he was too carefully groomed to be from Ghomikola.

I hopped down from the porch and headed toward him. At the back of my mind, alarm bells went off, but everything seemed to happen in a fog. The sky was blue and clear. A gentle breeze caressed the trees. A big blackbird angrily took off from a tree. As I approached the stranger, an inner voice was telling me that nothing good would come of this encounter. But I could not stop myself. I had to confront him.

I stopped about ten feet away from him as he stared at me with a blank look. "Salam," I said, but my voice caught in my throat. I wanted to be brave and strong, but I had choked up. I turned red in the face, angry and embarrassed at the same time. I swallowed hard and started again.

"Hello, do you have business with my father?"

The man looked me up and down, first the face, then my breasts, then my hips and legs, and then my face again.

"Is Mr. Lotfi here?" He managed to be polite and formal. Much to my surprise, he was after Reza and not AghaJan or me. The stranger took a step toward me and I retreated one step and half turned toward the house to shout for Reza just as he emerged onto the veranda, smoothing out his hair. He still had sleep in his eyes and his movements were slow. Our eyes met.

The stranger moved toward the veranda. "Mr. Lotfi?"

His voice cracked with authority, like a hand slapping a table. Reza stared at the stranger blankly. He then rubbed his eyes, as if hoping that once he stopped rubbing, the stranger would disappear like a bad dream.

"Mr. Lotfi?" This time much softer.

Reza stopped rubbing his eyes, but the stranger was still there and moving toward him. Reza now knew what was about to happen and he looked at me with panic in his eyes. Without a sound, he was transformed into a shell of a broken man. He went completely white in the face. His head sank into his neck, and he shrank a size or two—or maybe that's how I remember it now, because normal people don't shrink like that. Unless they are petrified. At that moment time stood still. It all became very quiet. The birds stopped their bickering and the rustling of the wind died down.

"Mr. Lotfi?" A third time.

Reza nodded.

"Well, get your stuff and come with us." The stranger's voice had a hard edge to it.

Just then everything became clear to me. The hairs on my arms and neck stood to attention as I realized the danger we were facing. Perhaps I had known all along, subconsciously, from the very instant I saw the stranger, that this was not going to end well. I knew then that the stranger was a member of the security services. I didn't know which branch of the security apparatus, but I had heard the stories—everyone in Iran had heard a horror story or two—and now an undercover agent stood in our yard about to arrest Reza and me.

I looked at the stranger, expecting him to tell me to get my things, too, but he showed no interest in me.

"I have all my stuff with me," Reza said in a low voice, without emotion. "There is nothing else."

I ran back to the porch and faced Reza. "Let me wake up AghaJan. He'll sort it out. He knows people," I said. "He's a basiji. He has connections."

"No." Reza grabbed my wrist. "Don't do that. Don't tell anyone. You'll make it much worse." He was almost in tears. He didn't want my father to see him being dragged away by the security police.

I nodded.

"Go and wait by the gate," the stranger commanded Reza. "Get going."

Reza limply let go of my wrists and whispered, *"Khoda hafiz"*—good-bye—and headed to the gate, where a second security guy was keeping guard.

I wanted to hug Reza and hold him, not out of love or affection but just to deny the security guards the satisfaction of taking him. The stranger walked past me on the veranda and to my great horror entered the room where AghaJan was sleeping. I followed behind him, not sure what was going to happen next.

My father slept on his back on a futon on the floor, wearing pajama bottoms and a work shirt that had partly rolled up, revealing a patch of his belly. Even though the room was shrouded in semidarkness, he had covered his eyes with a piece of cloth. He could only sleep in complete darkness.

The stranger looked around the room, and I followed his gaze and began to see the room afresh, the threadbare machine-made carpet, the pile of futons in one corner, the bare walls, the absence of any furniture. Yes, we are poor, I wanted to shout, but we are proud, and you can't treat us this way. But I kept my thoughts to myself. The only decoration was in one corner. I had framed a picture of a goat with a wispy white beard and a caption: "I think, therefore I am." Without a word, the stranger took the picture out of the frame and folded it, placing it in his pocket.

He knelt and gently tapped my father on the shoulder.

"Hajj Agha, Hajj Agha, wake up." "Hajj agha" is an honorific for those who make the hajj pilgrimage to Mecca, but it's also a way of addressing men from traditional and conservative families.

Father snapped awake immediately. For a few moments he stared at the stranger, and then he sat up quickly. He could sense there was danger afoot. I sensed he was embarrassed that a stranger had found him sleeping and had woken him up, and now he was going to be in a foul mood. He frowned at me.

"Hajj Agha, your groom, your son-in-law, well, we have to take him in." The stranger guided my father out of the room. "He's been doing things that have not been in the nation's best interest. He was plotting against the Supreme Leader."

Without warning, AghaJan turned to me. "What about her? Are you taking her, too?" he asked the agent as he glared at me.

"We are still investigating, but I'll do what I can to save her."

"Everyone in Ghomikola knows I'd give my life for the Supreme Leader," AghaJan said. "Ask around, everyone here will confirm it."

The stranger took out the picture he had removed from the frame and opened it in front of me.

"What is this supposed to mean? What is the meaning of this?"

"It's just a goat," I said.

"So you are not trying to mock the Supreme Leader?" he said in a friendly voice.

My father erupted in anger. "Arrest this one, too," he said, pointing in my direction. And then, to me: *"Oof bar to."* Shame on you. He raised his hand to slap me, but it just stayed in the air. "You are so wicked, you'll make the devil blush with shame. You have brought me nothing but dishonor."

All he wanted was for me to be a normal girl, get married and have kids, but now everything had turned sour.

I ran barefoot to the gate to say good-bye to Reza before they took him away, but I arrived too late.

"Reza," I yelled, but he never turned back. I watched him meekly get into the backseat of a white Paykan with the security men.

A group of boys some fifty feet away took turns riding an antiquated bike, oblivious to the drama playing out. They shouted and laughed and fought as multiple arms and legs and heads blurred into one. Close by, an exhaust pipe from a different car backfired; it sounded like a bullet from a revolver, startling me and sending the birds out of the trees. Maybe about a hundred birds flapped their wings and soared into an oval orbit around the trees in our yard.

"What about the wedding?" Mother asked worriedly. "When will they let him out?"

What she really wanted to know was whether I was going to be arrested, too. That was an excellent question. The security men had left, but the stench of fear was in the air. We all worried about what would come next. Father has always been a true believer in the Islamic Republic, but his children didn't share his belief.

"The devil can take her. Let her go to hell," Father said to no one in particular, pacing up and down the veranda. He was seething. "I'd take her to jail myself if the Supreme Leader tells me to. My own daughter mixed up with antirevolutionaries."

Nothing like this had happened to him before. He was used to being the one enforcing the Islamic laws; now he was confused and upset. He looked at me with real anger. When I was younger, I used to feel safe with him; I knew his moods and could predict his actions just by observing little signs, like how many chickens he sold on his trips to Babol, the way he took off his coat and boots, the way he called for his cup of tea to be brought to him after a day in the fields. He could be obstinate and scary, but for the past year I'd lost my ability to read his moods. He hadn't changed that much. I had—and in the process, I had become inattentive to his little signs.

"Oof bar to," he said again. Pretty soon everyone in the village would start talking about AghaJan losing control of his family. The humiliation of it all.

I had my own worries.

Usually, I am absentminded to the nth degree—I'm always forgetting my books, or losing my bus money, or leaving my keys in the door. But I realized I had to alert Ali the and other Kaveh members about Reza's arrest. Others could be arrested, too. Ali had started military service in Urmia, the second-biggest city in Azerbaijan, near the Turkish border, and it was impossible to contact him during basic training.

I needed to warn Leila, Reza's sister, and her family, and make sure there was no incriminating evidence left behind. We didn't have a telephone in our house. In fact, no one in our village did. There was a telephone exchange in Noushiravankola, the closest village. Often, we'd walk or take a bus there and fill out a form for the operator, writing down the phone number we wanted to contact. Once it was our turn, we'd be called into a small kiosk with a glass door that had a telephone inside.

"I have to let Leila know about the arrest," I said.

"Not your responsibility," Mother said. "You need to stay here with your family."

Nothing was going to hold me back. I threaded my arms through my jacket, hopped into my white sneakers, and took off. I sped past the boys still taking turns on their bike and then slowed to a steady jog along the dirt paths and unpaved roads next to the rice fields and fruit orchards. A few cars and vans sputtered past me without paying me any attention. It was just me and my thoughts. They had taken Reza, but who was next? I wondered. I didn't stop at Noushiravankola but continued on to the next village, Sheikh Mahaleh. I'd never used the telephone exchange there and hoped no one would recognize me. By the time I got there, I was exhausted, thirsty, and dusty.

I called Reza's parents and through sheer luck Leila answered. Before I could tell her the news, she blurted out: "The police were here this morning. They were looking for Reza."

"He was with us. They took him," I said grimly. The kiosk walls were thin, and I was suddenly conscious that the exchange center had gone very quiet. "I'll tell you the rest when I see you."

I took a bus to Babol and walked to Reza's parents' house. I had butterflies in my stomach as I reached for the doorbell, unsure of the reception that awaited me. Reza's mother, Banoo, was quite traditional, always wearing the chador whenever she left the house, just like my own mother. She doted on Reza, her only son, and was suspicious of me because I had usurped her place in his heart. Banoo thought I was loud, ugly, and too thin—a country girl wanting to be a city girl, always arguing, always talking.

But today, I had no one else. I felt alienated from my own family. I badly needed a friendly face. There was the sound of footsteps from the other side of the door and Banoo pried open the door to peek outside. Her eyes were red from crying, but she smiled when she saw me and I fell into her arms, unable to control my sobs.

"They took him away but he was so brave," I said as I described the day's events. I don't know how long I cried, but it was comforting to be somewhere I felt safe.

I had to repeat the details several times and answer many questions about Reza's arrest before Banoo was satisfied. At the end, she hugged me hard. I smelled of sweat and the dust of the road. Banoo could only take so much before she sent me to take a shower. But even then, as steaming water poured over me, I could not relax. The dirt and smell may have been gone, but the fear remained.

Later, as I sat in the kitchen over a cup of tea, I could barely keep my eyes open, but something was bothering Banoo. "Why would they take him away?" she kept asking. "What were you guys really up to?" She refilled my cup and warmed up a plate of food. "What did you do? You must have done *something*."

"We didn't do anything," I said. "We read some books and

wrote about them. That's all we did, I swear." I started crying again.

"Do you love my Reza?" Banoo asked suddenly. She was unmoved by my tears. She cupped my face in her hands. "Reza is a follower, not a leader. What trouble did *you* get into? How could you lead my son into trouble?"

Banoo was convinced that I was behind the trouble. I refused the food and begged her to let me sleep.

"Why didn't they arrest you?" Leila asked as she rolled out a futon for me.

It was a good question.

She wanted to talk more but I passed out in exhaustion.

Next morning, I headed to school as if it were a normal day. But it wasn't. On the way, I kept looking behind me, dreading every time a white Paykan came near me. There were lots of Paykans on the road, but not one paid any attention to me. I don't remember much about my classes, because throughout the day I expected to be arrested at any moment. I vowed to myself that if the police came for me, I wouldn't be taken without a struggle. In my head, I played out different scenarios of how I'd resist the security men, maybe even run into the oncoming traffic and throw myself in front of a car. I could barely sit still in class. Not that I was a good student at the best of times, but my nerves were on edge.

I returned to Banoo's house rather than going to Mina's or returning to Ghomikola. I just couldn't face my sister or Ramzoon. No one knew what had become of Reza. Banoo and Hormouz, Reza's father, had tried the police and the Intelligence Ministry, but received no information. Both denied they held Reza. This meant we were in serious trouble. Banoo tried to be kind, but I would catch her staring at me with a scowl on her face. She didn't say it exactly, but she blamed me for Reza's disappearance.

The next morning, I skipped school and instead took a bus to Ghomikola. I knew Father would be out peddling chickens and eggs on the street and so it was safe for me to go home to change clothes and talk to my mother. I felt so lonely.

"Masoumeh, where have you been?" Mother said with obvious relief. She was really happy to see me, and at that moment, I forgot all my other worries and was happy to be her little girl again. "We were worried. Where have you been staying?"

"I was at Banoo's. They can't find Reza. We're all really worried," I said quickly.

My mother grew quiet.

"Don't worry, I'm not going to get arrested," I reassured her. "It's all a big mistake."

Mother didn't look convinced. I didn't care because it was good to be home. I changed into clean clothes, and mother made some tea to drink and brought me a plate of fresh bread and cheese and vegetables. As I ate, she lectured me about obligation and duty and family honor. It was a lecture she had given many times before, but I was not in the mood to listen.

I knew that my mother loved me totally and absolutely, and I was sure that I was her favorite daughter. And I loved my mother, but I didn't want to end up like her. My life was just beginning, I thought as she lectured me. I wanted to experience it to the fullest, unbowed, unafraid, because I only had one life to live and wanted every day to be a new adventure. For Mother, family and reputation had special meanings that were lost on me. Her days were predictable, while I wanted mine to be full of surprises. Because of Reza's arrest, she was now on uncertain ground, and it worried her.

Mother desperately wanted to protect me, but there is a price to pay for being safe and secure, just as there is a price to pay for being daring. I didn't want love of earthly possessions or binding family ties or even fear of failure to stop me from doing what I thought was right.

A loud banging on the front door reverberated through the house. Mother had locked the front door after Reza's arrest so no one could enter unannounced and uninvited. She pulled her chador around herself and headed to the door. People dropped by our house all the time, and so there was no cause for alarm. I watched her open the door and then take a couple of steps back. A security service agent not many years older than me walked through. He wore an untucked shirt and had a beard and thick black hair. This was the unspoken uniform of security service personnel. His eyes wandered around till he saw me, still holding a glass of tea in my hand.

The moment I saw him, I knew that he had come to arrest me. He looked like a hunter who had found his prey. My childish hopes that somehow I'd be able to escape the attention of the security agencies were dashed.

"Khanom Masoumeh?" He had addressed me as Ms. Masoumeh. "Please get your things and come with me," he said brusquely.

"She has done nothing." Mother answered in my place. "She knows nothing, you took her fiancé, you can let her be."

"It's okay, Mother jan. Don't worry, we just need to ask her a few questions."

"They had just decided to marry, but they weren't really that close. She is a simple girl, she knows nothing." Mother continued to plead.

"It'll be very quick, Hajj Khanom. We don't need her for long—we are just going to ask her a few questions and we'll bring her right back." The agent smiled at Mother to reassure her. He was careful not to touch her, because touching a woman you are not related to is tantamount to a sin.

I had said nothing, hoping that Mother would somehow persuade him to let me stay.

"Khanom." He looked at me again. "Put your chador on and let's go."

"I'm not going to put a chador on," I said loudly, and stalked off without waiting for a reply.

"You have to put a chador on if you are to enter government offices," the agent shouted. "If you make a scene, I can radio for a woman agent to come and put a chador on you." He paused uncertainly. "You are making it worse for yourself," he added as an afterthought.

Mother was in a frenzy and rushed after me. "Please put your chador on, don't make him angry." She had tears in her eyes. "He said he'll bring you right back. Don't make it worse for yourself."

She didn't want to lose face in front of a stranger. Somehow, getting arrested was less worrisome than not wearing a chador.

"I hate the black chador. I don't wear a chador at school, and I'm not going to wear it now," I said. "It makes me look like a crow."

I didn't want to sacrifice my principles. I had fought against wearing the chador and had worn down both my parents so that I didn't have to wear one when I went to school. It was more than a fashion statement. It was about my identity. I didn't want to pretend to be someone I wasn't. I hated wearing the chador even then. I could sense it in my body—being forced to wear the chador was wrong.

"They can arrest me for not wearing a chador. Either way, I'm going to jail," I said with an anger that surprised even me. "They get to choose what to charge me with."

"Masoumeh jan, please don't do this." Mother held my soft and smooth fingers in her rough hands. "Don't make a scene. If our neighbors see…"

Tears streamed down her cheeks. I stared at her lined face and the calluses on her hands. She wasn't supposed to cry. I knew how she had toiled every day, on the farm and in the kitchen, and she never complained how hard life had treated her. I couldn't stand to see her cry. I felt guilty. My resolve weakened.

The fight had gone out of me. Now it was my turn to cry quietly. I wasn't worried about getting arrested, but I was upset because I knew that I had to give in and wear the hated chador.

Mother rushed to a corner and came back with a white chador with a flowery pattern she had removed from a wooden chest. "This was to be your wedding chador. It's white with a nice pattern," she said triumphantly.

"I wasn't planning on wearing a chador at my wedding," I said. I forgot my current predicament and the security agent waiting outside. "We never discussed this. You knew I wasn't going to wear a chador to my own wedding."

"You are going to be blessed in this chador," Mother said as she wrapped it over my head. "This chador will protect you. I know no harm can befall you now that you are wearing your wedding chador."

For Mother, it was as if I were putting on a suit of armor on my way to battle, like the legendary heroes in history books. I'd be safe as long as I had my chador, she said. In a way, I was going to war, but I needed more than a piece of cloth. Mother led me to the front gate. The agent walked in front of us and opened the back door of a white Paykan as we said our teary good-byes.

"The gentleman said you'll be back soon," Mother said. "Tell the truth and you'll be home for supper."

I hugged her so tightly that I could feel her heart beating in her chest.

CHAPTER SIX

I walked unsteadily to the white Paykan. The car door shut behind me and the driver took off as soon as a second agent got in. A third man sat in the driver's seat, and the front windows were open.

"Bend your head," the agent said, and as I did, he blindfolded me and everything went dark. I didn't even get a chance to turn back for a final look at Mother. I was scared but determined not to show it. In fact, whenever I'm scared, I get bolder.

"How long do you plan on keeping me?"

"Be quiet," said a stern voice—the driver's, judging from the direction it came from.

"The prisoner must keep quiet," the agent nearest to me said, to make sure I hadn't missed the point.

"My mother is expecting me soon."

"Shut up," the agent ordered. "I'm not going to warn you again."

After that, we drove in silence for a long while. The driver zigzagged through the narrow lanes and dirt roads of Ghomikola, taking corners with some speed, which made me bounce around on the backseat. I tried to imagine the roads that I had often walked on and the tiny villages that dotted the road to Babol. A pleasant breeze cooled the car. Being in total darkness was at first alarming, but then I lost myself to the beeping of the car horns, the grind and squeak of car brakes, and the revving of motorbikes zooming past.

The driver began honking the horn and then braked suddenly. The next thing I knew, I was hurled at full speed into the back of the front seat as the car ground to a stop. I bumped my head against the door. Crying out in pain, I reached up to remove the blindfold.

"Don't touch it," the agent said. "You must keep the blindfold on at all times."

"The way you are driving...don't go so fast," I said as I leaned back.

Eventually we came to a final stop and the engine was shut off. One of the back doors opened and I was told to get out. The agent beside me handed me a piece of cloth twisted and rolled into a rope.

"Hold on to this and follow me," he said.

As I held on to the rope, I used my free hand to half lift the blindfold to get my bearings. We were headed toward a four-story modern building that had a huge sign above the entrance: BABOL INTELLI-GENCE MINISTRY. I dropped my hand and followed the agent inside the building. We walked through a long corridor, our footsteps echoing on the hard surface, and then took two quick left turns before I heard a key entering what sounded like an old-fashioned lock.

"Get in," the agent commanded, encouraging me with a push. Once I was in, the door slammed behind me.

I took off my blindfold cautiously and found myself in a tiny cell with a red metal door. I tried the handle. It didn't budge. The cell was about five feet by six feet, the floor was hard and dirty, and graffiti covered the stained walls. It was odd the number of prayers written on the walls to a God that had abandoned those who had scrawled them. If I stretched out my arms I could just about touch two of the walls at the same time. A dim lightbulb attached to the corrugated sheet-metal roof provided little comfort or light. The air was dank and stale—a four-inch gap between where the red door ended and the roof began provided the only flow of fresh air. I took three steps and bumped against one wall. I turned and three steps later I was at the other wall. I paced back and forth for a few minutes but soon I was tired.

I wasn't scared anymore. I had been scared in the car, but that feeling had passed, and now that I was in the cell, my immediate worry was that the floor was too dirty to sit on. I actually thought I was having a big adventure; I still didn't think I had done anything wrong and expected to be released fairly soon. Just answer a few questions and I'd be out, the agent had assured Mother.

Minutes went by and I walked around the cell some more. Still no one appeared. Gradually, a sense of unease crept in. It was very quiet. Not a sound could be heard. Nothing—no muffled voices, no hum of machinery, no sound of doors being slammed. What I distinctly remember is the silence that descended. In one of my science classes, I'd learned about absolute silence in space, and now I felt as if I were there. I leaned against the wall, not moving a muscle, and slowed down my breathing. I desperately wanted to hear another sound so that I knew I was not alone. The silence was eerie. It was so powerful that I didn't want to make a sound, either. Morbid thoughts entered my head—what if there was an earthquake? I was all alone and no one knew I was here. Would they remember to rescue me? I wondered.

Minutes ticked by. The air was heavy with humidity and I was covered in sweat.

Suddenly and with no warning, an almighty thunderclap exploded above me. Millions of drops of rain drummed against the corrugated metal roof, like bullets fired from a celestial machine gun into my cell. A second thunderclap cracked and then a third and a fourth, all in quick bursts. The artillery of the summer storm.

The first explosion of sound made me jump, and in a panic, I rushed to the heavy red door and started pounding on it with my fists, but the barely audible noises that I made were drowned out by the sound and fury above my head.

"Let me out of here," I screamed. No one came. I wasn't sure if anyone could hear me. I started crying and punching the door. I squatted by the door, hoping to be rescued, but no one came to help me.

Just as quickly as it had arrived, the storm departed, and with it the torrent of rain on the roof of my cell petered out. To this day, I get nervous and jittery when there is thunder and lightning.

Sometime after the rain stopped, I heard noises outside my cell, doors opening and shutting and the sound of voices—but too far away and muffled for me to make any sense of them. Soon came a rattling of keys outside my door, which opened briefly. A guard put a metal tray containing a bowl of *ab-goosht,* meat soup, and a piece of bread and a glass of water on the floor. It was a welcome sight. A piece of meat floated in a sea of greasy water. The soup's aroma was far from pleasing, and as for the taste, well, it was nothing like what my mother made for us. I broke off small pieces of the stale bread and threw them into the soup and greedily ate it all up. The meat was tough and tasted undercooked and I chewed for a long time before I could swallow it.

If there was a mattress there, I'd have happily taken a nap. Instead, I banged on the door demanding to be let out to use the toilet. I must have made quite a lot of noise because footsteps approached.

"Someone should have told you the rules." A guard spoke from behind the locked door. I could only use the bathroom three times a day, he explained, so I had better use my visits wisely.

"Each time, before I come in, I will knock on the door, and you must put on the blindfold, wear your chador, and sit on the floor with your back to the door. Then, you must say 'Ready,'" he said, stressing the last word. "Only after you say the word will I open the door. Understood?"

"I really need to go to the toilet."

"Did you hear what I said? Do you remember what I just told you?"

Reluctantly, I put the blindfold on, wrapped my white chador around me, and gingerly sat down. I hated getting my beautiful white chador dirty, but there was no way around it.

"READY," I yelled at the top of my voice.

The door opened and the guard entered. He touched my shoulder with a thick cord.

"Grab this," he said gruffly. "Didn't they tell you to wear black?" He seemed put off by my white flowery chador. "Follow me."

I held on to the cord with one hand, and with the other I held my chador tightly under my chin and followed him slowly. I felt very vulnerable. So this is what it must be like to go blind, I thought. He guided me to the toilet, where I could remove the blindfold. For now, my cell and the toilet were the only places where I didn't have to wear it.

I returned to my cell and the hours dragged by. I wasn't scared, just bored and restless. In any detention boredom is the real challenge. I sat and stared at the ceiling. I read the graffiti on the walls; I even sang to cheer myself up. Some time later, another tray with more food appeared, along with two blankets. I rolled one heavy blanket under me to lie on and pulled another over me and, still wearing all my clothes, tried to go to sleep. I spent a sleepless night tossing and turning, trying to get comfortable. The blankets were rough and coarse and the light stayed on all the time. I feared there might be mice or cockroaches or, worse, centipedes roaming around the cell if I were to doze off. I've always been squeamish about mice and bugs and now I checked constantly.

I hoped Mother and AghaJan were worried about my absence. I missed my family and I wanted them to be concerned about me and make a big fuss. I wondered whether Mother had ever imagined that my wedding chador would see the inside of a prison. Probably not.

The next morning, the clank of a metal breakfast tray roused me. A piece of bread, a tiny cube of salty cheese, and some tea. A guard hollered from behind the door, "Hurry up, put your blindfold on, you are going to meet the *bazjoos*"—the interrogators.

I was filled with dread, and yet at the same time I felt a sense of relief. I wasn't naïve, but I didn't think my crimes were serious, and I imagined that my ordeal must almost certainly be nearly over. After spending most of the day before all by myself, I looked forward to talking to another human being. The guard kicked the door three times.

"You have the blindfold on?" he shouted.

"Yes," I replied.

"You've got to say 'Ready.'" He sounded exasperated.

"READY."

The guard nudged me with the cord, and with him in the lead we walked into another part of the building, turning a couple of corners before entering a room.

"Sit down," said a gruff voice I had not heard before. I could not see him, as I had my blindfold on, but my other senses were working overtime. The room smelled like it was coated with nicotine and fear.

I gingerly sank onto the floor and wrapped the chador around me, like a cloak, and held it tight. There were two *bazjoos* in the room, both standing behind me. As the days went by, I came to think of them as the scary *bazjoo* and the consultant *bazjoo*—the word he used to describe himself. The consultant had a sad voice and said that he was going to be my friend. It was the good cop, bad cop routine, with the difference that the good cop was pretending he wasn't even a cop.

The two men conferred in hushed tones. I tilted my head toward them, hoping to catch a word or two that might set my mind at ease. At last, one of them dragged a chair along the floor slowly until it was directly behind me. Sitting on the floor, I felt very vulnerable, especially with the scraping of the chair so close to me.

"Everyone talks eventually. I'm going to ask you lots of questions and you're going to tell me the truth," he said matter-of-factly. "I can always tell when someone lies to me. Don't waste my time. Tell me the truth and we will be done very quickly."

He waited for me to speak but I kept quiet.

"Put out your hand," he barked.

Nervously, I stretched my hand out from under the chador. I felt something cold and heavy.

"This is a heavy-duty chain that I use on those who don't cooperate," he said. "Just think about how much damage this chain can do to you. Just think about that."

He and the other man walked out, leaving me by myself holding the chain. I am not brave when it comes to enduring physical pain. Was he actually going to beat me with that chain? I wondered. I was so scared that even after he had left I didn't dare to take off my blindfold.

After a while, the door opened and the consultant *bazjoo* returned. He sat in the chair behind me. I had my blindfold on still but could sense his movements.

"For your sake, please tell him the truth," he said. He leaned in close to me. "See, I'm just an observer, not an interrogator. I'm here to make sure the procedures are followed correctly, but my colleague, he has a terrible temper. Tell him what he needs to know and you'll be fine."

He spoke in a soft voice that made me want to trust him. I almost asked him if he was from Ghomikola. It sounds stupid, I know, but I felt that if he was from my village, then he would look after me, make sure I would come out in one piece. I needed a friend, someone to be in my corner, during the long hours of questioning.

The scary *bazjoo* came back and the interrogation began. In a monotone, he asked a number of basic questions, such as my date of birth and home address, as if he was filling out a form, before moving on to questions about my brothers and other family members. He asked about my schools and why I had switched.

"Are you a popular girl?" he asked suddenly. "Who is your best friend?"

"I just changed schools. I don't have many friends," I said.

"What about your previous school?"

"I've lost touch with them," I said stubbornly. I wasn't about to snitch on my friends.

In the afternoon, he picked up the pace as he grilled me about my political views.

Was I a communist? I shook my head.

"What was Kaveh, if not a communist cell?"

"It was a reading group, to educate ourselves."

"Your reading list contained many books about communism."

"I never got around to reading those books. I like poetry books."

"Tell me about how Kaveh was formed. Who created the group?"

"It just came together. I don't think anyone created it." It was better to act dumb, I told myself.

He kept asking and probing for the next few hours, and then at the end of the afternoon, instead of being released, I was led back to my cell.

"I want to go home," I yelled through the cell door. "I've told you everything."

"This is your home now," the guard shouted back, laughing.

Cut off from the rest of the world and stuck in the dirty cell, I prayed for a way out of my ordeal so I could return home. I kept wondering why no one from my family had tried to find me. Had I been truly abandoned by Mother? I wondered. For the next two days, a pattern developed. Breakfast was followed by a session of questioning in the interrogation room that was halted for lunch, and this was followed by more questioning before I was led back to my cell. I cried myself to fitful sleep every night.

By the fourth day, my head was spinning from the constant questioning and lack of sleep. That morning, in the stifling heat of the interrogation room, I dozed off. I was sitting as usual on the floor, my eyes shut tight under the blindfold and covered by the chador. As the *bazjoo* went on a long preamble before a question, I fell asleep. It was all too brief, but I dreamed of floating over our garden in Ghomikola. In my dream, I saw myself sleeping under a tree with the rest of my family, all my brothers and my sister and my cousins and aunts having a picnic next to me. Everyone was happy, eating and being merry, even though I was sleeping under the tree. Then without warning the mood changed; dark clouds gathered, the wind picked up, and a rainstorm sent the family indoors. Lightning crashed around the tree as the rain rolled in like a blackout curtain. "Wake up," I yelled at my sleeping self to get her out of the rain.

"What are you shouting about? Have you lost your mind?" The scary *bazjoo*'s shout brought me back to the interrogation room. "Stop acting like a crazy woman."

I heard the door open, and the other *bazjoo* rushed in. "What happened?" he asked.

"Nothing. She started shouting for no reason," the scary *bazjoo* replied.

Only then did I realize that I must have yelled loudly enough to alarm the other interrogator. The two men conferred. Truth be told, I was scared of them both. Even the sound of their breathing scared me. I had never been alone in a room with two men who were not family before. I had always had another female or a male relative, like my brother, present. Even with the chador wrapped tightly around me, I felt as if they could see my naked body and were ready to violate me. I felt truly miserable and sobbed quietly.

After some discussion, the scary *bazjoo* left, and his soft-spoken colleague addressed me in a kind voice.

"I don't know what happened, but my colleague didn't mean to scare you." He squatted down next to me. He was almost whispering. "I want to help you to get out of here, but I need your help. Because *he* doesn't think you are being truthful."

"I just don't know what to tell you," I said, whimpering. "I'm tired. I've told you all I can."

"Take off your blindfold," he commanded.

Slowly, I reached up and took the wretched cover off. After my eyes had adjusted to my surroundings, I turned to look at the nice *bazjoo*. He had a friendly face, with neatly cropped dark hair and gold-rimmed glasses.

He handed me sheaves of paper with the saying, in Arabic, *Al-Nejat fi Al-Sedq*—"The truth shall set you free"—at the top of each page.

"Write down everything about yourself and how you got involved with Kaveh. Tell us about your friends, your family, anyone who was involved with Kaveh." He spoke without any sense of urgency. "Tell us everything." And he left me.

I sat on the carpeted floor and wrote out my confession. I didn't know it at the time, but that was only the first draft, and I would end up writing many more versions before I was finally released.

After what must have been hours, the door opened and the scary *bazjoo* entered—a short, swarthy man with small eyes, wearing a pinstripe jacket that was cut too long and a shirt buttoned to the top without a tie.

I handed him my confession. He quickly scanned it and swore under his breath.

"You think you can fool me?" he roared. "Your innocent act doesn't work here. You are going to write and tell me everything, or you'll never leave here."

"I don't know any more. You've got to believe me, agha." I lowered my eyes. "We only produced a pamphlet, that's all."

"Put your blindfold on and get out," he growled. A few minutes later the guard appeared and took me back to my cell.

The next day, the scary *bazjoo* was waiting for me. "Don't you want to get out of here and return home? Your poor mother must be worried about you."

"She knows I'm here? Is she coming to visit me?" I screamed with joy. "Please let me see her." Then, overwhelmed with emotion, I started to cry.

"You are a stupid peasant girl," he said scornfully. "No one knows where you are. No one even knows if you are alive or dead."

I cried into my white chador that was supposed to bring me happiness. I wanted to go home.

"I will write whatever you want, I swear to God I will," I pleaded. "Just give me the papers, just like the ones you gave me before."

"Let's start again. Tell me about Kaveh. Who had the idea to start the group?" he asked.

Once I had finished a page, he'd take my confession and leave the room, only to return, demanding details that I had held back.

He seemed to know all the secrets of our group and was just toying with me.

"Who paid you? Where did you get the money? Tell me about your finances."

"What money?" I said indignantly. "You think if I had money, I'd steal books?"

He left the room and returned some minutes later.

"You had a printing machine, a copying machine, to produce the pamphlets." He paused. "Who paid for that?"

I tried to act dumb to buy time to think. I didn't want to tell them that my brother Ali had supplied it. So far, I had downplayed his involvement in Kaveh. I desperately tried to think of some subterfuge, something to trick him with, but he read my mind.

"We know everything already. This is for your own sake, so that you are saved."

I bit my lips nervously. I didn't want to betray my own brother.

"Who bought you the printing device?"

"No one."

He persisted. "Where did Ali get the money to buy the device?"

So, they knew about Ali, I thought.

"Ali stole it from his university," I told him.

"Where is it now?

"In the marshlands on the outskirts of Babol."

That afternoon, when I returned to my cell, Leila was waiting for me.

"What are you doing here?" I was startled. "Are you here to get me out?"

But she burst into tears as she held me tight. Leila told me she had been picked up two days after I was arrested but held at another detention center and now had been moved here for questioning.

"I've told them everything," she sobbed. "I was so scared." She had not seen Ali or my mother or anyone from my family.

Seeing Leila gave me a lot of strength. I was going crazy sitting in that cell by myself in the evenings.

Sleep was a challenge that night. The cell was already too small for one person, but now, every time one of us moved, we collided with each other. But our real problem was the next cell.

It was occupied by a male prisoner. He was charged with killing his wife and faced the death penalty. He spent that night raving and ranting about his wife. He punched the walls and begged forgiveness from God for his sins. One minute he demanded to be hanged and the next minute he pleaded to be released so he could look after his children.

"I didn't mean to kill her, it was an accident," he said again and again. I often wondered if he was insane or just pretending. "Don't hang me. What will happen to my children if you kill me? They'll be left with no one to look after them."

Even though the walls were thick enough to protect us, Leila and I held on to each other all night as his voice reverberated around us.

"Leila, what will happen to us?" I asked. "What if they keep us for months?"

"I've already told them everything," Leila said. "I will tell them whatever they want to know. You should, too. I don't want to die."

It was only after the other prisoner quieted down that I fell asleep. When I woke up, there was no sound from the other cell. That day, it was the consultant *bazjoo* who took over the questioning. He greeted me pleasantly, like one of my teachers, and asked me to sit at the desk so I could write more of my confession. I had to keep writing my confession until the *bazjoos* were satisfied I had nothing more to give.

"Have you ever wanted to kill someone?" he asked quietly. "Like someone important, like one of our leaders."

In all my confessions, I had made no mention of Ali and me firing a gun. That would have elevated our little protest group into something much more sinister. That was a secret I had to keep at all costs.

"No. Violence only begets more violence," I said. "Killing doesn't solve the fundamental problems of our society," I continued in a monotone. "We wanted to educate the people, change their thinking."

"My name is Mr. Sadeghi," he said out of the blue. "And I'm trusting you with my name and I want you to trust me."

He was tall and lean and wore a brown suit. He played with a set of red worry beads in his right hand. The door behind me was shut, and for a few moments I feared that he was going to force me to have sex with him.

"I'm not an interrogator, not like my colleague." He waved toward the door. "As I've told you before, I'm an adviser, a consultant. I'm here to make sure things go smoothly and easily."

Many years later, I discovered that it was all lies. His name was not Sadeghi, he was not on my side, he was not my friend. In fact, he was in charge of all the interrogations in Babol.

Mr. Sadeghi consulted a folder on his desk. "You've been good, but there are a few gaps in the story that we have to clear up before my partner loses his patience."

We had reached the tipping point of the interrogation. Where the scary *bazjoo* would threaten to beat me up, Sadeghi, a sophisticated interrogator, was looking for a different way to get me to confess.

"I've told you everything, I swear it on the Quran, on all the saints," I said. "There is nothing more to tell."

"Do you belong to the Mojahedin?" he casually asked.

"No," I said in alarm. "I swear I do not."

"Good, I believe you, but what about Ahmad?" he asked.

"When we realized Ahmad was a former Mojahed we broke up. He was too radical for us. I've told you that."

"Mojaheds like to assassinate people, especially our leadership—you know that, right?" he asked. He sounded reasonable and friendly.

"We didn't want to associate with the Mojaheds."

"Have you thought about a situation where someone might use a gun?" he asked. "To assassinate our leaders."

"No. I never did. It'd be illegal."

"So, why would you fire a gun in your backyard if not for the purpose of training to kill someone?"

Someone must have betrayed me, I thought.

"Ali gave the gun back," I said, and immediately regretted it.

"So, Ali had the gun."

"We had only two bullets. Ali fired one bullet and I fired the last one. We gave the gun back."

"So, you did fire a gun." Mr. Sadeghi gave me a hard stare. He looked disappointed. "Why would you do that?"

He had finally gotten what he wanted.

For the afternoon session, the scary *bazjoo* was waiting for me in the interrogation room.

"This time, we want everything."

I wrote and wrote and then wrote some more. I had resisted for as long as I could not to implicate anyone else, but all my defenses were down. I was done.

The next morning, a guard knocked on the door three times. Both Leila and I were ready, wearing our chadors and blindfolds, with our backs turned to the door.

"READY," we shouted.

The guard tapped me hard on my shoulder with a coil of rope. "Grab this," he said harshly. "Don't let go."

I followed the guard, and Leila had her hand on my shoulder. We walked down a long corridor and I could hear cars on the street and voices of the people on the street as fresh air hit our lungs. It was good to be outside and I squeezed Leila's hand. We're going home, I thought.

We sat in the back of the car with our blindfolds on and the car took off. I wanted to scream and shout and laugh but was afraid that if I showed any joy, we might be sent back to the detention center. I was on my way home and didn't want to do anything to be sent back to that dank cell. I looked forward to seeing my family. I wanted to hug my mother really hard and never let her go. I missed my family so much. I had confessed and now my ordeal was done, I thought. I could still get to finish high school and marry Reza. I was sure that he was also being freed at the same time. Maybe I'd see him in a day or two after I had washed the stench of prison from my hair and body. I kept squeezing Leila's hand and she squeezed back.

I was so naïve.

We kept driving for a long time.

Finally, the car stopped. The men in the front exited the car, leaving Leila and me sitting anxiously by ourselves in the back. After a few minutes, someone yanked open the car door and ordered us to remove our blindfolds.

A young soldier with not a mark of life on him, but with a big automatic rifle hung over one shoulder, stood in front of us.

"You are not planning on escaping, are you?" He grinned. "This way."

We weren't in Ghomikola at all but in Sari, the state capital. The soldier marched us quickly to a side entrance of the Intelligence Ministry's offices, and we entered and headed down a set of steep, narrow stairs. I thought we were being released, but instead we had been upgraded to a fancier detention center.

At the bottom of the stairs, the soldier handed us over to two women guards, also wearing the chador.

"Name?" The female guard in charge walked toward us with a clipboard in her hand. She was a big woman, bigger than some of the men I knew.

"What is this place? What are we doing here? We were being sent home." I was angry and tired.

"Home?" She grinned. "This is your home until the court decides what to do with you."

The court!

It sounds foolish now, but I never did think that my actions were all that bad. All we had produced were a few pamphlets. I had thought our actions would be viewed as high school hijinks and we'd be released with a warning or some mild rebuke. A court date sounded ominous.

"Hurry up, turn out your pockets. If you have a purse, money, or jewelry, you have to hand it over. No knives or sharp objects—you have to leave it all outside. No belts, either," the guard said.

In prison, it's always "Hurry up, hurry up." No matter how fast

I moved, it never was fast enough for the guards. It's not as if they had other pressing engagements that I was keeping them from.

After being processed, we were taken to a large central hall with lots of cell doors leading off it. At the far end of the hall, a table tennis table was pushed right up against the wall, and beyond it, a corridor led to a toilet and shower unit. Farther down was an interrogation room.

Leila and I were put in the same cell—bigger and cleaner than our previous resting place. We had three blankets each, a *sofreh* to eat on, and a small bucket for trash. Fluorescent light made the room brighter. This was a major step up.

I stared at the walls and felt abandoned. I'd never been away from my family for this long, and I was getting restless and anxious. Why hadn't they come to see me? Why hadn't they contacted the authorities? Why had they abandoned me?

As political prisoners we were not allowed calls until our court appearance. There was no way to contact my family to tell them where I was.

There was a hush in this prison. The walls were thick, and the heavy metal door blocked all noise from the outside. The blindfold rules were more relaxed. We had to wear the blindfold when going to the bathroom or to the interrogation room but could always sneak a look.

A female guard took me to the bathroom for my first shower in a week. I climbed a short staircase and opened the door. A cloud of steam, like the warm breath of a cow in the early morning, hit me in the face. That happened every time I went to use the toilet, a cloud of steam and the smell of cheap soap would greet me. It was as if I was following right after someone who had just finished showering.

A squat, open toilet sat on one side and the shower on the other. A washbasin stood in the middle. The toilet floor was blanketed in thick, curly hair, and yellow stain marks covered the wall. I used a hose to clean the whole area before I touched any of it. The shower unit was also covered in coarse, curly hair. Men's pubic hair. It was disgusting. Again, I cleaned the shower floor before stepping onto it.

Before I had finished showering, the guard knocked on the door and exhorted me to get out. Other prisoners wanted to use the toilet, she grumbled. Only one prisoner at a time could move from their cell to the toilet or the interrogation room.

"This is not a women-only prison," I whispered to Leila on my return to the cell, as if I had discovered a special secret. "There are men here." The idea that we were sharing a prison with men filled us with dread.

All my life I had been told that men would take advantage of me, molest and rape me, if I wasn't covered up, if I didn't wear a head scarf—and now I had to share the same shower with them.

Again, I faced daily interrogations in the morning and afternoon. The new *bazjoos* made me repeat my earlier confessions and write and rewrite everything I had said before, making sure no names had been omitted. It was quite tedious. After interrogations, it was back to the cell. Pretty soon, Leila and I ran out of stories to amuse ourselves. We devised word games, but soon lost interest and became quiet and sullen.

During my time in the Sari prison, I saw another prisoner just once. I was on my way to the toilet, escorted by a guard, a young woman not that much older than me. As I held the rope that connected the two of us, I heard incessant coughing and wheezing. Another prisoner was out in the hall gasping for air. That person is dying, I thought, and I lifted up my blindfold to sneak a look.

It was Reza.

I felt as if I had been hit by a thunderbolt. He was the last person I had expected to see. I froze.

He was squatting by the far wall, chained to the table tennis table, coughing into a cloth. He looked terrible, his face bruised and pale. He had been beaten up badly.

"REZA," I shouted, letting go of the length of rope and my chador. I took my blindfold off and started wailing. "What have you done to him, you animals, you filth—you are killing him."

I ran to him, brushing past the guard. I didn't dare touch him even though I wanted to hold him, so I just screamed at the guard to get Reza medical attention. The interrogation room door was yanked open, and a *bazjoo* stepped out to see what was going on. For a few seconds, my eyes locked with his, and he ducked back inside his office and called for more female guards to come and deal with me.

I was hysterical. Even Reza, from his prone position on the floor, felt compelled to tell me to calm down. But after weeks of pent-up emotion, I was out of control. At the end of my outburst I collapsed on the floor. The male guards took Reza to the infirmary and the female guards gave me sweetened hot tea to revive me.

I didn't face any interrogations that day.

A day later, early in the morning, one of the *bazjoos* banged on our door and entered quickly, barely giving Leila and me time to put our chadors on. He put a basket of apples on the floor.

"You should have told us you were pregnant. Why didn't you?" he said with a wide smile. "Your husband told us you were expecting." The apples were a peace offering. "We don't want anything bad to happen to you and your baby."

PREGNANT! Me?

Leila and I stared at each other in amazement. That was how I learned about my condition. In jail. From my guards. I'm too young to be pregnant, was the first thought that ran through my mind. I was so naïve then. Reza and I had fumbled around in bed a few times, but I never talked with my mother or my older sister about such things as sex and what to expect after I got married.

I had rejoiced when my periods had stopped a couple of months before, relieved there were no more excruciating pains or messy bleeding episodes. I never thought that meant I was pregnant. Besides, this wasn't something I was comfortable discussing with my mother or any of the other women around me. Somehow Reza had figured it out.

It just seemed wrong to be pregnant in jail.

"How can you be pregnant?" Leila asked after the *bazjoo* left. She examined me closely. "You don't look pregnant, and I'm too young to be an aunt."

We laughed and munched the apples, the first fresh fruit in ten days. It seemed such a crazy idea at first. Me, pregnant? I wasn't ready to be a mother. I had dreams of traveling and exploring the world, and now before I had even left Ghomikola I was trapped. My destiny was already set.

"Did you ever imagine a *bazjoo* giving you the news that you are pregnant?" Leila asked, laughing uncontrollably.

"What if it's a trick?" I said, as I rubbed my stomach. "I don't feel a child inside of me." I laughed. "It's too late to worry about that. We ate all the apples."

But I was worried. I had to explain away another mark of shame to my parents—I was pregnant before being properly married. That was my biggest concern.

The interrogations went easier after that. The *bazjoos* walked me through my confession again and again, until I knew it forward and backward. By this stage, I was numb to the proceedings and wanted everything to be resolved so I could know my fate. Like all teenagers, I got bored easily, and I was bored with this new prison.

One day a guard took Leila and me in the direction of the interrogation room, but instead we walked past and climbed a set of stairs at the back of the building. I felt a cold chill. What if they were going to kill me and my baby? I thought. Maybe they thought I was a Mojahed after all, and they were going to hang Leila and me. For the first time, I thought protectively of my unborn child. I held the rope with one hand and with my other hand held the chador tightly under my chin. Leila held on to the hem of my chador as she climbed behind me. My thoughts turned morbid as we climbed higher and higher. I tried to remember if under Islam pregnant women could be hanged, but that was not a subject that had been covered in my studies.

Finally, we stopped climbing and the guard opened a door and led us into a large room. I could hear lots of voices, some familiar. I tore the blindfold off.

All the members of the Kaveh group sat around the one room. Some had bruises on their faces. I waved to Reza, who was sitting by himself, and he cheered up. My brother Ali sauntered over as if he didn't have a care in the world. He had yellow and purple bruises under his eyes and he was thinner than the last time I had seen him. Ahmad, the former Mojahed, stared out the window and didn't look in my direction. Even the guy who had loaned us the gun was there.

"I tried to warn you," I told Ali. "But—"

"There is nothing to be sorry about," Ali said calmly. "I had already been arrested before they picked you up." He led me to a long table at the other end of the room as he recounted how he had been picked up at his military camp.

Cardboard nameplates bearing our names and "titles" had been placed on the table. Ali was listed as head of the armed wing, Reza was head of the ideology section, and I—well, I was head of the women's wing. It was comical to see such lofty titles.

Before our eyes the room was turned into a makeshift film studio. Technicians unpacked video cameras, hauled heavy tripods and stands, and hooked up special bright lamps. "Now they want us to put on a show," Ali said. "They plan to film our confessions."

Amid all the activity, Mr. Sadeghi, the nice *bazjoo*, quietly entered the room and beckoned to other guards to bring in a basket of fruit and jugs of water. He stood in front of the room and asked for quiet without even raising his voice.

"You have a chance to cooperate and receive a reduced sentence," Mr. Sadeghi said. "Most of you have admitted to your crimes. Now you need to do it in front of the cameras. Do it and the court will be merciful."

"Mr. Sadeghi, this is not right," I complained. "There were only two women, Leila and me. How can I be head of a women's wing? This is a joke, right?"

"You, more than anyone else here, should think about your future," Mr. Sadeghi said. I was sure he was referring to my pregnancy.

We all sat at the table and one by one, we faced a camera and made our confession, repented, and asked for mercy. Ahmad was the only one who didn't say anything in public apart from his name. In a quiet moment later, I asked him if he had told them anything.

"Never confess." He smiled sadly. "If you do, they'll keep you forever."

As a former Mojahed, he didn't expect any mercy. We later found out that he was hanged.

A day or so after that, we were back in the white Paykan. Mr. Sadeghi sat in the front with the driver. Now, I thought, I'm going home. Instead we stopped in the middle of Sari. We followed Mr. Sadeghi out of the car and toward the dreaded Revolutionary Court buildings. Convened in secret in 1979 to hand out punishments to officials of the Shah's regime, the Revolutionary Courts dealt with offenses of national security. The court did not allow juries or defense lawyers to be present, and cases would be decided by special judges. The United Nations Commission on Human Rights had condemned Iran's Revolutionary Courts for denying defendants legal representation and the right of appeal.

A confession was the best evidence for the judges of the Revolutionary Courts, and that's why the *bazjoos* were so keen on fine-tuning our stories.

As we got closer, I noticed a throng of women in black chadors sitting on the pavement outside the Revolutionary Court building. I recognized my mother, but Mr. Sadeghi stopped me from running to her. My mother eventually reached me and hugged me tightly, and we both started to cry. Mother said she had tried to find me but was told to wait by the court building. She had waited there for the past three weeks.

Inside the building, Mr. Sadeghi took Leila and me to a waiting room. "Don't worry, the worst is over," he said.

I was desperately impatient to return to my family. I squirmed in my hard-backed chair as we waited until, at long last, our names were called. Leila and I were escorted to the judge's chambers while Mr. Sadeghi waited outside.

In the chambers, everything about the stern-looking judge was dark, from his brown suit to the dark spot on his forehead to his tinted glasses. As we entered, he kept himself busy reading our files.

On the wall behind him, the double portraits of Khomeini and Khamenei seemed to rebuke me personally, their faces staring out disapprovingly. The judge's bookshelf contained nothing more than copies of the Quran and prayer books. A large potted plant sat neglected in a corner; its leaves had turned yellow.

"You seem to be curious about this room. You'd be wise to pay heed to your own case," the judge said.

"Is this the court?" I asked incredulously. I had expected something grander.

"You've confessed to some serious offenses against the Islamic Republic. You could face a heavy sentence. A severe punishment awaits you."

I stared at him uncomprehendingly. I didn't even know what charges I faced. No one had read the complaint against me. I had no lawyer to defend me. I was forced into giving a confession, and now all that remained was for this judge to pass a sentence. It didn't sound very just. Later in life, I discovered that there is not much justice in the Islamic Republic.

"We were told you'd be lenient." I had no fight left in me. "We confessed. Is that not enough?"

"The punishment for your actions can be severe. I could even sentence you to be hanged," the judge said slowly, looking into our faces intently to see if we were scared. "This is not a joke. Your confession is enough."

"I'm pregnant," I whimpered. "I promise to be good. I made a holy vow in prison to go on a pilgrimage to Mashhad once I'm released. I wanted to go with my husband."

The judge wrote out my sentence by hand and then he read it out loud.

He had sentenced us both to five years in prison and seventy-four lashes. The sentence, however, was to be suspended for three years. The moment he said "five years in prison" I burst out crying. I stopped listening. All I was thinking was that I didn't want to give birth in jail. Even after he stressed that the sentence was suspended, I still kept on crying, because I didn't understand the process. The judge took his time to explain that the prison term was suspended, meaning that if I stayed out of trouble for three years, the sentence would be wiped clean.

After I realized that I would not be going to jail for five years, my mood switched completely. Just then a thought occurred to me, even as I was thanking the judge for his kindness. Why had he sentenced me to seventy-four lashes? I asked. That's for mixing with boys, the judge said. Had our political group been segregated, there'd be no need for the seventy-four lashes. I rushed out of the chambers and ran past Mr. Sadeghi, but the guards barred the door.

"You have to be processed," Mr. Sadeghi said. "Then you can go home."

The guards took us to the women's section of the Babol municipal prison, where common criminals, from petty thieves and burglars to drug smugglers and murderers, are kept. Leila and I were put in a separate section so as not to mix with the general crowd. Two days later, just after dawn prayers, we were released. On the way out, we stood against a white wall, and a guard took our mug shots.

The prison door finally opened, and Leila and I stepped into the sunshine of freedom. The authorities had not informed our families about our release, and there was no one to greet us when we walked out. The first thing I did was take off my white chador, which was quite filthy by now, and roll it up into a ball. For a brief moment, I remembered that it was my wedding chador.

"I hate the chador," I screamed, and dumped it in a trash can.

I had a craving for nectarines. I guess it's normal to have cravings when you are pregnant. I also, more than anything else that day, wanted to terminate my pregnancy. I had a mission: find nectarines and find a doctor to terminate the same pregnancy that had given me this craving for nectarines. I wanted to be free and start fresh. The pregnancy was tainted because I had heard the news in prison. I didn't know when Reza would be released, and I didn't want to have to look after the baby by myself.

Most of Babol's doctors had their offices in a particular neighborhood, and that morning Leila and I went to see almost every one of them. At each, I explained that I wanted an abortion. I told the truth: I had just been released from prison for political crimes; my fiancé was still in jail and might be there for a long time, for all I knew. I felt no twinge of sadness at what I was doing. I spoke in a detached and impersonal manner, as if describing something that had happened to another person.

Some doctors turned me away without examining me. Others examined me first before refusing my request. "Your pregnancy is too advanced for a termination," one doctor said. "I cannot do it, and I suggest you don't try to find anyone else to do it, either."

I was too tired to even cry.

We headed to Leila's house. Of course, no one was expecting us, but Banoo was ecstatic to see the two of us. Plates of cakes and fruit appeared in front of us as Banoo asked about our ordeal. I was overjoyed when she produced a plate of nectarines as if by magic.

I told her every detail, such as seeing Reza in jail, but I was embarrassed to tell her I was pregnant. What will she think of me? I wondered. I was exhausted and went to bed early, hoping that Leila would give her the news.

It felt great to be in clean sheets and surrounded by sounds that were familiar and comforting to me. I was barely asleep when Banoo burst into the room and reached down and hugged me. She started calling me her sweet daughter and told me how happy she was to have a grandchild. "Remember not to sleep on your stomach. It may hurt the baby," she said.

That night I had my most peaceful sleep in a month.

CHAPTER SEVEN

I sank into the deepest sleep. All my fears and memories of the interrogations and humiliations of the past three weeks, the sweaty *bazjoos* and their foul-smelling breath, the dirty prison cells, were now in the past. I had a small life beating inside of me. For the next two days all I did was sleep and take long showers, obsessively scrubbing myself to get rid of the prison dirt. What I couldn't do was wash and rinse away the shame I felt. It wasn't just the prison; being pregnant was never part of the plan.

I needed to think clearly about my next moves, but that was easier said than done, as hundreds of different thoughts bounced and ricocheted around in my head. Usually I'm a chatterbox, but I was moody and didn't want company and certainly didn't feel like talking. Could I go back to high school and finish the final few weeks and graduate? I couldn't show my face at school, and there was no chance that I would be allowed to graduate.

I'd be staring out the window at the rain and then I'd remember that I was going to be a mother and curse my luck for not knowing how to find a doctor to perform an abortion. I didn't think I could handle being a mother. I couldn't escape the thought of having a baby and I was both excited and unnerved by the idea.

It was more than that, though. I was terrified of telling my parents about my pregnancy, and that day of reckoning could not be postponed for much longer now that I was out of jail. I had a pretty good idea how AghaJan and Mother would react to the news. Above all else, I felt ashamed. Even in Tehran, the most cosmopolitan city in Iran, very few women get pregnant before their wedding night, so you can imagine how much rarer it was in Babol or Ghomikola. I was bringing dishonor to my family. I could tell that Reza's parents were taken aback by the news, but they were also excited about the arrival of their first grandchild. As for my parents, well, I hoped they might be excited, too, once they accepted the fact that I was pregnant.

My other worry was how Reza felt. I hadn't had a chance to discuss the pregnancy with him, and we had never talked about having kids. I had only agreed to get married to escape Ghomikola and have adventures in the wider world, but now how could I? I fretted that my stomach was going to bulge out almost overnight. Like almost immediately. After my first shower as a free woman, I examined myself in the mirror. I was still pretty skinny; maybe I had a tiny bump around my tummy but nothing noticeable at this stage. It wasn't easy for me to accept that my body was going to change and I'd be bringing a baby into the world. A big, prominent belly was a step closer to being a chained woman. All around me I saw young mothers washing soiled and smelly diapers, breast-feeding their babies, and becoming trapped inside their homes by the never-ending list of daily chores. Banoo told me that soon I'd feel nauseous and this would last for months. I just knew I was going to hate being pregnant.

Tuesday was visitation day at the Babol detention center. Reza had been moved out of the Intelligence Ministry's prison to the local jail where they kept common criminals like burglars, drug smugglers, and embezzlers. Leila and I got up early, around 6:00 a.m., to get ready. We got the taxi to drop us as near as possible and then walked anxiously toward the jail, holding hands. I was feeling morning sickness on top of my anxiety, which made every step a battle against throwing up on the side of the road. Just three days earlier, Leila and I had been released from the women's wing of the same dreadful building, and now here we were, mingling with other visiting families, waiting to reenter it. I felt like a criminal who returns to the scene of her crime. With my other hand, I gripped my chador tightly, holding it just under my nose to partially cover my face. I was sure the guards would recognize me even under the cover of the chador.

But the policeman at the gate just waved us through without even looking at me. Leila and I walked as closely as possible to the other families, as if we were part of a larger group and not just two lonely young women. My heart was beating wildly, and I thought that any moment a hand would tap me on the shoulder and I would be asked to return to my cell. I kept praying silently to the Prophet Muhammad and all the major Shia saints. Please God, Ya Muhammad, Ya Ali, Ya Imam Reza, don't let them arrest me again, I pleaded silently. It wasn't that I was religious, but the more help I could get the better, I reasoned.

Inside, the men were searched in one room while a female guard patted the women down in a separate area before we were allowed to enter the reception area. We all lined up to sign a form requesting the prisoner we wanted to see. I filled out the application asking for Reza. There was a blank space left for the applicant's "relationship" with the prisoner, and after a few moments of hesitation, I put down "wife."

The guard behind the counter slowly eyed me up and down as if he had X-ray vision and could see my naked body through all the layers of clothing. I felt so uncomfortable that I wrapped my chador tighter around my body and turned sideways away from him.

"Don't worry yourself. Your husband will be here for a long time." The guard smiled suggestively. "It can be pretty lonesome for a fine young wife like you."

Then he pointed to a door, adding, "Booth number nine. You've got thirty minutes. Next."

All the visiting families were shepherded to a large room with rows of hard-backed chairs that were scratched and chipped from years of neglect and overuse, facing a pane of thick glass. I sat down in booth #9 and waited nervously. A telephone sat idly on the side panel. All kinds of thoughts raced through my head. Had Reza recovered from the beatings? Did he still want to get married? Did he want our baby? What did the guard mean when he said that Reza was going to spend a long time inside?

Soon enough the prisoners started arriving. I watched with fascination as sounds of weeping and lamentation rose over hushed whispers floating through the telephones.

All of a sudden Reza appeared and grumpily sat down. At the sight of his gaunt and still-bruised face, tears welled up in my eyes. He looked unkempt, and his stubble had grown into a beard as dark as night. He didn't seem particularly happy to see me. I put the tip of my index finger on the window, and he stretched his index finger and put it opposite mine. Maybe I imagined it, but I could feel the heat of his finger through the thick glass. I opened my hand and stretched my palm against the pane; after a few seconds he did the same. We didn't talk, just held our hands against each other as if the glass weren't there.

I could barely see him through the tears in my eyes. When I picked up the phone next to the window to speak with him, his first words were: "Don't be scared. It's our kid and we'll take care of the baby. No matter what happens we'll take care of each other."

That was all I wanted to hear, and it was such a relief. My hormones were kicking in, and I was feeling very teary. I started crying, and Leila came and took over talking with Reza. I was emotionally spent.

After Reza, it was time to visit my elder sister Mina and let her be the first member of my family to learn about my pregnancy. All the excitement had taken its toll, and by the time we rang Mina's doorbell, I was close to fainting from hunger—and the hard part of telling my sister still lay ahead. I rushed inside with a cursory hello and just sat on the floor, leaning against the wall.

"Hey, hello, little sister. You don't say hello anymore to your family?" Mina wasn't expecting us to drop by out of the blue. Normally, she was calm and in control, but now she was flustered. "When did you get out? Did you get out just now? Today?"

"I need something to eat," I managed to say. "And some water. Please, one of you, can you get me some water?" I was ashen and could barely move. "And something sweet. I need something to eat."

"What's the matter with you?" Mina asked me, and then, without waiting, she turned to Leila. "What's the matter with her? Is she okay? Is she sick?"

"No. She's just really very hungry." Leila rushed to the kitchen and came back with a glass of water and a piece of flat bread she'd found on the counter. She took an orange from the table.

Mina stared at me in silence for a long time, trying to figure out what had happened. "Did she get sick inside?"

"She'll be fine. It's just her condition." Leila had an apologetic smiled spread across her face as she peeled the orange. She was enjoying not telling Mina the news. "Once she eats something, she'll be fine."

"What condition?" Mina took a step back, worried that I might have caught a mysterious ailment in prison. She stared at me, waiting for me to make a confession. Mina and I used to be close, but now she was too much of a fundamentalist for my liking. "Is she diabetic? Or is it... What is it?"

"She is pregnant," Leila answered calmly as she fed me an orange slice. It was amazingly sweet and juicy. "She is three months pregnant."

Mina stared at Leila as if she'd gone mad.

"Pregnant?" Mina shouted. "Who? Our Masih? Pregnant?" She took a step forward and looked like she might slap Leila just to get a different answer. "Who's the father?"

"It's Reza," Leila said indignantly. "Who do you think it is?"

It dawned on Mina that maybe we were telling her the truth, and that's when she slowly sank to the floor as if her legs were unable to support her weight any longer. I munched greedily on the bread and orange and smiled peacefully at the two of them, content to let them sort out a solution for my woes.

"I want to slap that smile off your face," Mina said. "What the hell did you go and do that for?"

"I know it's a bit of a shock, but Reza will come out soon and they'll get properly married," Leila chirped, happily unaware that Mina could explode any minute. "You are going to be an auntie. That'd be nice, right?"

Mina did not look pleased at the prospect. She fixed me with a disapproving look.

"How did you get pregnant? Oh, never mind," Mina didn't want to know the details. "This is ruinous. How are we going to show our faces to the rest of the family and our friends? What are you going to tell AghaJan? What are you going to tell Mother?"

That was the big problem, for I was afraid of going to Ghomikola and telling my parents that I was pregnant. Iranian weddings are two-part affairs: there is the *aghd* (legal part) and the *mehmooni* (reception or party). The two parts together constitute a marriage. We had signed all the paperwork at the notary public to get married, and technically we were married, but as far as Iranian customs, and our families, were concerned, we were still only engaged until we had the *mehmooni*. Before our arrest, I had said I didn't want to spend money on a reception and instead we could use the money for other purposes, like traveling. AghaJan wouldn't hear of it and fixed it so the *mehmooni* was to be held a few days after my high school graduation.

"It's tradition," AghaJan said at the time, dismissing me with a wave of his hand. "After the *mehmooni,* I'll put your hand in Reza's and you'll both have my blessing."

It had all gone belly-up, so to speak. Given my condition, by the time Reza was released, my stomach would have swelled to the size of a house. Of course, if Reza misbehaved in jail and his sentence was extended, I'd be holding the baby in my arms at the *mehmooni*. It'd be a big blow to my father. My being pregnant before the wedding day was not only a stain on my reputation, but it would shame my father. He'd never be able to live this down. He had been a basiji who never tired of lecturing everyone in the village about being a good revolutionary Muslim.

"I can't tell them," I told Mina. "I'm afraid it'll break their hearts. It will really hurt them."

"If you really cared about our parents, you wouldn't have gotten pregnant," Mina said meanly. She always enjoyed scolding me.

"AghaJan will be devastated if I tell him, but you can tell him."

"You've always wanted to play by your own rules, but you've done it this time. Are you sure you are pregnant?"

"I didn't want to get pregnant," I said petulantly. "This wasn't supposed to happen." Tears poured down my face. "When I was younger, I wanted to be like Mother, the village tailor. But I don't want to be like her or like you or anyone else. I want to be myself. I want to be different, and I didn't want to get pregnant, but I am."

"Well, my parents were shocked, too, but they are happy they are getting a grandchild," Leila said, finally coming to my defense.

"That's not going to pacify AghaJan." Mina stood up and forced me up as well. She examined me carefully. "You don't look pregnant."

Before I could protest, she put up her hands to stop me from saying anything.

"Calm down. I believe you, but you are so damn skinny," Mina said with a look in her eyes that meant she had a plan. "If AghaJan can get a special furlough for Reza, you could get married quickly, then no one would need to know you are pregnant."

Mina looked especially pleased with herself. Mina and I were no longer close, but she was my big sister, and her idea was brilliant. Only someone had to sell the idea to AghaJan.

"You are my only hope." I held Mina tight.

* * *

The next day, Mina took the bus to Ghomikola to break the news to Mother. When she heard, Mother was not overjoyed but devastated. She slapped herself on the head and sobbed.

"What have I done to deserve this? What am I gonna tell Agha-Jan? What will the neighbors say?" Mother kept repeating as she cried.

When AghaJan came back, Mother gave him his regular cup of tea as he sat on the carpet on the terrace, resting his back against the wall of the house. After he had drunk his tea, she told him the news of my pregnancy. At once, AghaJan's face became crimson. He looked up uncomprehendingly.

"Pregnant? How? How is it that your daughter brought shame on our family?"

As the last child, I was pretty rebellious, and AghaJan had had to deal with a lot of mischief from me, especially after I became a teenager. I'd fought against wearing the chador, and he had only grudgingly accepted it. He had kept quiet about my arrest so as not to lose face in the village. But the pregnancy was a step too far, he said.

AghaJan had told the rest of our extended family and neighbors that I was staying with Mina in Babol while Reza had gone to the city of Mashhad to finish his teacher's training. There had been rumors in the village that we had been arrested, but AghaJan denied them all. Now his lies were going to be exposed. However, Mina had a plan.

The next morning, AghaJan didn't take his chickens to the market but instead put on his best clothes and headed to Babol's Intelligence Ministry and met with a number of officials there to find a solution. AghaJan had not been a high-ranking basiji official, but he figured his past service counted for something. He begged for a three-day furlough for Reza. Not that he liked Reza or approved of his political views, he explained. It was so that we could get married, then Reza would return to finish his sentence. It had to be done quickly.

That day, he went from the Intelligence Ministry to the Justice Ministry and then saw the police chief before finally getting Reza a three-day furlough.

As AghaJan was doing the rounds in Babol, I took a bus to Ghomikola. Normally the thirty-minute bus ride went pretty smoothly, but that day my insides were in a turmoil, and I felt every bump and pothole in the road. I dreaded the prospect of facing my parents.

Mother tried not to even look me in the eye, but she couldn't keep it up for long.

"Masoumeh, what are we going to do with you? You were always so rebellious. If this news gets out, I can't show my face in Ghomikola anymore," she said amid tears.

Her tears always moved me to tears, and we had a good cry. I was relieved to be united with my family but jittery with all the hormones running wild in my body.

That evening, AghaJan burst into the house looking very pleased with himself. He had a massive self-satisfied smile on his face as he sat down on the terrace and looked me up and down. I had been dreading this moment. I feared that he was going to scold me or even take the broom handle to my back, though he hadn't raised a hand to me since I was a teenager.

"From what I can see, you have a lot of work to prettify your looks." AghaJan laughed at his own comment. "I'm gonna give you a wedding feast and then you are not my problem anymore."

"What wedding?" Mother and I both said at the same time.

My face was puffed up from all the crying, my nose was red from the sniffling, and I looked a right mess.

"Next Thursday. It's all been arranged. Reza will get a three-day furlough. And then he'll go back inside. It's all arranged."

In great detail AghaJan told us of how he had saved the family's honor once again from the mess caused by his children. Once we were married, he'd put an end to all the rumors of the arrests. All I cared about was that Reza was going to be freed for three days, and I wanted to spend all that time with him and not with a collection of old relatives whom I had not seen for many months.

"I don't want a wedding party," I told my parents firmly. "I don't want to feed all the uncles and aunts I hardly see. It's my wedding and I only want a small gathering of my friends. People my age. Three days is not a long time, and I want my time with Reza to be with our own friends"

"*Inshallah* [God willing] you will have many decades together," my father said, "so no need to fret about just three days. He'll be out in four months and the rest of his sentence will be suspended."

"I still don't want a wedding. I hate weddings."

"It's not for you. The wedding is for the family, to show that we have raised a fine daughter, even though you've given us so much grief."

AghaJan hardly spoke to me in the week before the wedding, but he was busy making sure everyone knew about the *mehmooni*. He complained about the cost of the extra rice he needed to buy for the guests, the chickens he had to slaughter, and how no one ever thanked him for his sacrifices.

Village weddings are odd affairs. They're different from what you see on television or in movies. They're different from city weddings. In the village, the custom is for the bride's family to have a party for their own family at the father of the bride's house. The groom has a party at his house. Later in the afternoon or early evening, the groom and his family, along with some friends, visit the father of the bride with flower-laden cars and take the bride away. The party continues at the groom's house, where the bride receives wedding gifts. In the cities, especially in major places like Tehran or Isfahan, some families have only one wedding reception that both the bride's and the groom's relatives attend. At those events, the bride and groom sit in front of a *sofreh aghd* (wedding spread), an elaborately decorated tablecloth spread on the floor and decorated with flowers, flat bread, honey, crystallized sugar, gold bracelets, and of course mirrors and candelabras, representing light and fire in the ancient Zoroastrian religion. To ward off evil-sayers and evildoers, espand seeds are burned.

My ceremony was a much simpler affair.

The day of the wedding, I went behind the cowshed, where Agha-Jan had built a stand-alone shower, and scrubbed myself clean. Afterward, one of my cousins sat cross-legged on the floor in front of me to work on my face, using a cotton thread to pluck and thin out my eyebrows. My only attempt at makeup was using some kohl around my eyes.

We didn't have much money to splurge on the occasion. Mother made *fesenjoon,* a stew with chicken, walnuts, and pomegranate sauce, along with large dishes of steaming-hot white rice. She also made homemade yogurt with honey for dessert. All the men sat in one room and the women in the other room. An aunt drummed a local Mazandarani rhythm on a tub to amuse the children. That was our music! The children were the only ones who danced.

I wore a long black skirt as a protest against having a party. This was only the second time in my life that I had worn a skirt. The first was for the *khastegari* (matchmaking), when Reza's parents came to our house. Everyone thought it was strange that the bride was wearing a black skirt, but AghaJan and Mother just wanted this day over with and didn't object. Just to be different, I also put on a pink head scarf.

As I mingled, I could hear some women whispering about the rumors of my arrest and jail, but no one was quite sure. They could have asked me, but they didn't have the courage. Mother was a nervous wreck, wondering if Reza was going to show up.

In the other room, AghaJan had his doubts, too, but he cracked jokes and laughed. He was telling everyone in a loud voice that Reza was finishing his training, which explained his absence recently.

After the wedding lunch had been cleared and tea had been served, everyone sat around talking. Again men and women were in separate rooms, and only the children ran from one to the other and out onto the terrace, where most of the men had retired.

From the distance came the sound of car horns approaching.

Beep beep . . . beep beep beep . . . beep beep . . . bee beep beeeeep . . .

"They'll be here soon," Mother said. She had a big smile on her face, but her eyes were sad. I was the last child, and now I, too, was leaving the nest. The wedding had so far been a triumph. No one knew I was pregnant, and Reza's arrival would scotch rumors of his arrest. AghaJan had saved face.

Beep beep beep beep beeeep . . .

I had already packed a small bag containing gifts and money. I put on a white chador, another gift from my mother, and waited anxiously.

Beep beep . . . bee beep beeeeep . . . beep beep . . . bee beep beeeeep . . .

By tradition, the groom would enter our house and greet my father and kiss his hand, and then my father would place my hand in his and give us his blessing.

BEEP BEEP . . . BEE BEEP BEEEEEP BEEP BEEP . . . BEE BEEP BEEEEEP . . .

The car horns sounded right outside our house. The men all piled outside onto the terrace, and AghaJan stood proudly at the top of the stairs, waiting for Reza to approach. The iron gate was opened, and some women stood on a separate part of the terrace and started ululating.

The car door opened and Reza stepped out. My heart skipped a beat as I saw him, but I sensed there was something horribly wrong. Reza was not wearing a suit. Even in Ghomikola, grooms typically wore a suit. Instead, he had a green shirt tucked inside a pair of black jeans and a black baseball cap tightly jammed on his head. He didn't look like a groom ready to take his bride. AghaJan's face turned crimson as he stared with amazement at Reza, who was walking shyly through the yard.

Everyone sensed there was something wrong. The women stopped their chants, and most retreated back inside the house, taking me with them.

"It's not right for the groom to see the bride's face before it is time," an old aunt told me.

If only she knew that the groom had seen much more than my face already. But this was not the time to tell her that.

When Reza reached the bottom of the steps leading to the veranda, he took off his hat. There was an audible gasp from the men on the porch.

Reza's head was completely shaved. As if he were a common convict.

In Iran, common criminals, like thieves or smugglers, have their heads shaved as a form of punishment the first time they enter prison. Political prisoners, by contrast, are left alone. Reza was a political prisoner and by rights he should not have had his head shaved. But that seemed to be the price for obtaining the furlough. The Intelligence Ministry hadn't wanted to play along with AghaJan's little ruse, and Reza had to pay the price. It was now obvious to everyone that Reza had been in jail.

In my heart I felt for AghaJan. He had trusted the system that he believed in, but the security forces had a dark sense of humor. AghaJan's face remained beet red as he stared at Reza in disbelief.

"Salam, AghaJan," Reza said. He didn't look at my father but instead stared down at his shoes.

"Salam. Welcome." All sorts of emotions must have run through AghaJan, from anger and hurt to shame. But he was the family elder and he shook Reza's hand and patted him warmly on the shoulder. They both had tears in their eyes.

Without looking at anyone, AghaJan turned around and came into the room where I stood with the other women, watching the drama.

"Get your stuff; the groom is here." AghaJan then went to the other room and shut the door.

I wrapped the chador around me. All the family were talking and whispering. I didn't care. I was just happy that Reza had been released and the *mehmooni* was over.

On the terrace I found my mother. Her eyes were full of tears. Shame and joy mixed together. She took my hand and put it in Reza's.

"I'll leave Masoumeh in your hands. May God look after both of you."

AghaJan couldn't do it, but Mother had come through in the end.

The afternoon had not turned out as we had planned, but it was over.

"Don't worry. It's gonna be fine, and I'll come and visit every week," I promised Mother. I hugged her tight. She cried softly into her hands.

"You always wanted me to get married; you always said a man will look after me and give me protection and comfort," I whispered to her. "I've not been easy, but you did it. You found me a husband."

Another long hug, and then I walked demurely behind Reza to his car, making sure I wasn't about to trip and twist my ankle and cause another disaster. The caravan of cars took off again, this time toward Babol.

Beep beep…bee beep beeeeep…bee beep…bee beep beeeeep…

Reza explained in the car how the guards had taken him to the prison barber and forcibly shaved his head just before his release. After that, he didn't feel like putting on a suit or getting dressed up. He kept apologizing for ruining our wedding.

I didn't care. I kept rubbing my hand over his shorn head. "I guess I'll get used to it."

At Reza's parents' another party was in full flow, but here it felt more like a celebration than the one at my parents' house. Men and women danced to music from a portable tape player, even though some of the bonhomie and laughter were forced. My new family was gaining a daughter.

The next night, I accompanied Reza back to jail. He had to serve the rest of his sentence. That meant spending four months away from him.

I didn't care. I had left village life forever and I wasn't going back.

CHAPTER EIGHT

On a windy November morning in 1996 Reza walked out of the prison, looking gaunt and pale but otherwise unharmed after his four months inside. I, on the other hand, was definitely looking like a whale, and although I was as hyperactive as ever, I had stopped climbing trees as a concession to my pregnancy.

The first thing we did as a married couple was to go on our honeymoon—on a pilgrimage to the holy city of Mashhad to visit the shrine of Imam Reza. Mashhad, and the golden-domed shrine, the largest and busiest of its kind, was not what I had in mind for a honeymoon. But sitting on that hard-backed chair outside the judge's chambers, I'd made a vow to make the Mashhad pilgrimage if we escaped the death penalty. Now, I wanted to fulfill my obligation as soon as possible. I'm not really a pious person, but I figured it wasn't wise to renege on a promise made to the Almighty, especially as I was due to have a baby in less than two months. No point in making enemies in high places.

After a few days' rest in Babol, Reza was ready, and on a chilly morning we boarded a bus heading to Iran's second-biggest city. Reza's clothes now sagged on his broomstick body; he was never the bulky, athletic type, but prison had drained him. I was excited and even giddy to be going on a trip, my first as an adult, without Mother and Father keeping me in check. I loved how people paid attention to me and made a fuss over me because of my condition. After about five hours, the bus pulled into a motorway diner serving kebabs and tea. We ate our homemade boiled eggs, bread, and green vegetables. Throughout the trip, I kept looking at Reza and wondering if the two of us would remain happy together and in years to come would remember this trip as the start of our own journey.

Surprisingly, the city was packed with honeymooners, though I doubted that their experiences were similar to ours. We found a guest-house dedicated to serving pilgrims with modest incomes that suited our budget. It was near a major thoroughfare, and all day and night we heard the roar of the traffic and smelled the noxious exhaust fumes.

Mashhad was jammed with Afghan migrants, pilgrims, and even a few Western tourists. I had never seen such crowded streets. The city is very conservative because of the giant shrine, which is open day and night. Each day, beggars line the streets, their numbers increasing the closer you get to the site. Almost all the women in Mashhad wear the chador on top of their long coats, along with baggy pants and head scarves. Religious tourism is the city's biggest industry, and the foundation in charge of the shrine is one of the wealthiest corporations in Iran, with billions of dollars in annual revenues.

Mashhad's skyline is dominated by the soaring gold-and-turquoise dome of the great mosque of Goharshad, flanked by two tall golden minarets. The massive shrine complex is made up of verandas and courtyards, some covered by Persian rugs where anyone can sit and rest. Inside the halls, almost every inch of wall space is decorated with tiny mirrors that reflect the light from massive chandeliers. I went in through the female entrance, mindful of my bulging tummy, but it was impossible to reach the golden cage that protects Imam Reza's tomb. I had to get past wailing throngs of women, shoving and push-ing to reach the bars. Many people threw money, gold coins, or jewelry through the bars as part of their vows, crying one minute and kissing the enclosure over and over again the next. They all wanted Imam Reza to intercede on their behalf to help cure an illness or find a missing child. I tried getting close enough to grab the bars at least once, but the crush of bodies was impregnable. In the emotional intensity of that moment, I, too, joined in the lamentations, shedding tears freely. It was an emotional release of the highs and lows of the past few months. I felt scared and excited. I was leaving the safety of my parents' home for a new adventure but carried scars of prison, and an unexpected baby. An elbow to my side jolted me from my trancelike state. I pulled myself away from the crowd and headed back outside.

We went to a crowded and noisy kebab restaurant for a late lunch. This was the first time I'd ever been in a restaurant. I looked around, amazed at how so many strangers could sit and eat in the same room. A plateful of steaming white rice with two skewers of kebabs arrived in front of me. The mound of rice had a saffron necklace and a golden raw egg yolk nested at its peak. I stared openmouthed at all the food, as the waiter put down a plate of flat bread with little packets of butter wrapped in tinfoil, a plate of herbs, and two glasses of doogh. I wrapped up the bread and butter in a handkerchief and stealthily put it in my bag for our next day's breakfast. I figured we had already paid for the bread, so what difference did it make if we ate it now or later.

Throughout lunch, I had a silly grin on my face. I'd traveled to a metropolis like Mashhad without AghaJan and Mother and was eating in a restaurant. This is what being a grown-up is all about, I thought.

Six weeks after returning from Mashhad, on the afternoon of December 18, I started having pain in my stomach and back. I thought if I rested and took a nap, the pain would go away by itself. When Banoo heard my quiet moaning, she immediately realized it was time to take me to the hospital. Except now, after nine months of carrying my baby, I didn't want to give birth.

"I'm not ready yet," I pleaded. "Just give me a few minutes and I'll be fine." But I couldn't even get up because the pain was so intense.

Fortunately, Banoo didn't pay me much attention. She quietly packed a small bag and hauled me into a taxi to the city hospital, which was for poor people who couldn't pay. Private hospitals were nicer-looking, but Reza and I didn't have any money.

I stayed in an open ward with twenty other beds at first and then was taken to a small room with white walls and a pervasive smell of disinfectant. When I arrived at the hospital, the pain was unbearable, but the doctor barely gave me a glance.

"You'll be here for another ten to twelve hours before your water breaks," he said.

I had no one with me but Banoo, who sat next to me and nervously squeezed my hand. The room was full of women all getting ready to give birth. There was nothing heartwarming about the experience. Thirty minutes later, I felt a trickle of water down my leg.

"I'm so sorry, but I can't control my bladder," I told Banoo. "My leg is all wet."

Banoo raced to fetch a nurse, who bundled me into a wheelchair and rushed me to a private delivery room. I searched for Banoo, but there was only a doctor and two nurses in the room with me. The doctor jabbed me with a syringe.

I was happy once the drugs washed over me, making me numb to the pain. I felt very lonely among the strange nurses and the doctor as they examined me, poked me, and attached wires to my body. I wanted it to be over with. I had never felt so vulnerable in my life. I wanted my own mother to be with me, but that was impossible.

Soon enough, it was over. One of the nurses wrapped the baby in a white sheet and put him on my chest without bothering to clean off the blood and gunk. I was so weak that I couldn't move my arms and felt paralyzed. Then another nurse came over to clean up the baby. Banoo came in with apple juice and some fruit and I regained some strength. Reza was allowed to visit me for one hour the next day. I released myself the following day. That first night at home, I woke up constantly in the middle of the night to check on my son, whom we named Pouyan. Of course, as soon as I fell asleep, he would wake up and demand to be fed.

Reza was very proud of himself, as if he were the one who had carried our son for nine months. He helped where he could, but I had to do most of the heavy work, like hand-washing soiled diapers and clothes and feeding my son. Soon, like all new mothers, I got the hang of things and started taking him with me everywhere, wrapping him in a blanket close to my bosom.

Yet I seemed to be more disorganized than other mothers. One day, I bundled Pouyan up across my front and grabbed Leila, who by now was my best friend, to head to the bazaar to check the price of gold bracelets. I needed to sell some of the jewelry I'd received as wedding presents. By the end of the afternoon, we left the bazaar, exhausted and thirsty. Suddenly I felt panic in the pit of my stomach.

"Where's Pouyan?" I clutched Leila's arm. "We've lost him. We left him behind."

Leila screamed, and we both raced back along the mazelike passages. She was punching herself in the face as she ran, calling herself all sorts of names. I lifted my long skirt to run faster, gripped by an overwhelming fear. I couldn't imagine a life without Pouyan. We burst with a loud clatter into the last jewelry shop we had visited, startling the old man behind the counter. He looked first at me and then at Leila. A few minutes earlier we'd been here pricing gold bracelets. Now we were wild-eyed, with loosened head scarves and out of breath.

"Where's . . . have you seen"—I took a gulp of air—"my baby?" My lungs were bursting from running so fast to get here, and now I couldn't speak. "Did we leave my son here? We've lost my baby son!"

I must have sounded like an idiot. The man might as well have been deaf—he kept staring at me and then at Leila, his head calmly moving back and forth.

"Please tell us . . . did we leave him here?" Leila asked loudly, half turned to the door. "If not here, we have to go to the next store."

Very slowly the man raised a bony finger to point to my midsection. "You don't mean that baby?"

I looked down and there was Pouyan, sound asleep and wrapped in his blanket around my body.

"What are you, blind?" I screamed at Leila as I slapped her on the forehead.

"We are really sorry," I said to the jeweler. "Thank you. I don't know what I'd have done if you hadn't found him. Thank you, you saved my life."

Leila followed me and we stood outside the store, laughing so hard that tears rolled down our faces. I laughed so much that I got hiccups.

"How can you call *me* blind?" Leila said, and then started laughing again. "You were carrying him all this time."

"I've got used to carrying him so much that I don't feel him anymore, but you were LOOKING at me. Didn't you see him?"

"I panicked."

Just five months after Pouyan's birth, twenty million Iranians voted for Mohammad Khatami, a mid-ranking cleric with an easy manner and a kind face. Always elegantly attired in navy-, chocolate-, or cream-colored robes, he looked nothing like the other clerics, who wore wrinkled, dusty robes and plastic sandals as a way of demonstrating their revolutionary credentials. He was the first cleric to introduce a note of elegance, and it was pleasing to see a leader who had a smile on his face, in contrast to the scowls of the other officials.

Of course, this man who smiled a lot was not supposed to win. The country's political machinery, the religious elites and Supreme Leader Ali Khamenei, had given their blessing to Ali Akbar Nategh-Nouri, Speaker of Parliament. Khatami was an outsider, the dark horse candidate.

Iran's political system is a complex, unhappy marriage between theocracy and republicanism. The real power lies in the hands of unelected clerics, but they need elections to legitimize the system. Only a select few get to choose the Supreme Leader, but the people get to vote for the president.

Iran's first president, Abolhassan Banisadr, fled the country after clerics moved to impeach and arrest him. The next president, Mohammad Ali Rajai, was killed in a terrorist attack by the Mojahedin—the same Mojahedin that Ahmad had belonged to. Khamenei, who came next before assuming the Supreme Leader role, brought some stability during the war with Iraq, and he was followed by the canny Ali Akbar Hashemi Rafsanjani, another cleric and reputedly one of the richest men in Iran.

Rafsanjani had played a role in every major event in Iran since the revolution. He had now finished his two terms and was not eligible to run again.

Islamic Republic elections are not meant to be competitive. AghaJan voted at every election, and if you asked him who he voted for, he'd say, "I voted for whoever Rahbar [the Supreme Leader] wanted. I voted for Islam, I voted for the Islamic Revolution."

That year, AghaJan could relate to Nategh-Nouri, the overwhelming favorite, who, as it happened, was born in Noor, a small city in Mazandaran, not far from Babol. But the favorite secured only seven million votes, crushed in one of the biggest political landslides in Iran.

Why?

The children of the revolution had come of age and wanted a new Iran. They voted for the candidate promising change: Khatami. He wasn't supposed to win, but he did.

I was one of those children who had come of age—but I was too busy with Pouyan to vote. I have never voted in any election. The Iranian system is rigged at the most fundamental level. No matter how many votes the president gets, the Supreme Leader still controls the security services, the judiciary, and the military. He has a big say in foreign policy and controls a vast financial empire made up of religious foundations—charitable trusts and endowments with billions of dollars in income that only report to him. Besides, the candidates are preselected, and no secular candidates are allowed to run.

We ourselves had more immediate concerns that the president could not solve. Reza could not officially be employed as a teacher because of his conviction for a political crime. We built a one-room extension in the front yard of his parents' house and turned that into our bedroom. Reza spent most of his time composing verse after verse of poetry. Of course, that didn't make him unique. Writing poetry is almost the national hobby in Iran. We have a proud poetic tradition, from the classical works of Omar Khayyam and Ferdowsi to the romantic love poetry of Saadi and the mysticism of Hafez and Rumi. Most Iranian homes have a copy of the Quran and many volumes of poetry. To quote poetry is a sign of sophistication in Iran.

The other national hobby is singing, and all Iranians think they have a great voice. As I've said, I don't just think it. I know I have a great voice. More on that later.

My favorite poet was Forough Farrokhzad, often compared to Sylvia Plath. Born in the last days of 1934 to a middle-class family, she broke conventions both in her private life and in her poetry. In an Iran grappling with modernity, she wrote about being a woman—about the shopping basket, a pair of earrings, a cup of milk: the daily objects in a woman's life. In a society where sex outside of marriage was taboo, Forough wrote about her sexual relationships, about "sinning" that pleased her "in arms that trembled with ecstasy." She wrote about sex and love and relationships from a woman's point of view.

I'd get goose bumps reading her candid poems. It was as if she were writing about my life as a woman. Forough's life was tragic. She married an older second cousin at sixteen and quickly gave birth to a boy. Her first collection of poetry was published in 1952, when she turned eighteen. Two years later she fell in love with another man and divorced her husband, even though that meant losing custody of her son. Forough also directed documentaries, including the award-winning film *The House Is Black* (1963), about harsh conditions at an Iranian leper colony. She died in a car crash at the age of thirty-two.

> I am that candle which illuminates a ruin
> with the burning of her heart.
> If I want to choose silent darkness,
> I will bring a nest to ruin.

I wanted to be like Forough, to write poetry and live life to the fullest. Reza laughed at my efforts; he dismissed them as nothing more than sappy adolescent love poetry. Reza always saw himself as superior and more learned than me and was frustrated that his talents could not get him an important position.

My twenty-first birthday hit me hard. I had become what I had feared most—trapped in a vicious cycle of breast-feeding Pouyan and hand-washing his soiled diapers, on top of cooking and cleaning and all the other household chores. That's not what I wanted in a marriage. Reza gave lessons as a private tutor, but it did not bring in much money.

A week or so after my birthday, I sold what remained of my wedding gifts—a few gold bracelets—and bought a camera. I approached all the photography studios in Babol that specialized in wedding photos. Although some wedding ceremonies were mixed, most parties were segregated, with men and women in separate rooms. Male photographers were not allowed to enter the women's section. That created an opening for me. There was huge potential in becoming a wedding photographer.

My own wedding was not a glamorous affair, but I quickly realized that in Babol weddings were about the women, and that as long as the brides were happy, the grooms agreed to pay the bill. I had little competition and learned quickly from my mistakes. After a few months, I was a much-sought-after wedding photographer. I even bought a video camera to create wedding videos and made my own business cards to promote my services. Soon I was earning four times what Reza was making from his teaching assignments.

At the end of 1998, the Ministry of Islamic Cultural Guidance, better known as Ershad, issued an edict demanding that all professional photographers be registered for an identity card and a work permit that had to be renewed every year. Naturally, I applied, but my fingerprints revealed my prison record and no permit ever came my way.

There is a predictable cycle in Iranian politics, as predictable as the weather. Every year, for a few months, the government relaxes its grip and some actions are tolerated—women can show a few inches of hair under their head scarves, or men and women can actually walk together without being married, or the newspapers can publish mildly critical articles. Then, just like the dark clouds that gather in late autumn, the freedoms are taken away and transgressors are punished.

After turning a blind eye to mixed parties, the morality police began raiding mixed wedding parties, arresting all the guests. As the photographer, I wouldn't get detained, but my camera would be confiscated for a few days. I had to visit the local police station and wait most of the day before I could collect my gear. Making a living was becoming more precarious without an Ershad card.

Teaching bored Reza. With my earnings, I bought him a computer, and he became adept at computer graphics. Mohsen owned a small publishing company in Tehran and offered Reza a job if we joined him there. Ali had finished his prison sentence after almost three years, and he was going to Tehran, too. With the crackdowns on photographers, it seemed a good time to try our luck in the capital. Suddenly, a new adventure beckoned.

All I knew about Tehran was what I had heard from Mohsen and what I had seen on TV. I was very excited to move to Iran's biggest city, but my first impression was how it was dotted with murals of stern-looking warriors who had died in the war with Iraq and giant billboards with portraits of the founding father of the revolution. Every street was named after a martyr or a revolutionary cleric, or so it seemed to me. Tehran, a city of seven million souls, was bustling and noisy; everyone was always moving fast and no one ever had time to talk. It felt alien. Tehran's concrete urbanity, which included motorways that slashed through the city and an army of construction cranes promising more high-rises, was like nothing I had seen before. I was a village girl with a funny accent for which I was mocked nonstop till I managed to lose my strong northern accent.

The affluent Tehranis lived in the northern neighborhoods of Niavaran, Fereshte, and Saadabad, where most of the city's parks are located, the streets are wider, and the air is cleaner. The poor lived in southern Tehran, made up of more conservative and religious neighborhoods.

With Reza working for Mohsen, I found myself a stay-at-home wife again, much to my chagrin. I looked for jobs, but everyone could tell by my dress and accent that I was not a Tehrani, and no one wanted to hire an unknown photographer with a loud voice and a funny accent. Besides, there were plenty of female photographers in Tehran, which meant that I was not unique. Instead, I became a market researcher for the state-owned radio and TV station, Seda-va Sima (Sound and Vision), asking people in the street or in their homes to fill out questionnaires about the station's shows. I got paid a fixed amount for each completed form.

Although most weekends Reza and I headed back to Babol to spend time with our parents, we had started making new friends in Tehran and joined a literary circle that met once every two or three weeks. We read and discussed books by contemporary Iranian novelists, like Abbas Maroufi, and modern poets, like Fereydoon Moshiri. At other times, members brought their poems and short stories to read to the group. At these small gatherings, Reza was treated as a celebrity because he had been jailed for his political activities. No one, including Reza, liked acknowledging the fact that I, too, had been part of the same political gang. Reza began to be cold to me. In time, I was seen merely as his wife, an appendage, and stopped going to the gatherings.

It didn't help matters that Reza continued to look down on my poems and short stories. Our free and easy life became fraught with petty jealousies. He persisted in his belief that I had no talent as a writer or a poet—that he alone was the poet. There was no room in the marriage for another literary talent.

Both of us were working, which meant that for the first time we had some money. Our small apartment, on Resalat Avenue, in the east of Tehran, was on the top floor of a decrepit building. All day long, I would go around the streets of Tehran, knocking on people's doors to fill out Seda-va Sima questionnaires. Back at home, I barely had any energy left to climb up four stories. At the end of our first year, I wanted to move to a more central location; I was bubbling with ideas about such a move, but Reza was uninterested. He seemed preoccupied.

A new item had been added to the list of my duties. On my way to work, I'd drop in on real estate agents and scour the newspaper postings for a new home. I also left word with all our new friends to be on the lookout. Eventually, I found an apartment in Yousefabad, an area with mixed housing in the heart of Tehran. The apartment was in a shantytown, surrounded by high-rise buildings. It goes without saying that this part of the neighborhood wasn't great, but at least Yousefabad was more central than our current place.

The day before we were supposed to move, Reza began dressing as if he was going out to a special event. He seemed miles away as he got ready. I reminded him that we were moving the next day and said I couldn't pack the apartment by myself. "Don't you want to help with the packing?"

"There is an event in honor of…" He mentioned the name of a famous modernist poet. "I have to go and meet people."

He carried on getting dressed.

"I can't pack it all by myself."

Reza stared at me as if I had caused him immense pain.

"I was perfectly happy here," he said. "We could have renewed the lease. This is your doing, not mine."

He put his shoes on and left.

I asked my sisters-in-law Fozieh and Mohadesseh to help me pack. Both women rolled their eyes when I said Reza wasn't helping. I had to keep a close tab on Reza to make sure he was being a good husband, they lectured me.

"He is doing what he thinks is important to him," I said. "I can't put a leash on him."

By the time Reza came back in the evening, everything except the bedding and the sofa had been packed. He looked around, slowly taking in the room that was devoid of furniture but full of cardboard boxes.

He plopped down on the sofa and lit a cigarette, inhaling deeply.

"Look at how efficient I was today," I chirped. "Just three women did all this." Naïvely, I expected some praise.

"I'm in love with another woman," he said calmly. "I want to marry her."

CHAPTER NINE

Another woman... You love another woman," I whispered.

I felt as if he had punched me in the stomach. Reza nodded without looking at me. At least he had the decency to look guilty. My mouth was dry and I could barely speak. I was numb to every sensation apart from the ache in my heart.

"You said I was your only love," I managed to say. "You said I was the one with a crown of thorns."

I felt foolish even as I spoke.

A new muse. That's what Reza wanted.

He began talking slowly at first, but words tumbled out of his mouth and he became more animated. He waved his hands a lot and smoked furiously, extinguishing one cigarette only to light another one almost immediately. He said he felt trapped in our marriage.

"My poetry only flows when I'm in love," Reza said with a sad look in his eyes. "Our marriage has become loveless."

I was holding him back because he didn't love me anymore. It was my fault, he said.

"This marriage is a chore," he said, gesturing to all the boxes that he hadn't even packed. "This is not what I want."

I stared with tears in my eyes. For once, words failed me.

"There's no passion in our marriage."

Unless he felt the ecstasy of love, he couldn't write. In that respect, he was the exact opposite of me. I write when I'm sad, when I've been hurt, when my heart has been broken. I write to cure my blues. He wrote when he was in the grip of passion.

He had fallen in love with Nasrin, a woman from the literary group. I knew all about Nasrin—she was a colleague from Seda-va Sima who had ambitions of having her own poems published. At meetings, she paid way too much attention to Reza. In recent months, he often attended poetry readings with her while I stayed home with Pouyan. One time, I opened one of Reza's notebooks only to discover that he was working on a poem about her. I trembled as I read the unfinished poem. Reza had once composed a poem about me—that's how our relationship had started. It didn't matter that there was nothing romantic in his poem about Nasrin; at the time, I still felt angry. When I confronted him that night in the kitchen, he laughed it off.

"It's nothing," he said with a chuckle. "It's just an intellectual exercise. To be honest, Nasrin's poetry needs a lot of work."

"I want to be your muse forever," I said. "Am I not enough for you anymore?"

Reza was amused by my jealousy. He pecked me lightly on the forehead and started drying the dishes.

I let the matter drop.

That was then. Now he wanted out of the marriage. We kept talking and talking about what had gone wrong. Mostly he talked and I only half listened. He was still the same young poet who had fallen in love with me five years earlier—except that he was no longer in love with me. He was moving on and so should I.

"We should get a divorce," he said quietly.

"Divorce?" I whispered. I hesitated to say the word out loud. It was almost a taboo word. "What will happen to Pouyan?"

The acrid cigarette smoke in the room made my eyes water. I was close to tears anyway, but I stubbornly refused to believe that my marriage was over. I walked over and opened the window, leaning out to get some fresh air. With a burst of new energy I waved my hands rapidly to push the smoke outside. If only I could push all my troubles out the window as easily. Far above Tehran's silent streets and buildings, a galaxy of stars from millions and millions of miles away blinked invitingly. I wished I was far away, too.

Looking back, I know that our marriage was never really us. Reza and I thought we were going to make us into a family unit, but the life we had made wasn't what either of us wanted. He left because he didn't think there was anything worth staying for. He wanted to leave the washing-up, the dirty linen, and the wilting flowers and write his poetry. I would have quit us, too.

I was not worried about being left destitute, the fate of many women in Iran after a divorce. I had been the main breadwinner in Babol and in Tehran and was confident I could look after myself. But that night I felt terribly weak and defenseless. I dreaded explaining the divorce to my parents, to my brothers and everyone else. Once again, I had notched another family first: The first woman in our family to be arrested, the first to be jailed, and the first to be pregnant before her wedding, I would now be the first in all of Ghomikola to be divorced. It didn't matter that Reza was leaving me; everyone would think that it was somehow my fault.

"Please don't do this," I pleaded. "We have a good life, we have Pouyan. We'll have more kids if you want, I promise. And I'll even stay home more."

He stared at his feet and said nothing.

I racked my brain, flipping through millions of memories to find the right one to make him change his mind. I wanted him to want me. At that moment, I was ready to give up my own ambitions and become a housewife just to save our marriage. It does not bear thinking about, but I was hurting so much that I was ready to promise anything, even becoming the type of woman that I had rejected all my life. I'm sure I wouldn't have kept my promise, but that night my heart ached like never before. I didn't like being discarded.

Reza didn't say a word. His silence cut through me like a blade. I was ready to grasp at anything to save the marriage. Eventually, I made the ultimate offer.

"Go with her for a while," I said with the last ounce of energy left in me. "Go with her. I don't have a problem with that. You'll tire of her soon enough and I'll be here for you."

Reza stubbed out his last cigarette in the overflowing ashtray and stood up.

"I wish you wouldn't do this," I pleaded with him one last time.

"I can't stay here tonight. It doesn't feel right. Don't worry, I'm not going to her, but I have to sort things out for myself."

I silently watched him pack a few items of clothing and his notebooks into a suitcase. He took one last look around the room and promised to call me in a day or two after he had cleared his head and heart.

The door swung shut behind him.

The next morning, I woke up to the incessant ringing of the doorbell. I sat up fully dressed on the bare floor in the bedroom, where I had cried myself to sleep. The apartment stank of stale cigarettes and failure. My back hurt and the muscles from my arm had cramped from yesterday's packing. There are too many boxes for a soon-to-be divorced woman to own, I thought as I opened the door.

Ali had come to help with the move, but one look at me and he knew something was wrong.

"It's over, he's gone," I said as I headed to the kitchen to boil some water for tea. "He's leaving me for another woman."

"That ungrateful bastard," Ali spat. "He has no honor. I'll kill him."

I burst out laughing. Ali, the meekest of my siblings, was now acting like a typical macho Iranian male. I was in pain, but this was not a fatal blow.

"Reza has found someone who offers him more love. I wasn't enough for him." I smiled bravely at Ali. Each word hurt me deeply, but it needed to be said.

"He found someone he could love more, and if he's happier that way, I'm not going to stand in his way." I poured him a glass of strong tea.

"It's just not right for him to abandon you like this," Ali muttered as he blew on his tea to cool it. "He's ruined your future."

"We'll manage. If he doesn't love me, why should he stay?"

My mother had shown me by her actions never to be afraid of adversity. I remembered one particular incident a while back, before I had moved to Tehran. There was a public holiday, and the whole family had gone to visit Ali at his prison, some three hours away. The prison had granted special permission for families to visit the prisoners in the yard rather than from behind the glass. Mother spent days making special meals and pastries that Ali liked. AghaJan brought along fresh figs, which Ali loved. We got up before dawn to catch a special bus, carrying our food and bags of fruit to have a picnic with Ali.

We patiently waited in the prison yard, along with all the other families, for the inmates to be released at noon. Everyone came out, but not Ali. AghaJan dispatched Mohsen to go inside to see what had happened. He was worried that Ali might have taken ill and could not meet us. Soon, Mohsen returned looking glum, accompanied by the deputy prison chief.

"Ali has lost his visiting privileges," the official said in a superior manner. "I'm sorry, but rules are rules, and he is not an easy prisoner." He didn't look sorry. In his left hand, he absentmindedly counted off the green pellets on his string of worry beads.

"We've come a long way," AghaJan said. "It doesn't seem right."

"Ali has refused to join in the Friday prayers. He is refusing to take our Quran study classes," the deputy said. He towered over AghaJan. "I'm sorry you've come a long way, but we have to punish him."

I wanted to punch him, but that would have done no good. No matter how bad we felt, I was sure Ali was feeling much worse. Mother pushed AghaJan aside and stepped in front of the deputy. What happened next is as vivid to me as if it happened just yesterday.

"If you've read the Quran, you know that wasting food is a sin, but this sin is on you," Mother said, her voice shaking with emotion. She took a thermos out of her bag bursting with food and poured out the boiling tea on the ground in front of the official. Steam enveloped her. Next, she took out the fresh figs and threw them forcefully on the ground, and then she took out the fresh bread she had made.

"I baked this bread before dawn because I love my son, and now I've thrown it away and you are responsible," she said. "The sin is on your head."

"But Madar jan…" Taken aback by the vehemence of her tirade, he had addressed her as "dear Mother." But she was not finished.

"On Judgment Day, the fires of hell await you for breaking a mother's heart."

"We have rules, and if you break them there are punishments. Otherwise we'll have anarchy," he said. "If he had behaved himself, he wouldn't be here."

"Punish my son. But you can't control my son, so you punish me." Mother was unstoppable. "I've traveled three hours just to be here." She opened a pot of steamed rice and poured it on the ground. The deputy hurriedly took a few steps back.

"If my son misbehaves, punish him, give him solitary confinement, whip him, beat him, but today is a special visitation day." Mother gestured toward the other families. "Today is not for our sons but for the families. Today is my day. You are punishing me. A mother. Come Judgment Day, you will be sent to burn in hell." She spat the last words out in fury.

The other families could hear what was happening, and they shouted their support for my mother.

"Show some mercy," one man shouted. "Let her see her son."

"She is a mother. God doesn't like it when you break a mother's heart."

"Show some mercy."

The deputy and the guards exchanged nervous looks, and then the deputy cleared his throat to address Mother again.

"Why don't you step into my office and we'll see what we can do for you?" he said, making his best effort to smile benignly.

"No, I've seen what you've done for me already." Mother was still steaming mad. "We are done here."

The deputy stared hard at my mother and then the fight went out of him.

"I'll make an exception this time, because you remind me of *my* mother. It is a holy day, and as the Prophet Muhammad, peace and blessing be upon him, says, 'Heaven lies under the feet of mothers.' I'll get your son for you now."

Victory, I thought. I glanced at my brothers Mohsen and Hamid. Big smiles all around. Mother had rescued the day. I wanted to go and hug her. But she wasn't finished.

"I don't need your charity," Mother said. "I don't need your pity."

The smile froze on my face.

"I had a right to see my son. You took away my right. I'll come back next week by myself and I'll see him through a glass screen. But I'm not going to beg for what is my right."

She turned and walked back out the prison gate.

"Please...It'll only take a...We'll fetch Ali now...." The deputy's voice trailed off.

Without a word, we all trooped out behind Mother. No one said anything about that visit again.

Mother always regarded pride as a mortal sin. Always be humble toward other people, she drummed into our heads as we were growing up. Yet even though she didn't have a formal education, and lived just above the poverty line most of her life, she didn't want to be belittled.

As Ali blew on his tea, I was transported to that day, remembering how we all sat on the bus heading home, hungry and thirsty, and yet no one complained. I was sad that my marriage was over, but if Reza loved another, then I had no claim on him.

Reza and I met a few more times over the next few weeks in public places like Laleh (Tulip) Park and in cafés to talk. The marriage was over, but it needed a postmortem.

Mohsen and Ali fell out with me for a while because I refused to take my full share of the *mehrieh*—the 20,000 tomans, 12 gold coins, and Quran that Reza had said he would pay me in the event of a divorce. My alimony. Mohsen had fired Reza, and I didn't want to impoverish him.

Mohsen always felt protective toward me and acted like my second father. He still saw me as a teenager who needed to be told what to do. I would go to Mohsen's office after work so he could take me back to his house and feed me. He warned me that my parents would regard the divorce as bringing shame on the family. Again. No matter that it was Reza who was unfaithful—society would blame me.

"Don't think Iran is a modern country," Mohsen said, sitting on the edge of his desk. "Divorce still carries an awful stigma. You are young enough to remarry, but it's not going to be easy."

His solution was for me to remarry as quickly as possible.

"Men will see you as a piece of material, a commodity, that was used and then returned to the store. Even if you were blameless, society blames you." Mohsen paced back and forth as he put manuscripts in his briefcase. "Nobody ever blames the husband. It's not fair, but that's the reality."

Later I discovered that being divorced made me more desirable in the eyes of certain men—the ones already married and looking for sexual favors outside of their own marriage. To put it crudely, these men thought that since my husband had left me, I must be ready for sex. Very few families wanted a divorcée to marry their sons.

I should not leave the marriage empty-handed, Mohsen insisted during our talks.

"I don't need his money," I said to Mohsen. "I don't want the gold coins he doesn't have. I don't care that the law is on my side—I'm not interested in Reza's money."

A month after he first broke the news, Reza, Pouyan, and I sat on a bus to Babol together to talk to our parents and resolve the issue of the *mehrieh*. I was not looking forward to seeing my family.

I went to see my family by myself first. The visit did not go well.

Mother cried the moment she saw me, as if I had caught an incurable illness and faced imminent death. "You are ruining your life," she said through her tears. "You'll have no man to look after you. A husband can protect you." She hit her head, and tears poured down her face. Mother could be tough as steel when it came to defending her family, but she had had a rough childhood. Her own father had died, and her mother had abandoned her to the care of an aunt. Mother's marriage to Agha-Jan was not perfect, but it had provided stability. Without a husband, it was like drifting in the middle of the ocean, at the mercy of big waves and wild sea creatures, she often told me.

"The world's not safe for a woman to be by herself. Don't be proud. Go and beg Reza to take you back."

AghaJan simply shook his head. "You managed to ruin your life again."

"If Islam didn't approve of divorce, there'd be a holy edict against it," I replied. "Lots of people divorce nowadays."

"You'll have to come back to Ghomikola and wait till you are married again," AghaJan said firmly. "You'll only bring more shame on me and your mother if you stay alone in the big city."

It didn't matter to AghaJan that I was an independent woman and made more money than the man who was soon to be my ex-husband.

The next day, Reza and I sat on a park bench in Babol to discuss the issue of who was going to get custody of Pouyan. As we talked, I became distracted by a figure moving furtively among the bushes, some fifty feet away. I observed the figure closely. To my horror, it was my own *mother*. Somewhat surprised, I walked toward her, followed by Reza.

"Mother? Are you following me?" I asked. "Please come out."

Mother, looking smaller than usual, kept wiping away her tears as she emerged from the shrubbery. She didn't even look at me but instead appealed to Reza to take me back.

"For the love of God, don't divorce Masoumeh," she begged.

"She's always been difficult, but she has a kind heart and she'll learn to be a better wife."

Reza looked uncomfortable.

"Stop spying on me," I told her. "We are getting divorced. It'll be fine."

"You can have two wives, it says so in the Quran." Mother continued to address Reza as if I weren't there. "Keep Masoumeh as your wife *and* take a new wife. Just don't abandon my Masoumeh, don't let her be alone."

Reza made some excuse and practically ran out of the park. There was nothing to be said to Mother. She and I walked to the bus station in near silence.

Later, I heard that Reza had been keen on having two wives but that Nasrin had killed the idea.

About two weeks later, Reza and I waited our turn to see the district divorce judge, who was also a cleric. Ali and Mohsen found an excuse not to show their faces. So much for their moral support. I had to recruit two bystanders to act as my witnesses to the proceedings.

At the court, I came face-to-face with the grim reality of being a woman in the Islamic Republic, where laws are devised by misogynists who find guidance and precedent in the seventh century. When it comes to the matter of ending a marriage, a man can divorce his wife, but the woman has to ask her husband's permission to ask for a divorce. How odd is that!

Reza came with his friends and parents.

Banoo took me aside in a corridor before the judge arrived. "The judge is unlikely to give custody of Pouyan to you," she confided. "I'm telling you this so you don't get upset."

"He's not even four. The judge knows in his heart that a mother has to look after her son."

"We have to think of what's best for Pouyan." She squeezed my hands gently and smiled. "Pouyan needs a father so he can grow up to be strong. Reza wants to get remarried very quickly, and you are still young and can get remarried more easily if there are no complications."

"I don't want to get married. I want to look after Pouyan by myself."

"In Tehran? All by yourself?" She sounded incredulous. "Who's going to look after him when you are working? Suppose something goes wrong and you lose your job? Pouyan needs his father."

I didn't answer. We went into the judge's chambers.

"Are you pregnant?" the cleric asked.

I tried some humor. "Once was enough."

"Are you pregnant?" the cleric repeated sternly.

"No."

"You have signed a note saying you are giving up your full *mehrieh*; you're giving up twelve gold coins. Do you understand?"

"I understand. I don't want his money."

The cleric made some notes, filled in some blank spots on a document, and then looked up.

"It's always sad when couples divorce. At these moments, I must think of the children, and here"—he looked down at his notes—"I have to think of Pouyan's interest. I'm going to give custody to Reza, but every week Masoumeh can have him for a twenty-four-hour period."

Banoo quietly whispered in my ear that she would take Pouyan back to Babol with her and I could visit him anytime. She grabbed him and walked out of the room.

I left the courtroom in a daze. I was all by myself. It was September 2000, a week before my twenty-fourth birthday. My marriage was over and I had lost custody of Pouyan.

CHAPTER TEN

I blossomed after my divorce. It was painful, but I was suddenly free to grow and be myself. I wasn't looking for new directions in my life, but I had little choice. The hardships I went through forged me.

At first it was not easy.

I moved into the new apartment in Yousefabad by my lonesome self, of course. One part of Yousefabad—a large, sprawling district in the northwestern corner of the center of Tehran—had gentrified over time, becoming a very desirable location for upper-middle-class families. At the other end was Halabi Abad, or Tin City, a slum that had mushroomed recently. Houses had been erected of stone and concrete, with little planning or design or order. Ali didn't like the area at all.

"You can get your throat cut in this neighborhood just for looking out of place," Ali said the first time he visited.

The apartment, near Kurdistan Highway, consisted of a long hallway leading to a bedroom and a kitchen. The hall was so long that it remained cold throughout the winter, despite the best efforts of an old Aladdin kerosene heater I bought. The national gas company refused to lay gas pipes in the neighborhood, despite its central location. I did have free electricity, thanks to residents having set up illegal hookups to steal electric power. This was the first apartment where I lived by myself.

The neighborhood was started by homeless villagers who had streamed into Tehran in search of jobs after the Islamic Revolution. They made makeshift shelters by piling oil cans on top of each other. Since then the area had expanded and modernized somewhat: You could find all kinds of buildings, but the construction quality was uniformly shoddy. Some dwellings had corrugated tin roofs; others had a curtain for the front door. Most walls were crooked or on the verge of crumbling, yet you could thrive if you learned to ignore the dirt and garbage strewn everywhere. It was the rough part of town, and I dreaded going home late after work. But at least it was my own place.

AghaJan kept sending messages via my brothers that I should return and stay with the family until he found me a husband.

I was never the obedient girl.

One day AghaJan himself called me.

"People talk. I have a position in the village." He was a former basiji, he reminded me. "How can I show my face at the mosque, where everyone knows my daughter is divorced but living in Tehran by herself?"

"I'm twenty-four, not a child anymore. I have a job and I'm not doing anything immoral."

"You need a new husband. Come home and we'll find you another man to take care of you."

"I don't plan on having a man look after me, and I don't plan on sitting at home in Ghomikola."

We might have moved into a new millennium, but in Iran divorced women had no identity of their own. My father was not unique; he was a reflection of Iranian culture. In many villages and small cities, there is an expectation that a divorced woman should sit at home and wait for her next husband. Only now, as divorce rates have climbed in Iran, is there greater tolerance for divorcées—and then only in Tehran and other major cities.

There was one thing I was sure of: I wasn't going back to Ghomikola. Eventually AghaJan gave up.

I went to see Pouyan, who was at Reza's parents' in Babol, as often as the law permitted. It was very painful. Many times it ended in tears. He didn't want to let me go and I was reluctant to part with him, but Reza had won custody. I kept promising Pouyan that once my situation improved, I'd come and take him away. I didn't know how, but I knew that one day I'd take him back.

I liked my independence, even though I was not ready for the single life. I stopped cooking and instead took to spending time at Ali's house, eating dinners there and taking home the leftovers. At other times, I hid in my apartment after work, feeling sorry for myself. What I needed to do was figure out what to do with my life. I was surrounded by darkness and needed to keep my eyes wide open.

I had started my job at Seda-va Sima when we had first come to Tehran and it was very easy to do. I was still visiting different neighborhoods and knocking on doors—of houses, apartments, shops, and businesses—to get folks to answer questions about their viewing habits and attitudes toward the TV station. I hauled a stack of questionnaires around with me and I found that I was good at connecting with people.

I could talk to anyone, young or old, man or woman. It must have been part of my rural upbringing. I'm pretty easygoing and like to strike up conversations. The job was a great education for me, as I met thousands of ordinary Tehranis and learned how to talk to people from different social classes and backgrounds.

One of the more interesting people I met was Fouad, a sixty-three-year-old travel agent who had lived in many countries in Europe, as well as in Singapore and Japan. Fouad was tall and distinguished-looking, with thinning silver hair, and he was full of stories of his travels. One night as he closed up his office, he called his wife and told her he was bringing a special guest for dinner. It was a cold winter evening when we trudged through the snow to his house. Until that day, I had never met anyone who had visited Western countries.

We talked in his kitchen as his wife stirred a pot of rice and chopped green herbs.

I'm very bad at keeping secrets. When I was a kid, my cousins refused to share their secrets with me because they knew I liked to talk and never kept information to myself for long. Even though I had just met Fouad and his wife, I told them my life story as I tucked into a plate of rice and vegetable stew. I expected some sympathy, but none was forthcoming.

"Stop feeling sorry for yourself," Fouad said. He piled my plate with a second helping of steaming rice. "There really is a big world out there, and you need to move on."

"When I was in Ghomikola, Babol was a big deal. Now I'm in Tehran. This is big enough."

"Tehran is big, but you should travel and see other countries, too."

"It's easy for you to say. You are the first person I've met who's flown on a plane," I said. "Tehran is big enough for me." I shrugged.

"What? You mean to tell me you haven't flown on a plane before?" Fouad was incredulous. He looked at his wife and they both laughed. "Are you serious? We've never met anyone who hasn't flown before."

"Why are you surprised? Perhaps you should travel among your own people more often." I hate being belittled. "In fact, no one in my family or among my friends has ever flown."

Fouad became all apologetic. "I want to be the one who buys your first airplane ticket," he said. "People forget what you tell them, but they never forget what you did for them."

It was a few days before the Iranian New Year, Nowruz, which starts on March 21. Ali had arranged to visit our distant cousins in Isfahan, a city rich in history and culture, for the holidays. They had asked me to join them, but I didn't feel any New Year's joy. Pouyan was going to be with his father. I also didn't want to explain to my brother's friends why my marriage had fallen apart and answer questions about getting remarried.

I had told Ali I would not be joining them.

"Can you get me to Isfahan?" I asked Fouad. "That will surprise my brother."

The next day, Fouad handed me a round-trip ticket to Isfahan. I would be flying out the same day Ali and his wife took the bus. I made sure I called Ali before he left to wish him safe travels.

I wore my best outfit and took a taxi to Mehrabad Airport, so excited I think I could have flapped my arms and flown there myself. I walked triumphantly to the gate, thinking everyone must be looking at me. Once the plane started taxiing, my bravado vanished and I became a nervous wreck. *What was I thinking?* I gripped the armrests and started praying with my eyes closed tight, begging the Almighty to get me out of there. In my panic, I even called over one of the stewards and told him I had changed my mind.

"I've had enough of flying. I want to get off now."

The steward smiled and ignored me. My biggest fear was that if the plane crashed, I would have had no chance to tell my friends I had flown on a plane. I only opened my eyes when the plane was at cruising speed. Just as I was getting comfortable, we landed. I was so disappointed—I wished we had stayed in the air longer.

Back on the ground, I couldn't wait to surprise my family. I got a taxi to our cousins' house and waited. Two or three hours later, Ali and his family rang the doorbell. I raced to open the door.

Ali was stunned. He couldn't believe his eyes. He kept on touching my arms, my head, just to make sure it was me.

"How did you get here so fast?" he kept repeating. "I spoke to you this morning before we left."

After six months of being depressed about my divorce, I finally felt like having fun. I felt special because I was the first person in my family to have flown. Finally, an achievement that was not shameful for the rest of the family.

As the New Year got under way, I had new concerns. My employment contract was coming to an end and I had to undergo a more rigorous application process, including a security background check, which included having fingerprints taken. If my prison record became public knowledge at Seda-va Sima, I was going to be fired.

Time to look for a new job. Besides, I didn't like my new work schedule. Some days I had to start in the late afternoon and work till late in the evening to catch whole families at home. I'd knock on doors at dinnertime, when the husbands had returned from work. One evening, at the end of a long day, I twisted my left ankle and fell down on the side of the road. Exhausted and in pain, I invited myself to my friend Mahsa's apartment for dinner. We'd known each other when I had just married Reza, and it was one of the few friendships from that time that had survived the divorce. Mahsa was finishing her university degree in foreign languages.

Everyone knew what a terrible cook I was, and Mahsa loved to cook. While she chopped onions, cooked some mincemeat, and made a pot of rice, I told her about my job-hunting efforts. My ankle was badly bruised and it hurt a lot. After dinner, Mahsa offered to take me home and stay at my place. It was around ten o'clock when we left her apartment, and every step was torture for me. I hobbled along, clutching my bag, which was filled with questionnaires, and with every painful step I cursed my clumsiness and my general bad luck. I was feeling sorry for myself and close to tears.

Mahsa distracted me by talking about her plans to leave Iran for Europe, probably Italy, and settle there. President Khatami had been a big disappointment, she said. Reforms had not arrived. I didn't care. All I cared about was getting a taxi, because I could no longer walk. That night all the taxis we saw were either full of passengers or sped past us with no intention of stopping. Plenty of private cars cruised by, which was not unusual. In Tehran, some men, and occasionally women, drive their cars like private taxis as a second job. Many people in Iran have second jobs to make ends meet. For safety reasons, women don't often get into these private taxis, but if they do and the cars are stopped by the police, it can lead to some awkward questions.

We waited by the curb. A dark Paykan stopped, and the driver leaned across the seat and examined us. His features were hidden in the dark, and he had a scarf wrapped around his neck.

"How much? How much?" he hissed. "I don't need you for the whole night. Just one of you. You are too skinny, but I'll take her." He nodded at Mahsa.

I retied my head scarf, tightened the belt on my manteau, and looked away, ignoring the man.

"Your loss," he shouted, and sped away with his tires screeching.

Mahsa and I burst out laughing. We were shocked—we hadn't been exposed to this part of Tehran culture before.

An orange Paykan stopped short of us. Another man leaned over, grinning lasciviously. "How much for both of you. In the car?"

"Get lost," Mahsa said.

Before the Islamic Republic, Tehran had its own red-light district, known as the Citadel of Shahr-e No, or New City. By all accounts, it was a miserable place. After the revolution, part of the Citadel burned to the ground and the rest was flattened and converted into a park. Prostitution was forbidden, but no one had been able to stop the practice.

We could now see, from across the street, that there was a specific spot where cars would stop and a female figure would get inside. The car would then speed away. We didn't want to be near that unsavory scene and walked about a hundred yards away to wait for a proper taxi. We thought it was funny that we were being mistaken for prostitutes with our long coats and head scarves.

As the minutes ticked by, I became aware that we were being watched—two men on a motorbike across the road had their eyes on us. They were probably purse snatchers, I thought. Recently the newspapers had been full of lurid stories of thieves on motorbikes snatching women's bags and speeding away. In one incident, a woman was hit on the head with a steel chain after she had left the bank. The robbers took her bag and she needed more than thirty stitches. I tightened my grip on my bag and we slowly started toward the next intersection, in search of a taxi and hoping to leave the men on the bike behind.

The motorbike drove away and then turned slowly to come behind us, stopping a few feet short. The driver pointed the bike at us, his headlight flooding us with white light as he played with the throttle, revving the engine higher and lower. Mahsa and I gripped each other's arms and kept walking, too scared even to talk.

Suddenly the bike sped past us and then the driver sharply braked and turned to block our path. The passenger, wearing an untucked white shirt and a Palestinian keffiyeh, or checkered scarf, wrapped around his neck, jumped down and sauntered toward us, stopping inches away from me.

"What are you waiting for, you piece of garbage?" He screamed wildly as he flung the keffiyeh open. He was about eighteen years old, hardly old enough to shave. "What the hell do you want here?" He screamed with unexplained rage.

"Take it, take it all, it's yours." I offered him my bag. Mahsa stood behind me. Neither of us felt very brave. "Just don't hit me. Please take it."

He slapped the bag with such force that he sent it flying out of my hand. It landed with a thud several feet away.

"I don't want your filthy *najes* money," he shrieked, using the word for "impure." "What the hell are you doing out on the streets at this time of the night? Turning tricks?"

I realized, a little belatedly, that these two were much worse than robbers. They were the paramilitary, the Basij. The keffiyeh had been worn by basijis in the Iran-Iraq war. The Supreme Leader, Ali Khamenei, often draped a keffiyeh over his shoulders.

Just when I thought the night could not get any worse, a car braked beside us and the driver opened the passenger door wide.

"Hey, ladies, jump in here. My car's more comfortable than that bike," the driver said.

With two long strides, the young man with the keffiyeh reached the car and violently kicked the door shut.

"Get lost, you filth," he yelled.

The wheels screeched as the car took off, leaving only smoke behind.

I had been questioned by basijis before, once or twice at road-blocks in Babol, but never at night. If we weren't careful Mahsa and I could be arrested for immoral activities. That would be disastrous for me—because of my record, I'd be sent to jail to serve the rest of my suspended sentence.

I had no time to think of a plan. The man in the keffiyeh raced back and kicked me savagely in the shin. I thought he had broken my leg—a flash of pain tore into my body and I crumpled and sat on the ground. I was in so much pain that I could not even breathe.

"You must be a very expensive whore—is that why you are turning down these men?"

Tears poured down my face as I gulped for air. My attacker bent down and punched me in the ribs. Again, and again.

"Help! Don't hit her. Let her go," Mahsa screamed.

"When will you whores learn not to sell your filthy bodies on the streets?"

"Please don't hit me." I found my voice as I raised my arms to fend off yet another blow. "We want a taxi to go home."

"No taxis stop here—only cars for you whores." He stepped back as his rage subsided.

The basiji who had remained seated on the motorbike now got up and walked into the middle of the road. He put both his hands out and stopped an empty taxi that had just turned off Vali Asr Avenue, less than a block from where we were standing. The driver, an old man, probably was on his way home but didn't want to risk trouble with the Basij.

"Get in there," my attacker shouted as he lifted me up roughly by my arm and threw me in the back of the cab.

"You said you were looking for a taxi—well, here it is," he said with a sneer. "If I see you again, I'll kill you."

Mahsa sneaked past him into the cab. She had picked up my bag.

My attacker leaned into the taxi and told the driver, "Take these 'ladies' to wherever the hell they want to go."

The driver turned and carefully examined us. We were a sight— eyes red with tears and streaking makeup running down our faces. Our head scarves halfway down our necks. I was grimacing in pain.

The old man shook his head in disapproval as he put the car into gear and moved on.

"Please, ladies, fix your head scarves. I need you to respect the hijab laws."

We had just been brutally assaulted, and this driver's only concern was about our loose head scarves. We meekly obeyed him as we cried quietly in the backseat. Perhaps he thought we really were call girls. But there is something wrong with a country where people are more concerned about a few loose strands of hair than a brutal assault on defenseless citizens.

For a few days, I limped around the apartment, my ribs bruised, and called in sick to work. I didn't feel like facing the world. It was time to make changes in my life. I vowed that no man was ever going to beat me again, and that if a man laid a hand on me, he would suffer ten times the consequences. I also needed to be serious about getting a new job, a new apartment in a better neighborhood, and above all else a car, so I wouldn't have to wait for taxis. It was a long list. I would start with getting a new job.

I had always wanted to be a writer, but I never thought I was any good at it. Mother had the gift of poetry. She could compose complex poems, dealing with themes of loneliness and love, in her Mazani dialect. My teenage writings had gotten me into jail.

It was time to call Mohsen for help. His small publishing house printed mostly academic books about natural history and science, but he knew a number of journalists whose ambition was to become a writer.

About a week or two later, I had an interview for an intern position at *Hambastegi,* a daily newspaper affiliated with the reformist political parties, meaning that their views were to the left of center and they supported President Khatami. Most journalists liked Khatami, who had opened up the cultural space to allow dozens of new publications to flourish.

The world had changed a lot in the 1990s, from the advent of the Internet to the collapse of the Soviet Union and the demise of apartheid in South Africa; but change had not penetrated Iran, especially as far as women were concerned. Khatami, with his ever-present smile, said he wanted to reform Iran. He had been born into a religious family and wore a black turban rather than the more common white, signifying that he came from the line of the Prophet. His father and his grandfather were both ayatollahs.

Khatami had allowed more newspapers to publish, greater numbers of books were available, and censorship was somewhat curtailed. But there were limits to his reforms. Secular political parties or newspapers advocating for a separation of religion and politics were still forbidden. Only candidates approved by the Guardian Council—a body made up of six clerics and six lawyers that vetted laws passed by Parliament—were allowed to operate, as long as they did so within certain guidelines. At that time, the Iranian political scene was a struggle between Khatami's reformers and the conservative factions. In reality, these were two wings of the same religious party. It's as if in the United States the only political opinions permitted were those of the Tea Party and the moderate Republicans, with no other political views allowed. It was ridiculous, but in Iran only religious political views were tolerated. Khatami only promised reform within the Islamic framework, and he was very much against any secularization of Iran. Even though he had won reelection in 2001 in a landslide, the real power, as always, resided in the hands of the Supreme Leader, Ali Khamenei.

Hambastegi, which backed Khatami's agenda, was based in a nondescript building in downtown Tehran. The building's security guard, a bored-looking old man with leathery skin and a blue short-sleeved shirt, sat on a rickety stool just inside the door. He took short puffs on his cigarette as he examined my papers. Without uttering a word, he waved me through.

I climbed up a flight of stairs, marveling at the dirt accumulated on each step and wondering if I had made the right decision. All my worries disappeared once I stepped inside the *Hambastegi* offices. A long table dominated the rectangular newsroom, with three smaller desks set in different corners. Around each table, young men and women huddled over notepads, writing stories in longhand or conducting interviews over the phone. An adjacent room contained a telex machine, which constantly spewed out news items from the state-owned Islamic Republic News Agency (IRNA), the official voice of the government. There were no computers or laptops to be seen. I'd never seen a newsroom before, but there was energy in the room; I stared in awe as male and female journalists were constantly in motion, some taking copy to the typing pool on a different floor, others exchanging the latest story items for the next day's newspaper.

This was where I wanted to be, I decided. I didn't know how to be a journalist, but I wanted to be part of this team. This was going to be my new life. I just had to make it happen.

I sat on a hard chair observing the newsroom for more than three hours before I was led in to see Mr. Q., a member of the editorial board. He wasn't a real journalist, but as a former reformist member of Parliament he had political clout and connections. That morning, he seemed at a loss for what to do with me, since I had neither.

"Your application letter says your name is Masih. The Messiah? Are you Christian?" he asked hesitatingly.

"My name is Masoumeh, and I'm a Muslim."

"I thought Masih was a man's name. So, did you pick that name for yourself or was it your father?"

"My fiancé gave me that name. My father is a devout Muslim and he never calls me Masih."

"What happened to your fiancé?" He seemed interested.

"We got married and then we divorced." I blurted it out.

Mr. Q. took some notes on the pad in front of him.

"Do you have a university degree?"

"I never went to university."

"A high school diploma?" Mr. Q. asked patiently.

"Not quite," I said.

He made some more notes, but he wasn't looking so interested anymore.

"Do you speak any foreign languages? English? French, perhaps? Our foreign desk is always looking for translators," he continued.

"I'm from Ghomikola. Persian is our second language," I joked. "I speak Mazandarani and a little Gilaki." (Gilaki is another northern dialect). "Does that count?"

He didn't even crack a smile.

"Any references? Anyone who can vouch for you?" Mr. Q. asked. "Politically, I mean. We are a reformist publication."

I meekly shook my head. If I had any patrons, I wouldn't be asking for an entry-level position, I thought.

"We are looking for candidates with experience. You look like you are hardworking and devout. I'll think about it," Mr. Q. said, and ushered me out of his office.

I knew that apart from my enthusiasm, I had nothing going for me. I had to make him think more urgently about me. I had to try one more time. The next morning, I was up before dawn and I walked into Mr. Q.'s second-floor office with a speech I had prepared.

"There are more qualified candidates," I began, my voice shaking a bit. "There are those who have the right family connections, and some can speak a foreign language or two. But I am a true product of the Islamic Revolution. My family are the *mostazfain*"—the downtrodden—"the ones who made this revolution and are the bedrock of support for the Islamic Republic. My father and brothers fought in the war. We don't have connections because we are too busy working to feed our families. This revolution was about giving opportunity to people like me, to the have-nots, not to the insiders."

"I like your nerve. You are a gutsy woman."

"I can learn to be a journalist. Just give me a chance. Let me be here for three months to learn," I begged him. "If it doesn't work out, I'll leave quietly. And you don't have to pay me."

"Journalists have to be bold, and we have to remember why we are in this business: to look after the people's interest." Mr. Q. sounded noble that day.

He recommended that the board hire me as a trainee without pay. I later learned that other interns received a weekly stipend, but I didn't care. It wasn't the first time I had worked for free, and I had gotten my foot in the door.

Mother always used to say: "If they lock the front door, go in through the back door. If the doors are barred, go through the window. If they shutter the windows, climb in through the chimney. Never let them lock you out. Always try to get in."

I've tried to live by those words. Ali and Mohsen offered to help me till I could get paid. I spent my days at the office and took classes at the Media Studies Center in the afternoons to learn the craft. I quickly discovered that as an intern from the provinces, I was lower than low in the hierarchy.

Marjan Sheikholeslami, *Hambastegi*'s senior political writer and the head of the political desk, agreed to take me under her wing. In the male-dominated world of journalism, the tall and beautiful Marjan was one of the rare women to rise so high. She had put in years of hard work to secure her reputation; she was well respected and knew all the right people, including those who owed her favors. Still, she could not gain entry to the *Hambastegi* editorial board, which gathered every morning to determine the key stories of the day and which ones were deemed worthy of front-page coverage. The board was made up solely of men. Though Marjan was excluded from membership in that particular club, almost all her stories ended up on the front page.

After three months, I had published only a few short items. There was nothing to make me stand out. I was apprehensive and needed to turn my internship into a full-time position. I needed a big break. Ironically, a dispute over press freedom came to my rescue.

While I struggled to adjust to life as a single woman and learn to be a journalist, a different struggle was taking place among politicians in Tehran. The reformist members of Majlis (Parliament) urged President Khatami to open up the society and make radical changes to the country's press and family laws, and to curb the powers of the Supreme Leader, Ayatollah Ali Khamenei.

Amid the wrangling, the Majlis passed a law to cut the budget of the national television broadcaster, Seda-va Sima, which was under the purview of the Supreme Leader. This was a test of who was in charge—the Majlis or Khamenei. Under the Iranian Constitution, the Majlis had oversight of Seda-va Sima, the only broadcaster allowed in Iran, but it was unclear whether the Majlis could actually limit its budget.

A few hundred years before, the king of England, Charles I, lost his head after he quarreled with Parliament. No one expected Khamenei to lose his head, but relations between the Supreme Leader's office and Majlis were very tense. Former president Rafsanjani had offered to mediate and find a middle way to calm matters.

On a quiet day with no news happening, Marjan went home before lunch. I had an idea for a story as I flipped through the desk's contacts book, which contained phone numbers of key political players. As an intern, I had to run my story ideas past Marjan, but I figured it was better to act first and apologize later. I started cold-calling Majlis members to get their opinions about Rafsanjani's meddling. I called the most radical lawmakers and played up the fact that I was an intern in search of guidance. It's funny how often male politicians can be relied upon to be patronizing to women, but they also provided me with great quotes. Two hours later, I filed a story on how the reformist MPs, itching for a confrontation with the Supreme Leader, were set to turn down Rafsanjani's mediation offer.

"This is from the political desk," I said, handing my copy to the news editor. The article's byline was "From the Majlis Team," which was standard procedure when we had a sensitive story. This way the author was somewhat protected.

As a trainee, one of my duties was to carry news copy to the editors. No one suspected anything unusual was happening.

I went home with butterflies in my stomach. I was so nervous I hardly ate any dinner and barely slept that night. Early the next morning, I raced to the news kiosk, where I bought a copy of *Hambastegi,* even though I could get a free one at work. I couldn't wait to see my story in print, but I got a big shock—it was on the front page.

I was on the FRONT PAGE.

My name was not there, but it was my story. That's when I started to panic. I was sure I was going to get into deep trouble. I had expected the story to be tucked away on an inside page, but this was very different. Marjan would be angry at being left in the dark. Instead of the bus I usually took to work, I hailed a taxi so I could intercept her and beg her forgiveness. The driver had the radio switched to a news station, and as he weaved through the morning traffic, I heard the announcer talk about the dangers of a political row over the Majlis dispute. The main news item on the radio was about the fallout from my story. Other politicans were reacting. Now I was sure I was going to get fired. When I arrived, the newsroom was buzzing with excitement about Marjan's great scoop. I sat silently in my chair, my eyes glued to the door as I waited for her. When she strolled in, I rushed to her, dragged her to a corner, and told her the truth. I kept apologizing for not checking with her and for not respecting the chain of command.

"I didn't think it was going to be this big," I said with a silly grin on my face.

She listened to me without saying a word and then walked straight to her desk. I'm going to be fired, I thought. Other reporters and section editors flocked to her to congratulate her for the big news. Even the editor in chief came out of his office to greet her.

Marjan held up the front page and turned to me.

"This is Masih's story. You should all congratulate her."

CHAPTER ELEVEN

After a few months on the politics desk, I was made the Majlis correspondent and entered a strange new world. The sixth Majlis, in the hands of the reformists, would be remembered in Iranian history as one of the most radical. Most newspapers and news agencies in Iran are affiliated with a political group. We had reformist newspapers (*Aftab Yazd* and *Etemad Melli*), conservative newspapers (*Kayhan* and *Resalat*), and a few, like *Hamshahri,* that claimed to be bipartisan and hovered between the two positions. I was in the reformist camp.

Soon I took a second job as a Majlis correspondent for the Iranian Labor News Agency (ILNA). I would spend mornings in Majlis working for ILNA and in the afternoon head to *Hambastegi* to write the day's analysis story. Being in ILNA gave me greater visibility, since many newspapers across the country subscribed to its news service. Suddenly my stories were being carried by dozens and dozens of local and provincial newspapers. I needed the extra money to escape from my shantytown.

I moved five times in three years, eventually renting an apartment in a building that had its own janitor. That was a relief. I'm always losing my keys, and the janitor soon learned to keep spare keys for me. I threw out everything that reminded me of my old life and relegated the sofa and bedding to the dustbin of history, selling most of the items and buying new ones. It drove Mother mad that I was wasting money rather than saving, but I had turned twenty-six and did not want to keep any signs of my old life around. I learned to live light. All my belongings could be packed in suitcases and cardboard boxes to make the moves easier. I rarely invited friends over, because I didn't want to talk about my private life, especially the divorce and losing custody of Pouyan. I didn't hang any pictures on the walls and only put photos of Pouyan in frames that stood on tables—easier to hide when, on rare occasions, guests did arrive.

As for food, I still didn't really cook. It's not much of an exaggeration to say that I relied on sandwiches and the kindness of family and friends, continuing to drop in at Ali's or Mohsen's place and leave with the leftovers. Whenever there was a party with homemade food, I'd turn up with the mere hint of an invitation and would be the last person to leave the table.

Still, I couldn't escape my past. To get a Majlis press card, I had to be vetted by a special management committee, which required a background check on me from the Intelligence Ministry, the Ministry of Justice, and the Revolutionary Guards. The Intelligence Ministry report recommended rejecting my application on the grounds that I had a record for political activities. Even though that was for a minor infraction when I was eighteen, the ministry still gave me the thumbs-down.

I reached out to Ahmad Borghani, a Majlis member and former journalist, for help. Borghani was a former Ershad deputy minister who had resigned in protest over a law to limit press freedom. Once he heard my story, he arranged for me to see Mehdi Karroubi, then the Speaker of Parliament and the most powerful figure in the Majlis. I felt very self-conscious as I was ushered in to meet Karroubi, who had been arrested under the Shah and had served in several roles since the revolution. Now in his sixties, he had retained the radicalism of his youth and wanted to be the next president of Iran. His distinctive white beard, which matched his turban, was often prominently displayed on newspaper front pages.

Wearing a cream-colored robe and gold-rimmed glasses, Karroubi spoke with the thick rural accent of his birthplace, the agricultural province of Lorestan. We exchanged stories about how hard it was to like the pretentious Tehranis. He immediately put me at ease, like a favorite uncle. I told him about my unsophisticated political activism as a teenager and my arrest and suspended sentence. Karroubi listened in silence. He called in his aide and told him to write a letter to the accreditation committee to help me get a press pass.

"You've served your sentence. There is no need to keep punishing you," Karroubi said.

The Intelligence Ministry had the last laugh, though. I received my Majlis press accreditation, but it was only a day pass, like those given to members of the press visiting from the provinces. The regular Majlis reporters were issued cards with a #400 stamp that gave them access without daily security checks. Every day, I had to inform the Majlis media office to put my name on a list so that the guards would allow me in.

I kept my divorce and having a son a secret at work and especially at the Majlis. I would sneak off to a pay phone outside the newspaper offices or outside the Majlis to call Pouyan. I wasn't ashamed but knew men would look at me as easy prey. In the male-dominated Majlis, if I didn't keep up my shield, there were lots of men ready to take advantage of me.

For a while, every morning I'd drive to a café on Saadi Street, in north Tehran, for a breakfast of *kalepacheh,* a thick, greasy soup with an entire sheep's head in every bowl: tongue, eyes, cheeks, and everything else. *Kalepacheh* is a traditional Iranian breakfast, full of fat and protein, and is now favored by the working classes and hipsters needing to refuel after skiing or a night of illegal partying. I liked this café because it was modern and chic and nothing like the old greasy spoons in south Tehran, where cooks in stained undershirts labored over industrial-sized vats of steaming liquid.

Here, the shiny white tiles gleamed, the cooking was done in a kitchen hidden from view, and the waiters wore spotless white shirts. I loved *kalepacheh,* but it is a workingman's dish. The sheep's skull has to be boiled for hours so that the meat becomes soft and slippery, floating in fat. I frequented the café till Mother warned me that I might get a heart attack from such a rich diet.

Now that I was a Majlis correspondent, my parents forgave all my earlier transgressions. My mother would call me every morning without fail to make sure I was awake and then proceed to give me advice on how to behave in a ladylike manner. Don't embarrass us anymore, was the message.

"These lawmakers are important people," she'd say. "You can't misbehave now."

I bought a used car, thanks to a loan from my brothers. Mother called the car my Iron Man.

"Your car is your protector now," she said when I told her how much I enjoyed driving for hours in Tehran and beyond. "There's no need to get married."

Women cannot walk the streets at night, as I had painfully found out. Many Iranian women have had the experience of being sexually molested, harassed, or targeted with sexual insults.

The morality police were more visible these days, patrolling certain neighborhoods with renewed vigor, using more brutal techniques. Plainclothes policewomen harassed women who wore makeup. There were also special patrols, the infamous *amr bah ma'ruf va nahy az munkar,* in which pious Muslims see it as their duty to encourage virtue and discourage vice. These patrols by semiofficial agents cracked down on women whose hijab was less than satisfactory. Confrontations could be problematic, and that's why my car was more than just my mode of transport; it was as if I were putting on a suit of armor every time I entered it. I felt safe and protected. Every day I'd park the car, hoist my bag strap over one shoulder, and fix my black manteau and head scarf to make sure that not even one strand of hair had fallen loose to cause me trouble with the morality police. Only then would I walk briskly into the Majlis building.

I wanted to stay away from trouble, but trouble seemed to find me on a regular basis.

After three months or so in Majlis, Mr. Q.'s replacement at *Hambastegi* called me into his office. He was also a lawmaker at Majlis, and another political appointee at the newspaper.

"People are complaining about you. Members of Majlis, my colleagues, have complained to me—they are upset with you," he said, pointing to a seat in front of his desk and beckoning me to take it.

"I haven't had a chance to make mischief," I said with a laugh.

"I don't think you realize that this is a serious job. The Majlis is the People's House and deserves respect."

"I respect the deputies, but I have a loud voice, and when I ask questions, maybe they think I'm being rude. But I'm not."

"You are not dressed appropriately. Just look at your shoes," he said. "That's not correct or proper."

I looked at my red leather shoes, which had straps across the front. Okay, some of my friends complained that they looked like a little girl's shoes, but I have small feet.

"What's wrong with my shoes?" I whimpered.

A "senior lawmaker" had complained that I was wearing "Pinocchio shoes."

"You cannot wear red shoes," he thundered. "This is the Majlis of the Islamic Republic. What is the matter with you?"

I was suspended from attending the Majlis for three months. I could still cover Parliamentary news, but only from the office. So I was on the telephone all day calling the deputies and my contacts in search of news. Maybe the editors hoped that my replacement, a male reporter, would do a better job, and that then they could fire me. Fortunately, he didn't work out, and soon I was back in the corridors of Parliament, chasing lawmakers and looking for scoops.

"No more Pinocchio shoes," the editor told me grumpily when he announced the end of my suspension.

* * *

I once read that news was something that the powerful wanted to suppress. I didn't want to be part of the pack. I wanted to go after the stories that mattered. A great majority of reporters preferred to wait for the Majlis spokesman to feed them news items or hand them official press releases, which they then would rewrite as "news."

I didn't want to be one of those reporters.

The powerful didn't have a monopoly on the truth. I wanted to break news and investigate areas other reporters were not interested in. As I had discovered before, I had a talent for getting people to talk to me. I could get words out of a stone, as we say in Persian, and in the Majlis we had 290 characters, many of them consumed with self-importance. As a parliamentary journalist, I had found my true vocation, and although I made a few gaffes, within a year I had established myself and often had stories on the front page.

Still, I rarely got calls from the editor in chief, and when I did, it was bad news. One day, he asked if I could possibly drop by his office if I was not too busy. He sounded worried. Immediately, I checked my shoes. They were black and very boring. At least I was safe on that front. I was ushered into a meeting with all of *Hambastegi*'s top editors and the lawyer representing the newspaper.

The atmosphere in the room was electric. The moment I walked in, everyone started talking at the same time. Eventually the editor in chief cleared his throat.

"I don't know if I should congratulate you or fire you," he said. There was nervous laughter around the room.

Iran's General Staff of the Armed Forces, the most senior military body to advise the president, and responsible for coordination of activities within the armed forces, had filed a complaint with the judiciary against me. For the first time ever, the military high command was suing a journalist. The military argued that I had insulted the honor of veterans and the memory of their sacrifices.

Four years earlier, in 1999, a paramilitary force of about four hundred and members of the security forces had raided a Tehran university dormitory, beating up students, smashing doors, and even setting fire to rooms. Some students were thrown off third-story balconies; at least one died, and three hundred were injured. Students in other cities, such as Tabriz, Mashhad, and Shiraz, held protest marches, and there were clashes, followed by arrests, beatings, and jail for thousands. That was four years ago, but now a parliamentary committee was holding an investigation to punish the security services for their brutal overreaction. In covering the committee's actions, I had mocked the Basij as an organization that once fought off Saddam Hussein's tanks but was now beating up students. I compared them to a bunch of thugs.

"You can't fire me. You should give me a raise," I said. "I'm the only reporter ever to be sued by the military. This will be big news."

I wasn't wrong. Other newspapers covered the complaint against me. Overnight, I had moved from covering the news to becoming the news. Of course, everyone knew that if the complaint succeeded, I could face jail and *Hambastegi* could be shut down.

In the spring and summer of 2003, the Iranian political leadership was nervously casting an eye westward. Hundreds of thousands of U.S. soldiers, marines, and pilots had amassed on Iran's borders, all set to launch Operation Iraqi Freedom, President George W. Bush's 2003 Iraq invasion. The Iranian military leadership expected the Americans to be bogged down in Iraq, but the fighting was over in seven weeks. There was talk that the Americans could continue their eastward march and invade Iran as well.

In late July 2003, I received a summons to appear before Saeed Mortazavi, the notorious prosecutor general of Tehran. My earlier bravado disappeared very quickly. All journalists in Tehran were well aware of his nickname: "Butcher of the Press." His name struck fear in most of us. He was the former chief prosecutor of the Islamic Revolutionary Court, in charge of the section that investigated press complaints. He routinely interrogated journalists, had jailed dozens, and had shut down about a hundred newspapers. He used the law as a cover for putting down dissent. Khatami may have loosened press restrictions, but Mortazavi was in charge of tightening the screws, and he reported to the head of the judiciary, who was appointed by the Supreme Leader. He had connections at every newspaper and he could cajole or bully his contacts to withdraw critical articles.

There was another reason to fear Mortazavi. He had gotten away with murder. He was said to be responsible for the murder of Zahra Kazemi, an Iranian-Canadian photographer who had died in prison after interrogation by his men. Kazemi had gone to take pictures outside Evin prison, a giant complex built during the Shah's time, in the north of Tehran, by the side of an expressway. The prison has had a grim reputation for more than fifty years, especially for being the place where thousands of political prisoners were executed in the decades after the revolution. For many Iranians, the name "Evin" conjures fears not unlike those associated with "Bastille" before the French Revolution. Even today, families hover outside its impassive iron gate and massive walls, waiting for news of their children held inside.

Kazemi had a photojournalist permit, but on June 23, 2003, she was arrested as she was taking photographs of families. Interrogated for three days, she was taken to a military hospital coughing blood and lapsed into a coma. She had extensive bruising on her arms, back, and breasts and a broken nose and fingers, and she had been raped. The examining doctor said that she had suffered a severe blow to the head. She died nineteen days after setting out to take pictures. Iranian journalists got a chance to cover the case only because the Canadian government mounted a protest.

Ironically, Mortazavi, the main suspect, was appointed by the judiciary to head an "independent investigative group." Reporters could only hint at a cover-up. Two interrogators were tried, but both were found innocent. Mortazavi liked to boast that he was one of the "untouchables"—the Islamic Republic needed people like him to do their dirty work.

My summons to see Mortazavi became yet another news story at other papers, and the Association of Iranian Journalists hired me a defense lawyer.

* * *

On the day of my interview, *Hambastegi* managing editor Ebrahim Asgharzadeh and a Mr. Kaveh, from management, joined me as we trooped off to see Mortazavi. Asgharzadeh had a colorful history—he was one of the student leaders who organized the occupation of the American embassy in Tehran in 1980, taking 52 diplomats hostage for 444 days. Now close to fifty, he was no longer the firebrand of his youth but had come along to show moral support and thought he could exert some influence over the case.

After a short wait, we were led to a large office decorated with framed photographs of Khamenei and Khomeini. Behind an enormous desk sat Mortazavi, in a light-gray suit that appeared too small for him. He was short and stocky, with a thick black mustache and medium-length black hair combed to one side. I remember most vividly his thick eyebrows, which rose theatrically as he made wild assertions against me. The combination of his short stature and the large desk made him look like a cartoon despot, especially with his large square-framed glasses completing the picture.

I was scared.

We took our seats in front of him. He did not acknowledge our presence, pretending to be absorbed in reading a report in front of him. As he read, he absentmindedly—or on purpose—brought a chubby finger to the middle of his face and started to pick his nose. It was as if we were not in the room.

Minutes went by. Finally, Mortazavi lifted his head. Ignoring our pleasantries and my two senior defenders, he fixed his eyes on me.

"So, who is behind you, really? Who writes your articles?"

"I write every single word myself." I pointed to my managing editor sitting alongside me. "The distinguished Mr. Asgharzadeh can vouch for me."

Before Asgharzadeh could speak, Mortazavi fired off another accusation against me.

"You haven't got a degree, you've not even got a diploma. You went to jail before you could finish high school." He made a point of reading slowly from the papers in front of him. "From what I can see, you've only been at *Hambastegi* for a year or so."

I had no response. I couldn't understand why he was trying to humiliate me.

"You are not qualified or experienced enough to be a real journalist." He thumped the table with the flat of his plump hand. "Someone is using you, someone is writing your articles for you, and you're letting them so you can be famous. Who are they?"

"I didn't know you were such a keen fan of my work," I said sarcastically. Mr. Kaveh coughed to signal for me to shut up.

"Make a confession and I'll go easy on you. I promise."

"Give me a piece of paper and I'll confess. I wrote every single word. I confess to being the author of my own articles. That's all I will confess to."

"So you are saying Mostafa Tajzadeh and Mohsen Armin don't write your articles for you?"

"I know of them, of course, but they have nothing to do with me." Armin was a reformist member of Parliament, and Tajzadeh was one of the intellectual leading lights of the reform movement.

"You think we are yokels or idiots at the judiciary. We know everything about you. We have lots of files on you." Mortazavi stared into my eyes. He looked ready to pounce. "You are having lots of affairs. You are committing adultery and we can prove it."

The monstrosity of his accusation shocked me. He had switched from attacking my work to going after my personal life. I turned red in the face from shame. Adultery was a capital offense. Women could be stoned, flogged, or hanged.

But that was not my concern. Mortazavi was trying to humiliate me by throwing these vile and deceitful accusations at me in front of my boss and his deputy. Asgharzadeh and Mr. Kaveh both looked embarrassed and at a loss for words.

"We have lots of files on you," Mortazavi repeated, waving a piece of paper that he held in his hand. "We know that you have sexual relations with three men every week and that they are the ones who pay for your upkeep."

"That's ridiculous. That's the most crass thing you've said today. Show me those names. I want to see the files." I blurted it in a rage.

Mortazavi waved his hand at the door and a thin man sitting in the corner taking notes got up without a word and headed out the door. An uneasy silence descended on the room. Mortazavi glared at the three of us. The aide returned and put a thick folder bursting with newspaper clippings and other pieces of paper on Mortazavi's desk. He dipped his head to consult the file.

"He has no right to shame you like this," Asgharzadeh whispered quietly. "Your private life has nothing to do with *Hambastegi*."

"You are going to confess to having illicit affairs," Mortazavi said triumphantly. "With married men. It will be front-page news, I promise you."

"Go ahead and publish." I stood up and spoke in a loud voice that some people have mistaken for shouting. "I've never been with any married men."

"Keep your voice down. Who do you think you are?" Mortazavi said just as loudly.

"Sit down. He has the power to send you to jail," hissed Mr. Kaveh, grabbing the hem of my coat and pulling me back down on the chair. "Do you have any money to post bail? If not, keep calm and don't raise your voice."

I didn't have any bail money. I kept quiet but I fumed on the inside.

Mortazavi resumed calmly. "Or you could write an apology. And we'll forgive you for now."

"I'm not leaving this room until you have named these men, my imaginary lovers."

It was preposterous that he was trying to delve into my private life as if he controlled me.

"Why did you divorce your husband? Who pays your rent now?"

I'd been divorced for three years and I paid my own rent.

"So, you are not having sex with Armin? You are denying that Tajzadeh is writing your articles for you?"

"No and no and a thousand times no. I don't know Armin or Tajzadeh." This was turning into a very bizarre interrogation.

Again Mortazavi consulted a document on his desk before asking yet another question about my private life. This pattern was repeated again and again. Not once did he bring up my article that had offended the military high command so much.

After an hour of questioning about my private life, he closed the folder abruptly and got up. He asked my two silent colleagues to accompany him outside but told me to stay behind and wait for him.

"I'm expected at court. Stay here till I come back."

He left the room and, much to my surprise, locked me in. For more than an hour I sat in his office alone, confused as to what was going on. Eventually, an aide opened the door to let me leave. I was dismissed but had to return the next day so that he could resume his questioning.

Outside his office, a group of journalists were waiting for me, but I had no idea what to tell them. I had been charged with insulting the armed forces, but I had fended off questions about my private life.

The next day, I turned up at Mortazavi's office alone. Both Asgharzadeh and Mr. Kaveh said they didn't think their presence could be of any help to me. Mortazavi continued prying into my private life. On and on he went, referring to secret dossiers about my sexual activities, but he never produced any evidence.

"Are you having relations with Mr. X?" Mortazavi would name a member of Parliament.

"No."

"We have lots of documents about your affairs."

"Show me some proof. At least tell me the names of these men," I retorted.

Again after three hours or so, he dismissed me but told me to return the next day. This went on for five days. Each day, I'd return to work and try to figure out just exactly what was going on.

"You need to write a letter of apology in *Hambastegi* for insulting our brave and selfless armed forces," Mortazavi said at the end of the week. "If you refuse to write it, I'll shut down the newspaper. I'll also make sure all the other newspapers publish a report that you committed adultery with three men."

This was no idle threat. He could ruin my reputation by strongarming publications to do as he asked. He had arrested and jailed my friends and colleagues.

Still, I couldn't resist firing back.

"My father and two brothers fought in the war. My brothers and my in-laws were all *janbaz*"—veterans who were injured. "I have a lot of respect for our military. I don't respect the folks who never served for even one day using the veterans for their political gains."

"Shut the hell up," he yelled. I had touched a nerve. Mortazavi had never served on the front lines during the war. "You have turned your back on the revolution, and if your brothers are like you, then they, too, have abandoned our cause. Their war effort counts for nothing."

With a wave of his hand, I was dismissed.

"My job is to protect the revolution," he said.

"My job is to protect the people," I shot back.

I didn't know it then, but our paths were to cross a few more times.

Back at the newspaper, I told Asgharzadeh about Mortazavi's demand.

"Thank your lucky stars." He grinned. "It's a small price to pay. Write it quickly for tomorrow's edition."

"But I've not done anything wrong," I said petulantly.

I knew there was no way out. Still, I delayed it as long as I could and eventually came up with an apology in which I lamented the fact that the reputation of veterans was being tainted by *lebas-shakhsi* (undercover) paramilitary organizations acting as professional hoodlums.

The next day, Mortazavi called Asgharzadeh to complain. "That was no apology. That article itself is grounds for a second complaint against the author and the newspaper. You'll be hearing from me."

Nothing came of his threats, and pretty soon I stopped fretting about getting arrested. I had to prepare for my first overseas trip.

A parliamentary delegation was going on hajj umrah, and the Majlis press corps was going to accompany them. Hajj, one of the five pillars of Islam, is an annual pilgrimage—millions of Muslims go to Mecca, the most holy city of Islam. The pilgrimage is in Duh a-Hijjah, the last month of the Islamic calendar, but you can also go on a hajj umrah, or minor hajj, which can be taken at any time. I wasn't particularly keen on going on a religious pilgrimage, but this would be my first trip abroad, and all the reporters were going, so I submitted my application form for a passport and in due course received my documents.

Like millions of Iranians, I had never traveled outside the country or gone abroad—*kharej*. When I was growing up, I thought that *kharej* was the name of a neighboring country—that there was Iran and then there was *kharej*. Later, when I became aware of countries and continents, the idea of *kharej* never lost its magic for me. I desperately wanted to visit these countries I'd only read about in novels. But only the rich could make such trips. Now here was my chance to visit Mecca, in Saudi Arabia—though that didn't sound exotic.

About fifty or so journalists were going. My friends joked that I should start learning how to pray in case the organizers decided to test my religious studies knowledge. It'd be a disaster if I failed. At the airport, all of us in the press corps felt as if we were kids going on a school trip. We exchanged gossip and cracked jokes in the departure lounge. Just then, to everyone's surprise, my name was called out on the loudspeaker.

"Masoumeh Alinejad, please report to airport security. Masoumeh Alinejad, please report . . ."

I jumped up from my seat. Some of the other reporters jeered.

"What trouble have you caused now?" said one.

"Did you forget to turn off the cooker? Your house has burned to the ground." The sound of laughter echoed around.

With a theatrical bow, I sauntered over to a door marked SECU-RITY. Behzad Nabavi, the Majlis deputy speaker, came along with me. The guard took me inside but politely barred Nabavi, a former government minister, from entering. I was taken to a windowless room that contained a table and some wooden chairs. Two plain-clothes security men came in and told me that they were from the Intelligence Ministry. Not again, I thought.

"This is just routine, but we have some questions for you," said one of the men. Clearly his role was that of the good cop. The bad cop kept himself busy with his worry beads and sullenly stared at me. In reality, there was not much difference between the two.

"Normally I'm the one asking questions." My smile froze on my face and disappeared. "I'm a journalist, you see."

"We know who you are. You don't think so highly of us, do you?"

"I don't know you. I have nothing against you."

"We are the men who protect this revolution," he said. "And we protect the people," he added as an afterthought.

I immediately thought of Mortazavi. Was this payback for my column? Was I going to be detained?

"My brothers fought in the war—"

The bad cop cut me off. He had a rough voice and an Azerbaijani accent, meaning that he was from the northeast of Iran.

"We know all about you."

"Then you know that I'm a Majlis correspondent going to Mecca for hajj umrah." I retied my head scarf very deliberately. "I am going to visit the House of God."

"How is it you work at the Majlis when you have a criminal record for political agitation? You are a national security risk."

"You are not serious. I've been working at the Majlis for a year and a half."

"I'm not sure we can allow you to leave now," the good cop said. "We have to check everything to make sure."

I stared at them in amazement. Of course, I had heard of being made *mamnoo-ol-khorooj*—forbidden to leave—a ban on critics from leaving the country. But dissidents usually wanted to head to the West—to Europe or the United States. I had never heard of any Iranian being banned from going to Mecca, the holiest site in Islam. This just went against the foundations of the Islamic Republic.

"This is silly. You are preventing me from going on a hajj." There was a knock at the door. Nabavi stuck his bald head through the doorway.

"Can I be of any help?" Nabavi smiled disarmingly. "We have a flight that we need to catch."

"You and your party can go, Mr. Nabavi," the good cop said, pouring on the charm. "We have some questions for her."

"If the news leaks that you prevented a Majlis reporter from visiting Mecca, it will not look good," Nabavi said, standing with his back against the door.

Now the bad cop chimed in.

"Ms. Alinejad is a political risk," he said, speaking in a very formal manner. "She was arrested for political acts against the *nezam*"—the regime. "How is it possible that she was granted her press credentials when there is a black mark against her name?"

"She is a former Mojahed," the good cop added, for good measure.

"I was never a Mojahed," I protested. "Besides, I've served my punishment."

"There is a black mark in her files," the bad cop said triumphantly. "Why was she hired?"

"Maybe someone countermanded it," Nabavi said.

"Or someone took a bribe to do it; if a journalist owes you a favor that can be useful."

Nabavi and the good cop stared at each other without saying a word. The security guys thought that Nabavi was the one who had obtained my pass for me, and that he had come to protect me once again.

"Mr. Karroubi approved my press credentials," I said, finding my voice. "He knows everything."

"That settles it, then," Nabavi said. "Now she can come with us."

"We can't just take her word. We'll have to check ourselves."

After some haggling it was agreed that if Karroubi vouched for me, I could go on the trip. I joined the rest of the group in the lounge. The women journalists hugged me as I burst out crying. I was sure this was payback by Mortazavi. After a long while, Nabavi came out to join the crowd of reporters.

"Hey, *shahr-ashoob*," he joked, affectionately referring to me as a mischief maker. "You are going." For the next few days everyone called me *shahr-ashoob*. Nabavi later told me that Karroubi himself had called in to support me.

After all the pre-flight excitement, Mecca and Medina, the second-holiest city in Islam, where the Prophet Muhammad is buried, were a letdown. It didn't feel as if I'd gone to *kharej*. We all had to wear Islamic dress, everyone was wearing a chador, and there were all kinds of other restrictions. It was as if I had not left Iran. Two other female reporters and I had decided not to wear chadors but instead wear long white manteaux, white head scarves, and maghnaehs. If we were fully covered up this way, there was no need to wear a chador, too, especially since it was scorching hot. We stood out in our all-white outfits, in contrast to the other women, who were all in black.

Some of the male reporters didn't appreciate our choice. One day, in Medina, we visited the Al-Masjid an-Nabawi mosque. Originally built by the Prophet Muhammad, it is the second most important site in Islam, after the Kaaba in Mecca. Some of the male reporters from the conservative newspapers could not believe that we were not wearing chadors. They became agitated—their eyes were bulging out of their sockets and their faces were red. That's because women are expected to be fully covered up at all times, even outside Iran, according to them.

"You are shameless," a reporter for the conservative newspaper *Kayhan* said vehemently. "You have brought shame on the Iranian delegation. You three are the only women without hijab in all of Medina."

There were many other women, from countries like Turkey, or

from the Far East, who were dressed modestly but were without chadors. The only people who complained were male reporters from conservative newspapers.

"Chador is our culture and you should put it on proudly."

"Before the revolution, our culture was a lot more flexible," I said.

"You are a secret royalist—I should've known," he replied, sneering.

It was funny: Some called me a Mojahed, and now I was labeled a royalist.

"If I'm doing something wrong, then God can send me to hell. Worry about your own salvation, and leave me alone."

My birthday came in the middle of the trip. I was turning twenty-seven and wanted to have a dinner party at the most daring location possible.

Naturally, I chose a McDonald's in Mecca.

I'd never seen one, but McDonald's was as big a symbol of America as you could get. I was going to get into trouble for visiting one, but I didn't care.

I wanted to try a Big Mac and fries.

In October, I became embroiled in a controversy involving the Nobel Peace Prize.

It began innocently enough. President Khatami had been nominated in 2003 for his efforts to open up Iran. For some reason, all the opinion makers in Iran thought he was going to win. In the aftermath of the U.S. invasion of Iraq earlier that year, everyone thought the Norwegian committee was going to award the prize to the Iranian president to snub George W. Bush.

When the news came it surprised us all: The human rights lawyer Shirin Ebadi was named the 2003 recipient of the Nobel Peace Prize. Ebadi, a judge during the Shah era, had been dismissed because she was a woman. The sweet justice of it all: Ebadi became the first, and only, Iranian, and the first female Muslim, to win the Nobel Peace Prize.

I felt ten feet tall when I heard the news. Actually, I screamed in joy. I didn't know Ebadi personally, but an Iranian woman was getting recognition for her achievement, and that was good enough for me. The fact that she had won acclaim outside the country added to my joy.

The whole world was congratulating Ebadi, who was in France on vacation, but in Iran the official response was to ignore her achievement. The state-owned radio and TV stations were ordered to keep quiet about it. Her victory was a slap in the face of the Iranian political system—the Islamic Republic always claims to be a beacon of virtue. How could the government explain that a human rights lawyer had won? Iranian officials often deny the existence of political prisoners and prisoners of conscience while referring to them as "security prisoners."

Khatami, no doubt, wished that he had won the prize himself. He made no public or private statements on the issue. Four days after the announcement, Khatami visited the Majlis to meet with reformist lawmakers to discuss the legislative agenda. At the press stakeout, I elbowed my way to the front of the pack.

"Mr. Khatami, the whole world has been congratulating Shirin Ebadi. Do you intend to congratulate your fellow citizen?" I just couldn't help shouting the question at the top of my voice.

"In the name of God, the merciful...as an Iranian, I'm pleased that a Muslim woman has won the Nobel Peace Prize—"

"But that's not what I asked you," I said, interrupting him. "As THE PRESIDENT, you should by now have sent her a congratulatory message."

Everyone in the room knew that Khatami had deliberately ignored the award.

"Does the president have to send a message for anything and everything?"

I persisted. "But, Mr. President, the Nobel Prize is a very important event." I wasn't going to let him off the hook.

Khatami was normally calm and unflappable. But not that day. He gave me a flinty look. "The Nobel Peace Prize is not very important. The ones that count are the scientific and literary prizes. Everyone knows that. It was awarded to her on the basis of totally political criteria."

That was a huge gaffe, and the television cameras captured the exchange. Khatami's comments were big news. Iranian hard-liners loathed Ebadi for her human rights activities and her refusal to wear the hijab outside of Iran. Conservative newspapers repeated Khatami's comments. That night, I watched the exchange dispassionately on the nightly news. Even the foreign news agencies covered the story, as did the *New York Times,* among other major papers.

I had embarrassed the president in public and I should somehow apologize, Khatami's allies demanded. Mohammad-Ali Abtahi, Khatami's rotund vice president, described me as an "inexperienced young lady," and the meaning was obvious—how dare I, as a woman, challenge the president?

Was it my fault that the president had lost his temper? I wondered.

For days, Khatami's blunder, and my role, received top billing in the news cycle. I tried to put the whole incident out of my mind when I drove to Ghomikola that weekend to spend time with Pouyan. Only seven, he, too, was worried. I wasn't sure who had told him about my troubles. He spent most of his time with his grandparents these days.

"Will you lose your job?" he asked.

"Of course not," I said crisply.

"I hate Khatami," he said.

I laughed it off. But later, I began to fret that maybe I was in trouble. When I returned to Tehran, I sought out my editor.

"Are you going to fire me?"

"It's your job to ask tough questions," he said reassuringly. "The president should be smart enough to handle them."

About two months later, the president's office called to invite me for a private audience. My first thought was to call Pouyan—to reassure him about my job security.

"Sweetie, I'm on my way to meet the most important man in Iran."

"You are meeting Baba?" For Pouyan, his father was the most important person in the world.

"No, I'm meeting President Khatami," I said, with a lot less enthusiasm than before.

"You should slap him," Pouyan said. "He was going to fire you."

Pouyan's advice was on my mind when I was finally led to the president's office. Khatami said he was troubled about speaking sharply to me at the press conference, which had provoked the calls that I be fired. He hemmed and hawed about the challenges of being a president and how words can be taken out of context. He had calculated that he faced a crisis once every nine days.

He was lucky my son wasn't with me, I told him. "Pouyan wants to slap you for trying to get me fired." He looked surprised, and I realized that he didn't even know I'd been married, let alone divorced. I quickly explained my marriage and divorce.

"Men try and take advantage of you once they know you're a divorcée," I continued. There were rumors that I was having an affair with a deputy who was using the code name Pouyan. "Now everyone thinks my lover is called Pouyan," I said to Khatami, "because I've been overheard on the phone."

Khatami looked uncomfortable hearing about my personal issues. He was rather shy and reserved, but now he wanted to give me a gift.

"I was sharp with you at the press conference and want to make it up to you." I could ask for anything within reason. "Ask me a favor, and if it's reasonable, I'll grant it."

I really wanted to get a stipend to pursue a university degree. But something stirred inside of me. I didn't need his charity, my pride said.

"*You* should ask *me* for a favor," I replied. "A president who wants everyone to like him is not tough enough for the job. You are the one who is in big trouble. You need my help more than I need yours." I ended with a smile.

It was true. Khatami was too nice to be president. Having been re-elected by a huge margin to his second four-year term in 2001, he was ineligible to run again. Instead of driving a reformist agenda in Parliament, he continually reached out to appease the hard-liners. He had backed down on a number of issues, from women's rights to press freedom, whenever he faced opposition from the Supreme Leader and the Revolutionary Guards.

As 2003 came to a close, both the reformists and the conservatives geared up for the February 2004 parliamentary elections. Khatami may have lost his progressive zeal, but the reformist lawmakers, fully expecting to win the election, again announced plans to introduce new legislation on press freedom, on women's rights, and on greater transparency of government finances.

Then the conservatives changed the rules. On a chilly winter's day, the Guardian Council disqualified about 2,500 candidates, most of them from the reformist faction, saying that they were not sufficiently dedicated to Islamic values and lacked revolutionary zeal. Such a move had never been seen before in Iran's history.

There was an uproar in the Majlis. Deputies wandered the corridors, complaining that a coup had taken place. Not that the conservatives cared: In the Islamic Republic, they said, the Supreme Leader and the Guardian Council have the final say. The victims of the ban included several leaders of the reformist faction, like my former *Hambastegi* managing editor, Ebrahim Asgharzadeh; Mohammad-Reza Khatami, the president's brother; and Jamileh Kadivar, a radical female representative. Iran's baby steps toward democracy had abruptly been halted. Thanks to the ban, the reformists couldn't even line up enough candidates to compete in all districts.

For journalists, it was an exciting time. Every day there was a new upheaval.

More than one-third of the Parliament resigned to protest the ban and staged a sit-in in the huge Majlis building, threatening to plunge Iran's political system into chaos. The banned deputies occupied the ground floor of the Majlis building and were joined by other political activists and student leaders. In scenes never before witnessed in the Islamic Republic, the resigning MPs read fiery statements from the podium of the Parliament that were broadcast live on Iranian radio. Member after member accused the conservatives of acting like the Taliban. Some wrote an open letter to the Supreme Leader, accusing him of humiliating the Majlis, obstructing legislation, and interfering in the electoral process.

The sit-in lasted more than a month, but the decision could not be reversed. The Guardian Council stood firm, and Supreme Leader Khamenei said that it was the MPs at the sit-in who represented bullies and "tough guys." Everyone waited for Khatami to make a move and challenge the Supreme Leader.

Instead, Khatami backed away from his reformist allies. He would not support the sit-in. He appealed for calm and asked people to go to the polls "despite the unfairness of the election."

It was a huge act of folly.

The conservatives cruised to victory in 2004. Having taken 195 seats out of a possible 290 in the 2000 elections, the reformists now could only manage 39.

During the crisis, I practically lived in the Majlis building, covering the events on an hour-by-hour basis. Witnessing the events from the front row, as it were, I wrote my first book, *Tahason* (*The Sit-In*), about the crisis.

The new Majlis was going to be more conservative, more interested in pushing back women's rights and clamping down on the press.

Gholam-Ali Haddad-Adel, a conservative politician who was related to the Supreme Leader, replaced Karroubi as Speaker of Parliament. That was not good news. It was he who had complained about my red "Pinocchio shoes."

CHAPTER TWELVE

The young conscript standing in the parking lot behind the Majlis building gave me a secret wave. He looked comical in his oversized boots and baggy green uniform, which hung on his scrawny body. As I pulled up to the security barrier, he even gave me a salute, as if I were a military officer.

"I've saved you a place," he said with a grin, pointing to a spot in the near-empty lot.

"I told you he has a crush on you," Mahnaz, a fellow reporter whispered. "Time for you to drop your lover Pouyan and settle down. He's a yokel just like you."

"That's the only smiling face I'm going to see here today," I muttered.

Inside the Majlis building, the departing lawmakers were busy packing up, and you could hear drawers emptying from inside various offices. The newly elected members were on their way. The *click-clack* of my leather shoes on the stone floor echoed in the corridors. A few days earlier, I received a message that my application for a press pass to the new Majlis inauguration ceremony had been denied. Intriguingly, however, I had been summoned by the security office. Again.

The security offices were deserted, apart from a young man with a thin black beard, his shirt buttoned all the way up to his chin. He had been expecting me. He walked me past empty offices to a small, carpeted room with a blanket spread in one corner. He signaled for me to take off my boots and sit on the floor on the blanket. I was embarrassed as I removed them, because I'd forgotten to wear socks that morning—as usual.

I've never been fond of small, windowless rooms—they remind me of my detention cell. The young man left, and a few minutes later, from outside the door, there were cries of *"Ya Allah . . . Ya Allah."* God. Conservative religious men utter the phrase loudly before entering a room to warn women inside to put on their hijab. A few seconds later, the door opened and a cleric heaved himself into the room. He had a pudgy face and a big round stomach, as if he were pregnant. Beads of sweat had formed on his face, which was half covered with a bushy black beard. With a chubby hand, he wiped his brow.

I stood up to show respect. He was not wearing any shoes, and the stink of his socks filled the room. He sat on the floor and invited me to do the same.

"I've been informed that you've written a book and you smuggled your book inside the Majlis," he said, leaning back against the wall and pulling out a copy of *Tahason*. "Without permission," he added, emphasizing the words ominously.

"I am a writer. Does it matter if I write an article or lots of articles or a book?" I shrugged.

"You were only issued a press accreditation because of your newspaper. You are not accredited as a book writer."

"I received permission from Ershad." The Ministry of Islamic Cultural Guidance was the censor's office—everything from books and films to magazines and music had to be approved by Ershad.

"We don't coordinate our activities with Ershad," he said in a snobbish tone.

As usual, I couldn't help myself.

"Not my problem. I assumed you talked to each other."

He rubbed the soles of his feet as he pondered his next move. He was not done with me yet.

"No matter," he continued. "We have witnesses who say you smuggled your books into Majlis in the trunk of a car. Do you deny it?"

He was acting as if he had caught me smuggling drugs or guns rather than books. With great difficulty I stopped myself from rolling my eyes at him. Instead, I breathed in deeply and decided to be more tactful.

"Your colleagues all wanted a copy. Maybe you should buy a few for the Majlis library."

More than anything else, the meeting was a warning that I was being watched. After a half hour or so I was dismissed. On the way out, the young man at the security counter handed me an envelope. Inside was my invitation to the inauguration ceremony.

Back at the parking lot, the young conscript was leaning against my car. His face lit up when he saw me. It was as if he suspected deep down that I was still a village girl pretending to be a political reporter.

"You left the window open. Again," he said, staring at his shoes and avoiding my eyes. "But I stayed by the car to make sure no one stole anything."

On the day of the inauguration, I headed to Haft-e Tir Square, in midtown Tehran, one of the largest and busiest shopping districts in the city, to look for something new to wear. The conservative lawmakers had vowed to turn back Khatami's reform agenda and crack down on the recent easing of social freedoms. Stricter enforcement of hijab laws and press laws were in the cards. Even Mother, as part of her morning alarm call, warned me to mind my manners and "buy a long black dress that covers everything."

As always, Tehran's streets were packed with cars, each trying to squeeze a few inches forward to find a path through. Naturally, everyone honked their horns. Typical Tehran traffic. I tried to keep calm, but I was aware that in a few hours' time I was expected to be at the Majlis for the ceremony and I still needed something decent to wear. In the shopping district there were no parking spaces to be found.

Except one. Right under the NO PARKING sign. Sometimes you

have to bend the rules a little. I squeezed my tiny Renault hatchback into the space, darted out of the car, and crashed into a traffic cop.

"Hold it, *khanom*. You have entered a restricted traffic zone and"—he nodded toward the sign—"you have parked right under the sign. You can't do that!"

I flashed my press pass at him and smiled as pleasantly as I could.

"I'm on a mission for Majlis. I'll be back soon . . . real soon."

"You can't park here—"

But I'd already veered into a side street in search of clothing shops. Mentioning the Majlis connection usually worked, I'd found. I tried a few shops but discovered that buying a black gown was a complicated business. Most of them had too many frilly decorations and sequins. In one store, the manager, seeing my agitated state, cautiously approached me.

"Salam. What type of gown are you looking for? Is it for a special occasion?"

"I'm going to a ceremony . . . an inauguration," I said distractedly.

"What kind of ceremony? Religious? Private? Is it mixed group? We have all kinds of gowns, and not just in black," he said, smiling, then added, "Nobody wears black for a party anymore."

"It's for the inauguration of the new Majlis," I said with a sad smile. "The new Islamic Assembly."

He glared at me, trying to figure out if I was joking. I shrugged and went back to the racks. The manager went to the storeroom and returned with a long, draping black gown from the back.

"Try it on in the back," he urged.

It made me look like a scarecrow. The gown could have fit two of me, but time was short.

"May it bring you blessings," he said, as I rushed out still wearing the gown, clutching a bag with the clothes I was wearing when I entered the shop. I didn't have time to go home and change. I quickened my pace as I tried to retrace my steps to the place where I'd parked the car. As I reached my car under the NO PARKING sign, I fumbled around in my bag, looking for the car keys, but came up empty.

No keys.

Not again. It drives all my friends crazy, but I'm always losing things.

"Just how did you GET your driver's license?" a voice demanded.

It was the traffic cop, and he looked furious. I was so busy searching my bag that I hadn't seen him.

"I cannot believe you ACTUALLY passed," he said with heavy sarcasm. "Before leaving the car, it's a good idea to turn the ignition OFF and take the key with you."

I looked at my car. I'd forgotten to roll up my windows as well. NOOO! The key was still in the ignition, though he had had the decency to turn off the engine.

"I'm really sorry, but I had to..." I tried to explain, but the cop handed me about half a dozen tickets, including one for "wasting his time by making him guard my car."

After all that, the ceremony was a joyless affair. Almost all the conservative legislators wore a keffiyeh over their shoulders to show solidarity against the United States, aka the global oppressor. All the women wore dark chadors. A sea of black greeted me as I arrived. Even the few remaining reformist female politicians, who in the past had normally worn colorful head scarves, had switched to black. I looked for familiar faces but found none. Last year's minority faction now ruled the roost. Everything about the new Majlis felt different, even the way the reporters looked. All the women were wearing long black gowns and chadors. Gone were the fashionable knee-length manteaux worn over jeans.

"Are there no legislators representing women who don't want to wear the chador?" I whispered to a fellow reporter.

In the new, or seventh, Majlis, it wasn't going to be easy asking tough questions. The critical journalists were ignored, while the reporters from conservative publications received access. I started taping all my interviews as a precaution. The last thing I wanted was to be accused of making up quotes.

* * *

A few days later, I sat in the press gallery observing the Majlis proceedings as usual—writing, with my chin resting on my other hand. I was wearing the new gown, with its too-large sleeves, which tended to droop, revealing my bony wrists and forearms. I caught Speaker Haddad-Adel's eye as he sat at the Majlis dais. He tapped his arms to indicate that I should cover mine, lest I excite a male lawmaker. That night I sewed my sleeves, taking them in so that this wouldn't happen again.

Haddad-Adel did not appreciate my reporting. "If one of us picks our nose," he once said of me, "she'll write a story and complain that the conservatives cannot manage the country because they have their fingers stuck up their nose!"

Trouble was that the members of the new conservative coalition were incompetent and pompous. As a parliamentary journalist I had a front seat to their buffoonery and, later, their corruption and graft.

In the new Majlis, women reporters frequently received admonitions to improve their appearance, to conform with hijab laws. We all received verbal warnings about strands of hair sticking out and the length and thickness of our outer garments. Written notices were posted about the evils of nail polish. We were constantly reminded that the new Majlis was different from the one controlled by the reformists. "This is not the sixth Majlis."

One day I was standing in one of the Majlis corridors chatting with two deputies. The corridors were the ideal place to grab a lawmaker to get a quote for a story. It was all harmless small talk that day, when suddenly a rather plump cleric lurched into view. He swayed from side to side as he approached me.

"Cover your hair," he said, waving a fat fist in my face, "or I'll punch you out of here."

I jumped a step back and reached with both my hands to check my head covering. He didn't look as if he was joking.

"There is no need to punch or kick anyone," I said meekly, looking for the two deputies for backup. They had disappeared.

"A kind and friendly warning would have sufficed," I added, hoping to mollify him. He glared at me.

I found two strands of hair sticking out from under my maghnaeh. Was this the cause of his anger? I could not believe that such a small slip, hardly noticeable, had offended him. The two deputies I had been speaking with had seen nothing wrong with my appearance.

"All this fuss for two strands of hair," I said, regaining my composure. "You should be ashamed of yourself for wanting to punch me."

"How dare you?" he roared, and lumbered toward me. "I'm going to teach you a lesson." He made a fist almost as big as my head.

"Even if you managed to punch me, what about the women outside of Majlis? Have you walked on the streets of Tehran? Are you going to punch them all? There are thousands of women—"

"Shut up, shut up." He went red in the face and waved his arms to swipe at me. "I'm going to teach you a lesson."

I was retreating even as I spoke, and I had to be quick to avoid getting hit. The commotion that we had caused alerted other reporters and deputies, and suddenly the corridor was full of people, including a photographer from the Iranian Students' News Agency (ISNA), who started snapping away with his camera.

My heart was beating so hard in my chest I thought it was going to explode. I was shaking with rage and humiliation.

"All the fuss was because of this?" I held the strands of hair that were sticking out and addressed the crowd around me. "Do I deserve to be punched for this?"

My would-be attacker kept raising his fists to pound my head, but he was held back by other reporters and lawmakers.

"What right does he have to attack me, to beat me just because a few strands of my hair are showing?" This was madness.

Eventually, Ahmad Nategh-Nouri, the brother of the former presidential candidate, led the cleric away.

From age seven I had put on the hijab, always covering my hair, like other women in Iran. The conflict over compulsory hijab is an issue that cannot be wished away by the country's clerical rulers. I was raised in the Islamic Republic and had known no other political system, and yet I and millions of women like me detested the humiliation of compulsory hijab laws. I am a product of the Islamic Republic, and like millions of my fellow Iranians I am rejecting that system.

"First cover your hair" is a retort familiar to all women in Iran. It's a way of putting women down. I bet every woman has heard that putdown at least once in her life. I have heard it a number of times. Women, like me, who have too much hair always have a problem covering it. As a teenager, my parents would sit me down on the floor to tamp down my hair before tying a scarf around it.

But fighting compulsory hijab is about much more than hair and dressing modestly, just as Rosa Parks refusing to give her seat to a white man on a bus in Montgomery, Alabama, in 1955 was about more than an unjust seating policy. It's about fighting for what is right.

Nothing demonstrated the absence of rights for women more than when, early in the new session, the main Majlis dining room was segregated so that only men could eat there, and women deputies were relegated to a room in the basement of the building.

A few days after my confrontation with the cleric, I was called into a meeting with the head of public affairs at the Majlis. "As a parliamentary reporter," he said coldly, "you should know that you cannot have too much hair on display."

"Why are you telling me this?"

"This is part of my job."

"What about all the girls on the streets of Tehran?"

"Everyone should deal with their own area of responsibility. This is mine."

Hijab was a red line.

CHAPTER THIRTEEN

The road to expulsion was paved with pay stubs.

I loved being a Majlis reporter. Let's get one thing straight: Politicians lie. They make too many promises, and they know that they cannot fulfill all of them. For me, holding politicians accountable and exposing their lies were all part of a day's work. In Iran, that was dangerous work. In the game of Iranian politics, truth was a highly prized secret. Revealing that truth could land you in jail.

The daily political jousting was exhilarating. I felt immensely excited about going to work. In my private life, I was disorganized and absentminded, but when it came to covering politics, it was as if a switch had been turned on. I was diligent. I memorized the phone numbers of all the MPs and knew their personal histories. I had a loud voice, which meant my questions could not be ignored.

My social life was rather limited. Most weekends, I'd drive up to Babol and Ghomikola to see Pouyan and my parents, who had forgiven my teenage indiscretions and were now proud of me for working as a journalist in Majlis. Only a few people in Tehran knew that I was a divorcée and had a small son. The conservative newspapers referred to me as "the Ugly Duckling." It hurt, but I took it as a badge of honor. It meant my articles had an impact.

Deep down, I was still the same mischievous girl I had been in Ghomikola. Once a month, the twenty or so women reporters who covered the Majlis would have a get-together to exchange gossip and talk about behind-the-scenes political jockeying. These meetings had an added bonus: home-cooked food. I got into the habit of taking a plastic container and sweeping up all the leftovers for my next lunch and dinner. It got to the point where the host would serve my plastic container first, giving me a special portion to box away before we had even started eating. I was always hungry and would shovel the food into my mouth as fast as I could. One of my colleagues, Shahrzad, tried to teach me manners—to be more feminine, or at least learn the etiquette of eating in public.

"A lady's spoon should not be full to the brim," Shahrzad admonished me. "Don't move your big head toward the spoon, like a crow—move the spoon toward your mouth. Do it slowly and remember: You don't have to swallow up the whole spoon."

Covering the seventh Majlis was like hitting the mother lode. The newly elected conservative deputies had vowed to be a can-do Parliament; they promised to cut waste and corruption and create jobs. They made plenty of other pledges, too, from ending cronyism to reducing the wealth disparity between different social groups.

A new Majlis building was inaugurated in 2004, to replace the original Parliament building, which dated back to the 1906 Constitutional Revolution. The old building had plenty of charm, but it was designed for a different era. The new building offered a better sound system, a giant television screen—so that everyone could see the members at the podium, no matter how far back they sat—and more office space for the deputies.

Having spent a fortune on the new building, four months after the move the new management committee of the Majlis decided to throw out the carpeting that had been installed and order about 270,000 square feet of new carpeting from Austria.

"The current carpet created static electricity that could disrupt the sound system at the Majlis," Haddad-Adel explained reluctantly.

"Exposé: Another Big Perk for the 7th Majlis Deputies" was the headline of my story.

The new conservative deputies prided themselves on their shabby and ill-fitting suits, chosen to show solidarity with the underclasses. But they still demanded extra perks such as free mobile phones and rent subsidies. Some deputies employed their own family members as bodyguards or their wives as researchers and collected their income. The Majlis parking garage was full of Citroën Xantias, regarded as a luxury vehicle in Iran.

I was constantly warned: Exposing hypocrisy and graft was no way to win friends. "It is not in the interests of the country for you to write about corruption."

Days after my carpet exposé, I was standing in a huddle with the other reporters in a Majlis corridor when I noticed that one of the new deputies kept staring at me. I thought, Not again. I quickly checked my outfit and head scarf. No strands of hair had escaped.

"Incoming. A deputy's coming your way," another reporter warned.

I didn't want another earful about my hijab or a lecture about respecting Majlis deputies. I headed back to the press room, but he kept following me. I quickened my pace.

"Ms. Alinejad, hold up," the deputy called after me.

I turned slowly, my defenses up, ready for another confrontation, but I needn't have worried. The deputy limped toward me in obvious discomfort. Now I regretted having rushed away. I recognized him as a new member of the conservative caucus, but I had never spoken with him before.

"I would never have caught up with you if you hadn't stopped," he said, slightly out of breath. "A gift from Saddam Hussein," he continued, smiling as he tapped his leg. He had lost part of it in the war.

"I need to tell you about a delicate matter," he said conspiratorially, looking around. His eyes darted back and forth along the empty corridor. Clearly he was checking to be sure that no one saw the two of us together.

I tightened my head scarf knot under my chin and waited for him to speak.

"This letter has been on my mind for days now," he said, pulling a creased piece of paper out of his pocket. It had obviously been folded and refolded many times.

"I'd hoped my colleagues would come to their senses, but now I have no choice but to appeal to you."

He waited for me to say something, but for once I kept my big mouth shut. I didn't even reach out to grab the letter from his hand.

"I would like you to write a story, in a delicate way, mind you, to stop this foolishness," he said. "Nothing too sensational."

He pushed the letter into my hands and limped away.

I immediately wondered if he had the right reporter. I was not known for my "delicate" style.

I sat at my desk in the press room and excitedly read the letter. It was an invitation for the deputies to attend a special meeting of a newly created home-lending bank so that they could obtain mortgages that charged lower interest rates. During the elections, conservative candidates had berated the reformists for not building affordable housing for low-income earners. Now, according to this letter, the new deputies were busy lining up cheap mortgages for themselves. A sweetheart deal for the MPs.

I rushed back to the newspaper's offices. A few phone calls later, the information was confirmed, and my story led the front page: "Exposed: Another Perk for the Majlis Deputies."

On the international stage, Iran's fledgling nuclear program was uniting Europe and the United States against it. Iran claimed that its program was to develop peaceful nuclear energy, but the West suspected that the Islamic Republic wanted to build nuclear weapons, and as a result it threatened sanctions.

Hassan Rouhani, a mid-level cleric and the secretary of the

Supreme National Security Council, arrived at the Majlis to update members and deputies on his negotiations with the UK, France, Germany, and other European countries.

"Do you think," I asked him, "the deputies have enough knowledge of nuclear issues to understand your briefings?"

Rouhani paused for a long time. His eyes twinkled and then he laughed deeply.

"Please, don't get us into a fight with the Majlis."

In those days, the nuclear dispute was a distant problem. Graft was the main issue. In late 2004, there were rumors of secret payments to MPs. Most denied the existence of these "bonus" payments, while others said that they had been sworn to secrecy. The conservative deputies talked of social justice, and it would look bad if they were lining their own pockets. Other reporters had heard similar vague rumors of graft, but my usual sources denied any knowledge.

As I contacted various MPs, I reached out to Shokrollah Attarzadeh, a lawmaker from a small town in the south. I had met men like him in Babol and Ghomikola. He came to Majlis dressed in green military fatigues, with a keffiyeh hung loosely around his neck. He always looked as if he were on his way to enlist—ready to pick up a gun and head to the front.

I asked him about rumors that the MPs were getting secret bonus payments above and beyond their salaries. Perhaps he could show me his pay slips to prove that nothing improper had happened, I suggested.

"Get out," he said. "I don't have to show you anything."

I had a feeling I could intimidate him. Not because of my size but because he loved being in Majlis and would do anything not to lose his position.

"There is a recession in the country, and high unemployment is hurting everyone. Perhaps you do have something to hide," I said. "That's not going to make you very popular back home. You may even get recalled."

It was a bluff. I had no leverage over him, but he didn't know that.

"Or you can share the bonus details with me, and I'll keep you as a confidential source. No one will know."

He took a pay slip out of his desk drawer and ripped out his name.

"My name will not get out."

"I promise."

I rushed back to *Hambastegi*. The pay slip showed that the deputies had received a million tomans (about $1,100 then) from the Speaker of Parliament "for consideration of the Deputies' Expenses."

As I held the pay slip in my hand, I recognized that this was an important moment in my life. I had the first evidence of a slush fund to make undeclared payments to the deputies. There'd be no going back. I would be marked, but the story was worth it. It was for moments like this that I had rebelled against my family and endured all sorts of hardships. I wasn't naïve. I knew there'd be a price to pay later.

My front-page story caused an uproar, and other newspapers followed our lead. Conservative newspapers claimed I had stolen the pay slip.

"I found it on the floor," I said jokingly. "I have confidential sources I cannot reveal."

My editors trusted me not to pass off fiction as fact or make up quotes. They also knew I had good sources in the Majlis who were giving me tips to pursue.

With the arrival of March, everyone was thinking of Nowruz. It was time to focus on visiting with my family and buying presents for Pouyan. But the news flow didn't stop. Every journalist knows this truism: Some days you are chasing the news, and other days the news is chasing you. This time, a reformist deputy, Valiollah Shojapourian, a mild-mannered man, sought me out. He was a former university professor, and I had interviewed him once or twice but otherwise had had no contact with him. Now he wanted to share his secret.

"You know it wasn't just one bonus payment," he said, smiling knowingly. "There are lots of payments, but if anyone finds out I've helped you, then I'm done for."

"If you have pay slips in your pockets, I'm not putting my hand there," I said, laughing. "People will start talking."

"I'm taking a big risk. Can I trust you?"

"No one is better at keeping a secret," I said, giving him my most confident smile. "But if you are worried, then don't share it. I'll find other means to confirm it." When in doubt, bluff—that's my motto.

"I can't give it to you in the open, but I'll hold the paper behind my back and I'll drop it as I'm walking." He stressed every word, as if talking to an imbecile. "I'll drop it and then you have to rush and pick it up."

He acted as if we were characters in a spy movie. I wished he could just hand the paper to me, but I played along, nodding eagerly.

"Just make sure you pick it up quickly. And don't use my name."

Dramatically, he crossed his hands behind his back, holding a crumpled piece of paper. As casually as I could, I strolled a few paces behind him. It was comical. I walked really slowly and pretended that I wasn't following him. I was close to bursting into laughter at the sheer craziness of it. Finally, the paper fell out of his hands. I ran and snatched it while he veered off.

This time the bonus was more substantial—3.5 million tomans for "religious duties," paid from funds under the control of the Speaker of Parliament. We had another explosive front page. My story ran in both ILNA and *Hambastegi,* as had been the case the first time, and dominated the news cycle. It is no exaggeration to say that the coverage of pay slips overshadowed all other domestic stories. There were no official denials.

Instead the officials focused their anger on me. I was accused of stealing the documents and being "flirtatious" with the deputies. The suggestion was that I had offered sexual favors in order to gain the information. Some deputies were calling for the security services to investigate me.

My editors at *Hambastegi* were also concerned about the latest exposé. They feared that the Speaker might seek an injunction and close the paper.

"How did you get this pay slip?" my editor asked at an editorial board meeting.

"I found it on the floor."

"How come you are the only one who keeps finding these pay slips on the floor?" he asked.

"Don't worry, it's not as if I'm using my feminine charms," I joked.

Everyone in the meeting burst out laughing. Judging by how hard they laughed, I guess none thought I had any such charms.

Just as things were quieting down, Shojapourian turned up with another pay slip.

"We received three bonus payments, and this is my final bonus to you," he said, handing me his pay slip, with his identification details torn off. "Make sure it can't be traced back to me."

The government had approved New Year's bonuses for all government employees—civil servants, the military, and teachers—of between 100,000 and 250,000 tomans. The deputies were getting 1.1 million tomans, or four to ten times what the civil servants would receive.

Once again, the story dominated the news cycle—this time for three days. The whole country was talking about the gall and arrogance of the deputies for accepting such large bonuses. In shops, in taxis, in offices, it was all everyone was talking about. Even my janitor stopped me one morning.

"I read the news. It's a disgrace. I've never seen one million tomans in my life."

A group of teachers held demonstrations outside the Majlis building, holding placards that said they wanted the same bonus of 1.1 million tomans.

I headed to Ghomikola to see AghaJan and Mother during Nowruz, when everything shuts down for thirteen days. I could also see Pouyan, though only for part of the time.

AghaJan had prayed for the victory of the conservatives. He had gloated when the hard-liners had captured the Majlis the year before. Now even he was upset that they had disappointed him. On the first day of the New Year, like many Iranian families, we gathered around to watch the televised public messages of the country's political leadership. First the Supreme Leader would address the nation, followed later by the president, from his official residence, and then the Speaker of Parliament. My interest picked up only when it was Haddad-Adel's turn. I had to beg everyone to be quiet, and what he said about the pay slip scandal sent a shiver down my spine.

"You may have heard the lies about Majlis deputies getting million-toman bonuses," he intoned, staring at the camera. "Don't believe them. These lies are promoted by one disgruntled journalist. The deputies of Majlis are good and honorable people."

I was puzzled by his defensive tone. New Year's messages normally contain a lot of clichés and homilies about a better future. It was rare to use the occasion to defend the record of the deputies. I had assumed that the bonus story would fade away after the Nowruz break, but maybe Haddad-Adel wanted to continue the debate. It'd only mean more stories for me, I thought.

At the end of New Year break, on the fourteenth day, to be exact, I headed to Majlis. I still had a day pass and as usual presented my name to the guard at the security gate to check against his list of those to let in. This was the exact same procedure I had followed for the past three years.

"I'm sorry, Ms. Alinejad, I can't find your name on the list," the guard said apologetically.

"Not a good way to start the New Year if the press office forgets my name on day one." I laughed as I reached for my mobile phone.

I didn't think too much of it and called the press office. After exchanging New Year's greetings, I asked the man on the other end of the line to send a note to the guard to let me in. There was a pause and some throat clearing.

"The management committee has decided to rescind your Majlis press card."

I was stunned.

"You mean I can't come inside? When was this decided? Who decided this?" I was in shock.

"The management committee felt your exposés had damaged the Majlis. Your work was deemed as going against the good name of Majlis and its deputies."

What nonsense, I thought.

"You can't come in. Your pass has been revoked."

I next called Mohsen Kouhkan, of the Majlis management committee. He confirmed the news. I was not allowed to enter the Majlis as a journalist.

"You are expelling me from the Majlis building? Seriously? I was only doing my job." I was too angry even to cry.

"You had been warned not to write your incendiary material. You did not listen," Kouhkan said firmly. He didn't sound particularly sorry. "The management committee has made its final decision."

I walked out the security gate in a daze. Majlis was my home. I had established myself, and I was now thrown out without a trial. Even in those first moments of shock, I knew that I had to turn my expulsion into a news story. I stood outside the entrance and told every reporter going in that I had been expelled. Everyone was appalled that this punishment had been meted out to me for the crime of performing my job. I had a lot of sympathetic journalists on my side that day. I also approached every deputy going in. Almost all said they had no idea that a decision had been made to expel me. I was encouraged to appeal the decision and try to win my place back.

My criticisms of those in power had not won me many friends, but I was working within the law and within the restrictions imposed by the Islamic Republic. Putting tough questions to politicians is part of the job description of every reporter. In many countries, I'd be praised and lauded for exposing corruption, but instead I had been expelled for doing my job. At least I hadn't been jailed. The Islamic Republic had a history of imprisoning journalists.

Distraught, I headed to ILNA. As I walked into the newsroom, the managing editor came out of his office and I was surrounded by colleagues all wanting to hear the story. By then, all the domestic news wires—ILNA, IRNA, ISNA, and the Fars News Agency—had run pieces about my expulsion. The Majlis spokesman had issued a statement in response, saying that Parliament had no issues with *Hambastegi* and ILNA and encouraged them to send a new reporter in my place.

"We will not send a replacement for Ms. Alinejad," the ILNA managing editor told those assembled. "This is censorship."

Battle lines were drawn. ILNA issued an official statement condemning my expulsion. Later, *Hambastegi* followed suit.

On the day of my expulsion, the journalists at ILNA and *Hambastegi* stood with me, challenging the Parliament of the Islamic Republic. It was one of the most daring acts of the Iranian press, which, sadly, had given up all attempts at being a watchdog in recent years and instead had become an echo chamber.

I had been expelled from the one job I really loved. Uppermost in my mind was Mother's advice. They had thrown me out unfairly. Now I needed to find a window.

CHAPTER FOURTEEN

Early the next morning, I was up and ready as if the gut-wrenching experience of the day before had been part of a nightmare. The sun was shining, and I was determined that all was going to be fine with the world. I warmed up a piece of sangak, a flat bread, and wrapped it around a piece of feta cheese to munch on in the car. As usual, I drove to my regular news kiosk to pick up a number of newspapers before heading to Majlis. The day's newspapers were piled in stacks on the ground next to the tea-and-sandwiches stand: The Supreme Leader's face stared up from some of them, others showed Khatami's beaming smile, and four had chosen to put me on the front page. Headlines spoke of "Martyrs," "Resistance," "America," and the "Expelled Journalist."

My expulsion made the front page of *Hambastegi, Etemad,* and *Aftab.* I bought a copy of every daily newspaper I could find and decamped to my car to go through each of them. Another fourteen daily newspapers had covered my story on inside pages.

Repeated in every story was the line "the first journalist to be expelled from the Majlis." I had notched another first. I wasn't sure if I should be happy about the achievement. I threw the newspapers on the backseat, put the car into gear, and took off. Driving relaxed me, and I sped around the streets of Tehran without a thought in my head about where I was going.

An hour or so later, I found myself in the parking lot behind the Majlis. The young conscript beamed at me. "I've found a good place for you," he said, smiling bashfully and running ahead to show me the spot. "Make sure you roll up the window and lock it, too." He chuckled. "I've got no one helping me today and can't stay by your car all day."

I dangled my keys at him with a big smile and said thank you. He hadn't read the newspapers.

It was a beautiful spring day, and all was well with the world. Maybe today I'd be allowed back in the Majlis, and maybe I'd get an apology, too. After all, I was on the front page of four newspapers. If the Majlis thought they'd avoid bad press by getting rid of me, then they must have gotten a shock with all the coverage. Yes, all was going to be well with the world, I said to myself, as I marched confidently, with long strides, to the Majlis gate. Inside, the guards eyed me curiously. I walked up to the counter.

"Ms. Alinejad?"

I realized by the way they looked at me that I wasn't welcome. I felt very embarrassed about my foolish dreams of returning.

"I need to get in. I need to clear my desk." I was tearing up. "I have a lot of my stuff in the press room."

"Your name is not on the press list," the chief of security said. He sympathized with me, but rules were rules. "But"—he brightened up—"you could go as a member of the public, as long as an MP signs you in."

How embarrassing, I thought. I had to stand by the gate and ask the MPs, many of whom supported my expulsion, to sign me in! It was funny, but I didn't feel like laughing.

A number of deputies did come by, but they all shunned me. Eventually, Nategh-Nouri arrived. He had often warned me that my journalism would get me into trouble. Now he shook his head at me in sadness. "What are you doing here?" he asked in Mazani. He and his family were from the town of Nour, about forty miles or so from my village. "I didn't think you'd show your face here again."

"I still have my stuff inside," I said in a pleading voice. "I'm not going to cause trouble or make a scene, but I have lots of notepads, cassette tapes of interviews, lots of stuff in my desk."

Nategh-Nouri walked me in. It felt strange to be inside the Majlis corridors. I quickly packed my bag and said my good-byes to the reporters in the press room. I walked into the press gallery, a balcony overlooking the Majlis floor, for a final look. The Majlis was in session and I looked for familiar faces below.

"You should stay for a bit—they're bound to be discussing your expulsion," one of my colleagues said.

My heart skipped a beat. I dared to dream: What if the deputies voted to have me back?

Eshrat Shaegh, a conservative with a seminary education, a hardliner and no friend of mine, asked to speak. This didn't look too encouraging. Shaegh, with her thick, dark eyebrows that bobbed up and down as she spoke, was in a state of perpetual disgust. Only a few months earlier she had called for all prostitutes to be publicly hanged.

"This reporter is immoral," she declared, when the subject of my expulsion was raised. She looked scary in her black chador, which covered her from head to toe. "She is depraved. I have confidential information that she was jailed in Babol for political activities against the Islamic Republic. How is it possible that she became a Majlis reporter?"

There was a sharp intake of breath in the press gallery, as all the reporters turned and stared at me. Only a handful of people knew about my prison sentence, but now it had become part of the public record, broadcast on the radio. I kept my eyes focused on the Majlis floor.

Another deputy followed. "Good riddance to her, because she was also a thief. She stole those pay slips, and I've got a lot of complaints from my constituents about my bonus payments because of her."

Now Shojapourian signaled that he wanted to speak. My heart sank. Was he also going to denounce me?

"She is not a thief, because I am her source. I was the one who gave her the pay slips, because I don't like the hypocrisy of the new deputies. She did not steal my pay slip."

There was an uproar in the Majlis. Lots of deputies started speaking all at once, shouting at each other and at Shojapourian. In the press gallery, I smiled broadly, feeling I had been vindicated. The deputies below had no idea I was watching the proceedings.

"She was flirtatious, and everyone knows that she got the pay slips by her immoral acts," shouted a cleric in a long brown robe reaching almost to his ankles. "That's how she got her stories."

My face turned red with shame. I had spurned the sexual advances of some of the same deputies over the past three years.

Deputy speaker Mohammad Reza Bahonar banged his gavel to bring order.

"Even if some deputy gave her the pay slips, that doesn't change matters. She was rude, and many members complained about her."

"We can't expel a reporter for doing her job," another deputy said in my defense. "A reporter is like the thermometer—we can't blame the thermometer if we don't like the weather."

"This thermometer is *kharabe,*" Bahonar shot back quickly as he banged the gavel once again, pleased with himself. The word means "broken," but when it is used for a woman, it means she is a prostitute. "Good riddance to her," he repeated.

The giant television screen in the Majlis was positioned behind the Speaker's chair and projected onto the screen was the image of whoever was speaking. No matter how far back you sat, you could always see the person speaking. The Majlis had at least three camera crews to monitor the floor and make sure they covered everyone.

Absorbed in the debate, I forgot myself and leaned slightly over the balcony to get a better look. The noise from the floor intensified. I looked around and realized that I had been discovered. One of the cameramen had focused on my face in the balcony and my features now filled up the TV screen. I felt like a cornered animal, staring at my own image just as all the eyes from the floor below turned toward me. A low chorus of boos and hisses rang out. It grew and grew.

"Booooo...Boooo...Get out..."

I wanted to run away, but my legs would not obey. Defiantly, I stood up. I didn't dare look down at the deputies. Instead I looked straight ahead at some distant pillars. Bahonar again hammered his gavel to bring order. I was shaking on the inside but held on firmly to the edge of the balcony. I was not going to run away. I stood and stood for what seemed like an eternity and then turned around and walked out slowly. The deputies had spent an hour debating my expulsion.

I didn't care anymore. I left the Majlis on April 4, 2005, and never set foot in there again.

Both ILNA and *Hambastegi* once again issued public statements against my expulsion. My colleagues had thought that the Majlis would rescind the decision and that I'd be allowed back, but the day's hostile reaction convinced me that Majlis was closed to me. The BBC website reported that eighty conservative deputies had signed a letter demanding my expulsion. The news received international coverage.

The next morning, as usual, I went to my favorite newsstand. Three newspapers put the Majlis confrontation on their front pages. Almost every newspaper in Iran covered the story. Even old adversaries now came to my aid. Just six months earlier, Vice President Abtahi had berated me as an uneducated yokel for challenging Khatami over the Nobel Peace Prize. Now, on his personal blog, he blasted the Majlis: "285 Deputies Against One Journalist."

He wasn't the only one. A week after my expulsion was confirmed, eleven reformist papers boycotted Majlis coverage and published a blank page instead of their regular coverage of Parliament.

Rather than demoting or firing me, ILNA promoted me, making me a Majlis editor, essentially overseeing all parliamentary news coverage. Now I was in charge of setting the agenda, assigning stories, and managing a team of reporters. I didn't need to go to Majlis to do my job. But management was not for me, I decided. I wanted to write a book about my expulsion. Writing is my therapy. After the Majlis debacle, all I wanted to do was telll my side of the story. I wanted to tell the story of my son, Pouyan, and my divorce, and the pressures that women face every day. Soon, my living room floor was covered in stacks of notes and newspaper clips. I wanted to write while the memories were still painfully fresh in my mind. Memories can fade, and in the end, nothing endures but words. I already had a title in mind: *Taj-e Khar* (*Crown of Thorns*). I had been crucified, figuratively, in the Majlis. Now I needed my own crown.

"You have more than enough material to write a book," Ali said one evening, carefully stepping over the stacks. He was carrying a plastic bag full of homemade food. "Now you have to get it out quickly."

The publicity I received worked both ways. The articles about my expulsion could create momentum for book sales, but Ershad (Ministry of Islamic Guidance) would not issue a permit for the book to be published for the same reason. I was too controversial.

"This is your chance to tell your side of the events," Ali said. He had gotten a job as an editor, and he saw the potential for such a book. "Don't blow it."

Words poured out of me as I wrote *Crown of Thorns*. I had to get my Majlis experiences out of my system and show everyone that I was not "flirtatious" or *kharabe*. I was an investigative journalist punished for documenting corruption.

In one month I finished the first draft of the book. All that remained was to get a permit. As it happened, a few days after I finished the manuscript, President Khatami opened the Tehran International Book Fair, in which hundreds of Iranian and foreign publishers from fifty-one countries took part. Mohsen had a stand promoting the academic books from his company, and I made sure I was with him on the first day. From the podium, Khatami, looking serene in his cream-colored robe, cited verses from the Persian poet Hafez and then launched into a lengthy address about freedom of expression and the need to have a critical press. He didn't know I was in the audience.

As is the custom, after he had officially opened the fair he went on a tour of the different book stands, accompanied by the Ershad minister. At each stand, he exchanged a few pleasantries with the publisher. When he reached Mohsen's stand, I jumped on a chair so he could see me above the throng of men who had formed a cordon around him.

"Hello, Mr. President. I hope you haven't forgotten me. *I* am the expelled journalist."

Khatami did a double take. He clearly hadn't expected to see me.

"Of course I remember you. I was just speaking about you. We need to protect the rights of journalists."

"Mr. President, I appreciate your kind words. But I need action. Can you tell your Ershad minister to green-light my book? I need a permit to publish my new book."

"Of course, of course, just go and talk to the ministry and they'll sort it out."

"It'd be easier if you gave him an order"

Khatami just wanted to get away from Mohsen's stand, but the throng of onlookers made it almost impossible. There was no guarantee that the minister would honor a verbal recommendation by Khatami. I pushed a piece of paper and a pen toward the president.

"Can you write a note for the minister?" I asked. "If you write an order, then it will be done."

Khatami looked very uncomfortable. He turned around, looking for an aide to come and rescue him.

"It's not an official piece of paper," he said, trying to wriggle away. "It needs to be a proper presidential paper with letterhead. I can't just sign anything."

"A note from you to expedite matters," I said, persisting. "Not an official order but a friendly reminder."

Grumpily he took the paper and wrote a one-line note to the Ershad minister to issue me a book permit.

I didn't tell Khatami that I had finished my book already. Almost immediately, Mohsen got to work, managing to get the book into print in just four days. He rushed a dozen copies to the book fair to be displayed on his company's stand. Within a day, Ershad officials dropped by the stall and asked him to pack the books away because he didn't have a permit to sell the book! Having a permit to publish the book was not enough, we were told; he had to apply for another permit. That process took another four days, but on the last day of the book fair, we could finally display the book legally.

After my book was published, a number of strange things happened. I now lived on the sixth floor of a high-rise, having moved yet again. One evening, I heard the sound of pebbles bouncing against my window. When I looked out, my neighbor signaled that I should meet her downstairs. Puzzled, I raced down the stairs and waited for her in the lobby. She grabbed my arm and dragged me outside to the street, and after the usual greetings told me that my apartment might be bugged.

"*Lebas-shakhsis* went to your place," she said, nervously looking back at the entrance to the apartment block. She meant undercover agents.

"My apartment? How did they get in?"

"They came to my place. First they asked for the building manager, but he wouldn't give them keys, and so they came to my apartment to see if I had spare keys." She wasn't that much older than me. I had seen her around with two kids and sometimes a husband. "The building manager called the police, and two uniformed policemen showed up to check their story."

"Why didn't anyone call me?"

"The policemen said the undercover agents had a special permit to enter your apartment," my neighbor said, looking sheepish. "We were warned not to tell you. You don't look like you are one of those antirevolutionary types."

"I'm a journalist," I said.

"Yeah, one of the neighbors said. I don't follow the news, but I wanted to tell you not to say anything, you know, bad in your place."

I called Ali, and the two of us went through the apartment inch by inch examining every nook and cranny for bugs and other alien electronic devices. Even though we didn't find anything, I didn't want to spend much time in my place. Every time I took a shower, I worried someone was spying on me. Soon I moved again.

I became very watchful of my surroundings from then on, and became convinced I was being followed. I thought I saw the same cars in my rearview mirror following me. One evening, as I met with two activists from Jebhe Mosharekat, a reformist political faction, to arrange a book reading at one of their events, I shared my fears. I wanted help but couldn't go to the police.

"My apartment's been bugged, I'm being followed, and I'm going to get killed," I told the activists.

"Why would anyone follow you?" one of the men said, exchanging looks with his colleague, a former adviser to the president.

I told them that a silver Samand, a make of car ubiquitous in Iran, where it is made, had been following me all day. "And it was there yesterday and the day before," I added.

"Let's see if anyone follows you now," the former adviser said. "We'll go for a ride and see who shows up."

We got into my car and took off. A silver Samand soon showed up. The adviser turned around to monitor the other car.

"Take a left," he barked sharply.

I braked and turned into a quiet street.

"Speed up," he said, looking through the rear window. The silver Samand also turned and followed us.

"Turn right...now another right...now a left..."

Every turn I made, the Samand followed. After driving for a while, the activists told me to pull over. The Samand stopped about fifty yards behind us. Without saying a word, one of the activists left the car and walked purposefully toward the Samand. He bent down to talk to the driver.

"Who do you think you are?" he said, loudly enough for us to hear. "Let me see some papers."

The Samand took off.

"Congratulations, the security services have taken an interest in you," he said when he returned to my car. "And I think I'd better drive," he added, looking at my trembling hands.

I still visited Pouyan on a regular basis, but the trips had become more difficult because of the attention surrounding my expulsion. I told Pouyan as simply as I could about the challenges I was facing. I knew that others would try to turn his mind against me.

"I want to punch all those who called you a thief," Pouyan said during one of my visits to Babol. He was ten years old, and we'd go into the fields and run and play. I wasn't like other mothers, he said. I climbed trees with him and took him for rides in my car. I missed him terribly, but I couldn't do my job and look after him, even if I had won custody. On the days we spent together, it took an hour or two for him to warm up to me, and by the time I had to leave, the pain of separation would haunt me for the next day.

At ILNA one day I received a strange phone call.

"Khanom Shirin Ebadi, the winner of the Nobel Peace Prize, wants to talk to you," the voice at the other end said.

This must be a joke, I thought. Probably a prank to embarrass me.

"Salam," Ebadi said in her distinctive voice. "I want to represent you. The Majlis slandered you, and I think you have a case. I don't want to talk on the phone. Come to my office."

How could Ebadi help me? Although she specialized in labor and children's law, there was no harm in seeing her. She worked out of the basement of her apartment in north Tehran. In person, Ebadi was blunt and to the point and didn't waste time with pleasantries.

"I think we can file a case against Bahonar and Kouhkan," she said. "By saying you had loose morals and that you were flirtatious, they damaged your professional reputation. We have a good case."

Of course, Ebadi had heard, and read, about my confrontation with President Khatami over her Nobel Prize, and we had a good laugh about it. The news stories surrounding the incident galvanized nationwide support for her in the face of official hostility and apathy.

Ebadi's assistant, Leila Alikarami, another lawyer, took responsibility for preparing the case. We didn't know it then, but Leila and I would become best friends over my case, and our paths would cross again five years later when we were forced into exile in Britain.

After my expulsion, I also became more interested in learning about women's rights activists. Feminism was taboo in Iran. As a parliamentary journalist, I couldn't risk being seen to be involved in feminism and women's rights activism. To be honest, I didn't have the time; nor did I want to risk another black mark against my name.

But soon after my book was published, Shahla Sherkat, the founding editor of the influential *Zanan* (*Women*), Iran's first feminist magazine in the years after the revolution, called me. It is difficult to overestimate the impact of *Zanan,* founded in 1991, and the role of Sherkat, in shaping the debate over women's rights. Some of the country's most important feminists, including Mehrangiz Kar and Shahla Lahiji, had also written for the magazine.

Sherkat and I both came from traditional families, and we understood each other. She had obtained a degree in psychology before becoming a journalist. Now, as she started the interview, I could see that Sherkat didn't wear the chador, but she had a habit of fidgeting with the folds of her scarf over her forehead. I knew exactly how she felt. All women journalists constantly check their scarves for rebellious strands of hair stealthily popping out. Our constant checking was a tick—a habit to protect against suffering the admonition "First fix your hijab." Like me, her tiny frame was often covered by an oversized black manteau, except that I ached to be free. I didn't know if she felt the same.

The interview became a *Zanan* cover story. I wish I could say that my face stared out from the cover, but all you can see is my large northern nose and my mouth, wide-open. I am laughing, under the headline "The Ugly Duckling of Majlis."

Sherkat was deliberately playing up the nickname that the conservatives had given me. It was a badge of honor, I told Sherkat. I would not be intimidated.

Two journalists from the *Financial Times* interviewed me in May 2005, when the book was published. I hadn't heard of the *Financial Times* before then and was rather surprised that anyone in the West was interested in my story.

Away from my personal troubles, dark clouds were gathering. I needed to keep my eyes wide open. In June 2005, Iran held its wildest presidential elections ever. During the campaign season, it seemed as if the normal rules governing Iran were suspended. The morality police stayed away from the streets, men and women mingled, and women's scarves could slip back and reveal lots of hair. Women walked around wearing the tightest manteaux ever, revealing their curves.

The Guardian Council vetted seven candidates, all regime insiders, as acceptable. The best financed was the former president, Hashemi Rafsanjani—Rafsanjani, who drove everywhere in a bulletproof Mercedes-Benz and rarely traveled outside of Tehran. "Everyone knows me," he once said, dismissing calls to reach out to rural voters. Outside his campaign headquarters, young women wearing headbands with the word HASHEMI in English handed out campaign material to passing motorists. Barely observing hijab rules, they caused traffic accidents as drivers ogled their shapely bodies.

Election month felt like one long festival across the country. It was unlikely that any candidate would win outright, and all the political pundits predicted a runoff election between Rafsanjani and Mehdi Karroubi, former Speaker of the Parliament. As the results began coming in, city by city and state by state, that outcome looked more and more likely. Rafsanjani was comfortably ahead and Karroubi was second. With most of the vote counted, Karroubi headed to bed to get an hour of sleep. When he woke up, he had finished third and was effectively out of the race, bested by Mahmoud Ahmadinejad, the least-known candidate, who had squeezed into second place. Karroubi cried foul. He complained about voter fraud. To no avail.

A week later, Ahmadinejad, the son of a blacksmith, crushed Rafsanjani to become Iran's sixth and most controversial president. Ahmadinejad promised to produce plenty of drama for people in Iran and for me.

CHAPTER FIFTEEN

As a native of Lorestan, Mehdi Karroubi arrived at his worldview far from cosmopolitan Tehran. I learned this when the white-turbaned populist cleric and I traded stories of being rural outsiders and he helped me get my press accreditation. The Lors are famous for their simplicity, their stubbornness, and their bravery. Karroubi was convinced he had been cheated. Being headstrong, he appealed to the Supreme Leader, but that only got him a reprimand and a warning to keep quiet.

In protest, Karroubi immediately resigned his official posts and launched his own political party and his own newspaper, both called *Etemad Melli* (*National Trust*). Soon after the paper was up and running, the editor called to see if I wanted to join as a twice-weekly columnist. I missed writing, and said yes before he had even finished speaking. I named the column Damasanj (Thermometer).

Before the handover of power, Khatami gave his final press conference, in July 2005. About three hundred reporters crammed into the presidential offices for the occasion. Khatami was immaculately dressed in a fine-woven gray robe. He defended his policies and voiced his hope that the next president would respect the reforms he had initiated. The mood was somber; we all expected Ahmadinejad to tear up most of Khatami's policies. At the end of the meeting, journalists mobbed Khatami and took selfies with the president. I didn't bother with a selfie and headed outside. I was on the steps as his official car pulled up, and at that moment Mother called my mobile. When I told her that I had just witnessed Khatami's last press conference, she demanded to speak with him.

I looked behind me, and there was Khatami, walking toward me. I gently explained to her that this was not the right time, but Mother was insistent. Just as Khatami was about to get into his car, I handed him my mobile.

"Mr. President, my mother wants a word," I told the bemused Khatami.

He pulled back from the car and with a resigned look took the mobile phone.

"Salam, Madar jan" is as far as he got. Listening intently, he gave the phone back.

"I can't understand what she is saying," he said with a shrug.

"I will have to translate," I told him. Mother spoke in Mazani, our northern dialect. "She doesn't get a chance to speak proper Persian."

Awkwardly, with our heads inches away from each other, I held the phone between our two ears so the president and I could both hear, and as Mother spoke, I translated.

"You threw my daughter out of Majlis—you've damaged her name. If any harm comes to one strand of her hair, you'll have me to deal with," she said, and I translated. I had to laugh at her audacity. Here she was, with dodgy knees that needed replacement from years of working in a rice field, threatening the president of Iran.

Khatami, to his credit, mumbled something about how he, too, didn't want any harm to come to me. I don't think he expected to end his last press encounter being lectured by my mother.

With Ahmadinejad as president, Iran needed a Damasanj—Iranian politics was heating up. Change was immediate and obvious. The stylish Khatami and his men had worn tailored robes and suits;

Ahmadinejad's team delighted in their unkempt and scruffy attire. There was something comical about Ahmadinejad's weathered face, with his shiny black hair and absurd grin, as if he saw a joke that no one else saw. He made dubious claims, like the one that there were no gays in Iran and how if we returned to the piety and the zeal of the early revolutionary days we could solve all our problems. During a trip to New York City to attend the United Nations General Assembly, he was invited to address a crowd of students and faculty at Columbia University. Asked about the treatment of gays in Iran, he said: "In Iran, we don't have homosexuals like in your country. In Iran, we do not have this phenomenon." With those comments, he made himself a laughingstock in the eyes of the world.

He played up the fact that he was not part of the elite. His foes mockingly referred to him as Ahmaghinejad—*ahmagh* means "idiot." His doctorate in traffic management was seen as a joke. But he had street cunning: Ahmadinejad was a populist politician who knew that the country was full of people just like him—the lower middle class, those who didn't have the wealth, the education, or the connections to rise to the next level. He played on their sense of victimhood. He knew how to appeal to those who felt they were being pushed to the fringes of the new Iran, the war veterans who had not benefited from the economic boom. His campaign motto was *Mishavad va Mitavanim:* "It's possible—and we can."

He portrayed himself as a man in touch with the people. One campaign video showed him among the poor, and in another, he stood in line at a self-service canteen. Short, with hollow cheeks, he was considered unattractive, and he had no sense of style, unless you considered ill-fitting jackets and a perennial windbreaker an ironic fashion statement. Unlike Khatami, he had no clever turn of phrase and could recite no poetry. Ahmadinejad was an outsider if ever there was one. The political establishment was against him, and yet with nothing or very little going for him, he had won, using revolutionary slogans harking back to the early days of the Islamic Republic.

The country held its breath.

In his first few weeks as president, Ahmadinejad picked fights with the Majlis for rejecting some of his cabinet choices; he even attacked his own economic advisers, and he fired a number of seasoned diplomats because they were leftovers from the previous administration. He acted as if he were still a candidate rather than the elected president. Ahmadinejad was acting like President Trump before there was a President Trump.

Ahmadinejad toured the country, visiting some two thousand towns in two years. He all but threw money into the crowds that greeted him. His officials were churlish and uncouth war veterans with bad suits and rough manners. At the equivalent of town halls, he pledged federal funds on the spot to uproarious applause. He was like a game show host or a faith healer, the miracle worker who came bearing quick fixes and offering instant gratification. He had no strategy apart from dispensing cash and empty slogans.

At *Etemad Melli,* we were clearly in the anti-Ahmadinejad camp. We watched with horror as Ahmadinejad created chaos around the country with his nominations and proposals. I was still learning to be a columnist, rather than a reporter. But I found my voice, commenting on the new president's mishaps, complaining that the election was over but the winner was still in campaign mode.

After noting a few controversies of his tenure, I wrote: "Mr. Ahmadinejad, the whole country has come to terms with the fact that the former president Khatami is gone. We miss him but he is gone. The country knows that we have a new president and that president is you. Isn't it time you believed it, too? It's true. You are the president of Iran. It's time you came to terms with it and acted like a president."

Just months into his presidency, Ahmadinejad called for Israel to be wiped off the face of the earth. It wasn't as if he was initiating a new policy. Before the 1979 revolution, Iran and Israel had enjoyed warm relations, but the Islamic Republic's founder, Khomeini, had called for Israel's destruction. Ahmadinejad was just reiterating the policy. He isolated Iran further by denying the Holocaust. His statements were disastrous for Iran, I warned in a column, comparing the president to a "loudmouthed street thug" who hangs around street corners yelling at other pedestrians and cars. "Even as other thugs applaud his actions and slap him on the back when he gets back home, a storm has wrecked his house." Ahmadinejad's antics were isolating the country, and ordinary people would pay the price for his belligerence. If Ahmadinejad continued unchecked, a storm would wreck Iran.

Needless to say, I made no friends among Ahmadinejad's conservative fans, but a number of reformist publications, all opposed to Ahmadinejad, sought me out, and I was busier than ever. Some of the president's statements were bewildering, but they were all calculated to appeal to certain sections of the electorate. Ahmadinejad was unpredictable: One day, he even said that the morality police spent too much time monitoring the hijab, and that we should not worry about such affairs. On another occasion, he said that women should be allowed inside sports stadiums to watch football games. It was amazing that Ahmadinejad, with all his shortcomings, was standing up for women's rights. Of course, he was quickly overruled by the clerics in Qom. That was one of the rare occasions on which I praised Ahmadinejad—for tackling an issue that Khatami had ducked. Even though he had been overruled, Ahmadinejad had done the right thing. It is insane that Iranian women cannot attend soccer or volleyball games.

At the same time, Ahmadinejad introduced the Program for Social Safety, which called for morality police vans to be stationed in popular neighborhoods to harass improperly dressed women. He pushed legislation that eroded the status of women in marriage and set quotas limiting the number of women accepted to universities in certain fields.

In my article "The Government of Denial," I lamented how Ahmadinejad's denial of the Holocaust and the existence of gays, and his refusal to acknowledge the equality of women, were shaming all Iranians. Not many were laughing at Ahmadinejad inside Iran. In another piece, "The Government of Lies," I said that from an early age we are taught not to tell lies. With Ahmadinejad, the lies were so big and outlandish that the people believed them. Ahmadinejad specialized in big lies. All his lies were enormous. My columns won me lots of fans, but not among Ahmadinejad officials.

In May 2006 I visited Beirut as an *Etemad Melli* columnist. The idea was to write a series of articles on the relationship between Iran and Lebanon, and on Hezbollah, but I really wanted to visit another country and experience life beyond our own borders. Foreign travel was a big deal because Iranians were typically denied visas by almost every country—exceptions included Turkey and Afghanistan, and the city-state of Dubai—or given them reluctantly. Europe was out of the question, and we had no relationship with the United States due to the 1979 embassy takeover. Every year, on the anniversary of the event, there are massive demonstrations in Iran, especially in Tehran, to celebrate the takeover, a sign of defiance against the world's only superpower.

I cajoled the editors at *Etemad Melli* and eventually got my letter of accreditation to go to Beirut, regarded as the Paris of the Middle East—the most European city in the region. After obtaining the visa from the Lebanese embassy, I raced back to our office to brag about our good fortune. One of my colleagues quipped, "You're so excited, you'd think you'd got a visa for America." Everyone in the newsroom laughed. I could more easily have imagined traveling to the moon than going to the United States. Even though I didn't believe that the United States was the land of the Great Satan, as the regime propaganda called it, I was apprehensive about the place.

Beirut. That was the first time I felt I had truly left the Islamic Republic and experienced *kharej*. I stared in wonder at all the women; for the first time in my life, I was seeing women in public without the hijab, women without head scarves, women who were not veiled, and women who walked with no head covering of any sort—and no one attacked them or beat them or arrested them. The shock of the first day remains with me still. I was almost thirty years old, and

My brother and I used to fight every morning over who got to this bowl first, filled as it was with warm milk my mother got from our cow. We loved to scrape the cream off the side of the enamel with pieces of bread.

My mother was the tailor for the village, and she made me this beautiful skirt. I was so proud. I felt as if I was the prettiest, and the most blessed, girl in the world.

Naneh (my grandmother), mother, sister Mina, brother Ali, and me at age around six. My older brother Mohsen had bought a camera, and we were all dressed up and excited to have our picture taken.

A recent photograph of my father and mother at our home in the village. These days, I can no longer visit them and have to rely on my siblings to send their pictures to me.

The long path to the outhouse. Can you imagine walking along that path in the dark, with only a lantern? My mother used to say, "If you're scared of the dark, open your eyes wider."

This is where only the women would come to talk and gather water for the household. During my childhood, this stream was the source of drinking water for the entire village. I didn't know this was to be my last visit to my village.

All the women in my family always wore hijabs at home. From an early age, I rebelled against this tradition. Here I was already an established journalist in Tehran on a home visit. Pouyan is next to my mother.

My father and I often argued over politics. It was one of our favorite pastimes. This is one of my favorite photos from my last visit, in 2009. He would often say, "One day you'll understand that you don't understand anything." To this day his words make me smile.

Welcome to my mother's "office." She could always be found working hard in this little patch. My mother is a true feminist because she worked as hard as my father and earned her own money—she was able to defend herself and her children when she needed to.

My fight for freedom started in the kitchen—a place where you could take off your head scarf because it was not a space for men. The kitchens in the village are designed for women, with low counters to accommodate their height. I insisted my brother be supportive of my feminist ideology by helping in the kitchen. When he complained that the counters were too low, I got him his own chair. Here he is washing the dishes using a chair. He was the first male feminist in my life.

After my divorce, I got to see Pouyan on weekends at my house. I always say that Pouyan and I grew up together. We were big fans of hats and loved to dress up and be silly.

As Pouyan grew older, I came to rely on him more. He liked to make sure I got enough sleep. This was from my last visit to see him in Iran.

My last day at Majlis, Tehran, 2005. I faced angry MPs livid with my exposés of their corrupt practices. I was banned from the Parliament as a journalist.

Interviewing former president Khatami for a book project on the lives of politicians, Tehran, 2008.

I would rush to these phone booths at Parliament to send breaking-news headlines to my editors at ILNA news agency. Officially, the booths were reserved for MPs, but I had to get my story out, so I disregarded their rules.

It was customary for women reporters at Parliament to wear black, but I wore jean jackets and bright-red shoes to my job there. All the women looked the same, but there was no dress code for the men, and they could wear whatever they wanted. That didn't seem fair.

I was not allowed to study in Iran after my prison sentence. But in the UK, I graduated from Oxford Brookes University, where the rest of the students were the same age as my son!

In Iran, schoolchildren are forced to cut their hair to the minimum. Pouyan was so excited that he wasn't forced to shave his head in Oxford, and I didn't have to cover mine. It was all about our hair!

This is my true nature when I let my inner child take over. © *Toby Melville / Reuters 2013*

"I have too much hair, too much voice, and I'm too much of a woman." Being interviewed by Tina Brown at the Women in the World Conference, New York, 2016. © *Getty Images*

This is Shahnaz. Her son was killed during the 2009 fraudulent presidential elections in Iran. Shahnaz bravely campaigned on social media to give voice to the victims of those violent times and refused to be silent in her demands for justice.

Shima Babaei was repeatedly arrested for participating in my #WhiteWednesdays campaign. "By arresting me, you cannot keep me silent. I will continue to protest compulsory hijab," she told the court. A fearless and inspirational warrior.

One of the brave women who contributed their photos to the White Wednesday campaign, which I launched to protest compulsory hijab.

Another brave woman protesting compulsory hijab, from Azadi Square (Freedom Square) in Tehran. Women in Iran want to be free to choose and are engaged in a civil disobedience campaign the likes of which has never been seen before.

January 2018. Iranian women protested against compulsory hijab on the streets of Tehran and other cities by putting their head scarves on sticks. After almost four years, #WhiteWednesdays is the most recognized civil disobedience campaign for women's rights in Iran.

Vida Movahed ignited a new wave of protests when she climbed a utility box on a Wednesday and stuck her white head scarf on a stick on the busy Enqelab Street (Revolution Street). She was arrested and detained but later released. Other women took to the streets to emulate her act.

افتخار می کنم که رابطه نامشروع داشته ام

مسیح علی نژاد

An Iranian hard-line conservative website posted this picture of Kambiz and me. They labeled me a prostitute for appearing with Kambiz without a hijab. Ironically, the photo went viral, and my unveiled image was seen on all Iranian websites.

I told you my mother is a true feminist! She is driving a machine made for men. She's a strong believer that women can do anything men can do.

A street sign in Ghomikola. I am proud to be a village girl, and wish I could go back and visit one more time.

Two different passport photos from two different times in my life. Taking the veil off brought to the surface a younger and more beautiful me. The true me.

this was the first time I was seeing women walking, driving, running, shopping, all without head scarves. Along the Corniche, a seaside promenade lined with palm trees, many Beirut residents took brisk walks, women with and without the hijab strolling together without any trouble.

On the first day in Beirut, I kept expecting the screech of brakes to signal the arrival of vans loaded with morality police to arrest these women. I looked for signs of rough-looking men to berate and attack these women without hijab. But no one seemed to care. The Lebanese men had no reaction; they were used to it. I was the only one who was staring. How was it possible that a Muslim-majority country like Lebanon did not enforce compulsory hijab? I asked myself. Iranian media was always telling us about the power and influence of the Shiite political group Hezbollah, with its own armed wing, funded by the Islamic Republic. Yet social freedoms did not seem to be curtailed in Lebanon. Officials in the Islamic Republic insisted, and still do to this day, that the well-being of society demands that women wear the veil. In Beirut, women had a choice; some chose the hijab, but others didn't. And yet the fabric of Lebanese society had not fallen apart. Why can't Iranian women have the same freedom to choose? I asked myself repeatedly.

In Tehran, on a few occasions, when my hair was shorter, I'd dress like a boy, and with a baseball cap firmly pulled down over my forehead I'd go on hikes up the mountain trails. There was always an element of danger, and it was fun sneaking past checkpoints, surrounded by friends. Once I became established as a political journalist, I stopped taking such risks.

It took me a day or two in Beirut before I dared to remove my own head scarf. I worried someone would report me to Iranian officials and I'd face punishment on my return. I kept fidgeting with the knot, trying to decide whether to take the head scarf off or not. I even hoped that a strong wind might come and blow the head scarf away, taking the decision out of my hands. I realized that just by the way I was dressed, with a manteau and head scarf, everyone could tell I came from Iran.

I wanted to blend in and be inconspicuous, but I was racked with guilt that somehow if I removed my head scarf, I was letting my family down. I looked over my shoulder constantly as I wandered around the city, worried that undercover agents were monitoring my every move. It was silly, but I also felt a sense of great responsibility. After all, I was a columnist for *Etemad Melli,* a major newspaper published by a former presidential candidate. I couldn't let the newspaper down, and I didn't want to lose my job.

It was difficult not to be influenced by what I was witnessing. I befriended another Iranian also in my hotel. I could tell she was Iranian just by the way she kept her head scarf on all the time. We debated removing our head scarves. Each of us pushed the other to take the first step. Finally, after two evenings of fretting, we made a momentous decision: We'd remove our head scarves in public the next day. We felt daring and defiant.

We sat on my bed. "This must remain a secret for the rest of our lives," I told her. After wearing a head scarf in public for almost twenty-three years, I was almost feverish with excitement at the thought of walking around the city with my hair uncovered.

"I can keep a secret. It's you that I'm worried about. You are a journalist. You write about everything that happens," my new friend Parastou said.

"I promise." I raised my hand as if making a sacred vow but kept giggling.

"Even if we fall out and have a fight, we should never tell anyone."

We took sacred vows to keep our act a secret. I wish I could say that what happened in Beirut stayed in Beirut.

Throughout my life I had been told that my virtue, my chastity, my self-worth, all were wrapped up in my head scarf. I was brainwashed to believe that a piece of cloth over my head would protect me from the lusty desires of men. If I went out bareheaded in public, then I was not a moral person. The next morning, my heart was racing as we left our hotel as usual, with our heads covered. After a block or two, we halted and looked at each other. Without saying a word, we yanked off our head scarves. My mouth was dry. I held my breath, expecting to hear police sirens and loud warnings from the morality police.

Nothing happened. No sirens. No policemen raced to arrest us. Other pedestrians walked past without a second glance in our direction. I looked at Parastou—she had the same excited and nervous look on her face I must have had on mine. We laughed and hugged, relieved that no one had caught us. It was amazing to feel the wind blowing in my hair as I walked around the city, like most other women we saw that day. I constantly touched my hair and my head to remind myself that I was bareheaded. I had a number of meetings and interviews arranged that day, and when my encounters were with Hezbollah officials, I put my head scarf back on out of fear they might report me to the Iranian embassy and cause me trouble. Otherwise I kept my head scarf off.

That night, giddy from our day of freedom, Parastou and I decided to push our luck and investigate a nightclub. We'd only heard about them and had no idea what to expect. It required another vow of silence.

"We should do it," I said. "For research purposes, of course."

"Our trip would not be complete without a full exploration of what Beirut has to offer," Parastou said with a giggle.

"If we go, we must take another holy vow not to breathe a word of our nightclubbing to anyone, even if we fight and fall out," I said.

Parastou nodded in agreement. "May we burn in the fires of hell if we reveal this secret."

Giddy with excitement, we dissolved in laughter. We called acquaintances who had moved to Beirut and beseeched them to take us to a nightclub. Once again, I was amazed at how free the women were to dress as they liked without being harassed or attacked or leered at. We were like social scientists, observing everything and taking mental notes.

That night, my nerves got the better of me, and I'd dressed as conservatively as possible and even prepared a cover story, just in case I was recognized. Even in Beirut I constantly worried about being followed. I put on a pair of jeans and a long-sleeved green dress and wrapped a long scarf around my neck that could just as easily serve as a head scarf. I also took my backpack and carried my notepad and pen. I was a journalist, in case anyone asked! I was gathering material for a story.

The club throbbed with the bone-shuddering beat of the loud music bouncing against the walls. It was terrifying. I had never heard music that loud. The room was dark apart from the flashing colors and the strobe lights, which made my head spin. Men and women were dancing to this deafening music under these lights. These people were crazy, I thought.

The bar served alcohol and I was shocked at how normal it was to drink. When I was married, I had tried *aragh sagi,* a type of homemade vodka made from raisins. I hated the sharp and bitter taste and I never touched alcohol again. All around me young men and women were chatting, laughing, and dancing together, acts that are forbidden in Iran. The image that I had been fed—that there was rampant sex outside Iran, that drug addicts and drunk men preyed on women, and that nightclubs were places of sin—was proving to be wrong. In Iran, we were constantly warned that our hijab protected us from the evil that men do. Having gone to *kharej,* I had expected more lasciviousness; I wanted to see acts of lewdness to regale friends and family with when I returned home, but so far there was nothing like that to tell.

Parastou and I met a lot of people that night, and once they realized we were Iranians, the reactions were mixed. The Shiites were happy with Iran for providing Hezbollah with cash. One woman showed us her locket necklace, which contained a picture of Hezbollah leader Hassan Nasrallah. I stared at her in shock. "How can you wear that and go to a nightclub? It'd be like finding basijis or hardcore supporters of Khamenei attending illegal underground parties and drinking alcohol. It just doesn't happen." I shook my head at her.

My impressions of Lebanon had come from Iranian TV reports. I associated Lebanon with pain, sadness, and resistance against the Israeli oppressors; but they looked a lot happier than the average Iranian.

We have a saying in Persian: *Ta seh nashe, bazi nashi*—literally, "Until there are three (of something), there won't be play." More poetically, it is better translated as "Third time's the charm" or "Third time lucky."

We had already taken two vows of silence, and then came the third. During my stay I had driven a few times past the U.S. embassy in Beirut, a forbidding and forbidden building. On my penultimate day, with nothing better to do, I persuaded Parastou to go for a visit.

I was just three years old in 1979, when radical students occupied the U.S. embassy in Tehran. Today, anti-American graffiti and drawings cover the walls of the embassy. I had seen newsreels about the takeover: Mobs surrounded the compound, which was labeled a "den of spies" by the revolutionaries, and chanted "Death to America," calling the United States the Great Satan as blindfolded career diplomats were paraded—images seen on television around the world. The hostage crisis sealed the enmity between the Islamic Republic and the United States.

I'd never met an American, and here was a chance, I thought. I'd been led to believe that the Americans were the devil and wanted to take over our country. I figured that since Parastou and I had broken two taboos, by taking off our head scarves and going to a nightclub, we might as well meet the enemy.

The next day the two of us headed to the U.S. embassy in Beirut. Lost in our own thoughts, we hardly spoke in the taxi ride to the north of the capital. I was nervous and apprehensive about what might happen. In my backpack, just in case, I had a copy of some of my clips and a photocopy of the *Financial Times* article about me, which I carried everywhere. It was the first article about me in English and one of my most valuable possessions at the time.

Looking back, our visit was rather absurd, but we were too naïve to know any better, and curious to see Americans. Again, if the United States was so bad, why did Hezbollah allow it to operate its den of spies openly? The taxi dropped us outside a building with tall walls and a big metal gate with a small window.

We stood outside the gate debating what to do next. We didn't want a visa, and I couldn't even meet or interview any diplomats, like the consul or the ambassador, because any contact with American officials was strictly forbidden for Iranian journalists.

"Why did you pay the taxi? We have no way of getting back," Parastou said. She had gotten cold feet.

"We can make a call for a taxi from inside the embassy," I joked, but she wasn't in a mood to laugh. "It's too late to back out."

"If word gets out, we'll be questioned for days. We'll lose our jobs and go to Evin," she said.

I reached out and rang the bell. Having come this far, there was no point in going back empty-handed.

"I don't speak any American, so get in front of me in case someone answers," I said firmly.

After a few minutes, a marine opened the door.

"Hello, we are Iranians," Parastou said in English with a heavy Persian accent. "We wanted to see what the American embassy looked like. We don't have an embassy in Iran."

I gave the marine my most winning smile and showed him the *Financial Times* article about me, jabbing at the accompanying photograph and pointing to myself. He looked at us, said a few words, and shut the door.

"He wants us to wait." Parastou shrugged. She was learning English so she could apply to an American university. "He'll fetch someone to give us a tour."

It made no sense at all. Why would the Americans give us a tour of their embassy? I wondered.

After about six or seven minutes, the door opened and two young men in suits and ties came out and examined us. They had big smiles on their faces and looked very friendly.

"They are asking if we need any help," Parastou said. "What do I say now?"

I showed my *Financial Times* article again and held out my Iranian press card. "Tell them that we are famous journalists and are curious to see the American embassy because we don't have one in our country."

One of the men took my ID and the article.

"Also, tell them we're just curious, but it's not a big deal. If we can't see the inside, it doesn't matter."

"You really are Iranians," one of the men said with a laugh. "Wait here." Parastou quickly translated what he had said.

The two went back inside and again left us in the afternoon sun. "I hope they give my ID and the press clip back—that's my only copy. I can't honestly explain to people how I lost my ID," I told Parastou.

The door opened again and we were invited in. The two men showed us a few offices and led us to a conference room and served us tea and cold drinks and some snacks. After a few minutes, they must have realized that they were talking with two innocents abroad on their first trip out of the country. We kept telling them how scary it was for us to meet Americans, and that made them laugh. They handed us some tourist leaflets about the United States.

"You sure you don't want to interview us?" one of the men asked.

"No!" Parastou shouted. "We'd end up in jail."

As I looked for a final time around the conference room, another thought occurred to me. "Imagine if this building was in Iran. All the walls would be covered in 'Death to America,'" I said to Parastou.

"I'm not translating that. Do you always get such crazy thoughts?"

Outside, we walked calmly away from the embassy for a block, in ladylike fashion, in case we were being observed. Then we began running—screaming wildly with joy as if we were little children.

"We just met some Americans."

That evening, our last in Beirut, my friend Mohammad Javad Akbarain, a dissident former cleric, took us out for dinner. We told him about our adventure at the U.S. embassy.

"Don't ever speak of this again," he said urgently. "You'd be treated as spies. I've been here for three years and have never dared to even go near that building."

Parastou and I took our third and final vow of silence that night.

Lebanon opened my eyes to different possibilities. Here was a Muslim country where there was no compulsory hijab and where men and women could mingle without being arrested. There were signs of change in Iran, but we seemed to be decades behind our neighbors. For every step forward, sometimes we took two steps back.

I returned from Lebanon eager to learn to speak a new language so I could travel to other countries. I told Pouyan I had plans to steal him away, that we'd go and live somewhere far away, where no one could find us. Most weekends I'd race up the winding road north through the mountains to spend time with him.

"But my grandparents could find us," he said with a kid's logic. "They should come with us, too."

Reza had married Nasrin. But he was resentful of my success and unhappy that I had revealed details of our marriage and subsequent divorce in my book. As punishment, he cut my access to Pouyan from once a week to once a month. It pained me to be cut off from my son this way, but the law had given Reza custody of Pouyan. I wept when Reza called to tell me of his decision, but he wouldn't change his mind. It was tough for Pouyan to understand why I couldn't be with him as often.

My own romantic endeavors had not been too successful. I got engaged but left my fiancé after he cheated on me. After that, I focused on work—I wrote for a series of newspapers and magazines, in addition to *Etemad Melli*, and in my free time, I wrote my third book, *Man Azad Hastam* (*I'm Free*). This time Ershad refused to issue the permit necessary for publication. My second book had received critical acclaim but was perceived as too political. Reza wasn't the only one who didn't like the book. Most MPs also hated it.

As my access to Pouyan was now reduced to once a month, I decided to be the fun mother! His grandparents mostly looked after him, so there was no point in worrying about his day-to-day life or offering to help him with homework. Maybe limited access was better, I reasoned with myself. I might not be with Pouyan all the time, but when I was with him, I gave him 100 percent. I was determined to make every occasion as memorable as possible for us. When I arrived to pick him up, I was ready for all kinds of adventures: I'd take him on hikes in the forests around Babol, clamber up mountains nearby, and sing under the trees.

In late 2007, before Pouyan turned eleven, I left for a short visit to Britain, promising to get him the latest gadgets available only to English kids. I figured I could learn to speak English in a few weeks. The other reason for the trip was that I needed to find a publisher outside Iran to print my book, which I would then ship to Iran and sell privately. Without a permit from Ershad, it was too risky for publishers in Iran to accept the book. London was cold and wet and windy. The people were unfriendly, and I spent most of my time with other Iranians in London, which didn't help me to learn the language. I found a publisher who for a small fee printed my book. I shipped a few boxes back to Iran, hoping that they would not be seized. Soon after, I headed back to Tehran.

I hardly learned any English during my short stay, but I had an idea for a new book.

It was going to be about *Us* and *Them*. How the way our leaders lived differed from how the ordinary people lived. The book would be a series of interviews with current and former officials about how the other half lived. I composed a series of questions, on subjects ranging from hijab to music to the role of women. I chose former presidents Rafsanjani and Khatami; the current president, Ahmadinejad; Haddad-Adel; Karroubi; Speaker of Parliament Ali Larijani (a former presidential candidate); and former Iranian prime minister Mir-Hossein Mousavi, who called himself "the most principled reformist."

I wrote to all seven and hoped for the best.

Karroubi was the easiest to get a response from, since I worked for him. I pulled up to his political offices in downtown Tehran. Everything about his offices screamed he was from the countryside. There was a mishmash of furniture in the waiting area. Vases and carpets and other handicrafts from his home state of Lorestan were randomly placed around the room; his staff wore casual clothes, with shirts hanging outside their trousers. The men walked around in slippers or just plain socks. I, too, was asked to remove my shoes and once again realized I was wearing unmatched socks. I always have a problem with this—when I'm wearing socks at all, either they have big holes or they're unmatched.

My photographer and I were led into Karroubi's private office, in which almost every flat surface was covered in papers—newspapers, position papers, campaign posters, and charts of all sorts. Karroubi, politically sidelined since the Ahmadinejad victory two years earlier, was already planning to make another presidential run in 2009.

In the middle of the room, Karroubi sat in an armchair with his legs pulled up under him. "Go on, let's see what sort of mischief you have in mind for me this time."

I started with an easy question regarding hijab. France in 2004 had passed a law banning the wearing of head scarves at schools. The issue remained a hot topic, and many Islamic leaders feared Europe would impose more laws restricting what Muslims could wear.

"Imagine you travel with your wife, and upon arriving, your wife is forced to remove her head scarf. What is your reaction?" I asked.

"It's a great insult, because hijab is part of Islamic culture," he said. He talked in a slow and deliberate way, repeating himself and overexplaining. I allowed him free rein to say as much as he liked. Finally, he paused for breath. "The French law takes away my wife's right to choose the hijab. And not just my wife—all the Muslim women in France are denied this basic right, the right to choose."

"Really," I said with mock indignation. "So when the French president and his wife arrive in Tehran, why do you force his wife to wear the hijab? Why must she wear the head scarf? What about her right to choose?"

"You trapped me!" Karroubi screamed, only half joking. "You are being clever. You let me go on and on and on, but you were waiting to snap your trap. Get out! I'll lose my head if I answer your questions." He was smiling now to show his appreciation for my approach.

I tried another question. "Almost all Iranians listen to music, at least in the privacy of their homes. Have you ever listened to the voice of a woman singing?"

Karroubi was not happy about how the questions were shaping up. He laughed, but I could tell that he was beginning to have regrets about agreeing to the interview.

"Here is an easy one," I said. "All revolutions devour their children, so which one are you? The one who gets devoured or the one who devours?"

"Who would dare to devour me? No one," Karroubi thundered, turning serious. "I will not devour anyone or let anyone eat me." He became pensive. He had been imprisoned a number of times under the Shah during the 1970s and served in a number of key positions after the Islamic Revolution. "In every revolution, some people are eliminated."

Khatami was next. He was now based at the International Institute for Dialogue Among Cultures and Civilizations, an organization dedicated to his pet foreign policy project of greater dialogue, as the name suggests, between civilizations. The former president had pushed for greater outreach between Islamic and Western leaders since 2001, in the hope of improved U.S.-Iran relations. Apart from a few academic papers, not much came out of his efforts.

Even after his presidential term had ended, Khatami attracted trouble. In May 2007, he had landed in hot water for shaking the hands of at least two women during a visit to the city of Udine, in Italy, to participate in a seminar on dialogue between cultures. Khatami saw himself as a philosopher rather than a politician, but the conservatives were relentless in hounding him for the handshakes, one of which had been captured on video. He denied the incident and claimed that the video footage had been doctored by the CIA. It was a lie, of course, but Khatami couldn't admit to shaking a woman's hand. It was against the Islamic Republic's laws.

Khatami's neat and orderly offices, in an expensive part of north

Tehran, were in complete contrast to the ramshackle mess of Karroubi's. All his staff wore elegant suits or, if they were clerics, fine woolen robes. Everyone wore shoes indoors, where the floors were covered with handwoven Persian carpets. An Italian coffee table dominated the waiting room.

When my photographer and I were called in, I decided to play a joke on the ex-president.

"Buongiorno," I proclaimed loudly, holding out my hand to him. I wanted to let him know that I didn't believe his denials over the handshake.

Khatami's smile froze on his face, and with icy politeness he invited me to sit on a sofa in front of another elegant coffee table. Of course he did not shake my hand. I started my interview with my question about compulsory hijab for the wives of foreign leaders.

Just like Karroubi, he started to lecture me on Islamic values and how the West must respect the hijab as a right for Muslim women who choose it. The French had no right to ban the hijab, he finally finished.

"What if the French president and his wife came to Iran? Why would you force her to wear the hijab even though, as a Christian woman, hijab is not mandated for her?"

Khatami fidgeted with his prayer beads. He clearly regretted having allowed the interview, and he chose to argue for Iranian exceptionalism. "We have laws that say all women must have their heads covered and be modestly dressed. That's the law. We are an Islamic country, whereas France is a secular country, and there are no such laws."

His argument was that Western countries had to respect Islamic laws and customs, but we didn't have to respect Western laws and customs. Since Western countries were secular, they were not bound to religious edicts, but Iran had to follow its religiously mandated laws.

I plowed on to the next question. Ordinary Iranians listen to pop music, especially by female divas like Googoosh and Haydeh. All you had to do was take a taxi in any major Iranian city. Had the president ever listened to a female singer?

"No. I've heard women reciting the Holy Quran."

I raised my eyebrows. Surely, as a man of culture, he had listened to some music. "These women are iconic. They are part of the fabric of our society and you say you've never heard any of their songs?"

"I have never had occasion to hear a woman singing," he said, shrugging.

"I have a beautiful voice," I said. "I'll sing for you."

Before Khatami realized what was happening, I started singing a pop classic by Haydeh. He looked panic-stricken and nervously played with his prayer beads. He forgot all about my photographer, who placed her camera on the coffee table between us.

After four short lines, he clapped furiously to make me stop. It was a hilarious image. A former president of Iran nervously trying to silence my singing.

"You are good, but…you should focus on your writing." He leaned toward me, his hands firmly on the coffee table between us. "Don't tell anyone about this."

My next target was Rafsanjani, who held court as the chairman of the Expediency Council, an unelected body appointed by the Supreme Leader to adjudicate disputes between the Majlis and the Guardian Council. It had an advisory role but no real power. Ironically located in one of the former Shah's palaces, it suited Rafsanjani, who was one of the most powerful men in the Islamic Republic. After weeks of silence I received a thirty-minute notice to present myself. With Tehran's traffic, there was no way I could make it by car to the Kakh-e Marmar, or Marble Palace, where the Expediency Council was based.

I walked into an intersection near my home. Cars and taxis sped past, but I had my eye on something else. I raised my hand and hailed a passing motorbike. Usually you had to find someone reliable to be your motorbike taxi, but I had no time.

"Where to, sister?" The rider was young and wore a black leather jacket and jeans.

"The Expediency Council. I'm in a hurry."

He looked at me to see if I was joking. Seeing my stony face, he nodded. "You serious? Oh, God."

I held on tight as we weaved through the traffic. It was my introduction to taxi bikes, and I instantly regretted my decision. My driver constantly revved his engine to speed up and then braked as he zigzagged between cars. I closed my eyes, so I wouldn't see how close we were to getting killed.

At last the young man slowed down and swung sharply into a narrow street closed off by a metal gate. A number of armed guards became interested in us as I gingerly got off the bike. My driver took off without asking for any payment. One of the soldiers walked up to me with an amused look in his eyes.

"I'm here to see Ayatollah Rafsanjani," I said, in the firmest voice I could command after the nail-biting ride I'd just had.

I was escorted to an outer office that retained some of the opulence of the Shah era, even though the Marble Palace had fallen out of favor.

An aide took my notepad, pen, and tape recorder. "All conversations are taped. If it's deemed necessary, we'll provide you with a transcript," he told me.

He led me to a large inner room furnished with Persian carpets and Louis XV chairs. Rafsanjani sat in a large, straight-backed armchair, as if seated on a throne. He was no longer popular with young people, not just because of the allegations of corruption surrounding him and his family but because he had been linked to a terror network responsible for the killing of dissidents. He was then at one of his lowest points of popularity, but you couldn't discount Rafsanjani. He always bounced back.

He got up and took just one step toward me, a token gesture of welcome, and I raised both hands to signal surrender. "I'm entering like a disarmed soldier, without my tape recorder, pen, and notepad," I said with a big smile, hoping to win his favor. "I'm like a cleric without his robe and *imamah*"—turban.

Rafsanjani's face showed no emotion. With his hand, he indicated where I should sit.

"I have a number of questions," I began.

"Bepors." Ask. One word. To the point. No extras or polite chitchat. He didn't waste time. Other politicians would have used a politer term, like *Befarmaeed.* Be my guest. He eased himself back into the armchair and looked at me with cold, calculating eyes, almost daring me to take my best shot at him.

"How can I without my tape recorder and notepad?"

"You didn't ask for a press interview. In your letter you said you wanted to meet with the leaders of the country to benefit from their wisdom."

He had obviously read my letter and understood that it was just a way to get in. He was looking more and more like "Akbar Shah," a term used behind his back.

"If I told the truth, I was sure you'd never grant me an interview. Truth is, I'm a journalist." I quickly told him about myself—my career at *Hambastegi* and ILNA, and now at *Etemad Melli.*

"I've read some of your articles," he said. I waited, my heart beating fast.

"You've got a nice writing style. And I followed the news of your expulsion."

That was it for compliments. Please go on, I thought, trying to egg him on inside my head. I was quite flattered that he had read my articles. But that was it. He was done with his press reviews.

"I'm writing a book about leaders and ordinary people. I've got seven questions for seven leaders."

"Bepors." Again the one-word reply.

"What is the biggest lie you've told?"

"Next."

I was puzzled. He stared at me impassively. There was nothing for me to do but move to the next question.

"Have you done anything to cause you shame?"

"Next."

I moved on to my other questions, and each time the response was "Next." Until the penultimate question.

"You are on an official visit to France with your family, and the French police ask your wife to take her hijab off. What would you feel?" I half expected him to respond with a terse "next." He surprised me.

"My wife can take care of herself. Next."

"But in the Islamic Republic you force women from other countries to cover up. So why don't other countries do the same to us?"

I wanted to start a conversation, but Rafsanjani wouldn't look at me directly. He played with his worry beads.

"These are not banal, everyday questions. Next."

The issue of compulsory hijab was one of the pillars of the Islamic Republic, and for this reason it was very sensitive.

"Have you listened to women singing? Millions of Iranians have, but what about you? Has the leader of the country listened to the voice of a woman singing?"

He wriggled in his chair. Then he got up and thanked me.

"These are good questions. Please coordinate with my office to come again for a proper interview."

The door opened and an aide came to escort me out.

"But please remember," Rafsanjani said with a half smile, "you asked eight questions, not seven."

He was the only one who had caught on to the fact that I was asking eight questions and not seven, as I had promised. I never got another chance with Rafsanjani.

Ahmadinejad had taken one of his trips to a far-flung province, dispensing money and favors like an Indian pasha throwing coins to the impoverished masses. He loved those trips, showing off like a pop star on a nationwide tour. He enjoyed breaking the rules of financial planning and professed not to listen to economists. Behind the scenes, a team of bureaucrats scrambled to ensure that the books were balanced. Sort of.

Watching his performance on television, I was mesmerized by the extravaganza, the crush of people rushing his motorcade, and the applause as he handed out contracts and cheap money. I had grown tired of the television coverage of these visits. I had a vision of him as the trainer who throws fish to the seals or...

My next column, "Avaz-e Dolphinha" ("Song of the Dolphins"), was my most controversial ever for *Etemad Melli*. I compared Ahmadinejad to a dolphin trainer who used food to teach new tricks. At each location, the crowd had learned to coalesce around him and perform a "hungry symphony of stretched necks and tears" as they waited to get fed. Except that Ahmadinejad wasn't teaching us any new tricks—just different ways to beg.

The next day, I was at a deli picking up a sandwich for lunch before heading in to the office when I heard a news report from a radio on the counter.

"The article by Masih Alinejad is a huge insult not just to the president but the whole Iranian nation," the newscaster said.

"They are talking about my article," I told the sandwich maker. "I didn't insult anyone."

By now I had developed a thick skin and shrugged off the report as an overreaction on a slow news day. That lasted until I reached my office. Inside, it felt like a wake. Everyone was gloomy and depressed.

"Fars News has published five stories on their website already," one reporter told me. Set up in 2003, the news agency was closely aligned with the Revolutionary Guards and other conservative hard-liners. Fars published slanted news articles and pushed through the agenda of the Ahmadinejad backers. In this case, the position they took was that I had insulted all Iranians and that *Etemad Melli* should take action. "They are demanding that you be fired."

Karroubi was under pressure to act. It was not enough that he punish me; they also wanted to shutter the newspaper. To prevent that, Karroubi himself issued a public apology and distanced himself from me. Some people "didn't know the difference between criticism and insult," he said. One of his aides appeared on a news show and said that the column was written by an "inexperienced youngster, not even a full employee but a contract worker." The newspaper was going to end its relationship with me.

I was enraged and stunned. Did I just get fired? I wondered. I had not expected to be abandoned by my editors so readily. Parliament had expelled me and I had found my window, but now that looked to be closing, too. Some reporters, fearing the closure of the newspaper, said I had gone too far in my column. But when in doubt, attack. That's one of my core beliefs. "I'm going to Fars," I declared to the reporters assembled in the newsroom. I hurried down the stairs, eager to confront the architect of the negative stories against me. On the way down I bumped into a young woman about my age, on her way up. It was Nahid Siamdoust, a reporter from *Time* magazine. I told her my plan.

"You think I can come?" she asked. She subconsciously checked her maghnaeh to make sure that she was properly covered up for Fars.

"Sure. I can't get into any more trouble," I said, bluffing. I had no idea what I was going to do, but whatever it was, having another reporter along could be useful. Especially since she worked for a foreign publication.

At Fars, a doorman with a receding hairline puffed on a cheap cigarette, blocking our path.

"I want to see the managing director. Your reporters are telling lies about me. I'm here to tell him I never insulted the people."

He whispered into a telephone, keeping a close eye on Nahid and me.

"Sorry, they said they cannot meet with you," he said, grinning triumphantly.

"Let's see if you can stop me." I rushed past him.

He yelled after me but did nothing to stop me. After a beat or two, Nahid followed me. We walked into the newsroom and found our way to the desk of a junior editor. Of course, the doorman had called, and so the element of surprise was lost. I demanded to be interviewed.

"We don't interview spies," the young editor said.

"I'll wait," I said, and sat at his desk. After some time, the managing editor agreed to meet with me.

"To call someone a dolphin is not an insult," I insisted after the briefest of introductions. "You can call me a dolphin and I wouldn't be insulted. Dolphins are much smarter than humans."

"That's all you have to say?" The managing editor looked at me incredulously.

"I'm not going to apologize. It's Ahmadinejad who should apologize for treating people this way. His gimmicks only turn us into better beggars."

Back at *Etemad Melli,* I was given an ultimatum. Write a new column and apologize, or the newspaper might shut down. I thought of my mother's words: Even if they throw you out, find a way to get back in. The door was shut and the window was barred, but at least if I apologized I might get back in. I was sure that I had done nothing wrong, but I had to swallow my pride and write a mea culpa column. Karroubi was adamant. He also took my column away for two weeks, as a public punishment. Privately, he told me that he had apologized to save me, and that my job was safe.

Around midnight, with the apology written for the next day's paper, I sat at my desk, drained from the day's activities. I still had the sandwich I had bought for lunch, untouched in my bag. As I unwrapped the sandwich, my phone rang.

It was Ali Akbar Javanfekr, Ahmadinejad's media adviser.

"You blew it," he growled into the telephone. "There will be no interview with the president."

CHAPTER SIXTEEN

 F_{ar} from being a disaster for my career, the "Avaz-e Dolphinha"
column raised my profile. The piece was widely circulated and discussed, as if I were the first person to claim that the emperor had no
clothes. I was acclaimed by reformist activists and politicians. I knew
of journalists who had been detained and jailed for doing far less,
and I think that my notoriety saved me from arrest.

I didn't belong to any political party or faction. I liked having
the freedom to write what I pleased without partisan pressure.
Yet I was openly critical of Ahmadinejad, and as much as I chas-
tised the president for his ruinous politics, I was also tough on
the reformist politicians, calling on them to promise real political
change, to improve conditions for women, and to foster an atmosphere where we could have freedom of the press, without fear that
our publications would be shut down. My independence came at
a price—reformist politicians whom I had befriended warned me
that if I were to be arrested, they'd be powerless to protect me or
come to my aid.

Trying to balance my chaotic life and still have a say in Pouyan's
life wasn't always easy. I hated the fact that I could see him for only

one weekend every month. My absentmindedness didn't help, either. One evening, I drove to Ghomikola on my way to pick him up. My brother Ali greeted me at the door as I breezed in. He casually asked what present I had gotten for Pouyan.

"Why should I get him a present?" I asked blankly.

"It is his birthday," Ali said, laughing out loud.

Oh God! I had forgotten Pouyan's birthday. It didn't matter that we paid scant attention to birthdays; given how little time I spent with Pouyan, I was overcome with guilt.

"I'm a terrible mother. May God strike me down," I said a little overdramatically.

"Do you know what he likes? You can still get him something in Babol."

I had no idea. I knew by heart the names of every single member of Parliament and all the cabinet appointees and their contact details. But I was clueless as to what toys or games my son liked to play with.

Ali saw the panic in my face.

"Get him a PlayStation."

"What's that?" I had never heard of it.

"You are hopeless." Ali laughed at my befuddled look. "They play games on it. Everyone has it."

As usual, I didn't have enough cash on me and ended up borrowing money from Ali and the rest of the family, who had gathered for Pouyan's birthday party at AghaJan's house. I rushed to the only electronics store in Babol to buy the PlayStation as Ali fetched Pouyan.

Pouyan tore open the gift wrapping and showered me with hugs and kisses. He soon became immersed in the games, forgetting all about us. I didn't care that he wasn't paying me much attention—as long as he was with me, I was happy. The next day a dark cloud of despair descended over me after Ali took Pouyan back to his father. I refused to cry when we separated. At least not until Ali's car had turned the corner. Then I sank to the floor and cried and cried.

I missed Pouyan every day and every week. I dreamed about having a magic wand so that I could change Iran's divorce laws to get custody of him. I wanted to bring him to live with me.

Yet it was not safe for me to be in Tehran. Rumors of my arrest circulated. It was only a matter of time before I was picked up on a bogus charge. One solution was to leave Iran for a few months and return once matters had calmed down. I hoped the security forces would forget all about me if I was no longer in the country. Karroubi agreed to an arrangement so I could write my columns from London as I tried once again to learn to speak English. He didn't want to be responsible for me if I was detained.

Once I made my decision, I moved fast. I visited Pouyan for a tearful good-bye. I wasn't going to see him for a few months. I then packed one suitcase very quickly, handed my apartment keys to my brother Mohsen, and flew to London.

I've always hated making plans. Getting out of Tehran was the easy part of my journey, but once I landed at London's massive Heathrow Airport, I realized I had no idea where I was going to stay or to study. I had a list of phone numbers and started calling them one by one. A few hours later, I arrived at the dormitory room of Mohammad Reza Jalaeipour and his wife, Fatemeh Shams. I knew them both from Tehran. Jalaeipour had achieved a first in Iran's Konkoor Sarasari, the national university entrance exam. He was working toward his doctorate in sociology at the London School of Economics. Shams, a talented poet, was working toward a PhD. In reformist circles, they were the "it" couple—young, smart, and connected. A political career beckoned back in Iran.

The couple had only one room and one bed. With typical Iranian politeness, they let me take it while they slept on the floor. Over the next ten days, they showed me the sights of London, from Nelson's Column in Trafalgar Square to the Crown Jewels in the Tower of London. We spent the time discussing the political situation in Iran, as if we were still in Tehran and not in the heart of Europe. Fatemeh wore a head scarf at all times outside the house. I wore a black hat—a newsboy cap, which became my signature style out-side Iran for a while. I was not ready to shed my hijab.

Ultimately, I found London overwhelming. It was too big, too spread out, and too noisy. Instead, my two friends enrolled me in a language course in the city of Oxford, about ninety minutes north-west, which I found more manageable. They even were able to find me a dorm room.

The world's attention was focused on the U.S. election. Barack Obama faced Hillary Clinton in the Democratic primary. The Irani-ans watched the contest closely—on one side, the African American Obama, the soft-spoken senator from Illinois and a former law pro-fessor, stood to become the most powerful man in a country that was majority white. At least 40 percent of Iran's population is made up of minorities—Kurds, Turks, Turkmen, Baluchis, and so on, but I could never imagine one of them winning the presidency. I was root-ing for Hillary, the former First Lady and senator from New York. Women are barred from running for the presidency in Iran, and a Hillary victory could galvanize Iranian women to seek more political rights. Typically, Iranians don't pay much attention to the U.S. elec-tions, but the Obama-Clinton contest captivated almost everyone.

In Iran, the Guardian Council permits no secular candidates, no women, and no Sunni Muslim or other religious minority candidates to run for president. The twelve men who made up the Guardian Council had ruled that the Constitution barred women from the presidency. Token women were appointed to one of a number of vice presidency positions and charged with handling female and fam-ily affairs. Compared with the American political system, the Islamic Republic's idea of democracy didn't look very democratic.

I rooted for Obama in the general election against Republican senator John McCain. Ahmadinejad boldly predicted that Obama would lose, famously saying that America would not elect a black man to the White House, because the centers of power would not allow it. He must have thought that the United States had a supreme leader who could annul election results. I was deliriously happy to see that Ahmadinejad was proven wrong. I saw Obama's success as a symbol of hope to all people in the world, not just Americans.

The day after Obama's victory, I decided that I was going to try to be the first Iranian journalist to interview him. The idea was totally crazy, of course. Had I been in Iran, I'd never have even dared to dream about interviewing Obama. Contact with U.S. officials was forbidden unless officially sanctioned. However, I was studying in London, and emboldened by Obama's triumph, I dared to dream. One night soon after the election, I invited Sahar, a doctoral student who also taught at the University of London's prestigious School of Oriental and African Studies (SOAS), to help craft a letter to the White House. Over endless cups of tea and a box of *gaz*, a Persian nougat dusted with white flour, we wrote our first draft. I dictated in Persian, and she translated my words into English, as my command of the language wasn't great.

"Dear Mr. President, I'm a troublemaker and an infamous Iranian journalist," I said.

Sahar laughed nervously. "You're not serious, are you?" she asked in alarm.

"I need to get his attention. He's bound to be inundated with hundreds of media requests."

Still, Sahar did have a point. We struggled on all night, our hands and mouths covered in white flour from eating too many sweets. Even the letter itself was powdered white, and we laughed hysterically at the thought that this might be mistaken for some sort of poison.

I was convinced that Obama would be thrilled to be interviewed by me. I naïvely thought that he wouldn't be all that busy in the days before he took office and could easily squeeze me into his schedule. An Iranian national characteristic is that we think the world revolves around us, and that everyone is thinking and talking about us. I wasn't immune to this. Much to my surprise, the friends I had made in Oxford thought I had lost my mind when I told them of my letter to Obama.

Fazel, a Palestinian, joked that nothing ever was achieved through writing letters. "Why don't you fold your letter into the shape of a paper airplane and throw it over the Atlantic Ocean?" Fazel asked with a straight face. "Whatever you do, don't climb the embassy walls. They may mistake you for a hostage taker!" Everyone laughed, and I laughed the loudest.

Undeterred by the ridicule, I posted the letter, addressed simply to "President Obama," to the U.S. embassy—not without a great deal of trepidation. I soon forgot about it, as I was focused on my English-language assignments and my articles for *Etemad Melli* back in Iran.

Almost three weeks passed before I got an email from "Mike D." at the U.S. embassy confirming receipt of my letter. At first I thought that the email was a prank—that it had been sent by friends—and so I emailed back, asking Mike D. to call my mobile number for verification. He called, saying in a perfect American accent that he was a political desk officer at the embassy and wanted to meet me. I felt great relief that he sounded like an American official, with no trace of a British or Persian accent.

"I wanted to make sure you were genuine," Mike D. said. The embassy staff had been puzzled by my letter, and his job was to confirm that it was not fraudulent.

"I'm for real," I assured him. My English was so bad that I made him repeat himself a dozen times before I understood him.

"Meet in person is better. I'm just learning English," I said. "Am I meeting Obama?"

"We want you to," Mike D. said casually. "Your request is being seriously considered. I again had to ask him to repeat himself, this time three or four times, before I understood him.

Then he surprised me. "*Negaran nabash.*" Don't worry.

"*Farsi baladi?*" You speak Persian? I had never expected to meet an American who could speak Persian.

"Just a little," he said, reverting to English.

The moment he hung up, I called Sahar and screamed: "The Americans want to meet me."

Covering a full block in Grosvenor Square, the American embassy, a six-story building with another three stories underground, was an imposing structure in the heart of one of London's busiest shopping districts. On the roof, a giant bronze bald eagle kept vigil. Everything about that building spoke of the power and might of the United States. I dressed conservatively and wore my hat to cover my hair. I had butterflies in my stomach as I approached the entrance, fighting the urge to turn around and head back to Oxford. I was jumping into the unknown with my interview request without any backing from my editors in Tehran.

Mike D. came to escort me personally inside. He was tall, with thick, black, curly hair, a square jaw, and a firm handshake. When he extended his hand, I automatically shook it, but the simple act, taboo in Iran, felt awkward.

"My boss wants to meet you," he said as we walked up some stairs.

"This wasn't part of any agreement, meeting your boss," I said, suddenly panicking.

"We don't get a lot of Iranian journalists who want to interview a U.S. president," he said, laughing. "We thought your letter was a joke and had a good laugh about it. Now I gotta show you to my boss."

I wondered inanely if he knew that the letter was fueled by tea and nougat and sugar.

From his office, he grabbed a pile of papers from his desk and led me down a hall. I glanced at what he was carrying and my heart sank. Atop photocopies of newspaper articles about me was the *Financial Times* article about my expulsion from the Majlis. For a moment, I flashed back to Mortazavi's stacks of paper, "evidence" of my corrupt behavior. I remembered how the chief prosecutor would walk into my interrogation sessions armed with fresh piles of "proof" of my culpability.

"What's this?" I said, grabbing Mike D.'s arm.

"This is our research on you. It's my homework to see if you were real."

I was puzzled. *Research?* It may sound silly, but my English vocabulary was rather limited, and I took this to mean that I was to be interrogated. I stopped in my tracks. Realizing that something was wrong, Mike D. pacified me, using the Persian words he had learned and simple English words. Only then did I agree to meet his boss.

We entered a huge office for what turned out to be a brief meeting. I gave him a little speech, memorized earlier, about wanting to be the first Iranian journalist to interview President Obama. "It may be dangerous, but I want to do it," I concluded. I don't think they knew what risks I was taking by just talking to them at the embassy.

Afterward, over a lukewarm coffee, Mike D. asked me for my analysis of the political situation in Iran.

"I'm not giving away any secrets, but the truth is the reformists need to get their act together. They need one strong candidate, not three or four or five. Just one to go head-to-head against Ahmadinejad."

I'd been saying the same thing in my columns for a while. The meeting at least established that I was genuine. Mike D. said my letter was now going to be passed on to the State Department and the White House. I shouldn't get my hopes up, he added. Presidents rarely gave interviews to foreign press. Still, I was the only Iranian journalist seeking an interview with Obama, which put me way ahead of my colleagues.

A few days later, Mike D. invited me to the embassy Christmas party.

"Come and meet the ambassador. It can't hurt your case," he said with his American twang.

That's when I realized there was some interest on the part of the American embassy staff in helping me secure the interview. It didn't seem far-fetched that Obama, who wanted to break with George W. Bush's legacy of hostility toward Iran, wished to signal his intention to establish better relations. He could do it through an interview with me. Or so I dreamed.

I had never been to a Christmas party before in my life and

certainly never thought of attending one at the U.S. embassy. Sahar was very impressed when she found out I'd been invited.

"What are you going to wear? Do you have a dress? This is really a big deal."

"I don't care about what I wear. I only care about what I write and what I say in public."

It was true then and remains true to this day. I rarely wear makeup and have no love of expensive clothing. My life has never revolved around fashion, and I couldn't name a fashion designer even if my life depended on it. For the party, I decided to deliberately dress conservatively. I wore a long shirt over a pair of black trousers and a long raincoat, and jammed my hat over my unruly hair. I looked as if I had come straight from the streets of Tehran. As I walked into the party, I thought I was in the middle of a movie set—all the women were decked out in expensive-looking dresses, and the men wore tuxedos or suits and ties. Waiters wandered around the room with trays of finger food and champagne.

I looked for a friendly face. I knew only Mike D., and when I found him he seemed distracted.

"There is a lot of chaos in my life," he said, pointing to his wife and four kids who were hovering nearby.

"Excuse me, but what is this—chaos?"

"Are you practicing your English skills with me? You think this is homework?" He snickered at his own joke.

"Actually, the letter to Obama was my homework, but I got such a high mark that I decided to send it to you."

Mike D. stared at me in disbelief and then burst out laughing. Later, he and his wife and four kids walked me to the train station to see me off to Oxford.

I was more focused on the Iranian presidential election, some seven months after the U.S. presidential election, in June 2009. After almost four years of Ahmadinejad's disorganized and shambolic presidency, the reformists were gearing up. There was huge pressure on me to join the reformist campaign and write articles in favor of Khatami, who had hinted that he might return—and indeed did return—to challenge for the presidency.

I liked Khatami personally; he was erudite and had a kind heart. But he was a weak president who didn't like making decisions. In fact, in one of my columns I wrote that Khatami was "too kind and compassionate" to be president. He was too worried about hurting others—too worried about the judgment of others—whereas a president needed to make tough calls. I wasn't going to back any candidate.

By the end of February 2009, Khatami dropped out in favor of Mir-Hossein Mousavi, who had served as prime minster in the first decade of the Islamic Republic. Mousavi was an unknown to most Iranians born since the Shah's ouster. An Islamic leftist, he had been a colorless and dogmatically anti-American prime minister during the war years. He had quit politics some twenty years earlier, taught architecture classes, and painted in his leisure time. But now he was back, and he declared his candidacy on March 10, 2009, and Khatami immediately threw his support behind him.

I wasn't sure what to make of Mousavi. He had been active in the early days of the Islamic Republic, an era that tolerated no opposition; thousands of leftists were executed during his premiership. That was the stain on his candidacy. No one wanted to address the issue of the executions inside Iran. Outside, the diaspora could talk of nothing else.

"Can we trust him?" I asked Fatemeh and Mohammad Reza one evening, after hours of discussion over dinner.

"He is better than Ahmadinejad, and that's all that matters," Fatemeh said, echoing the sentiments of the reformists.

My publisher, Karroubi, also registered as a candidate. His political platform was the most progressive of all the candidates on the issues that mattered to me—women's rights, human rights, and press freedom. He even spoke about limiting the role of the Guardian Council and that of the Supreme Leader. But with both Karroubi and Mousavi running, the reformist vote would be split.

Amid all the excitement about the Iranian election, I forgot all about my request to interview Obama. I was completely surprised when, a few days after Mousavi's announcement, I got an email from Mike D.

"Congratulations," he wrote. "The State Dept. is ready to help you get a journalist visa." This was a big deal, since Iran-based journalists rarely received such visas, given the lack of relations between the two countries. Once I arrived in the United States, Mike D. suggested, the State Department and the White House would coordinate to work something out.

I should have been overjoyed by the news, but instead I agonized over it. My main problem was that I had not told my editors at *Etemad Melli* about my plans to interview Obama. Poor Karroubi would have had a heart attack had he known of my plans. Besides, I was on my way back to Tehran to cover the elections. The last thing I wanted was a journalist visa from the United States in my passport. That could have gotten me arrested.

I called Mike D. to ask him to put things on hold.

"I thought you couldn't wait to interview the president. Why the delay now?" Mike D. didn't sound so happy.

"I'll need to talk to my editors first and get their blessing, and only then can I go to America."

"Hold on. You mean your editors don't know you've applied to interview Obama?" Mike D.'s voice rose a couple of octaves in astonishment as he cut me off.

"If I asked for permission and the editor said no, then I couldn't proceed at all." I tried to sound confident. "This is how it works in Iran. But now I can tell my editors that I have a visa. They can't refuse me."

"What if they did?" Mike D. did not sound so confident. "From what I can see, your guys are not coming to power any time soon." Mike D. didn't think the reformists could beat Ahmadinejad.

"I just can't see how I can meet Obama without telling my editors."

Talking to American officials was a big risk, and I faced serious trouble if my contacts were revealed. Many forces in Iran, like the Revolutionary Guards and fundamentalist clerics, were against any improvements in relations between Iran and the United States. President Bush had been harshly critical of the Islamic Republic, especially its nuclear program, threatening sanctions and military action to prevent Iran from developing a nuclear weapon. During his presidential campaign, even Obama had warned of harsh measures against Iran's nuclear program. Iranian officials maintained that the program was for peaceful purposes. I didn't want to get mixed up in national security issues.

In the end, I decided to reveal my plans in my blog, which was widely read in Iran. I wanted to be the narrator of my own story, rather than through a leak of some sort.

"After months of studying, I am returning to Iran to cover the elections and apply for a visa for America so I can interview Obama. President Ahmadinejad has refused to grant me an interview. Maybe I'll have better luck with President Obama," I wrote.

It was no crime to meet with Obama, but I knew I was issuing a direct challenge to the Iranian authorities. Prior to the November U.S. elections, the Intelligence Ministry had detained eleven journalists and confiscated their passports because they had wanted to travel to the United States to cover the elections. Now I was daring the security services to make the next move.

In the days before I returned to Tehran, I attended a cultural event in London where former Majlis Speaker Haddad-Adel was the main speaker. At the reception afterward, Haddad-Adel casually made his way to me. He had orchestrated my expulsion from Majlis four years earlier, but I wasn't intimidated by him anymore.

"Don't put yourself in danger," he said quietly, so that no one else could hear. "Meeting Obama is not the right thing to do. *Salah nist.*" Not advisable.

"I'm a journalist. Interviewing people in power is my job," I replied.

He nodded and moved away. Haddad-Adel was no friend of mine, but he felt concerned enough to warn me. I had thought that by being transparent, I could avoid trouble. Except that transparency was no defense.

I was heading back to Iran no matter what. There was another reason for my return. My ex-husband and his new wife had fled to Germany and applied for political refugee status there, leaving Pouyan with his paternal grandparents. I now had a chance to claim Pouyan so that we could live together. I Skyped Pouyan to tell him that I was working on a plan.

In mid-April 2009, I flew to Tehran's Imam Khomeini International Airport, feeling nervous about what to expect. It was just after 4:00 a.m. when I made my way toward the very long passport control line. A young man peeled off from an adjacent line and hesitatingly approached me. My heart almost stopped beating. I thought he was a security agent about to arrest me.

"Ms. Alinejad?"

I nodded, fearing the worst.

"I recognized you from your photo above your column in *Etemad Melli*. I am a big fan and wanted to tell you."

"What the hell is wrong with you?" I said in a loud voice. "I thought you had come to arrest me."

The poor man went red in the face as everyone around burst out laughing. Getting picked up at airports is a fear shared by most citizens of the Islamic Republic.

I cleared passport control with no hassles. The officer barely gave me a glance and handed back my passport without so much as a question.

I had overcome the main hurdle, I thought. If they were going to detain me, they'd have done it at passport control. Jauntily, I headed to the luggage claim area.

"Masoumeh Alinejad...Masoumeh Alinejad...please report to..." A man's voice repeated the message in a monotone over the public-address system.

Two men in civilian clothing approached me, and I knew

immediately they were part of the security services. At that moment I lost all my good cheer and suddenly felt very tired.

"Ms. Alinejad? Please can you come this way," one of the men said politely. They led me to a windowless room with a plastic table and three chairs. The two men were polite, the younger of the two offering to bring me some water. He smiled a great deal. His partner was more serious.

"We just want to have a friendly chat," said the older man, who was obviously in charge. "This is not an interrogation. Actually, we need your help."

He reached out his hand for my passport and started flipping through the pages. He didn't ask about my political views or whether I had met any dissidents.

"Did you just visit England? How long have you been away for?"

"I was only there a few months to learn English," I said cautiously. "Have I done anything wrong?"

"I don't know about that," he said apologetically, putting my precious travel document in a folder. His colleague leaned back against the door, silently observing me, his smile now gone. "We need to keep your passport."

I knew that once they kept my passport I was effectively a prisoner inside the country. But I couldn't exactly fight them over it.

"There seems to be a clerical error," the older agent explained. "There is a passport issued for someone else also named Masoumeh Alinejad, and we need to keep your passport to sort it out."

He wrote out an address on Fereshte Street, in the affluent north Tehran neighborhood of the same name. The security services used many unmarked residential and office buildings to conduct their operations.

"You can pick up your passport there."

"Are you sure there's been a mistake? I'm the only Masoumeh Alinejad from Ghomikola. I know everyone there. It's impossible that such a mistake could be made."

"You could be right. Just go to this address in a couple of days and it'll be sorted out," he said, smiling in a friendly way. "Even with our sophisticated computers, these errors happen."

Two days later, my brother Mohsen and I braved the morning traffic to drive to the designated building on Fereshte Street. Judging by the Italian armchairs and leather sofas in the waiting area, this was not your typical Intelligence Ministry operation.

As I waited I thought how easy it is for those who have never faced interrogation to sneer at the compromises made by those who survive such ordeals. I had been questioned a number of times, but I was still scared of what awaited me. Just after ten, I was called in and left Mohsen in the waiting area to fret by himself.

A nicely groomed man got up from his chair and introduced himself. I didn't pay much attention to the name, because I knew it'd most likely be an alias.

"This is not an interrogation. We'd like you to help us in our investigations," he said, flashing a smile at me.

"Did you find the other Masoumeh?" I said, with a big smile of my own.

"I'm not sure what you mean," he said, flustered, as he flipped through the folder in front of him. "I'm sorry. I don't understand."

"At the airport, I was told because of a clerical error there was another person with the exact same passport as mine."

This was not my first time facing the men from the various security services, and I couldn't resist the impulse to have a little fun at their expense.

"As you know," I continued, "there seem to be a lot of clerical errors, because I keep reading and hearing about journalists and activists and freethinkers who end up in such places."

"I'm shocked," he replied, spreading his arms wide to show his innocence. "We just want a friendly conversation for the sake of the national security of our nation."

For a man who made his living by deception, he was very bad at lying.

"Now that there is no other Masoumeh to confuse us, I'm ready."

"Before we start, I want to remind you that this is all off the record, and that you will not write about what goes on in this room."

I said nothing. I knew I was going to write about my interrogation experiences in my blog, if not in *Etemad Melli*. I also expected the room to be bugged with the latest recording devices available.

He left the room and returned with a copy of the Quran.

"I want you to promise me one thing at the outset and that is that everything you say will be true. Then we can proceed."

"You lied to me to get me to come here," I blurted in outrage. "You brought me here under the false pretense of clearing up a clerical error. You took my passport illegally. But I've nothing to hide. Go ahead and ask."

He still made me put my hand on the Quran and swear to tell the truth.

He looked at a list of questions in front of him.

"Why did you leave Iran?"

"To study English."

"Why England?"

"It seemed more reasonable to study English there than in Turkey or Saudi Arabia," I said sarcastically.

He continued, undeterred. "Did you meet any Americans?"

"I've already said I plan to seek an interview with Obama. It's all in my blog. I'm sure you've read it," I said, answering a question he hadn't asked.

"Did you meet any political figures?"

"Sure I did. I met Haddad-Adel."

"No. No...I mean, did you meet any anti–Islamic Republic figures? Remember, you swore an oath on the Holy Quran."

"I met journalists who had been forced out of Iran because they feared jail or worse."

He started making notes.

"Did you go to the American embassy?"

"Yes, I did," I said brazenly. "How else can I apply for a visa?" All fear had gone out of me.

He stopped writing and looked at me with his eyes wide-open, shocked by my candor.

"Don't you know the U.S. embassy is enemy territory?" he snapped. "You cannot deal with our enemies."

"I'm a journalist, not a soldier. It's not enemy territory to me."

"Why are you here?"

"Iran is my country, and I work for Mr. Karroubi's *Etemad Melli*. I came to get his permission and blessing to interview Obama."

"You did the right thing to seek permission, but he has no say in matters of national security," he said magisterially. "If you insist on interviewing Obama, I cannot return your passport to you."

We sat in silence for a few minutes. The silence grew and grew.

"The leadership has decided that the United States is our enemy, and we cannot have people like you writing articles that may help them. That would be against the national interest."

This was a formal warning not to pursue the Obama interview. Now I had to sound apologetic.

"If the Supreme Leader doesn't want me to interview Obama, then I must rethink my plans," I said meekly. "But I do need my passport, because I'm thinking of applying to a university in England."

"It's always good to study. Are you going to cover the elections?"

The Mousavi campaign wanted me to officially join his team. Karroubi expected me to be on his side. I still didn't want to tie myself to a candidate. "I haven't decided," I said. "I want to see my son and my parents first. When can I have my passport back?"

"Ah, now that depends on you." The interrogator took several sheets of paper and a pen out of a drawer and pushed them over to me. "You must do your part."

The hairs on my arms stood up. I didn't want to be a collaborator. I expected him to ask me to write secrets about my colleagues and friends as the price of returning my passport.

"What should I write?" I asked weakly.

"I want you to reassure me, give me a *ta'hood*"—a pledge—"that you will not cover the elections."

"Just that?"

"I need something in writing, a *ta'hood,* that you will not cover the elections before I consider returning your passport," he repeated. "You are a writer, so you know what to write, and make sure you put the date as well."

I did as he asked and signed it. He lifted the paper close to his face and read my words slowly. He then looked at me triumphantly.

"Come back when you have an airplane ticket out of Iran," he said with a self-satisfied grin. "When you come back, you'll get your passport back. Make sure you are leaving the country well before the vote."

Outside, Mohsen was waiting patiently and he hugged me warmly. I quickly recounted what had happened as he drove me back to the newspaper.

"He asked for an assurance that I wouldn't cover the elections," I told Mohsen.

"What about Obama? Did you give an assurance on him as well?" Mohsen said, honking his horn at the cars in front of him.

"He warned me, but I didn't give him a pledge. I don't think he believed I'd go to America to interview Obama."

Mohsen turned to look at me. "Are you going ahead with it?"

"We'll see," I said. For once, I decided to keep my plans to myself.

Karroubi laughed out loud when he saw me. "What's this about you and Obama?" he asked. I told him about my interrogation earlier that morning and then, outlining my plans to interview Obama, asked for his blessing to apply for a U.S. visa.

"If you gave a written promise not to cover the elections, you can't break your word," Karroubi told me.

I had expected him to stand by me.

"How can you call yourself a newspaper owner if you can't defend your own reporter? Why do you want to be president when there is no fight in you? You've got to fight back."

Luckily for me, Karroubi was used to my tantrums and wasn't offended. I planned on staying, and covering what looked likely to be a historic election.

On April 29, the reformists held their biggest rally to unite the party behind Mousavi. Thousands of activists gathered at a convention center in north Tehran, near the Milad Tower, the tallest structure in Tehran, which looks like a needle with a tangerine stuck halfway up it. For the first time, both Khatami and Mousavi appeared at the same political convention. Thousands of Khatami supporters waved scarves and small green flags, and chanted political slogans. We all sensed that after nearly four years of Ahmadinejad's regressive policies, the reformists had a chance to win.

I was invited as a special guest to sit in the front row alongside Khatami and Mousavi and other key speakers. Unlike other politicians, who kept their wives at home or offscreen, Mousavi had brought his wife, Zahra Rahnavard, an artist and intellectual, into his campaign, and she joined him that night. A new Iran.

Khatami called Mousavi to the podium. He then draped his green scarf around Mousavi's shoulders, a symbolic move to show unity within the reformist faction. The crowd went wild, chanting and cheering for a very long time. With his thick glasses, silver hair, and beard, Mousavi looked like a college professor. Yet that night I thought it was possible to glimpse a chance of victory and an end to Ahmadinejad's presidency.

The official Iranian election cycle is four to six weeks long, and for that period, it's as if normal rules don't apply. Campaign rallies turn into street parties where everyone stays out late and police stay on the sidelines and do nothing. Newspapers can be more daring in their criticisms. It's as if the censors have gone on a monthlong furlough.

In that atmosphere, I didn't want to leave Iran; I wanted to stay and witness history being made—the first time a sitting president would be defeated. I ignored text messages and voicemails from the security services asking me to come and retrieve my passport. I was intoxicated by the energy of the election. I visited the campaign headquarters of the candidates and mingled with the volunteers handing out pamphlets and publicity material. The smiling faces of the four candidates stared back from every available space, and the city was covered in posters. At major spots like Vanak Square, in north Tehran, activists wandered on the sidewalks and danced between cars stuck in traffic to hand out leaflets.

As the election neared, I had forgotten all about Obama until I got an email out of the blue from Mike D. He had amazing news. Obama was going to deliver a major address on U.S.-Muslim relations at Cairo University on June 4, and the White House wanted me to attend. He said that I'd get my interview in Cairo or, failing that, I'd get to ask the president a question at his press conference. This was my "golden opportunity," he said.

Obama was almost within reach, but the security services held my passport, and I didn't have Karroubi's approval to interview Obama. So close, and yet so far.

A few days later, Karroubi's son Hossein came to find me at *Etemad Melli*. Unusually tall and slim, Hossein ran his father's campaign. He told me the security services were unhappy with me. "I gather you promised not to cover the elections," he said. "They are very insistent that you should leave the country." He loomed over my desk like a giant as he spoke.

I was also getting daily text and voice messages to retrieve my passport. "I'm not leaving and they can't force me."

"We can't protect you. If you get arrested...or..."

He didn't have to say it out loud, but the Islamic Republic has a bloody history of eliminating dissidents and critics.

"You don't have to be gone for long," he said. "Just till after the elections."

The reformists were likely to win, if the people's enthusiasm was a reliable gauge. I could return after a Mousavi-Karroubi government had been installed, he said.

"If you are forcing me to leave, then I want to interview Obama," I said, bargaining. "I need you to give me a letter of accreditation, so I'm covered."

Eventually, the managing editor of *Etemad Melli* wrote me an official letter authorizing me to interview Obama. At about the same time, I got another email from Mike D., urging me not to give up. He felt that the White House wanted to reach out to Iran and that an Obama interview was a strong possibility.

That night, spooked by Hossein Karroubi's warnings and a general sense of unease, I stayed with my friend Soudabeh, a fellow journalist at *Aftab Yazd*. The next morning, I discovered that my car, a silver Pride, had been vandalized, with the windows smashed in and the car stereo ripped out, but left fifty feet away. The contents of a backpack I'd left in the car had been strewn across the street. My press ID had been jammed under the wheel. The policeman who came to investigate had a quick look and said the incident looked suspicious, and it was odd that nothing had been stolen.

"Maybe you have enemies," he said. "This looks like a vendetta against you."

"My enemy is Ahmadinejad," I said. "Are you going to put that into your police report?"

"No, I'm not," he said, tearing the pages from his notepad and throwing them away.

I drove to the newspaper and called my political contacts. It was obvious that I was being watched.

"Leave now, before it's too late," a politician with close ties to former president Khatami said. "Right now, nobody can protect you."

The more people told me to leave, the more determined I became to stay. I booked a ticket and retrieved my passport from the building on Fereshte Street. I then canceled the ticket and returned to the newspaper. The next day, I got a call from the security services asking me why I had canceled the ticket. I knew my every move was being watched, and I took to sleeping at different locations each night.

On June 3, I joined my friends to watch Ahmadinejad square off against Mousavi in the first televised debate between the top two contenders. It was billed as the most critical event of the election, the first one-on-one debate to be shown live, just as in the American presidential contest. Right from the start, Ahmadinejad launched a barrage of accusations and taunts, as if he were the challenger and not the incumbent. He even fished out a photograph of Mousavi's wife, Rahnavard, and said: "I have a dossier on a lady. You know the lady. She sits next to you in your campaign."

There was a collective sharp intake of breath across the whole of Iran. No one attacked the wife of another candidate on television. Ahmadinejad was prepared to do whatever it took to win the election. Mousavi was plodding in his responses, but he showed that he was not going to be intimidated. He didn't promise any great reforms, only better management of the country. At least Mousavi didn't deny the Holocaust, so maybe there was hope.

After the debate, supporters of Mousavi and Ahmadinejad poured into the streets to confront each other. "Ahmadinejad, bye-bye," Mousavi fans chanted. A carnival atmosphere prevailed in the country. So much so that even Ahmadinejad backers from the poorer districts of south Tehran headed for the capital's fancier neighborhoods, not to fight but to join the street parties.

The night after that first debate, having booked a new flight, I headed to the airport just as a pro-Mousavi rally in Tehran attracted tens of thousands, who locked hands to form a twelve-mile-long human chain along Vali Asr, the longest avenue in Tehran. I hated the fact that I was being pushed out. I comforted myself with the thought that it'd be only for a few weeks at most and that I'd return with an exclusive Obama interview.

The pilot revved the jet engines and I fastened my seat belt and turned to the window, gripping the armrest firmly. The plane took off into the darkness, and as I looked at the glittering lights of Tehran I closed my eyes and drifted off to sleep, dreaming of my return.

That was the last time I saw Tehran.

CHAPTER SEVENTEEN

Once again, I arrived at London's massive Heathrow Airport. This time I felt no excitement, because I had left my heart and mind back in Tehran. The elections were going to be monumental, and I hated to be missing out on what I expected to be a great outpouring of joy once Ahmadinejad was defeated.

I headed straight to Leila Alikarami's apartment in West London. She was the lawyer who had assisted Shirin Ebadi on my case against the MPs who had expelled me from Majlis four years earlier. The case had been dismissed by the Revolutionary Court, not unexpectedly. Since winning the Nobel Prize, Ebadi had become a target inside and outside Iran and had been forced to leave the country. Both the reformists and the conservatives were united against Ebadi, who had agreed to defend Baha'i leaders under arrest. The Islamic Republic regards people of the Baha'i faith as apostates, and randomly arrests and executes them. In retaliation for her advocacy, security forces had raided Ebadi's offices and seized her computers and files. Ebadi had then left Iran for the sanctuary of Britain. Leila was also in London to pursue her doctorate.

I followed the election news online and through my own contacts. I was sure that the election fever I had witnessed in Tehran, which was echoed on Facebook and elsewhere, would result in a Mousavi victory. I submitted my passport to the U.S. embassy to get my visa application, hoping that I could quickly set up my interview with Obama. I wasn't naïve enough to think that Mousavi would win in the first round, but I figured that both he and Ahmadinejad would move into a runoff election and that Mousavi would win in the final round.

Friday, June 12, Election Day in Iran, was beautiful and sunny. Leila and some of our friends wanted to vote at the Iranian consulate, located in London's posh Kensington neighborhood, where special ballot boxes were set up. Too late, I realized that I couldn't vote, since my passport was at the U.S. embassy. The long line of voters snaked around the consulate. I took out my small video camera to film a short report I planned on making. I'd always dreamed of being on TV but never thought I could do it. I walked among the crowd and started asking people why they were there and who they were going to vote for. Just by the way I was dressed I stood out as an Iranian who had just arrived in the West—I wore a light-blue head scarf and very modest clothes covering every inch of my body. I planned on returning to Iran and didn't want to be accused of having a "bad hijab." Most of the Iranian women in London did not wear head scarves or any form of hijab. However, they carried head scarves with them and loosely donned them just before they entered the consulate.

It felt like a street party—more a chance to catch up with friends than to participate in an election. Even the presence of a few hecklers didn't dampen the mood. Across from the consulate, a dozen or so protesters had gathered, shouting slogans against the clerical regime, calling the elections a public relations gimmick designed to legitimize the Islamic Republic. They taunted those who had lined up to vote, and called them "traitors." In return, some among the line of voters responded with chants of "*Bi vatan.*" Stateless.

Apart from the competing chants, there was no real tension. Even the British policemen standing around the consulate looked bored. It seemed everyone in London was voting for Mousavi and felt more than ready to celebrate the end of Ahmadinejad. As I kept hearing Mousavi's name again and again, I thought, What if the unexpected happens? I didn't have any special knowledge, but I don't like to follow the crowd. All my life I have tried to make my own path. Now, surrounded by Mousavi supporters, I wondered: Were the real rulers of the Islamic Republic, the Revolutionary Guards, the clerics who never faced an election, willing to accept the changes that Mousavi supporters wanted?

"How can you be sure your votes will count? How can you be sure there will be no fraud?" I asked those standing in line to vote. Not one thought fraud was possible. Everyone that day thought Mousavi's victory was a foregone conclusion. With such an overwhelming level of support for Mousavi, any shenanigans would be spotted easily.

Back at Leila's, I quickly wrote my column for the next day's paper about the turnout in London. I spent twice as long as it took me to write the column on the phone arguing with my editors as to why it had to be in the next day's paper.

My editors sounded distracted, which was understandable. The country's SMS text-messaging network had been mysteriously shut down, a contingent of security forces had been deployed near the newspaper offices, and several of Mousavi's advisers had been detained. Some polling booths were still open when Fars, the same news agency that had run many campaigns against me, declared Ahmadinejad the winner, with more than twenty million votes. If true, that would be a landslide that no one had expected.

I dismissed the report out of hand. The polls were still open and would be kept open for another few hours to account for the heavy turnout. Most analysts had predicted that higher turnout should favor Mousavi, the challenger. Also, the count was usually labor-intensive and time-consuming, since there were no computerized or electronic forms of voting. Every voter had to write out the name of his or her candidate in full, by hand.

I uploaded my video to YouTube and then sat back, glued to my laptop, to monitor early election returns. Every few minutes, I'd get a new message from my friends and contacts inside the country. Each message was gloomier than the one before. Reformist activists and journalists had been rounded up, the security forces had shut down Karroubi's campaign headquarters and destroyed all the equipment, and Mousavi's campaign headquarters had also been raided.

When the polls finally closed at 10:00 p.m. (6:30 p.m. London time), Mousavi called a press conference and declared himself the winner. "Any result other than one indicating my victory will be wrong and manipulated," he told the mostly foreign media. When I read those comments online, I practically jumped from my chair in astonishment.

"Can he really declare himself the winner?" I asked Leila. "This is looking very strange."

The "official" tally was announced soon after. IRNA declared Ahmadinejad the winner, saying he had won 63 percent of the votes cast. Mousavi had won 34 percent. I turned white. I was shaking with rage. The "official" results were very close to what Fars had predicted, even with four hours of voting still left.

I called my *Etemad Melli* colleagues, only to be told that the security forces had raided the newspaper and arrested some of the reporters. I had to get the news out—but how? I quickly made another video report, which I uploaded to YouTube: "I am Masih Alinejad, a columnist for *Etemad Melli*. Our newspaper has been raided and my colleagues arrested. There is fraud in the Iranian elections."

Befuddled as to what to do next, Leila and I headed back to the Iranian consulate. A political crisis of massive proportions was unfolding before my eyes. I knew that the whole of Iran was watching the events nervously. I was sure that Ali and Mohsen had voted for the reformist camp, and just as sure that AghaJan had gone for Ahmadinejad. Once again, Father and I were on opposite sides.

I hardly slept that night, constantly checking the television and my laptop for the latest news. My political contacts and sources were either running for cover or had already been arrested. That would have been the fate that awaited me had I stayed. The next day, thousands of protesters gathered in front of the Interior Ministry, which is responsible for the running of the elections. They were met by riot police armed with batons and plastic anti-riot shields—our homegrown RoboCops. There were clashes, and security forces fired tear gas into the crowd before firing live bullets.

Meysam Ebadi, a sixteen-year-old assistant tailor, became the first casualty of the 2009 protests. He had called home to say he was meeting some friends and would be back soon. Instead he was shot in the stomach. Meysam was the main breadwinner of the family, as his father could no longer work due to an illness.

That afternoon, Khamenei congratulated Ahmadinejad, calling his reelection "a divine sign," and urged the losing candidates to accept the result and support Ahmadinejad.

"Khamenei can't do this. He has to wait until after the Guardian Council has certified the results," Leila, who was well versed in constitutional law, said. "He is making it impossible for the council to invalidate the results if there was fraud."

"It doesn't matter, because the Guardian Council will never dare go against Khamenei," I said. "He appointed all of them."

Inside Iran, Internet speed slowed to a crawl, which was frustrating. The riot police blocked Mousavi's headquarters, harassing his campaign staff and the foreign press. It was exciting as a journalist and an activist to witness history being made, and yet it was frightening at the same time. I couldn't eat and I don't think I slept more than a couple of hours a night, instead taking catnaps during the day. I cried in frustration and sadness as I followed the news. My mood lifted with every message of defiance from the reformist camp and sank with news of every arrest. I desperately wanted to be back in Iran but knew that I'd never make it out of the airport.

On Sunday, June 14, two days after the election, Ahmadinejad held a victory rally in front of hundreds of thousands of his supporters. Most had been bused in from outside Tehran. As I watched it live, my stomach turned at the sight of Ahmadinejad grinning and waving to

the crowd in his off-white windbreaker. He compared Mousavi voters who were protesting to supporters of a football team that had lost
a game but refused to accept the result. But he didn't care, likening
his opponents to *khas o khashak,* dirt and dust. "Forty million participated in the elections in Iran. Now four or five *khas o khashak*
creeping from the corners may do something. But you must know
that pure river that is the Iranian nation will not allow them to put
themselves on display."

Images of clashes in which riot police brutally beat up anyone not
fast enough to run or duck were shown around the world. "Where is
my vote?" the crowds chanted in protest of the election results.

The Tehran nights reverberated with chants of *"Allahu akbar"*
shouted by protesters from rooftops. The irony was not lost on the
clerical leadership. During the Islamic Revolution, some thirty years
earlier, Iranians had shouted the same slogan against the Shah's autocratic rule. Now the wheel had turned full circle. But the Islamic
Republic was proving to be more ruthless than the Shah's police. Two
more protesters were killed on June 14.

More than two million people marched in Tehran in support of
Mousavi on June 15, three days after the election. This was the
biggest demonstration seen in Iran since the 1979 revolution. In
London, I watched a video clip of some demonstrators trying to
storm a Basij base north of Azadi (Freedom) Avenue. At first, the
militia standing on the roof of the base fired into the air, but when
a group of demonstrators threw rocks at them, they fired indiscrim-
inately into the crowd. The *lebas-shakhsi* raided Tehran University
dorm rooms, lobbing tear gas canisters and firing pellet guns. Five
students were beaten to death and another two were shot dead.
Another hundred or so were arrested.

I survived on a diet of news, fruit, and coffee. It was impossible
for me to comprehend how the peaceful country I had left only days
earlier was suddenly on the verge of a civil war. The pre-election carnival atmosphere had turned into a nightmare of arrests and deaths.

Hundreds of thousands took to the streets the next day, June 16, to show their support for Ahmadinejad.

The whole country was waiting for Supreme Leader Khamenei to make a comment, which we had been told would come on Friday, June 19. This was an unparalleled constitutional crisis for the Islamic Republic. For the first time since the fall of the Shah, the streets were filled with chants of "Death to the Dictator." When the nineteenth arrived, my mouth was dry with fear. Deep down I knew that Khamenei would not back down, and he didn't disappoint me. In harsh tones, he scolded the protesters. Speaking in front of thousands of Friday prayers worshipers on the grounds of Tehran University, he dismissed allegations of fraud and blamed the troubles on the Western media and foreign agents trying to overthrow the regime. "Street challenge is not acceptable." He especially warned reformist leaders, saying, "They will be held accountable."

Mousavi had called for a demonstration the next day, June 20, but after Khamenei's uncompromising warning, it was clear that the security forces had been given the green light to crack down on protesters. But hundreds of thousands of Iranians poured into the streets in droves to challenge Khameini. I was so proud of my fellow Iranians for being so brave. Unfortunately, the security forces also put on a show of force. Riot police units, some accompanied by water cannon trucks, were determined to break up the crowds. Videos shot on mobile phones showed police and Basij units charging into crowds and beating protesters with their clubs and batons.

I could practically smell the fear and the violence in the streets of Tehran from my laptop. I updated my Facebook page every hour with news of the latest developments. Unable to file stories because *Etemad Melli* was barely functioning, I used my blog to disseminate information. The BBC invited me to be a guest analyst on one of their news programs to discuss the latest developments.

I relied on video clips, which popped up in my email with painful regularity. I kept thinking about the human drama of the protests. Who were the unfortunate ones who had been killed? Were they young or old? Married, with kids? We knew nothing about the victims. I covered the movers and shakers of Iranian politics, the mighty and the powerful, but they were not the ones on the streets risking life and limb. Now I wanted to know more about the ordinary people who had answered the call of Mousavi and Karroubi to protect the sanctity of their votes. I was tired of the powerful and wanted to tell the stories of the powerless.

As I waited in the BBC greenroom for my turn, I opened up my laptop for the latest developments and found a new video clip in my in-box. It was filmed by an onlooker on a mobile phone, but this one was different from all the others. It captured the last forty seconds in the life of Neda Aghasoltan, a musician, on the streets of Tehran after she was shot by a sniper. I watched, like millions of others, as she collapsed and died. Neda wasn't even political. It was the twenty-seven-year-old Neda's bad luck that she and her music instructor were caught in traffic as the riot police chased a group of protesters. Neda had left the car to see what was happening when she was shot by a basiji. In the video, she gently collapsed to the asphalt as others around her screamed in despair. A doctor rushed over and pressed his palm on her wound to stop the bleeding. Her eyes looked straight into the camera and she tried to speak. Instead, blood gushed out of her mouth as her life drained away.

The video went viral. Television networks around the globe aired it repeatedly. At least fifteen people were killed on June 20, later called Bloody Saturday, but Neda's blood-spattered face became the symbol of the Green Movement, the name given to Mousavi and Karroubi supporters.

As I watched Neda collapse and die, I screamed at my laptop. "Get up. Please get up," I begged her. I wanted her to move, to stay alive. Other guests looked at me in alarm, but I didn't care. Neda had just died in front of my eyes. I cried uncontrollably. When an assistant producer arrived, at first I waved her away.

"Do you need a visit to the makeup room?" she asked kindly.

I shook my head. I went on air that day to talk about the death of

Neda and other victims with my makeup wiped off, puffy eyes that bulged, and a nose that was as red as a tomato.

Amid all the troubles, I worried about Pouyan being stuck in Iran. He was safe with his grandparents, but I missed him terribly. The post-election violence made me realize that it could be a long time before I might be able to return to Iran.

"I'm going to get you out of Iran," I assured him during one of our Skype calls. I didn't know how I was going to do it, but that was another task on my to-do list. He was turning thirteen, and I had hardly spent any time with him in the past year or so. I wanted to get Pouyan to Britain, so I could get custody.

Amid the drama of Iranian elections, Mike D. called: My visa was ready.

"The protests in Tehran aren't working in your favor," he said. "The White House doesn't want to send the wrong signals."

"Obama should show that he is with us," I said.

"This is not how we expected things to turn out," Mike D. said. "Obama has to tread very carefully."

A few days later, with a great deal of trepidation, I boarded a plane full of British holidaymakers: families juggling bags into overhead bins and trying to keep rowdy children in check, and young couples holding hands and being romantic. I was not in a jovial mood. I also didn't know what to expect in the United States. Mike D.'s call had raised some doubts about whether Obama would actually grant me an interview. But I felt I had no choice but to move forward, like a shark that has to swim at all times to survive, I had to keep going. There was no going back to Tehran.

The immigration agent in New York took one look at my documents before sending me to a back office for a more thorough examination. I was tired, jet-lagged, and desperate to find a quiet corner to open up my laptop and get the latest news. I had been away from it for nine hours or more. A beefy agent in a blue uniform nonchalantly beckoned me over. He towered over me and could easily have crushed me to death if he'd fallen on top of me.

"So, you are from Iran?" he said, flipping through my documents and passport before punching keys on his computer terminal. He barely looked at me. My mind wandered back to my trip to Iran a few weeks earlier, when I'd had to hand over my passport for a similar examination.

"Yes, but I'm not a terrorist." I smiled weakly. I was trying to be friendly.

The agent gave me a long stare. In my black hat and manteau, I must have looked a little strange. I smiled again.

"Why did you say that?"

"My birthday, September 11 . . . It was a joke."

"Never joke about that. Take a seat and we'll call you."

Great, I thought. I haven't even entered the United States and I've already ticked someone off. After a half hour of waiting and fretting, the agent handed me my passport.

"Welcome to America," he said, barely giving me a glance.

It took a lot of self-control for me not to scream out in joy.

My enthusiasm waned considerably during the yellow cab ride to Brooklyn, to the apartment of Roozbeh Mirebrahimi and his wife, Solmaz Sharif, journalists who had escaped from Iran. Roozbeh had been jailed for a while in Iran for his journalism.

Brooklyn didn't look like what I had imagined America to be. I'd always wanted to ride in a yellow cab like the ones in the movies, but the Brooklyn streets were full of potholes, the afternoon air hot and sticky, and the honking incessant. I even spotted a number of women in hijab wandering the streets. To think that I had traveled halfway around the world just to end up back in Tehran.

After a day or two, my hosts took me to Manhattan to sightsee. The skyscrapers and touristy venues like Times Square looked familiar—more like what I had anticipated. I had told Ali to find a suitable time to tell AghaJan and Mother that I had gone to America. Ali was a supporter of Mousavi, while AghaJan, as I've said, had voted for Ahmadinejad.

My last conversation with AghaJan had not gone well. Don't go to Britain, he'd warned. "If you end up living there, I'll never visit you." He was in a foul mood that day. "You should stay here with your own kin. If you leave the country, I'll never see you again."

He was still upset that I had not remarried. Even Mother took his side.

"What's so special over there that you have to go there?" she asked me pointedly. "Stay in Tehran. Talk nice to Reza and he'll let you see Pouyan every week."

I didn't have the heart to tell them that Reza had emigrated to Germany.

Walking around New York surrounded by tall buildings made me feel as insignificant as an ant. The streets weren't paved with gold, but you could see the city's wealth and power. At the same time, I was shocked to see bags of garbage piled up on the sidewalks where big brown rats roamed the streets at night, especially in downtown areas. The army of homeless was another revelation to me. I was too restless to enjoy Manhattan. I felt strangely disconnected from everything now that I had been driven out of Iran. Away from my homeland, I felt like a leaf fluttering in the wind.

New York was a magical place, but I quickly realized that you needed money to enjoy the city. I was on a tight budget and stayed with friends, sleeping in guest rooms or on sofas.

After a few days in New York, I was invited for a meeting at the State Department in Washington, DC. When I got off the train at Union Station, my mouth fell open at the sight of the tall columns, ornate ceiling, and chiseled inscriptions. It made New York's Penn Station look third world. I couldn't wait to see Washington, the so-called heartbeat of U.S. imperialism. From my first steps at Union Station, I knew I was in the right place. I'd always wanted to see the White House and headed there through the National Mall, walking past historic buildings and monuments. Everything was so clean and polished! At the White House, I contemplated lining up with the other tourists who had come from all over the world for a look at the inside. I wondered if President

Obama was around and whether I could sneak into the Oval Office. Compared to Iran, there seemed to be hardly any security.

Everywhere I looked, there were dozens of giant American flags gently billowing in the wind. It was amazing to see so many American flags not aflame. Every schoolchild in Iran learns song lyrics such as *"Amrika, Amrika, marg bar nayrang to"* (America, America, death to your trickery). For years I had been told that the Stars and Stripes was the flag of the enemy, and here I was surrounded by hundreds and hundreds of them. It was very disorienting.

Eventually I arrived at the State Department. My heart beat fast, and I had difficulty breathing. It was unsettling, but I figured that if this was the path to Obama, it was worth it. I wore the same newsboy cap that had been my constant companion in London. Without it I felt naked. I was led into a room with three or four officials who were Iran experts and were curious to know if I had an accreditation letter from my newspaper. They all introduced themselves and I promptly forgot their names. They pumped me for information about how the political showdown was developing inside Iran.

"We are in uncharted territory," I said. "No one has dared to oppose the Supreme Leader before, but we have two credible figures who are standing up to him."

"How will it end?" one official asked.

"In Iran, we always blame you for everything that happens, so you tell me how it's going to end." I meant the Americans should know the ending.

We talked some more about the situation in Iran, before I turned the conversation to my request to interview Obama.

"It's complicated," the same official said. He'd like nothing better than to arrange a meeting, he said, but seeing President Obama wasn't so easy.

"The White House doesn't always listen to advice from the State Department," a second figure who looked more senior said. "How about if you attended one of Secretary of State Hillary Clinton's press conferences? You could even ask a question."

It was a tempting offer. I'd be the first journalist from the Islamic Republic to put a question to Hillary Clinton, but I hadn't come all this way for her.

"We'll take it step by step," the official in charge explained. "We may be able to get you a short interview with her. We'll see what reaction that interview gets, and then we can approach the White House again."

I knew they were trying to be helpful, but for all their expertise and know-how, they didn't seem to get the dynamics involved. Hillary Clinton was a hawk. She had made tough statements on Iran, whereas Obama had suggested he'd be willing to mend fences. Karroubi would never approve an interview with Clinton to appear in his newspaper.

"There is no guarantee that *Etemad Melli* will be around much longer," I said. "We are under pressure as it is, and I only have one chance, and that has to be with President Obama."

There was silence.

"Well, let's see if we can get you into a President Obama press conference," the one in charge said. He didn't sound too convincing.

The meeting was sobering. I had imagined that American officials would be falling over themselves to set up my interview with Obama. I had done my homework. I had read up on the president and prepared my questions. Yet the American officials seemed unsure as to how to proceed. Well, I was not ready to give up.

"I'm going to stay in the United States until I get my interview," I declared boldly at the end of the meeting.

It was unclear whether the street protests back home were helping or hindering my efforts to get to Obama. In the meantime, there was nothing to do but wait.

I flew to Boston and along with some activists launched *JARAS,* an online publication dedicated to the Green Movement. Now reformists had their own publication outside the country, to counter the lies of the Ahmadinejad government and to publicize the protests. I wrote many of the articles, some under a pseudonym.

I had one eye on political developments in Iran, another on the White House. I realized that I had to raise my profile to put some pressure on Obama's team. Back in New York, I met Laura Secor, a *New Yorker* writer who chronicled my attempts to interview President Obama. I prayed that the White House staff read the magazine. Secor summed up my dilemma: "For the White House, a request that looked, in the spring, like an opportunity for outreach now poses a conundrum." Obama was caught in a bind, Secor wrote. If he met with me, he might be seen as taking sides, and if he turned me away, he was turning his back on the Iranians who were protesting dictatorship.

After the *New Yorker* article was published, the State Department called to say that they were working on a plan to get me invited to the next presidential press conference in the White House where I would be given an opportunity to ask a question of Obama. Never underestimate the power of *The New Yorker*. Thank you, Laura.

I headed to the West Coast to speak at a protest rally organized by the Iranian community in San Francisco. I had never spoken in public before, but I brazenly accepted. I figured only a handful of people might show up and there was no harm in it. I had always admired Obama's speeches but when I was in Iran I had studied the speeches of civil rights leader Martin Luther King Jr., especially his "I Have a Dream" speech, which resonated with me through his use of stylized language and repetition. As part of learning English, I listened to the speech again and again.

I hardly knew anyone in San Francisco, and when I arrived at the rally, I truly looked as if I didn't belong, in my uniform of black hat and long raincoat—everyone else was wearing tee shirts and jeans. Thousands of Iranians had gathered in Civic Center Plaza, in front of San Francisco's city hall, to listen to speakers denouncing the crackdowns in Tehran. They spoke Persian, but most had left Iran many years, if not decades, earlier. I mounted the stage slowly as the announcer called my name to a smattering of applause. It was a warm day and I prayed silently that I could survive the heat. I said in a quavering voice:

> I've been jailed, beaten, expelled, was not allowed to finish my education, but I didn't lose hope. I am just a traveler from Iran, the same country where even if a lowly mosque watchman casts doubt on our faith, our lives would be ruined. But today, it is we who have doubts—we are the ones who doubt the validity of the elections which have ruined the reputation of this government.... People have lost their lives, many more have been imprisoned—but it is this government that is a prisoner of its lies.
>
> For thirty years we were afraid. Now it is the Islamic Republic who must fear.

The Persian-language service of the Voice of America (VOA) and other Los Angeles–based TV channels aired my ten-minute address repeatedly. No one had attacked the Islamic Republic so openly and in those terms before. Someone uploaded the speech onto YouTube and it went viral. Within a matter of days, many in the Iranian diaspora were talking about it. The website Iranian.com named me "Iranian of the Day." My activist friends in Iran were not too happy. Even Karroubi called to chastise me.

"You were supposed to criticize Ahmadinejad, not the whole of the Islamic Republic," one activist in Tehran told me. "You can't say that for thirty years the Islamic Republic has been a dictatorship."

The reformists didn't want to overthrow the whole regime. They just didn't like Ahmadinejad. I was cast off and abandoned by senior reformist leaders. Now, going back to Iran looked even more uncertain. Back in Brooklyn, I kept busy writing dozens of daily news items for my blog and Facebook page. I was listless and unsure of my next move. The State Department kept telling me to be patient. I didn't know it at the time, but my life was about to change. I got a phone call from Kambiz Foroohar, a Bloomberg journalist. I had vaguely heard of Bloomberg. I'd seen their TV programs, which all had a lot of numbers running at the bottom of the screen. After my San Francisco appearance, I was used to getting interview requests and assumed he had called to interview me. I launched into my well-rehearsed speech about how I'd arrived in America, but he stopped me short.

"What are you *really* doing here?" he asked.

"I'm going to interview Obama," I said.

"Seriously?" he said half mockingly. "You have it confirmed?"

"Well, no, but..."

"I work for Bloomberg, a major news organization, but even we have a hard time getting an interview with Obama. It's not as easy as you make it sound."

"Well, the State Department is helping me." I tried to sound upbeat. "Are you doing a story about me?"

"It's not very compelling for our readers," he explained. But perhaps he could buy me lunch and get some details about reformist politicians. "Maybe you could share your contacts."

I agreed and immediately forgot about it. The next day I was surprised when he called to remind me about our lunch.

"How did you get my number in the first place?"

"Remember, I'm a reporter. That's what I do. We're still set for lunch."

For the past three days, I hadn't left the apartment. I'd sat in front of my laptop monitoring political developments and coordinating coverage of the protests. I didn't feel like leaving now.

"I don't feel well. I've changed my mind. Why don't you come and have lunch here in Brooklyn?"

"Nobody goes to Brooklyn for lunch," he said. There was a long pause. "I bet you haven't left the house in the past twenty-four hours, or is it forty-eight hours? It will do you a world of good to get some fresh air."

He was persistent without being pushy, and two hours later I found myself on Lexington Avenue in front of the Bloomberg building. I wore a pink shirt and jeans, and would have been wearing my black hat, except that I'd lost it on the subway. On the sidewalk, a gust of wind caught my hair, blowing it in every direction. I was still wrestling with my hair when a voice said, "Khanom Alinejad?"

Kambiz looked very concerned.

"Where is your manteau? Your hat?"

"Outside Iran, I only wear them for official duties. How did you recognize me?"

"I didn't, actually. I just saw someone caught in a whirlwind of hair and was curious if it was you."

He took me on a tour of the Bloomberg offices. It was the most impressive building I had seen in New York. The elevator doors opened on the sixth floor, to a central area that resembled the flight deck of a spaceship, with natural light flooding through massive windows. The food court offered free soft drinks and a variety of fruits and snacks. As I wandered from the TV studios to the newsroom, for the first time I felt that I came from a third world country.

"Our newsroom at *Etemad Melli* is nothing like this." I stared at rows of computer terminals on desks. "We have to share computers, and they are really ancient compared to yours."

Kambiz was easy to talk to and he kept probing for information about different political factions. Over lunch, he asked if I could put him in touch with Mousavi or Karroubi so he could interview them.

"They will not talk to you directly. They cannot be seen talking to the Western media," I said as I stabbed a piece of chicken salad. "You may get their advisers but not the main players."

Five years earlier, Kambiz had written an investigative piece on the family fortunes of former Iranian president Rafsanjani. He won an international award, but the Islamic Republic let it be known that he was not welcome in Iran anymore.

"How is this going to end?" he asked.

"We've never had anything like this before. No one knows."

I needed a new black hat to replace the one I had left behind on the subway, and Kambiz took me to Barneys. He neglected to tell me that it was one of the most expensive clothing stores in the city. I picked out a black newsboy cap and headed to the cashier.

"That'll be two hundred dollars," the cashier said, smiling nicely.

I thought it was only worth twenty dollars, but didn't want to lose face in front of Kambiz. I took out two crisp hundred-dollar bills, thinking how I'd turned into my mother, worrying about losing face.

"You must be loaded if you can pay two hundred dollars for a hat," Kambiz said. He sounded impressed.

"How much would you pay?" I asked him later.

"I'd pay about twenty bucks to a peddler on a street corner."

Afterward, I sat on a bench in Central Park. It was a beautiful day. All around me runners jogged, bikers raced, and Rollerbladers zipped by. I was lost in thought. I had to get Pouyan out of the country—there was no way I'd be allowed back into Iran in the near future. The only question was how to get him out. If I could find someone to take him across the border to Turkey, then I could take him to Britain with me.

I filled my days filing stories for *JARAS* and *Etemad Melli* while waiting for the White House to make a decision. The confrontations in Iran continued. The Green Movement was not going away, but an impasse had been reached. Demonstrations were held even outside the United Nations in New York to bring attention to the disputed elections. Ahmadinejad was possibly coming to the United Nations General Assembly in September, but I couldn't wait that long in New York.

A week later Kambiz took me to a late lunch at P.J. Clarke's, an old restaurant in Midtown.

"You still looking to interview Mousavi?" I asked him as I attacked my medium-rare steak with some gusto. I'd skipped breakfast to work on a documentary about the post-election violence.

He nodded warily.

"I'm waiting for Obama. Both of us are waiting," I said. "One of us will succeed."

"Mousavi doesn't seem to be a media-friendly person," Kambiz said. "Why is he so popular?"

"He is not Ahmadinejad, that's why," I replied.

I loved being taken out for meals, perhaps because I don't like cooking. We chatted about everything, especially my plans after I got my interview with Obama.

"Maybe he's worried he'll face a real tough journalist. You Americans seem to be going easy on him."

It was lighthearted banter as well as the latest political developments. At the next table sat a woman, exotically dressed, with lots of pins and brooches on her jacket. She had been busy sketching in a notepad as she ate. We didn't pay her much mind, but she had been paying attention to us. As she was leaving, she asked for our names and wrote them on a sketch of Kambiz and me at lunch.

"You look like such a lovely couple. Hope you can remain this way for the rest of your lives," she said, handing the sketch to us.

Kambiz and I felt very awkward. I felt some attraction to him, but there were too many events vying for my attention.

The news from Tehran was not great. A show trial of one hundred former government officials, most accused of conspiring with foreign powers to stage a revolution against the Islamic Republic, began in early August. Most of the accused were either my friends or my political contacts. The trial was shown live on Iranian television, and it was shocking to see the former officials dressed in light-blue prison uniforms that looked like pajamas, their faces gaunt and haggard. A day after the trials began, Ahmadinejad was formally sworn in as president. Riot police, the Revolutionary Guards, and the Basij combined to stop protesters from joining together to form a massive rally.

I was interviewed on National Public Radio's *Tell Me More* program about my efforts to interview Obama. A few days after the interview, Tehran prosecutor Saeed Mortazavi ordered the closure of *Etemad Melli*. I no longer even had a publication to write for even if the White House gave the green light.

I went to DC shortly afterward to make a special program about the 2009 Iranian election. My State Department contacts called and offered me a chance to interview an assistant undersecretary of state for Middle East affairs. "The situation is very tense. Let's see how this interview goes and we'll see how things develop," my contact said.

I lost patience.

"I turned down Clinton before," I said. "Now you are offering me an interview with some assistant undersecretary. I don't think so."

"We just don't want to send the wrong signal."

That was my last contact with the State Department.

I could see his point of view. Ahmadinejad had been sworn in as Iran's president, and association with Karroubi and Mousavi put me in the opposition camp. Obama didn't want to antagonize the clerical regime.

On Friday evening, I called Kambiz from my hotel room in Washington. Of all the people I'd met in the United States, he was the easiest person to talk to. Raised in London, he was self-confident without being annoying.

"I've been trying to think of an excuse to call you," he said.

"I'm sitting in a hotel room by myself and I'm tired of all the people around me. You should come and rescue me."

"I'll be there tomorrow to bring you back to New York. Pack your bags."

"I have all these people who want to see me. What do I tell them?"

"Good-bye."

The next day, he turned up in a beat-up black Saab. Not exactly trying to win me over with fancy cars. We spent the next ten hours hanging out and figuring each other out on the way back to New York. He had two kids from his first marriage and was "kind of" seeing someone. It wasn't serious, he explained.

"Our timing is bad," I said. "I'm going back to London and then to Turkey."

I had arranged for a friend to bring Pouyan to Istanbul on a bus.

"I promised him I'd get him out of Iran by September. I don't need any more complications in my life. We can't get involved." We were standing outside the friend's house in Brooklyn where I'd been staying. It was past midnight and not the best time to make a major life decision.

"We'll work something out."

"You have two kids. I haven't seen my son for a long time."

"No rush, no pressure. Get your son out of Iran. We'll sort it out."

As he said good-bye, I reached out to shake his hand.

"Come and give me a proper hug. I don't shake hands." He embraced me tightly but made no effort to kiss me, which I liked. I wasn't ready for intimacy yet.

The next day, sitting in my plane seat, I couldn't stop texting him. Nothing important. Just stuff.

"You didn't get Obama but got me instead. That's a great deal," he texted.

"HA HA," I texted back.

I wanted to stay. But wheels had been set in motion in Iran.

Ali had arranged for a friend to take Pouyan to Tehran from Babol and then an older married couple was taking him to Istanbul.

CHAPTER EIGHTEEN

I landed in London and took off again the next day for Istanbul, excited that finally I'd be reunited with my little son.

Except he wasn't so little anymore. My sweet, tiny boy now had a wisp of a mustache, more like a caterpillar, on his upper lip. He was still slight and small for his age—but I was now the mother of a teenager. I couldn't help thinking of my own rebelliousness during my teenage years. But that didn't matter. I wanted to shout and sing and dance when I saw him. I had my son with me at last, and no one was going to take him away from me.

There was awkwardness. He resisted my attempts to embrace and kiss him at first. "You are embarrassing me," he protested, struggling to get away from me. "I'm all grown up."

I wanted to spend a few days in Istanbul to meet with friends and other journalists who had escaped the crackdown in Iran—and to bond with Pouyan. I hadn't been a full-time mom for many years, and it dawned on me that there was a lot to learn about my son. I bought him chocolate ice cream—everyone likes ice cream. Immediately, after one mouthful, Pouyan started sneezing. After the fourth or fifth sneeze, I looked at him quizzically.

"I'm allergic to chocolate," he said. "I love it, but I sneeze all the time." And he sneezed again.

"When did this begin? Why didn't I know about it?"

"Maybe you didn't buy me chocolate."

What else didn't I know about my own son? I wondered. I wanted to make up for all the years I'd not had him with me and create happy memories for us. I took him to Hagia Sophia, the Christian cathedral that became an imperial mosque and is now a museum. It wasn't that I had suddenly turned religious, but I wanted to show Pouyan how sophisticated I had become. It's funny how all I cared about was impressing my son. After lining up for quite a long time, we edged our way inside. Immediately I noticed the circular calligraphy panels that hang from the columns, containing the names of Allah; the Prophet Muhammad; his four caliphs, Abu Bakr, Umar, Uthman, and Ali; and Muhammad's grandchildren Hussein and Hassan. The names are in gold on black backgrounds. The Islamic art stood in striking contrast to the Orthodox Christian imagery of the mosaics: kings and saints with gold halos around them. It was shocking to see Christian and Islamic imagery next to each other. As we left the building, a call to prayer echoed around the square and suddenly I had a sense that I had been transported back to Iran. Only for a moment, though, because all around me were tourists without any head coverings.

Pouyan wasn't excited about museums and soon got bored with doing anything cultural. The next day, I thought I'd really impress him by taking him to Buyukada, one of the islands in the Sea of Marmara and only an hour's journey by ferry. The couple who had brought him from Tehran joined us and acted as our guides since they frequently visited Istanbul. Pouyan stood at the boat railing for the entire journey, transfixed. His first ferry. One unique aspect of Buyukada is that there are no cars on the island, only horse-drawn cabs with red leather seats. We hired one to take us on an hour-long tour. I told Pouyan about my life and my work since I had left Iran. He was my only family now that we were both outside Iran.

"Did you meet Obama?" he asked.

"The timing wasn't right," I said. I really wanted his approval. "Maybe next time."

Pouyan wanted to get to England as quickly as possible. That evening in the hotel, he asked if England was next to Germany.

"I want to go and see Baba Reza," he said. "Maybe I can stay with him."

I felt as if I had been kicked in the stomach. I couldn't really blame him. Pouyan had spent most of his life with his father, but I still felt hurt.

The next day we flew to Britain for our new life together. Once we cleared immigration, our troubles began. My command of English wasn't that great, and even Pouyan could see how often I asked people to repeat themselves before I could understand them. We got lost on the Underground and ended up in Earl's Court, a backpacker haven full of betting shops, fast-food joints, and liquor stores, not quite what Pouyan had expected. We lugged our heavy suitcases up two flights of stairs to the street level, only to discover that we were at the wrong station. After getting detailed instructions from Leila, we caught two different buses before we arrived in her neighborhood. Pouyan looked beat. He and I got kebab sandwiches at a fast-food diner, and since I love onions, I ordered extra onions for both sandwiches. Afterward, Pouyan confided that he hated onions and was almost sick in the diner. I had lived by myself for nine years without worrying about taking care of anyone else. Being a mother was tougher than I thought. Eventually, we reached Leila's apartment. Her son, Parsa, was eighteen months or so younger than Pouyan, and the two of them became fast friends and retired to Parsa's room.

"I don't think I can be a mother again," I confided to Leila. "I really wanted to have my son back, but now that I have him, I'm afraid. How do *you* manage it? I've got to cook every day? And I hate cooking."

There was another reason I was nervous. I'd always wanted my life to be impactful. I saw myself as a writer, a journalist, an activist. Iran was a mess, and this was a critical time. I wanted to make a difference.

"You'll get the hang of it pretty soon," Leila said

Even before my divorce, I'd been the breadwinner and hated being the stay-at-home mother. There was no escaping my new reality: I had to learn to be a mother to a teenager.

"I have to raise my son and earn a living by myself in a foreign country," I said in a panic. "I barely speak English myself."

I wanted to live close to Leila, but I had registered to get a university degree in Oxford and had to find a place there as soon as possible. I had to enroll Pouyan in a school pretty soon.

"You'll get the hang of it," Leila repeated.

"But when?" The more I thought about it, the more anxious I became.

After two days with Leila and Parsa, we took a bus from London to Oxford. I rented a room with a double bed for us to sleep in while I looked for something more permanent. I registered at Brookes University but had no idea how to find a school for Pouyan. As for finding a proper home, it was a struggle—real estate agents wanted letters of reference, my work history, and pay stubs. I didn't have anything like that.

"We have a nice house, but it's so small I keep crashing into Masih," Pouyan said to his grandmother on the phone.

Our room was rather narrow. I wondered if I'd made the right decision. A few weeks earlier I had addressed ten thousand Iranians in San Francisco, and only a few months before that, I had sat alongside Mousavi and former president Khatami at one of the most important political gatherings in recent history. Before the current political climate, I was a prominent columnist at an important newspaper, *Etemad Melli*, with all doors open to me. Now my newspaper had been shuttered, my friends arrested, and I couldn't even rent an apartment.

News from Iran continued to be bleak. A number of antigovernment protesters who had been detained at Tehran's Kahrizak prison had been killed, and some of the younger ones had been raped by guards. Every week more advisers to Mousavi and Karroubi were arrested. More than one hundred journalists and bloggers were jailed. Even though I wrote for a number of Iranian online publications, money was going to be tight. I asked my brother Mohsen to sell all my possessions left behind and transfer the money to Oxford so I could pay my tuition.

Amid the chaos around me, my thirty-third birthday snuck up on me. I had no desire or inclination to celebrate. I was far away from friends and family, forced into exile in a strange country. It was just Pouyan and me in a small room where we sat on the floor to eat. We ate a lot of McDonald's and other sandwiches because they were cheap and easy and required no cooking. I hadn't been paid for a while and my savings were running out.

Around noon on my birthday, there was a knock on our door. A deliveryman handed me a purple orchid in a ceramic vase and a giant box that contained all kinds of exotic fruits—pineapples, mangoes, kiwis—as well as pears and apples and plums. It was my birthday present from Kambiz. That basket of fruit lifted my mood immediately. No one had ever given me fruit as a birthday present. It was just perfect. Pouyan and I headed to the river that runs through Oxford for a picnic.

"You have friends who give you fruit?" Pouyan asked as he smashed a coconut on a piece of rock.

My luck changed after my birthday. Soon, through word of mouth, I found an Iranian couple who were renting out a house in the village of Kidlington, just five miles north of Oxford. They didn't ask for a reference or employment history. I enrolled Pouyan in a school nearby and settled down to life as a student, journalist, and mother.

I was deeply conscious that I was building a home and a new life for my son and myself while my country was in disarray. I now had my son close to me, but every day I interviewed mothers whose sons had been killed or arrested and most likely tortured. This dichotomy between my own life and the lives of these mothers weighed heavily on my mind. It was totally irrational, but I felt guilty because of the good fortune of having my son with me.

Pouyan spoke no English, so his school assigned a special teacher to work with him on his language skills, even as he attended class with other students. My life fell into a routine of sorts—I'd get up early every morning and call sources and contacts in Iran before feeding Pouyan breakfast and taking him to school. After that, I'd head to university, where I was working toward a degree in media studies.

I'd write my articles between classes in the cafeteria or in the evening once I'd fed Pouyan.

His teachers had asked me to read to him every night. My own English was not great, but it was at least better than his. I'd lie in bed with him and read. One night after I finished reading, I looked over and saw tears rolling down Pouyan's cheeks. I didn't think the story was particularly tragic, but he seemed to be moved by it.

"I'm so proud of you for paying attention to the end," I said, and gave him a hug.

"I'm crying because I didn't understand a word of what you were reading to me."

I tried to reassure him that if he worked hard enough, he'd pick the language up quickly. But he was not convinced.

"Isn't there some powder you can give me, like the vitamins you mix in water for me, so I can learn English?"

There were no magic pills or powders. I wanted special powers of my own so I didn't have to cook. Actually, I wanted a magic powder for Pouyan so he could cook for himself. He had seen me struggle in the kitchen and was keen on cooking for himself. There wasn't time to cook a proper meal every evening, and so our dinners sometimes consisted of pasta and pizza or rice and boiled chicken legs. I think my lack of enthusiasm in the kitchen encouraged Pouyan to learn to cook.

A year or so later, I attended Pouyan's school play. This time it was my turn to cry. Pouyan was onstage and his English was so good that I couldn't understand him. He played three different characters, and his drama teacher sought me out afterward to congratulate me. On the way home, Pouyan asked, in all seriousness, "Do you think you could work on your English? When you go on the radio, your accent is..."

"WHAT?" I screamed at him. "How dare you mock my English? I remember one night, because you couldn't—"

Pouyan didn't allow me to finish. "I don't remember," he said.

A few weeks after I had settled in Oxford, Kambiz flew to London to visit me. Anyone who sends pineapples for a birthday present can't be all that bad, I thought. I wanted Leila and her husband to check him out. They were my closest friends in England, and I had a feeling Kambiz was serious.

He wore a blue blazer over a white tee shirt and jeans and was checking his watch to see if I was late when I pulled in front of him in my used silver Ford hatchback and honked the horn. He did a double take when he saw the car.

"I thought you were poor. What happened?" he said as he buckled himself in.

"My paychecks arrived, and this is now the man in my life." I tapped the steering wheel. "Why do I need anyone as long as I have a car?"

"Where are we going now?"

"One of my favorite places in the whole world," I said as I pulled into a cemetery.

"How romantic…"

"Cemeteries are full of history and the dead don't talk back."

Even in Iran, I liked to visit cemeteries and walk among the graves and watch the mourners. The British were more reserved; there were fewer crying families. I spent hours at cemeteries, reading tombstones, trying to imagine the lives of the people buried around me; I always left a cemetery more energized, more determined to live life to the fullest.

"You better be on your best behavior," I warned him. "You are meeting Pouyan and Leila."

"I'll behave, but what about you?"

"I'm allowed to misbehave."

He charmed everyone. Pouyan was still young and was more interested in watching *The Lord of the Rings* on TV. After dinner, I drove Kambiz to the London Eye, across from Waterloo Station, to catch a train. My romance with Kambiz was sealed with a kiss.

"I guess I passed the audition," he said, winking as he left the car. "Next time, let's get together when there's just the two of us."

"I've already gone through one divorce. I don't want to go through that again," I said. "I have my son to think of."

"Understood. I'm in this for the long run. And so are you."

I liked his self-confidence. He was solid, someone I could trust. In December, Pouyan and I flew to New York, where we again stayed with Roozbeh and Solmaz. I spent most of my free time with Kambiz. We were now a couple.

One snowy day, he invited me over to meet his kids, Darya and Bahman, who eyed me suspiciously for one minute before deciding to include me in their role-playing game of fairies and pirates.

"I love your kids more than I care for you," I said. Playing with the children made me forget about the troubles in Iran. I had always wanted more children, and I was now faced with having three of them. "We're going to be a big family, if we make it."

"You passed the test," Kambiz said, grinning. "If the kids didn't like you…" He moved his finger across his throat in a cutting motion.

"All kids love me because I am like them," I said as I punched him in the shoulder. "Just bigger."

I wrote constantly for many publications and appeared on television programs to highlight the crisis. Often I'd be asked to defend Mousavi's tactics, because I wrote for reformist publications, even though I had criticized Mousavi many times before. As always, I wore my black hat, a nod to the hijab rules, and for the sake of my parents. I didn't believe in forced-hijab rules, but I wanted to be respectful of Mother and Agha-Jan. I had to shed my hjijab under the right circumstances, when the time was right.

The government vilified me for these articles and speeches. I was blamed for being behind the 2009 sedition, as the government referred to the protests.

I had started 2009 with hopes of interviewing Obama. In 2010, I was interviewing the families who had lost their loved ones in the crackdown after the Iranian election.

CHAPTER NINETEEN

Iran was in turmoil.

In 2010, my focus turned to highlighting human rights abuses as the protests and the crackdown continued. Much of my work was identifying those who had been arrested, shot, and killed, and interviewing their families. Unearthing this information was not easy. Often the families didn't know for some time that they had lost a loved one. To keep the number of casualties low, the authorities did not release information about those who had been killed. They also told families not to talk to the press and not to hold public funerals. Some families had to bury their dead at night.

But I wanted the world to know and not to avert its eyes. I wasn't the only journalist who was chasing these stories. Masoumeh Ebtekar, the Tehran City Council member, was secretly sending me phone numbers and information about victims of the crackdown. Ebtekar was one of the students involved in the 1979 U.S. embassy occupation. She had gained fame as the spokeswoman for the hostage-takers. She now worked to undermine Ahmadinejad. (Once Rouhani was elected, she stopped cooperating with me and cut me off totally.) Iran state television started producing programs on how I was one of the women behind the sedition. They said that I was making up fictitious deaths. Death threats became a constant feature of my life.

I was so busy I had no time to worry. I would get up in the middle of the night to monitor the news in Iran, and then wake Pouyan up and take him to school before heading to my own university. I would rush back from classes, prepare food for Pouyan, and begin working again. Money was tight, and I turned my living room into another bedroom and rented it out to make ends meet.

One morning, I had been up for a couple of hours working on a story, when Pouyan called out that it was time for me to take him to school. "Mammon...I'm gonna be late," he shouted from downstairs. In the mornings, he made his own breakfast while I worked.

"Coming," I yelled. "Put your coat on and get in the car."

I grabbed my phone and raced downstairs two steps at a time and jumped into the car, still focused on my own work. I drove as if on autopilot and didn't exchange a single word with Pouyan. In five minutes, I pulled up in front of the school. I was in a rush to get back quickly to wrap up the story before going to my own classes.

"Time to get out, sweetie," I said as I turned around. The words froze in my mouth. He was not in the car.

I was so preoccupied that I had driven off to the school without waiting to see if Pouyan was in the car with me. I couldn't believe I had left him behind. I screamed and punched the steering wheel before putting the car into gear and heading back home. Pouyan was standing in front of the house and looked relieved when he saw me.

"Where did you go? I went to pick up my jacket and—"

"Jump in, I went to get milk for your lunch." I wasn't going to tell him I'd forgotten him.

"So, where is the milk?" he asked innocently. "I'll take it with me."

"All they had was chocolate milk, and you're allergic."

Pouyan and I were getting to know each other. We were in a new setting—a new country, for him—and there was no knowing how long I'd be in Britain. I felt guilty for not having enough time for him, but I had to work. As a single mother, I had no choice.

One of the challenges during those days was that the Iranian authorities would pressure the victims of the crackdown not to talk to the émigré journalists, who were the only ones who could write about it without fear of retribution. All Iranian media is controlled by the government, to varying degrees, and Iran-based reporters acted more like cheerleaders than journalists.

Sometimes when a contentious article of mine was published in *JARAS* or *Kalame,* the authorities would pressure those who had given me an interview to retract their comments or deny ever speaking with me. The family would call me, often in tears, and hesitatingly ask if I could make the changes.

"Whatever you want," I told each and every one. "I'm on your side. When you are ready, we can always add those details back in."

Of course, it really hurt to take down an article. One day, I got a call at the university from Ladan Mostafaei, the wife of Ali Hassanpour, one of the victims of 2009. A father of two, he was shot in the face and killed in Azadi Square, but his body was kept by the security forces for 104 days.

I had interviewed Mostafaei for hours, but now she wanted me to edit the story or pull it down. She feared for her own safety; other journalists had warned her that she might get into trouble just for talking to me. It was nonsense, I told her, but I removed the article from the website. I stood by the veracity of my reporting, but the family had been pressured.

Every time this happened, government news sites would accuse me of publishing fiction. Otherwise, they crowed, why remove the offending article?

I started taping all my interviews. Transcribing the tapes was a laborious task that often had me in tears. Adversity forced me to find a solution, and I hit upon the idea of putting all my interviews on SoundCloud, a streaming service that at the time was revolutionary.

I think I was one of the early users of SoundCloud among Iranian journalists. No one else was broadcasting their interviews.

It was in this way that I started creating what later became the largest collection of audio files of interviews with the families of the victims of the 2009 protests.

I had no idea what I had was of any value until one day, Ali Hamedani, a bright BBC Persian reporter, arrived at my house. As I made him a cup of tea, he ran his finger along the windowsill to examine the accumulated dirt and quietly assessed the pile of unwashed dishes in the kitchen sink. I didn't have any other refreshments to offer him.

He offered to buy my collection of audio interviews.

"I can't sell them to you," I told him. "These are stories of loss and pain. I know these families. I've relived their pain. I've cried with them. I can't make money off these tapes."

That afternoon I played one tape after another for him, explaining the backstory of each case, how I'd found the family, what had befallen them since, and how they coped with their loss. Hamedani instead decided to make a program about me, as the keeper of the records of the crimes committed during the protests.

Soon afterward, Niusha Boghrati, the editor in chief of Radio Farda, a Persian-language radio station based in Prague, called to commission me to make a multipart documentary about those who had been killed in the protests.

I knew Niusha from our days in Iran when we were journalists on rival papers.

"I want a half-hour episode about each victim. Everything you can find about their lives and of course their deaths," he said. "We'll broadcast one every week and reruns, too. We can't let the people forget."

He quickly dismissed my protests that I had never made a radio program. "We'll assign you someone to teach you, don't worry."

A week later, I got a ten-minute tutorial on the art of making a radio documentary, and then I was on my own.

I wanted to get away from working for *JARAS, Kalame,* and other reformist publications. Living outside Iran, unfettered by self-censorship and freed of the red lines of the regime, I had moved politically beyond the baby steps proposed by the reformists. One time when I visited Kambiz in New York, a European radio station called to interview me about the continuing protests. I called Kambiz and told him that I wasn't sure my English was good enough, and that I needed some pithy quotes to make news.

"The people voted for change, but their vote was stolen," I told him. "The people are calling for change. What else can I say?"

"Tell them that the people want regime change and you'll be fine," Kambiz said, hanging up quickly.

The interview was short, and I thought it went well. I gave it very little thought till later that evening, when I received a call from Iran. Karroubi's son was not happy.

"You called for regime change. Have you lost your mind?" he asked. "We want Ahmadinejad to go. We don't want to remove the Islamic Republic."

I realized that Kambiz had tricked me. When I called him on it, he just burst out laughing.

"I didn't think you'd go ahead with it. Besides, you can't have a little change. You need to change the whole edifice, not tinker with the decoration."

For me, human rights were universal and not just limited to my own political group. I wanted to write about the female Mojahedin prisoners who were kept inside with their children. I thought it was a huge human rights violation. The editor in chief of *JARAS* thought that I should focus only on reformist prisoners. After a shouting match or two, I quit. I left *Kalame* at around the same time.

Money was going to be even tighter with my income limited to the Radio Farda programs and freelance pieces. I started making what turned out to be a fifty-seven-part documentary, consisting at first of a weekly half-hour radio program devoted to the life and death of each one of the victims. This had a big impact, with each episode including audio from the family, interviews, and my own narrative.

I was living on nicotine and coffee. When I sat down to work, only one thing calmed me, and that was cigarettes. Every morning, my in-box was full of painful messages, news of someone being tortured, someone missing or in a secret detention center. My head was filled with the voices of mothers crying as they told me in painful detail how their son or daughter was killed. They recounted the humiliation the family underwent to get their child's body back. Sometimes the father would speak. When I listened to their tales of loss, I'd light up a Marlboro Menthol just to steady myself. Sometimes I smoked one after another even as I was crying. It was my only vice, I told myself, because I didn't drink. Pouyan hated the smell of tobacco, and I took care to open all the windows and blow the smoke outside when he was at school. At other times, I'd sneak out on an errand just to smoke a cigarette. Like all smokers, I carried lots of chewing gum and mint to cover the smell.

One day, I stood by my bedroom window, smoking a cigarette and blowing the smoke out, when I saw Pouyan walking home with his friends. I'd lost track of time. I quickly threw the cigarette away, sprayed myself with perfume, opened more windows, and started waving my arms to clear the air. When Pouyan came home from school I was so frazzled that I called out, "Hi, sweetie, you want your cigarette now or later?" I'd meant to ask him if he was hungry.

His friends burst out laughing.

"I hate smoking, Mum," he said, hugging me when I got downstairs. "You think I don't know you smoke?"

Each episode of the documentary took a lot out of me. My room felt like a morgue. A digital morgue filled with tales of torture and death. All my stories were about prisoners, victims of the Islamic Republic's brutal clampdown on the opposition.

Parvin Fahimi became a major presence in my life for months and months. She was the mother of Sohrab Arabi, a nineteen-year-old pro-democracy student who went out one day to demonstrate against the election results and never came home. As Parvin told me, she assumed that he had been arrested. She went to the authorities but found no answers. Every day, clutching a picture of Sohrab, the youngest of four brothers, she climbed the steep hill to Evin prison, meeting other families also gathered there. "I'd wait outside, and as soon as a prisoner was released I'd run over and ask if they'd seen my Sohrab," she said. "I even made a video and posted it online on YouTube."

After twenty-six days of shuttling between prisons, hospitals, and courthouses, she was summoned to the Revolutionary Court and asked to identify her son from among sixty photographs of bodies. She was then shown a coroner's report, dated June 19, which said that her son had died of a gunshot wound to the chest. He had disappeared on June 15.

Parvin described her love for Sohrab in detail to me. His death was killing her; her pain was raw and visible. And she wasn't the only one.

With every article, interview, Facebook post, the chances of my returning to Iran became dimmer. I had hoped that somehow a solution to the political crisis could be found, but the situation grew more grim with each passing day. In February 2011, I received a panicked call from one of Mousavi's daughters. Security forces had come to arrest her father. I was the first reporter to break the news that Mousavi and Karroubi, the leaders of the Green Movement, had been put under house arrest. Many expected another wave of protests to be unleashed, but nothing happened.

To keep our long-distance relationship going, Kambiz and I would take turns flying to see each other. My routine in Kidlington was to take all my interviews and notes and occupy a corner at the Costa coffee shop, a Starbucks rival. Everyone there knew me because I'd often end up crying as I typed my notes and listened to my interviews. One week, Kambiz came during a particularly difficult period. I had a breakdown and couldn't face listening to another family. I told Niusha that I was going to quit the Radio Farda program.

"You've recorded thirty episodes," Kambiz said, holding me gently, as if I might break in his arms. I looked gaunt, weighing less than a hundred pounds. We were standing in line at Costa.

"Thirty-two, if you are counting," I said. I could not be consoled.

"Think of it as making history. You are making their history. You'll bring them to life; their families will always remember you."

"I know all that, but listening to their cries, stories of pain and loss..."

"You get the coffees and I'll hook you up," Kambiz said. He was determined that I finish.

I returned to my corner seat with two lattes. Kambiz looked pale and was busy wiping tears from his face.

"What happened?"

"I just listened to about thirty seconds. That's all I could take. I don't know how you can listen to their pain."

I patted his arm gently. As long as he was with me, I could handle it.

The series, called *The Victims of 88,* a reference to the Iranian calendar year 1388 (2009), when the election and the protests took place, won an AIB International Media Excellence award in the category of Investigative Documentary/Radio in November 2013. It was like winning an Oscar for international radio programs. At the award ceremony, I burst into tears when the announcer read the judges' commendation: "Superb research is its foundation." I continued crying throughout the gala reception, the tension of the past two years pouring out of me. In all the photographs from that night, I look as if I'm in mourning, with red, blotchy eyes and a dripping nose.

While making the program, I'd hit upon the idea of reaching out to the Islamic Republic officials and asking them to account for their actions. This may sound routine for those living in the West. In the Islamic Republic, asking tough questions was dangerous. In Iran, journalists never really challenged those holding the reins of power: the heads of security services, the Revolutionary Guards, the clerics, the top ayatollahs sitting on secret committees. But now I was out-side their reach, and all I needed was their personal mobile numbers. I decided to go after Saeed Mortazavi, the prosecutor general who had interrogated me in Tehran. The Butcher of the Press had by now shut down more than one hundred publications.

This time, I held the upper hand. He could not threaten me with prison, or shut my newspaper down, or grill me about my private life. He was under pressure, and I surprised him by calling him on his private line. Even if he slammed the phone down on me, that itself was newsworthy, and I could make a short, quick radio hit. But he didn't slam down the phone. Instead he engaged in a conversation.

The sound of his voice made my throat dry up. Here was a man responsible for arresting and torturing hundreds of protesters, someone who was implicated in the death of the Iranian-Canadian photographer Zahra Kazemi. And he had interrogated me for five days. I saw myself back in the interrogation room, and even though he was in Iran and I was in Oxford, my hand was shaking as I spoke to this thug thousands of miles away. Nevertheless, this time I was the questioner. And I was not alone. Friends were downstairs in the kitchen, cooking a meal, oblivious to my tussle with Mortazavi.

"How do you like being called a murderer?" I asked. "You are the most hated man in Iran. How do you feel about that?"

"You are counterrevolutionary," he said in an oily voice. "I'll grant an interview under one condition: Return to your country and re-pent. You'll be treated fairly."

"If I return, what guarantee is there that I won't end up dead like Zahra Kazemi?" I asked.

"If you repent, there'll be no problem."

"But you were the one who interrogated Zahra Kazemi, and she ended up dead."

He hung up. I stumbled downstairs and collapsed on a sofa. My friends made sweetened tea for me as I told them of the encounter.

I broadcast my interview on my own Facebook page, and BBC Persian rebroadcast it. For the first time, Iran's chief prosecutor had responded to a journalist in the diaspora. Iranian authorities had rarely given interviews to or engaged with journalists outside the country. They regard these journalists as the enemy. Islamic Republic authorities prefer to engage with reporters who can be bullied and threatened with jail or worse.

I joined Voice of America as a contributor, providing special segments mixing satire and politics. With this platform, I started a new trend of calling Islamic Republic officials on their private mobile numbers. Their numbers were sent to me by disgruntled lower-ranking officials.

AghaJan still refused to speak with me. When I left Iran, he turned his back on me. He also wanted me to repent for my opposition to the Supreme Leader. Until then, no communication. Even Mother refused to talk to me when he was around. Ali and Mohsen were on my side, but it was painful not talking to my parents. Ali kept them abreast of what I was doing. But news of my activities often reached them via other means.

"Sometimes I'm too late. One of the neighbors has already told Mother," Ali said proudly.

Times had changed in Ghomikola. Our neighbors had invested in satellite dishes and were watching banned television programs like VOA's Persian service. My most famous call was to Ayatollah Ahmad Khatami, a hard-liner and Tehran's Friday prayer leader. He had once said the country had to shed blood, if needed, to safeguard compulsory hijab. So I called him and asked him to explain what exactly he meant. Without giving me a chance to introduce myself, he blurted out the standard line—how compulsory hijab was part of the country's Islamic faith.

"But we are seeing women being attacked and beaten. Is that what you had in mind?"

There was a pause. He had never been challenged by a journalist before in his life.

"Where are you calling from? Which news organization?"

When I introduced myself, he went apoplectic.

"How dare you! How dare you call me? You are counterrevolutionary," he screamed. "You can't call me!" And he slammed the phone down.

I worried about his health. I thought he was having a heart attack.

The audio clip of the interview went viral on the Internet among Iranians and was passed hand to hand inside the country, saved on flash drives. Khatami—no relation to the former president—was a regime thug, threatening young people from his bully pulpit every Friday. Every Iranian enjoyed hearing him get his comeuppance.

By 2012, I was on three different diaspora television stations— I reported exclusive breaking news stories for Manoto, a new TV channel launched in London, and did weekly segments for VOA and occasional analysis pieces for BBC Persian.

I graduated from Oxford Brookes University that same year, after three years of study. In Iran, I had been denied a chance to finish high school and attend a university, and for years I'd been hurt by insults that I was "uneducated," but none of that mattered as I calmly climbed up to the stage in my graduation gown, my mortarboard precariously balanced on my head. Kambiz flew from New York for the occasion. I beamed at him as he filmed the ceremony on his mobile phone. More than anyone else, I wanted him to be with me at this moment, and he hadn't let me down. He was the rock in my life. He "got" me—he understood my need to be hyper and jump around and sing aloud in the streets. I asked for his advice first, and he was the person I listened to most.

With one caveat. I listened, but I didn't always follow his advice.

After graduation I applied for a U.S. visa to spend the summer with Kambiz in New York, as a sort of a trial run to see if we could move in together. He kept talking about marriage, but I didn't want to ruin our love by getting tied down with a formal contract. I had gone to New York many times during our courtship, and so I booked my flight even before my visa appointment at the U.S. embassy.

The interview was a breeze. The agent smiled cheerfully as we chatted about life, my graduation, and summer in New York. I was full of excitement about the next phase of my life. Within a few minutes we were done and he handed me back my passport. I quickly looked to double-check the visa stamp mark. Then I had the bright idea of confiding in him.

"My partner and I have been talking, just talking, about getting married," I said, grinning to let him know that the marriage plans were not entirely serious. "Would it be easier to get married here or get married in New York?"

"Your... your partner is a U.S. citizen?"

"Sure, he's..."

"You plan to get married?"

"He talks about it, but we haven't decided. I want to live with him first before deciding," I babbled.

"Can I have your passport back for a second, please?"

He stamped my passport again. He had canceled my visa.

"If you are thinking of getting married, you should apply for a fiancée or a marriage visa."

I was speechless and walked out, not quite sure what had just happened. I was almost on my way to New York, but now my application had been denied. I walked out of the embassy in a daze, and then it dawned on me what had happened. I let out a loud scream and hurled my passport back at the embassy wall. I sat down on the pavement and called Kambiz. It was early morning in New York, and I woke him up.

"It's your fault for living in that stupid country," I said, sobbing. I was angry. "They denied my application."

He didn't need to tell me that I had goofed royally.

"They thought I was trying to sneak into the country. I've never been denied before."

"We should get married first, then apply."

"I'm not getting married just to get a stupid visa. I'm not coming to America." I turned my phone off for the rest of the day.

I went to Leila's house and sobbed for a long time. I had been so excited at the idea of moving to New York, but now everything was up in the air. Kambiz flew over a week or so later. I couldn't visit him anymore, so he had to fly to London to see me every six weeks or so.

A year later, I went back to the U.S. embassy, this time with Pouyan, to apply for another tourist visa.

The immigration agent asked one question

"Are you still with the same partner?"

Pouyan gave me a soft kick in the shin. "Mom, give the right answer."

"Yes, I am."

The agent denied the application again. "You should apply for a fiancée visa."

I called Kambiz with the bad news. I had lost my enthusiasm for moving to New York.

"All you had to do was say you were no longer seeing me and you'd have gotten the visa."

"I'm not going to deny that we are together."

"It's not a denial," Kambiz said. "Why couldn't you have had amnesia for five minutes?"

"I couldn't physically bring myself to. I'm not going to lie."

It may sound pathetic, but it was true. Another year in the UK. Pouyan and I moved to London's Kew Gardens, full of green space and lots of trees and the massive botanical gardens of the same name.

CHAPTER TWENTY

In the 2013 presidential elections in Iran, reformists rallied around Hassan Rouhani, a so-called moderate. He went from outside candidate to outright winner in a field of six candidates in a matter of two weeks after promising to relax many social restrictions. A cleric with an easy laugh, he also promised to free the political prisoners, especially Mousavi and Karroubi. He was a regime insider involved in key security decisions. But in Iran, the elections are always a choice between bad, worse, and disaster. He was presented as the best of a bad bunch, and a number of reformist activists approached me to back him publicly. I couldn't in good faith advise anyone to back Rouhani or any candidate.

But I agreed to be silent and not to endorse a boycott movement. The day after the election, when it became clear that Rouhani had won, Tehran exploded in spontaneous parties. That week, my heart ached. I really missed Tehran; I wanted to be dancing in the street with my own people, honking my car horn, and hugging my friends and families. I didn't care that the Rouhani victory was a triumph of bad over worse; I missed Iran. I missed holding and kissing my mother; I missed exchanging gossip with my brother Mohsen and talking politics with Ali. I hadn't seen my mother for five years. And I couldn't see a way that I'd be able to.

"I can't see how you could go back to Iran," Kambiz said one night in London during one of his regular visits. "You've managed to annoy every political group. The clerics hate you, the royalists hate you, and the lefties hate you."

He was right. On my last trip to New York, in January 2012, I began to consider the idea of interviewing Reza Pahlavi, the son of the last shah of Iran. I tried the idea out on Kambiz.

"If you were advising Reza Pahlavi, how would you deal with an interview request from me?" I asked Kambiz in my most charming voice.

"I'd tell him no. I'd tell him to avoid you at all costs."

"How could you? And you call yourself a journalist? You are supposed to be on my side, on the side of the press," I said, mocking him.

"If I'm to be an honest adviser, I'd have to warn him that he'll come off second best."

I was livid. I picked up my mobile and called Pahlavi's office right there and then. After a few rings, his secretary answered.

"I'm Masih Alinejad, and I'm a freelance reporter. I wanted to arrange an interview with Mr. Pahlavi," I said. Many Iranians call him "His Highness," but I just couldn't bring myself to do it.

"He's not available, but we'll get back to you."

"Even if he agrees, it'll be for some time in the distant future, and you'll be back in Oxford," said Kambiz. "That was a call for nothing."

Three minutes later, the secretary called me back.

"His Highness will be happy to grant you an interview. Are you available next week?"

The look on Kambiz's face was priceless. "I heard her, but I can't believe he agreed."

I didn't want an interview for my website. The way to get maximum exposure was to make a video report. But the established Iranian television stations didn't want to commission me. At the time, I had no experience as a TV journalist or as a documentary filmmaker.

I called on Hasan Sarbakhshian, the former AP photo editor in Tehran, now based in Washington, to be my video cameraman. At Pahlavi's ranch, his secretary balked when she saw our camera equipment. The interview was not to be filmed, she said. "No one told us you'd bring a cameraman."

I had to bluff my way in. "You didn't think I would arrive here from the UK just for a print interview? If this is a problem, I'm happy to cancel our arrangement."

Reluctantly she agreed to let Hasan record the interview. Reza Pahlavi was all too happy with the camera. He wanted to be seen among the younger generation of Iranians who were my audience. He didn't ask for questions in advance; nor did he ask to check his quotes or see the final edit. He didn't blanch when I asked him how he felt about the fact that some Iranians hated his family.

"My father did a lot of good for this country as well," he said calmly. The Pahlavis created the modern Iran. "I'm not worried about history's judgment."

I put the interview on my own social media channels, on YouTube and Facebook, where I knew it'd be viewed many times. I got a great deal of abuse from supporters of the Islamic Republic but far more from Pahlavi supporters. My crime: I hadn't referred to Pahlavi as "Your Highness."

I like to make my own path, even if the rest of the world is against me.

I was getting comfortable in London and had my circle of friends and my routines. Kambiz still visited regularly, but we had to make a decision about our relationship. On one of his visits, in the spring of 2014, he dragged me out on a shopping trip lasting hours, even though we ended up buying nothing. We found ourselves at the tail end of King's Road, the chic artery of Chelsea. I was famished and tired and wanted to go home and have a long bath and then surf the Internet.

Kambiz suggested that we instead have an early dinner at some nearby restaurant. As we waited at the bar, the maître d' came over.

"Do you want to go to your table now, or do you want to wait for the other guests?"

"Later," Kambiz hissed and waved her away.

"What other guests?" I asked, suddenly alarmed. I hate surprises.

"Let me get you a coke. You must be very tired," Kambiz said. He looked guilty. Then it dawned on me. He had something planned.

"You are going to PROPOSE? No...no...you know I hate surprises. I'm leaving." I started for the door.

Kambiz grabbed my arm and led me to our table. "I've invited lots of our friends."

"Call it off. I'll call it off." I started phoning friends who obviously would have been invited and told them not to bother coming. Most were on their way and refused to turn back.

Kambiz had a smug look on his face. "I've even got a ring," he said, and burst out laughing.

"I'm not ready yet. Don't propose today. I'll be too embarrassed and may say no. I'll be stressed."

"The only way for us to be together is if we get married now or you get a fiancée visa," he said.

"Let's go for the visa."

When our friends arrived, there was no mention of a marriage proposal or a ring.

That night we applied for a fiancée visa.

CHAPTER TWENTY-ONE

In April, the howling winds ceased their screams, the icy rains stopped their pelting, and the dark clouds departed for even gloomier terrain. Finally, the skies over London cleared up and I could even spy bits of blue and hints of a golden sun. Spring was trying to break out at last. My mood also improved because Kambiz came over on his way to Vienna to cover the nuclear talks between Iran and the world powers. For the next two years, he often traveled to Vienna or Geneva to cover the negotiations, which had started the previous October. There was another reason for my happiness. My fiancée visa had been approved. Finally, I could move to New York. Of course, it only brought the idea of marriage that much closer. To be honest, I feared getting married again. I liked my independence and wanted to focus all my attention on my writing and on my work as a campaigning journalist.

"Marriage will kill our love," I told Kambiz. "Once people get married they are crushed by the daily chores."

Kambiz was used to my anti-marriage views.

"Let's see if we can stand each other after a couple of months, and then we'll make a decision."

I knew he was joking, but I was still racked with fears. I introduced him to all my friends and dared them to find his flaws. They all loved him. Even my family in Ghomikola and my brothers in Tehran were on his side, literally begging him not to give up on me. My mother, of all people, kept telling me to count my blessings. She'd take every occasion to lecture me on how I should learn to be an "obedient wife" and take care of my future husband.

"I say a prayer every day so that Kambiz's shadow will always protect you," Mother said. "You are lucky to have someone willing to marry you."

"I don't need a man to look after me. Don't keep saying this, it's embarrassing."

I was a women's rights activist and campaigner and my mother kept encouraging me to learn to cook and take better care of my future husband.

Mother also said AghaJan was relieved that I had a fiancé.

Spring in London can be quite energizing. Walking with Kambiz around the enchanting streets of Kew Gardens, I marveled at the pink cherry blossoms everywhere. I couldn't contain myself. I had a bounce in my step, a surge of energy, and I started running back and forth, gathering the pink blossoms that had fallen and throwing them up in the air and laughing like a kid. It was just fun to feel the warmth of the sun on my skin, the wind running through my hair; it was good to be alive. Kambiz was clicking away with his camera. My mood lifted.

I needed a change. For some time now, my writing had been about despair, the loss of my home in Iran, the detention and deaths of protesters. Although I had finished *The Victims of 88,* I was still covering human rights violations in the Islamic Republic in 2014. They had continued unabated despite the election of Rouhani a year earlier. Even Pouyan complained that my laptop contained too many stories of death and torture. Sometimes I had nightmares of blood seeping out of my laptop.

I wanted to write about my joy at being free to run and jump and shout and sing. I wanted to write about the parts of my life that were joyful. One day I flipped through recent photos and selected one of the ones that Kambiz had taken of me running freely in a street filled with cherry blossoms. I wore a bright orange down jacket, my arms held open, ready to embrace the world, the wind blowing through my hair.

On my Facebook page, I wrote a simple message:

> Whenever I'm running free and my hair is dancing in the wind, I remember that I come from a country where for thirty-odd years my hair has been taken hostage by those in power in the Islamic Republic. I know that the streets in Iran will miss me, miss my joyful presence, miss my rapid footsteps, miss my dance, miss my laughter. Of this I am sure.
>
> I come from a country where for thirty-odd years no one has been able to free their hair from the hands of the hostage takers, who keep saying, "The time is not right."

That simple photograph and message changed my life.

I had deliberately used the term "hostage," which obviously is full of meaning; the Islamic Republic had solidified its rule in 1979 through the management of the hostage crisis. The Islamic Republic had turned my hair into a hostage—and not just my hair but the hair of all Iranian women.

I had always found compulsory hijab one of the annoying attributes of the Islamic Republic, but when I was living there I could only gripe privately. It was a red line for the regime. As a journalist, I could push the boundaries a little bit, and in private sessions I gently probed the issue with senior political figures like former presidents Khatami and Rafsanjani; but all of them had dismissed my concerns. It was not a big deal, they said. "There are bigger issues that require fixing first." They all wanted to fix society's ills but didn't have time to listen to what women wanted. I could see that social freedoms for women just weren't on the agenda. Inside Iran, I had to obey the red lines and know when to back off. It was when I left the country that I realized how important the issue of compulsory hijab was for ordinary women. It irked me that Iran's Muslim neighbors in the region—Turkey, Pakistan, Azerbaijan, Turkmenistan, Iraq, Lebanon, Syria—did not enforce such a restrictive practice.

I had more than two hundred thousand Facebook fans, and my cherry blossom post almost immediately created a huge volume of comments. I seemed to have touched a nerve among my readers. My photo and the accompanying message were shared again and again, on Facebook and other social media sites. Even more interesting, a heated discussion took place in the comments section. I'm an advocate of creating online conversations, in getting people talking and bringing political transformation through shifting the culture so that reforms become permanent. I was very happy about the dialogue I had created on Facebook about compulsory hijab. Here was a forum for ordinary women, as opposed to women activists, to speak freely about the oppressive nature of compulsory hijab. The big surprise was that some women also posted photographs of themselves without the hijab in the comments section.

But I had more immediate concerns. On April 17, I was on my way to do some errands with Pouyan when my mobile rang. The moment I heard the voice on the other end, the hairs on my arms stood up. The call was from Ward 350, one of the wings inside the notorious Evin prison. I recognized the caller's voice: Siamak Ghaderi, a former top editor at IRNA now serving a four-year sentence for criticizing human rights abuses during the 2009 post-election protests.

Ghaderi's voice was shaking with rage. In the background were all sorts of screams and sickening sounds of violence. He described a chilling tale of almost one hundred security men in riot gear entering Ward 350 "for inspection." Prisoners were ordered to leave their cells. They resisted, saying that they wanted to be present during the searches. That's because on previous occasions, personal items had gone missing, and the prisoners didn't trust the authorities. When the prisoners refused to leave, the guards charged them with batons, whacking them on their legs, on their arms, and even on their heads, dragging some along the floor, ripping their clothes and beating them. Some prisoners were blindfolded and handcuffed before being beaten. More than thirty were injured; many had broken ribs and skulls, and four were injured so badly that they were transferred to a hospital outside the prison. The rest of the injured ended up in solitary confinement rather than being taken to the hospital.

Ghaderi told me this and much more. The guards were specifically looking for mobile phones that had been smuggled in, like the one that Ghaderi was using to call me. Ghaderi and a human rights lawyer, also imprisoned, agreed to be interviewed from inside Evin. I had a firsthand account of prison brutality.

I'm not the most tech-savvy person. I put my mobile next to my laptop's microphone to tape the interview. Pouyan, who had been standing in the doorway throughout my phone conversation, just rolled his eyes. "If people knew how you operated, no one would ever call you," he whispered, with the easy arrogance of teenagers toward their parents. I shushed him away but he stayed, quite clearly affected by the story emanating from my phone. Ghaderi and the lawyer, whose name I must protect, recounted the day's events again, for me to record.

"Were you just speaking with someone in jail?" Pouyan asked when I was through with the call.

"Yes, from Evin," I said distractedly, as I tried to write up my notes.

"How come they called you from inside of Evin prison?"

"People smuggle mobile phones inside jails and the guards can't find them all."

"How come in all of Iran, with all the organizations and all the journalists that are based there, these prisoners call you? Isn't there anyone in Iran who can help them? You are in London!"

Of course, there were organizations in Iran that cared for prisoners' welfare and journalists who were interested in covering this news. But the reality was that no publication in Iran would dare report on prison brutality. There are many red lines, and crossing them will get you in deep trouble. Writing about political prisoners is a red line, since the authorities deny having any political prisoners. If journalists tackled the subject, then they might end up in Evin themselves.

"I'm outside the country and the authorities cannot touch me. No one's going to arrest me, and it's my responsibility to spread the news."

I called BBC Persian and told them I had voices from inside Evin. BBC reporters didn't have the same contacts I did, and the editors quickly agreed that I should do a special program on the prison. The next day, as Kambiz and I sat on the Underground, another call came from Evin. We quickly rushed out of the train. I was juggling my backpack, my iPhone, and my laptop—something had to give. The laptop went flying and crashed to the ground and I fell on top of it. I was in agony, but the laptop looked in worse shape.

All my freelance money now had to go toward a new laptop. Not for the first time, I had taken one step forward and two steps back. I was mad at myself for my clumsiness.

"I promise I'll be more careful from now on," I said.

"Till next time," Kambiz said, rolling his eyes. He was getting used to my losing phones and credit cards and breaking electronic devices. In fact, less than a year later, I knocked a glass of water over my beautiful MacBook Air. But that's another story.

Although the Evin stories were sensational and received a great deal of publicity, the readership never matched the number of viewers of the photograph of me running free in London. That photograph and the accompanying text received more than 14,000 likes, was shared 741 times, and received more than 500 comments. My Facebook critics complained that such freedoms were not available in Iran. True, but millions of Iranian women find ways around the compulsory hijab laws. I knew I had. I found a selfie from my days driving north from Tehran to Ghomikola to prove it.

I wasn't being a rebel. Millions of Iranian women would do the same if there were no morality police. Given half a chance, millions of Iranians would remove their hijab, especially in the privacy of their own cars. I was sure that every Iranian woman had pictures like this, taken in private moments, alone or with friends. One day I even wrote the phrase *azadi yavashaki*—stealthy freedom—and knew every woman in Iran would get it. I just knew it. You cannot be a woman in the Islamic Republic and not be forced to live part of your life *yavashaki*. We think of this as our secret life.

If you are an Iranian woman, you've secretly fallen in love, stealthily removed your head scarf, quietly attended a party, and secretly gone on a trip. All the women who were now sending me their photographs without head scarves knew exactly what they were protesting.

They knew the guilty pleasure of breaking an unjust law. The more time I spent online with these women who were sending me their photographs and videos, risking detention, arrest, and perhaps imprisonment or worse, the more I realized we were all connected. It didn't matter that I was physically not in Iran. We were connected irrespective of class, wealth, profession, or geographical location. As women, we had all faced the same frustrations in the Islamic Republic. We were all required to hide parts of our identities—to keep parts of our true selves hidden. I didn't want to be stealthy anymore.

I posted the photo of me driving in Iran without the hijab on May 1. Again, with a message:

> If you are a woman who doesn't believe in compulsory hijab, no matter where you are you'll create your own Azadi Yavashaki—Stealthy Freedom—so you are not ruined by the weight of coercion and compulsion.
>
> Coercion is not just from the Gasht-e Ershad. Sometimes pressure comes from family, sometimes from the employer; and sometimes there is pressure to conform so we are not judged negatively. I have experienced all these forms of coercion, and I'm willing to bet that the majority of Iranian women who don't believe in compulsory hijab have tasted Azadi Yavashaki.

I'm willing to make another bet that these women have photos of their stealthy freedom moments that don't hurt anyone.

Shall we publish our photos of driving without head scarves, walking without a veil in the woods or by the sea, or on top of a tree or in the desert where we can breathe freely? Here is my stealthy freedom photograph on the Haraz motorway going north.

Almost immediately, a woman sent a photo of herself in a similar pose driving without a head scarf. "Please don't post my name. I'll be arrested," she begged.

I posted that photo on my own page and wrote another comment: "There are those who say hijab is a small concern and the country faces bigger issues. My in-box is full of messages from women who think this is a big concern. Let us respect other people's 'small concerns.'"

In a number of comments, I saw references to Azadi Yavashaki. The term seemed to have a certain appeal among Iranians. Everyone in Iran knew what I was talking about—the moments of small rebellion, the tiny acts of defiance that allow us to breathe, the guilty pleasure of breaking unjust rules that allow us a modicum of dignity. I thought that this was a great name for a new campaign.

As this was going on, a Facebook page called Azadi Yavashaki was created by one of my readers, who made me the administrator of the page. Two days later, on May 3, the Azadi Yavashaki/My Stealthy Freedom page was launched.

I immediately realized that I wanted to make our cause international and started asking friends to translate the text that was coming in. Our page exploded, with a great deal of interest coming both from inside Iran and from the international media.

A hundred years ago, Iranian women participated in public affairs and held important positions in teaching and journalism. Fighting for our rights is not a new phenomenon, even though the issue of hijab had always been a thorny one in Iran. In the 1930s Reza Shah

Pahlavi had banned the hijab as part of his modernization effort. When his son Mohammad Reza ascended to the throne, he did not enforce the ban, and the question of hijab became a matter of personal choice. Iranian women had a choice on the hijab; and they could attain top positions in the country, become cabinet ministers, and even serve as judges. Nobel Peace Prize winner Shirin Ebadi was a judge before the revolution but was demoted to secretary afterward. On March 8, 1979, just a month after the revolution, one hundred thousand women demonstrated against compulsory hijab.

In my own family, all the women wore head scarves, even in bed. But resistance to compulsory hijab is widespread in the country. I was not against hijab but against compulsion. I wanted women to have the freedom to choose.

Our first-ever picture on My Stealthy Freedom was of a tall woman in a cherry-colored knee-length dress over a pair of jeans, standing all alone in the middle of a deserted road. Chinar trees line the road as far as the eye can see. The mysterious woman holds her arms wide apart, as if nailed to an invisible cross, and her head is thrown back so that her face is not quite visible. Her brunette curls fall gently around her. She has no head covering.

We posted another photograph on May 5. The subject is letting go of her head scarf, which appears to be floating in the air. I continued to publish photographs of women throwing off their hijab. I was overwhelmed with the response. I was getting goose bumps as my in-box filled with photographs of brave women. The subjects had a sense of humor. An unveiled young woman stands in front of a sign that reads: SISTERS, OBSERVE YOUR HIJAB. This was the equivalent of giving the finger to the authorities. But with a smile! "Have they ever considered why women stand in front of signs about the hijab, and instead of observing it, take off their scarves?" the young woman wrote.

Another young woman with red hair and dark glasses stands next to the ruins of Persepolis, the capital of ancient Persia. Her message reads: "Freedoms that last only for a few seconds." In another post, two young women without the hijab dance happily on the shores of the Caspian Sea. Of course, the beaches are segregated in Iran. A day later we published group photos of women throwing their head scarves in the air. Something was happening right before our very eyes. In Iran, girls are always brought up to keep their heads low, to be as unobtrusive as possible—to be meek. Women, especially in small cities and villages, are admonished if they attract attention. Most women in Iran are always in low-power poses, but the women sending photographs to My Stealthy Freedom were the opposite— they stood tall, they held their arms aloft, they were showing the world that Iranian women were free, powerful, and not ashamed of their bodies. They were smiling, happy, not scowling—as if through this simple act of rebellion, women could be empowered.

Women who posted their photos without the veil on a public page could be arrested for breaking the law. But these women didn't seem to care. They appeared to relish their brief moments of freedom and defiance. The common theme was: Hijab wasn't my choice, and I want the freedom to choose.

The traffic to the Facebook page soared, going through the proverbial roof. Every day, thousands joined our campaign. Not bad for a niche page. In three days, we had more than 27,000 fans. Manoto TV was the first media organization to cover the campaign in Persian, and on May 7, 2014, Golnaz Esfandiari, a journalist for Radio Free Europe/Radio Liberty, got wind of the campaign and wrote a short piece about it.

Suddenly the media floodgates opened. *Vocative,* an online publication, produced a fabulous package around the campaign, which had received a major boost thanks to a tweet by George Takei, of *Star Trek.*

When I told Kambiz, he was silent—for a moment. "George Takei has tweeted about us? Seriously?" he said incredulously down the telephone from New York. We spoke five or six times on a normal day, but back then we were in continuous contact. "This is Sulu, the guy from *Star Trek?*"

"Who is *Star Trek*?"

"Not who but what. Classic science fiction TV series and Hollywood movies." He paused. "You have no idea what I'm talking about, do you?"

"I only watch *Friends*. *Star Trek, Star Wars, Star* whatever—is your territory. Can you deal with him?"

The workload was intense in the beginning. First, the volume of photographs sent from Iran was overwhelming, and I couldn't just publish any photograph. I had to research each and every one, making sure there were no fakes and no photographs sent without their owners' permission. One false move and we'd lose our credibility. I received a number of photographs from fake accounts. Unsurprisingly, Islamic Republic agents tried many times to discredit us by sending fake photographs.

In that crazy first month, friends like Ahad G., an aristocratic Iranian with a British accent, would drop by with food parcels to feed me. In campaign work, momentum is key. I rushed from one interview to another to explain that our movement was for women's choice. We were not against hijab; we were not against Islam.

"I'm not against hijab. My mother is a traditionalist; she wears the full hijab, as does my sister, but millions of other women don't," I said. As Iranian government–backed attacks on My Stealthy Freedom rocketed, women activists joined the campaign, answering emails, posting on forums, and tweeting nonstop. This was a cultural war, where the battle lines were drawn on social media.

Iranian women were telling the world that if they had the choice, they wouldn't choose hijab. That was the key message from my campaign, which was dangerous to the clerics in Iran. Until then, the Islamic Republic narrative was that Iranian women embraced compulsory hijab. Within three weeks, the page had 350,000 fans.

One of my favorite photos, published around May 20, is of a woman wearing a full-length chador and holding a small whiteboard in front of her face so that only her eyes are visible. Even though, following Iranian law, she is fully veiled, the explosive nature of the statement on the whiteboard makes this an extraordinary image: "I am an Iranian woman and I believe in hijab and at the same time I abhor compulsory hijab."

I spent many sleepless nights, worried that one of my "Stealthies" would be picked up. It never happened.

The government forces were just one of my worries. Even among the groups against the Islamic Republic, there is no agreement on any issue, least of all on hijab. Some radicals thought that I was not going far enough and that I should denounce hijab and Islam. The dogmatic leftists attacked me because they said that the hijab issue was not that important and that I should focus on solving poverty and unemployment. One group accused me of being a spy for Israel, while another accused me of being an agent of the Islamic Republic. Some said that they could not trust me because my parents were serfs and I had worked for reformist newspapers.

I was also never sure who was supposed to be paying me. Some said I was paid by the CIA; others said Israel's Mossad. Another group said that Ayatollah Rafsanjani was behind my campaign. I used to joke that I was owed so much back pay by these spy agencies that I could retire as a multimillionaire. In the real world, I couldn't make ends meet without turning my living room into a bedroom and renting it out.

Another group accused me of hurting Iranian women and setting back the cause of women activists. "Don't you know that freedom cannot be stealthy?" they taunted me.

The attacks got so bad in the first months that I even contemplated ending the whole project. I lost about twenty pounds, my weight falling to around eighty pounds. I was despondent and ready to throw in the towel.

"Are you crazy?" Kambiz said during one of our phone conversations. "Quitting now would be insane. You've just started. The ones who are sending you photographs and personal stories, they are all from inside Iran. They are real and they want you to be their champion."

"Okay, but I'm going to change the name from My Stealthy Freedom to My Clear Freedom, My Explicit Freedom..."

There was a roar of laughter. "I'm glad you got your sense of humor back. That's priceless."

The name stayed.

The truth was that the women I was reaching were not rich or academics or politically active, but they felt the pain of compulsory hijab. They felt humiliated by the morality police who told them to fix their head scarves or wear longer overcoats that reached their ankles. My fans were ordinary women with ordinary desires. They didn't want to solve all of society's problems but wanted to be treated with dignity. This was the first step; the rest would follow.

On one of my posts I wrote:

If by freedom you mean the freedom to always say yes, then that's not freedom. Freedom means being able to say no. If I only have freedom inside the four walls of my room, then that's not much of a freedom. I don't have freedom when I have to be meek, when unjust laws force me to be covered up, to have fewer rights than men, to be denied the right to travel abroad without the permission of my husband, when I am banned from sports stadiums. What worries the Islamic Republic is if women find their voice and talk loudly about their lack of freedoms in a loud voice.

When my critics said freedom cannot be stealthy, I had to be measured and calm. "Of course, freedom cannot be stealthy," I wrote again and again. "When you have thousands of Iranian women protesting in such a public manner, on Facebook and across the world media, there is nothing stealthy about our campaign. The My Stealthy Freedom Facebook page is meant to publicize the freedoms."

A number of political activists complained that compulsory hijab was a small issue that would be resolved in due course once

Iranian society was fixed. "You think we don't have bigger problems than compulsory hijab?"

It's not a small issue. It's the biggest issue. From the age of seven, Iranian women have to follow compulsory hijab laws, even if they are not Muslims. Unless they wear the hijab, they cannot receive an education, get a job, or even be seen in public without being arrested and jailed.

I needed a prominent name in my corner, and Iran's most famous human rights lawyer came to my aid. Nasrin Sotoudeh, who had defended activists arrested during the 2009 protests and had worked closely with Nobel laureate Shirin Ebadi, was herself arrested in 2010 and spent three years in jail. Released in September 2013, before Rouhani's trip to the United Nations General Assembly in New York, she was barred from practicing law or leaving the country.

Sotoudeh wrote a public letter to My Stealthy Freedom in which she recounted an incident from inside prison. When she was incarcerated in 2011, she refused to wear a chador. The authorities were trying to break her indomitable spirit, and she was given a choice: Either wear the chador or lose visitation rights. That meant not being able to see her children—her four-year-old son, Nima, and Mehraveh, her teenage daughter—at all for the next four years. As she recounted in her public letter, Sotoudeh did not back down but wrote a very private letter to her children, to prepare them for the worst and explain her decision. After telling them she loved them dearly and missed hugging and kissing them, she came straight to the point.

Whatever I do will be judged by you someday, whether I like it or not.

Therefore, I want you to know that I will not let them force me to see you with something compulsory on me. I prefer to be deprived of seeing you than give in to their unjust demands. I will not let them force me to wear the veil.

In the end, the prison authorities gave in and allowed her to see her children. "Your protest is not a small matter," she told me.

With Sotoudeh on my side, I felt confident enough to keep pushing.

"If you can't determine how to cover your head, you can't control what goes on inside your head," I repeated at conferences. The compulsory hijab laws were the most obvious sign of oppression against women.

Women in Iran have more rights than our sisters in, say, Saudi Arabia, but we suffer from discrimination just the same. Millions of Iranian women object to being treated as second-class citizens. From employment laws that discriminate against women, to divorce laws that give custody of children to men, to the fact that women cannot run for the top office in the country, or qualify to be judges, women are curtailed. If you are an unmarried woman in the Islamic Republic, you cannot travel abroad without the permission of your husband or your father. Iran's top soccer player was prevented from traveling with the national squad to an important game because her husband refused permission. The same restrictions apply to employment outside the home. A woman is worth half as much as a man: If a woman dies in a car accident, her family's compensation is half that of a man. The list of discrimination against women is endless, and the most obvious sign that women are second-class citizens is the fact that they cannot choose what to wear.

I wasn't expecting to change compulsory hijab laws immediately. I wanted to change the culture, to empower women to see the possibilities. A young woman from a farming community in Lorestan Province, a traditional bastion far away from the glitz of Tehran, sent me a note along with her photograph that brought back memories of my own days in Babol: "I come from a place where covering my hair even in front of my father, my brothers, and all male relatives is mandatory," she wrote. "In our society, everything is forced upon us. I don't want to force women to shed their hijab or be forced to wear the hijab. We all must have the right to choose."

In her small community, she had risked a lot to send me her photograph. She later contacted me to say that many friends had recognized her and that she had received threats and insults. But she was glad she'd done it and stood up to the insults.

We all have *yavashaki,* or stealthy, moments, but we become powerful as women the moment we stop living a lie. I could have pretended to obey the hijab laws in public and in private be without the hijab, but that would have been hypocritical. I wanted all Iranian women to be strong enough to demand their freedoms.

Women, even in the West, are forced into situations where they have to accept decisions that are made for them. Women become powerful agents of change when they start living their own lives.

By the end of May, in less than five weeks, My Stealthy Freedom had close to five hundred thousand fans.

The whole world was talking about the brave Iranian women who were risking seventy-four lashes or prison to protest the compulsory hijab rules. There was bound to be a reaction. I just didn't know what to expect. But I knew something was coming.

CHAPTER TWENTY-TWO

My mother often delighted in telling everyone how when I was a child, I'd poke the beehives with a little stick. Invariably the bees would chase me away, back to the house.

"I only gave them a little poke—why did they have to sting me?" I asked Mother.

"Even a little poke upsets bees," she'd say, as she picked the stingers out of my arms and covered me with lotion.

I had just poked the Islamic Republic with My Stealthy Freedom. I was about to find out how painful the regime's stingers could be.

It was a glorious Saturday afternoon in May, sunny and warm, with a cool breeze and low pollen count. I wanted to spend some time with Pouyan. I hadn't seen much of him over the past month, and we took a stroll in Kew Gardens, with its lush fields and tall, leafy trees from around the world. We just goofed around, playing silly word games and telling silly jokes. I'd always wanted to act like a "proper mom," but more often than not, I wanted to be a kid, too. Mother and son, both with curly hair—his was a short Afro style and mine was shoulder-length and wiry, coils of thick curls woven in every direction. Kew Gardens was a sea of green. It reminded me of home.

"This is just like being in Ghomikola," I said to Pouyan, getting emotional and homesick.

"This is what you say about any place you like," he said, laughing. "This is nothing like Ghomikola, apart from the trees, and they aren't the same kind of trees."

"Teenagers! They can be so cruel," I said, as I started laughing, too. "I'm homesick," I yelled.

"I bet if you go to Paris, you're going to say 'This is just like Ghomikola.'" Pouyan was laughing so hard that tears were rolling down his face. "Paris is just like Ghomikola..."

I don't know what other visitors at Kew thought of the two of us laughing hysterically near the Orangery, a greenhouse building in the middle of the park.

I was still in a joyous mood a few minutes later when my mobile phone rang and a slight shiver ran down my spine when I saw that my brother Ali was calling me from Iran. We typically spoke early in the morning; he rarely called me late in the afternoon.

As soon as I heard Ali's voice, I realized that something was not quite right. Ali was more than just my older brother; he was my best friend, my confidant and protector. I could sense tension and stress crackling through the earpiece. Ali sounded strange, agitated; he was speaking in short bursts, not letting me get in a word.

"Khobi?" Are you okay? The words sounded fine, but there was so much tension and hidden meaning. "Everything good? How's Pouyan? Is Pouyan with you? Is he okay? You gotta be strong. I told mother to be strong, too."

Suddenly, Kew Gardens, packed with tourists, families, couples, lovers walking talking, kissing laughing, giggling jogging, no longer felt like the friendly place it had been a few minutes earlier.

"What's the matter with you? You sound strange. What have you done?"

Pouyan, immersed in his own thoughts, had walked off a few feet away.

"Listen, you were in the news again just now, but you gotta be strong." Ali's voice struggled to reach me from over three thousand miles away. The tension was at odds with the air of playfulness around me.

"As long as you are safe...Just don't let them get to you."

Ali and I spoke two or three times a week, and we had always had a telepathic connection, especially when we were younger, but now I couldn't make sense of what he was saying.

"You are not making much sense. There is nothing to be upset about on the news. Let me speak to Mother."

I missed speaking with her. Maybe she would be more direct than Ali. He seemed deliberately evasive.

"Later. She doesn't want to speak with you just now. She is upset." He paused for a while as I digested that information. AghaJan had not spoken to me for more than five years, but Mother was always on my side.

"Go and see the news first," he said. "This will pass."

What will pass? I wondered. What had I done now? Pouyan and I ran back to our apartment, racing up three flights of stairs, out of breath and agitated. Frantically I searched online. Shabake Khabar, the news service of Iranian state television, had broadcast a ninety-second news report all about me. Ninety seconds...just a minute and a half. How much damage can you do in ninety seconds?

Too anxious to sit down, I stood in front of my laptop, arms folded across my chest, waiting for the clip to load.

"Masih Alinejad, one of the key journalists promoting sedition...," a female presenter's voice said over some archival material on me.

Sedition? That was how the Islamic Republic still referred to the street protests against the 2009 disputed presidential election that kept Mahmoud Ahmadinejad in power. Millions of Iranians thought the vote was rigged.

The presenter continued: "...now trying to deceive young women in Iran to shed their hijab....In the streets of London, Alinejad had been raped by three bandits after shedding her clothes under the influence of hallucinatory drugs." It got worse. According to the news bulletin, Pouyan, who may have been a witness, was now receiving psychiatric help.

A thousand thoughts flashed through my mind. The TV news said I had been raped, and if it was on TV, it must be true, right? I looked on in disbelief. After the word "raped," I froze in place, staring numbly at the screen, barely registering anything else. I hadn't been raped. Had something happened that in a perverse, twisted way had been construed as rape? Had I greeted someone the wrong way? It didn't make any sense. I was never comfortable with air kisses, and even hugging a male friend was out of the question. My mind raced through all my meetings and encounters over the past few days and weeks since Kambiz had left for New York.

If I had been raped, I'd have made sure the whole world knew about it.

I wasn't really scared. I was angry and confused and in a total state of disbelief. Ali, forever a gentleman, had not asked me if the TV report was true. He knew it wasn't, but he still felt angry at being powerless to stop such a lie.

Why would state-owned Iranian TV report a lie? The fact that the Islamic Republic murdered its critics was nothing new. I wasn't worth killing. But to create a fake news report and broadcast it on national TV—that was a new level of thought control. Apparently state television used George Orwell's *1984* as an operating manual. Fact and fiction were blended daily to create a parallel universe at odds with reality as you and I know it.

I had become used to getting death threats on the phone or via email. Two years earlier, after a particularly nasty death threat, I'd reached out to a special branch of the British police, who traced the call to a number inside Iran. Don't get me wrong. I'm not brave, far from it, but I just never thought I was worth the trouble. I'd always reasoned that my journalism was annoying, but not enough to get me killed. I was a gadfly. The TV news report was a signal that I had crossed an invisible line, from pest to threat. The rules had changed, but no one had bothered to inform me.

I ran to the bathroom and splashed cold water on my face. My hands were shaking. In the mirror, I checked my reflection and wondered: What crime had I committed to be subjected to this? Snippets from the broadcast circled around inside my head.

"...raped by three bandits...under the influence of hallucinatory drugs...disrobed in public..."

As a journalist, I pay special attention to words. Did they really mean bandits? Or did they have thugs in mind? I wondered. London hasn't had bandits for centuries. And certainly not in my neighborhood of Kew Village, with its ordered lawns and hedges, narrow streets, and friendly shopkeepers always wishing me a good morning.

In London, I was free to be myself without any fear of attack. I never felt I was in danger. But now, with Iranian state TV reporting that I had been raped...well, who knew what could happen. I felt hot with anger. In the space of ninety seconds, I had experienced shock, fury, hurt, dismay, defiance, and shame. Then I thought about how my family would react. I was saddened beyond belief.

As the minutes ticked by, I could imagine the shame of my mother. She would have seen the report, and I know she was humiliated. In Iran, rape is always the woman's fault. If you are raped, then you must have asked for it. Even though the report was false, still my mother had lost face in her small village in northern Iran, where everyone knows everyone else and all their dirty laundry. I started crying, and in frustration at being so powerless and so far away.

I called Kambiz in New York to tell him I was okay. Removed from the immediacy of it all, he laughed off the fake story. "Every time they open their mouths they lie," he said. "It's amazing the Islamic Republic has such a low opinion of its people that it lies so brazenly to them."

Pouyan played the broadcast again and again, fascinated by the lies and distortions in the report.

"You have won, Mom. If the best they can do is to create fake news about you, you have already won the argument. Keep fighting."

A free and fair debate is scary for the Islamic Republic. Especially on women's issues. There are no debates on why women cannot go to sports stadiums to root for soccer or volleyball or basketball teams. Deciding what you can wear is a form of freedom of speech. And that is a luxury not available in Iran.

Compulsory hijab is one of the cornerstones of the Islamic Republic. Admit that many Iranian women, as much as half the population, object to it, and that undermines the legitimacy of the regime. Faced with a tsunami of social media protest from women who object to being forced to wear the hijab, the authorities in Iran decided to aim their attack at me as the representative of the movement to reject this rule.

My friend Azadeh called to warn me against watching the TV report. Too late, I said, sobbing. "You've seen what they're saying about you?" she asked me. We cried on the phone together. She's one of my closest friends and toughest backers. A reformist activist, she, too, was shocked at the attacks against me. "I can't believe they'd sink this low."

Azadeh felt betrayed and was angry, but my mother's feeling of shame was typical of women of her generation. My mother thought that the mere suspicion of rape ruined a woman's reputation. Shame is a terrible thing for Iranians. Losing face is a horror. And quite frankly, I had done a lot that made my parents uncomfortable. My mother believed in the Islamic Republic. How could the clerics, who were men of God, make up such lies? Did she really believe that I had been raped? I didn't know.

The sad part was that the regime supporters were joyous at the news. I was shocked at how they could take pleasure from the news that one of their fellow citizens had been raped. When I tried to explain the situation to Western reporters, they were puzzled as to why the Islamic Republic would broadcast a fake rape story. I was repeatedly asked: Did they not get it that rape is a horrific assault on a woman?

CHAPTER TWENTY-THREE

Just over a month later, in July 2014, Kambiz headed to Vienna for the Iran nuclear talks. The plan was that once the nuclear accord was signed, we'd fly to New York together. The My Stealthy Freedom campaign was in full swing, and on top of that I was busy with a weekly program, *The Newsmaker*, on Voice of America Persian. I was also churning out news segments for Manoto television. It didn't seem to be the best time to be going to New York, but Kambiz and I had been in a long-distance relationship since 2009, and after five years, it was time to take the plunge.

The negotiations in Vienna were taking a long time. Iran held its collective breath, hoping that a deal could be struck to remove sanctions so that money could flow to the country. I had been badgering my producers at VOA to send me to make a program about the talks. I didn't want to miss out on the country's biggest diplomatic coup in more than a hundred years. They finally agreed, and I arrived in Vienna late on the evening of July 18. I rushed into a taxi and headed to Palais Coburg, a former royal palace and now a luxury hotel, where the talks were being held.

The diplomats were on the inside, the press cordoned off on the outside, and armed police formed an outer perimeter. Behind metal barriers, hordes of journalists and cameramen jostled as they waited for the random diplomat to dart in and out to provide the latest news of the talks. The Iranian journalists watched my arrival nervously. The government had essentially declared me an enemy of the state, but that didn't prevent many former colleagues from coming to hug me and say hello. I had worked alongside quite a few of them in Tehran, but I knew they were being monitored by Ershad minders and didn't linger. The minders had arrived as fake journalists, carrying identity cards from publications that served as a cover for the security services. At least two journalists from conservative news organizations reported to their desks that I was on the scene.

There was a sense of closure missing. I didn't think a deal was going to happen. The diplomats and their aides emerging from the hotel looked haggard, not elated—as they should have been if they'd just concluded the deal of the decade, if not the century. In my haste I'd forgotten to collect my press credentials, and in any case, as one of the protocol officials explained, he had no more press cards to hand out. Seeing the disappointment on my face, he gave me a diplomatic badge instead. Another hour passed, and close to midnight, the hotel's glass doors were opened and the press were herded inside the bar. The basement of the hotel was being hastily readied for a press conference. More waiting before Javad Zarif, the Iranian foreign minister, and Catherine Ashton, the EU foreign minister, headed downstairs. Just at that moment, a security guard holding back the journalists saw my diplomatic badge and lifted the velvet rope to allow me to follow Zarif and Ashton down the stairs and past long corridors to an enclosed hall with exposed bricks dating from the sixteenth century. I kept about ten feet behind them, but I'm sure Zarif would have had a heart attack had he seen me. I didn't want to cause a diplomatic incident and waited outside the room until the rest of the journalists arrived. Despite all the excitement, there was no historic accord that night. Instead, Zarif and Ashton announced another extension of the talks.

I returned to London, knowing that I was heading to New York to start a new life. My last few days blurred into one as I said tearful farewells. I closed out my accounts and gave away my possessions, with the exception of two tall wooden giraffes, which happen to be my favorite animal. Pouyan had decided to stay in London with some of our friends and finish his final year of high school, and he was already settled in their place. Leaving him again made me even more nervous about moving to New York, but I was traveling with Kambiz.

Our flight would take us from Heathrow at 11:00 on Sunday morning, July 24. Contrary to my usual habit of arriving early at the airport, I kept packing and repacking, trying to delay my departure. I always like to pack light, with just my laptop and a shoulder bag with a change or two of clothes, but I figured it would be bad luck this time if I left any of my clothes or mementos behind. Finally, I double-locked the door and dropped the keys off at the real estate agent's office with tears in my eyes. At check-in, my fiancée visa didn't cut much ice with the ticket agent, who eyed my documents suspiciously and politely asked if I minded if they called for a supervisor to take a look as well.

"If the visa is no good, can we stay?" I asked mischievously. "It's a sign from the heavens."

Kambiz just rolled his eyes and grunted his dissent. But he was smart enough to negotiate an upgrade, so we both ended up in first class.

"You only get married once," he said, handing me the immigration documents. "Well...twice, in our case, so we might as well arrive in style."

I joined a long line of passengers waiting to be body-scanned, holding my boots in one hand and the envelope with my visa documents in the other. I had gone through the routine many times, but somehow this time it felt different. I was going to find out if I was ready for a new life.

Once we were through security, we headed to the British Airways lounge so I could upload more photos to the site. Every day, I published tons of news and photos from women complaining about compulsory hijab. Today was not going to be any different. As the minutes ticked by, Kambiz cleared his throat.

"*Ahemmmm*...sweetie, we need to make a move."

I was in the middle of an online chat with a couple of volunteers who wanted to translate My Stealthy Freedom entries into French, and I was downloading a video from Iran that I wanted to upload to my page.

A few more minutes ticked by.

"If you've changed your mind, this is a good time to tell me. I can at least catch my flight."

"I'm coming with you but..." The Wi-Fi in the lounge was excruciatingly slow. "This is the final call for Flight...," a voice over the loudspeaker said.

Kambiz grabbed my laptop.

We raced to the gate, the last couple to board the plane.

There was a moment—when the plane left the tarmac and burst through the low clouds, reemerging into the glorious sunshine and blue sky—that gave me a great deal of hope. Really, it's very hard to be depressed sipping orange juice at ten thousand feet when the sun is shining and you are heading for an adventure. My nerves steadied. I watched a movie and dozed off, trying not to think of all the things that could go wrong.

I woke to find that we were making our final approach to JFK Airport. It was two in the afternoon. As we stood in line at immigration, I looked at everything and everyone with a different eye, trying to see myself as a new immigrant. It was my first time back after more than two years, but then I had been a tourist, and now I was planning to stay. Even the scowl of the officer behind the desk didn't faze me. He took one look at my paperwork and sent us to a back office with the minimum number of words possible.

"What if they reject us now?" I whispered to Kambiz. We sat on plastic seats in an open area facing a counter. The Department of Homeland Security agents in their distinctive blue uniforms stood and worked.

Kambiz half turned in his seat. "This is the easy part," he said, holding my hand. "After we get married, we have more paperwork and interviews." He rolled his eyes. "Remember, this is not the right place to talk about free love. I am bringing you as my fiancé, and if they"—he nodded to the officers behind the counter—"if they hear you are having second thoughts, they'll deny your visa. Pleeeeeze." He drew out the word. "Let's just get through this. This is not the place to share your doubts."

"You've become very funny now that you are in New York."

We sat in silence. Soon a bored-looking officer called out my name.

"Aaaleee Nejad…Komi? Forrrooa?"

We jumped up as if we had springs in our legs. The officer returned the paperwork to me and stamped my passport without any emotion.

"Aren't you going to say 'Welcome to America'?" I asked with a big grin.

"Welcome to America." The officer grinned back. "Don't forget to get married."

When we were through the luggage area, I was hit by both the chaos of JFK and the late July heat of New York. I stared in amazement at everyone as we navigated our way to the taxi line. The last time I was in New York I survived a snowstorm, but now I felt dizzy from the heat, the noise and surge of humanity. I tried to put on a brave face and look on the bright side, but JFK is not the most welcoming of airports. The taxi ride was no better. We pushed our way slowly through traffic. I had never used air-conditioning during my time in England, but now I desperately, absolutely, totally needed it. The taxi didn't have it, and rolling down all the windows didn't help. The driver pulled off the freeway onto a wide avenue. He appeared to be aiming for each and every pothole on our way. With each jarring bounce, it felt as if someone was banging a nail in the base of my spine.

"Are you sure we are still in New York, or have we secretly moved to south Tehran?"

"It's a bit nightmarish, but I call it home," Kambiz said with some pride.

I stared out the window at unfamiliar shops with signs that at first were populated with Cyrillic script and, as we kept going, gave way to Hebrew and then Urdu and even Arabic. I wondered if I was in America or some mishmash country.

We finally pulled up in front of a Victorian house on a tree-lined street in Brooklyn. Instead of being happy, I was overwhelmed as I walked in. Everything felt so alien. It looked huge, but in America everything looks big, or so I thought at the time. This was to be my new home, but as I went through the three floors, I just couldn't establish a connection with the house.

"You have so many pots and pans and plates. Why do you need so many knives and forks?"

"We need to eat on something," Kambiz said good-humoredly.

"All we need is two plates." I knew I was being difficult, but in London I had lived a minimalist existence, with as little furniture as possible.

"I've got kids. And we want to invite friends over, and they might object to sharing their plates with each other."

Kambiz gently led me by the hand outside.

"How about we do some retail therapy and see a bit of Brooklyn?"

He had a silver Grand Cherokee with 110,000 miles on it and a few dings in the side panels, and we got in. It was too late to go to Manhattan, he explained, but we could drive to the Barclays Center mall.

I burst into tears.

"Everyone is so big," I said. The people looked taller and beefier than Europeans. "Everything is so dirty and smelly. I might as well have moved back to Tehran."

We drove to the waterfront in Red Hook. In the distance, the Statue of Liberty provided more proof that I was in America.

The next day, we took a very noisy subway to Canal Street and then walked a few blocks to 26 Federal Plaza, a forty-one-story office tower where many federal agencies were located, including my colleagues from Voice of America Persian. A long line of people from many different nationalities lined up outside the building.

I was looking for a friendly face, but no one was smiling. It is a cliché, but everyone in New York seemed to me to be always in a hurry, always scowling. Once past security, we rode the elevator to the thirty-third floor.

I bounded out of the elevator with manic energy and went in search of my colleagues, whom I had met only via conference calls and online chats. Producer Saman Arbabi took me around to meet everyone, and we ended up in the office of Bob Leverone, New York bureau chief.

"When can you start? I have lots of ideas," Saman said.

"I have lots of ideas, too, and can't wait to get started," I said, sitting on a large sofa. Bob's office had an undisturbed view of columns of light across lower Manhattan, the effect of the sun striking the downtown skyscrapers. "How about now?"

"What's your visa status?" Bob asked.

He and Saman looked at me. I slowly turned to Kambiz.

"We are good, right?" I implored. "I can start?"

"She needs a couple of details to be sorted out—"

Saman cut Kambiz off. "Like what? Let's get it done. We have a show to do."

Kambiz paused as he pretended to be thinking.

"She needs to say yes."

"To what?" Saman asked impatiently. "What's the question?"

"He wants me to marry him, but we don't need to discuss our private life now," I said, jumping in to cut off Kambiz.

"We need to get married to get the green card so you can work," Kambiz explained patiently. It had worked out perfectly for him, even if he hadn't planned it.

"Go to city hall and do it now," Saman said, clapping his hands. "Do it today. What are you waiting for?"

"We're thinking about it," I said as I stood up to leave. The good-byes were not as warm as our reception had been. Everyone urged me to get my work permit as soon as possible.

Kambiz and I stepped into the elevator, and I waited till the doors clamped shut before turning on him.

"I'm not getting married for a work permit or a green card. I'd rather I never worked again in my life than get married for the sake of a piece of paper."

"Love alone is not enough to get you a work permit. The sooner we get married, the faster you can start working."

"I'm not ready to get married. Don't rush me."

Without my regular VOA show, I fell back to doing freelance articles and segments. I'd get up in the middle of the night to start my workday, making phone calls to Iran to interview politicians or human rights victims. But it wasn't the same.

My first month was full of tension as I adjusted to my new life. Since I wasn't working, money was tight, and I didn't want to rely on Kambiz.

And then there were the children. Darya, eleven, and Bahman, seven, were happy to see me again but also curious about what my role was going to be. I was the newcomer entering their world. The three of them had established a pattern, and now I was disrupting that pattern in a major way. Darya was friendly but sensitive to my presence.

"I'm happy you are here, because you make my father happy," she confided in me. Still, it wasn't easy for her. Bahman was happy as long as he had someone playing with him.

I wanted to change the world, to get rid of compulsory hijab, but I didn't know how I fit in. I took to carrying my passport with me everywhere. I had been an immigrant in Britain and was an immigrant once again, this time in New York. I was committed to my new life, but I also needed to know that I could always head to the airport and flee if things turned out badly.

One evening at the end of August, after six weeks of living together, Kambiz put the kids to bed and sat next to me on his ancient blue velvet sofa, a determined look in his eyes. I hated that sofa. It was twenty years old.

"We've wasted enough time as it is. We'll get married tomorrow at city hall."

"Oh, you are such a romantic," I said. "You know how to make a girl say yes!"

"We'll get a gown tomorrow and head into the city."

Next morning, we all piled into the Jeep and headed to a bridal outfitter in Flatbush that offered a multitude of wedding gowns, with lots of satin and lace. As I wandered around the shop, my stomach tightened and I found myself scowling.

"Let's pick something quickly, and then we can drive to the registry office and get it done," Kambiz said breezily as he picked different dresses for me to look at.

"Here comes the bride.... Here comes the bride...." Bahman and Darya were laughing and marching around the shop.

Their merriment added to my nervousness about getting married.

"Please make them stop," I pleaded. "It's not a laughing matter."

Kambiz chased the kids around the store, but that made them laugh even louder, as if this were a game. I couldn't see myself in a wedding gown. I shuddered as I thought about the black outfit that I wore at my first wedding. A young sales assistant came over to help.

"What are you looking for? Are you looking for a mermaid or a ball gown? Or a strapless?" The young sales assistant went through the various choices. "A beaded lace dress with a sash?"

I had no idea what she was talking about.

"Here comes the bride.... Here comes the bride...." Bahman and Darya were waving ribbons and rummaging through clothes racks.

I thought my head was going to explode.

"I don't feel comfortable buying a dress right now." I looked at Kambiz, but he was distracted by a tow truck across the street. The driver was putting a chain around the axle of a Jeep.

"Look at that, some poor guy is getting towed," he said, before turning to face me. "I know you didn't want a big wedding, but I feel we need to try and at least look—" He stopped. "Oh, shoot—that's my car. Wait here." He shouted this as he raced out of the shop. Catching up with the tow truck, which was moving slowly into traffic, he banged on the window to stop it.

"Why can't we say 'Here comes the goom?'" Bahman asked, still absorbed in play. "I want to say, 'Here comes the goom.'"

"It's *gROOM*, with an *r*," Darya said, correcting her little brother. "Besides, it doesn't rhyme. We can ask Masih."

Both looked at me expectedly, as if I could adjudicate. I was saved by Kambiz's return. He looked at me and at the children.

"You win," he said quietly. "We are not going to buy a gown today."

"Thank you." I hugged him tight. I was so happy I had tears in my eyes. The kids rushed over for a group hug.

"We'll drive to Manhattan and do something fun," he said as we all piled into the car.

"What happened? Why did you change your mind?"

"The Jeep was towed, but I managed to get it back."

"That's good."

"I still had to pay to get the car released. It's cost me one hundred thirty-five dollars not to get married—a bargain, I'd say." He laughed out loud.

We drove to the city and surprisingly found a parking space on a street in Midtown. I felt the weight of the world had lifted from my shoulders as we had a leisurely lunch and walked around Rockefeller Center. I was just so happy that I didn't have to wear a gown. It was early evening when we headed to pick up the car. Except the Jeep was not there.

"Did someone steal the car?" I said, staring at the empty spot where we had parked a few hours earlier.

"The Jeep is twelve years old. I don't think anyone is going to steal it," he said, approaching a street vendor who was selling hot dogs and pretzels.

A few minutes later he returned with a sheepish look.

"The car got towed again," he said, laughing. "Twice in one day. If that's not a sign not to get married, I don't know what is."

The following week, he took me to Saks and I picked out a silver dress. It was not a wedding gown, which was a major point in its favor. The next day, we headed to the city clerk's office—just the two of us. We had arranged to meet a photographer inside city hall—he would record the moment. No other guests or witnesses. Just the photographer. This time Kambiz put the car in a parking lot. "It'll be cheaper this way."

As we neared the building, I had butterflies in my stomach.

"I have a few questions I need to resolve. Let's grab lunch and talk it over and then get married." I knew I was stalling.

"There is a photographer waiting for us, and I don't want to rush the ceremony. We'll eat after."

"You care more about the photographer than you do about me? I'm hungry."

"Lots of people are getting married today, and we'll miss our chance if we dillydally," Kambiz said firmly.

I don't know what came over me, but I started crying and demanding to be fed.

"I'll wait till you've calmed down." Kambiz strode off to a bench and started to check his emails on his iPhone.

I stood to the side, crying inconsolably, so much so that a policewoman came to check if all was well. I had ruined my makeup. Once again I had puffy eyes, with black streaks of eyeliner running down my cheeks, and a dripping red nose.

"Are you Masih Alinejad? Oh my GOD, I can't believe it," a voice screamed in Persian. A young woman quickly wrapped her arm around my shoulders and with the other pointed an iPhone at the two of us. "Let me take a selfie—my mother and I are big fans."

"What are you doing here?"

"I met a guy a few weeks ago and just got married."

"Just like that?"

"Just like that. Gotta go." And with that she was gone.

I walked over to the bench where Kambiz was waiting.

"Let's get married," I said. I was determined.

We walked up the steps arm in arm, and then *crunch,* the heel of my right shoe broke.

For the rest of the day I was barefoot. Which was brilliant.

A calm settled over me as we waited our turn. I put my head on Kambiz's shoulder as he scanned an electronic notice board to see if our number had been called. Happy couples, young and old, giggled and laughed. Some were with their parents, others with their children. I felt serene about my decision. I was also glad that it was just the two of us. I didn't want to share these moments; didn't want to worry about what the guests were up to. I wanted our time together to be stretched forever.

My reverie ended when our number flashed on the monitor and Kambiz gently helped me up to my feet.

When it came to saying the vows, I felt as if I were in a movie: "to have and to hold...for richer, for poorer, in sickness and in health, to love and to cherish; from this day forward until death do us part."

And then I said, "Yes...very much YES."

I don't believe in wedding rings and didn't have one for Kambiz.

"In that case, I'll give you your ring later in the evening," he said.

A kiss and we were husband and wife.

We went under the Brooklyn Bridge, in Dumbo, to take our wedding photos, and had a romantic dinner at the Odeon in Tribeca. At the end of the night, Kambiz kept looking in his pockets and then went to check the Jeep a few times.

"Whatever it is, it can wait," I said. "It's our wedding night. Come and hug me."

"I've lost your wedding ring," Kambiz said. "I knew I should have given it to you in London."

He was devastated.

It was too funny. I was the one with the reputation for losing things, from credit cards to iPhone chargers to keys, but Kambiz had gone and lost the ring.

Now I didn't have to worry about losing my wedding ring.

CHAPTER TWENTY-FOUR

The hard-liners in Iran sometimes referred to me as "Joje Ordak Zesht" (the Ugly Duckling) in their articles, often adding a caricature that made me look like a monster. On more than one occasion, they referred to me by the initials JOZ. It was all part of an attempt to humiliate me. It also served as a warning to other Iranian women. The designation had always puzzled Kambiz, and one day after I moved to New York, he finally lost patience with it.

"Don't these people read books? Ugly ducklings turn into beautiful swans at the end. Don't they know?"

"I'm no swan. I'm happy to be a beautiful duck."

"They can't get away with it," Kambiz hissed. "This is personal."

He created the moniker "Ghomikola Eagle" for me and started writing updates of our life together on his Facebook page, which he knew was being monitored. Nothing serious, but he wanted to have fun. It was all tongue-in-cheek, but certain websites close to hard-liners in Iran took notice. I was ecstatic that I had someone in my corner who was not afraid. The Ugly Duckling references came to a stop.

One afternoon in mid-October 2014, I was using a coffee shop in Midtown as my office when Kambiz called, saying it was urgent that I meet him. Most days, I worked out of a coffee shop offering reliable Wi-Fi until my work permit came through. The My Stealthy Freedom campaign had grown exponentially, with lots of volunteers helping along the way. That afternoon I was in a good mood, because I had just taped a segment for a news program on Manoto TV back in London. And we were going to Hawaii for our honeymoon at the end of the week. Kambiz bounded up to me, barely able to contain himself.

"Do you know who Sheryl Sandberg is?"

I shook my head. "Does she work at Bloomberg?"

"Nooooooooooo! She is the number two at Facebook and...she loves My Stealthy Freedom."

"We have over seven hundred thousand fans. I can't know each and every one of them."

"You know nothing, Masih Alinejad," Kambiz said. He was referencing HBO's *Game of Thrones*. "At an editorial board meeting at Bloomberg, Sheryl Sandberg said her favorite page was My Stealthy Freedom."

Facebook was my medium. It was where I had more than two hundred thousand fans on my own public page, and it was the home of My Stealthy Freedom. We spent a great deal of time talking to Facebook engineers and support staff in the beginning to get their help to protect the page from hackers, trolls, and copycats, not to mention abusers. At first, Facebook engineers told me that for "freedom of expression" reasons they could not remove hateful posts. We had some tough negotiations till they began to see that there was a systematic pattern of abuse and hatred against the women who had sent their pictures.

Unbeknownst to us, Sandberg, one of America's best-known women leaders and feminists, and the author of the best-selling book *Lean In,* had mentioned My Stealthy Freedom at *Fortune* magazine's Most Powerful Women Summit. I had no idea who she was or that she was going to speak about our struggle. Until that moment, I hadn't fully grasped the idea that the struggles of Iranian women for their rights could find resonance elsewhere, with powerful women in the West and East.

I teared up as I watched a video of her speaking from the stage. "What drives me—and I'm sure it's true for so many of the amazing women in this room—you want to make a difference. That means making someone else's life better. What I love about Facebook is that we give people a voice," she said.

She then named My Stealthy Freedom as an example, getting a bit choked up when she talked about her favorite picture on the site, whose accompanying text she had someone translate for her. "The grandmother writes, 'I wanted my granddaughter to feel the wind through her hair before it goes gray.'"

It was amazing. I had tears in my eyes watching Sheryl Sandberg get teary-eyed about a campaign I had created.

"She has no idea who you are or the people behind the campaign," Kambiz said. "You need to write to her."

"And say what? She is busy running Facebook. She doesn't have time for me."

"She says you are her favorite page. Let's find out," Kambiz said.

That evening I watched a video of her on stage giving a TED Talk. Her talk was empowering—my heart was racing. I could relate to her and her easy and friendly manner. There was something powerful and at the same time feminine about her. She was in total control, saying the same things I believed in. I watched her in awe. Here was a business leader, totally at ease and self-confident on the global stage. Sheryl had said that my page was an inspiration to her, but as I watched her, she became an inspiration to me.

The next day I wrote to her, thanking her for her support of our campaign of social disobedience.

With some nervousness, I pressed Send.

Less than two minutes later, she responded. "Wow. Great to hear from you." I hadn't expected to hear back from her directly and so quickly. She then invited me to go to Facebook to meet in person.

Before I could make plans, I was sidetracked by a series of acid attacks in the city of Isfahan, Iran's top tourist destination, a few days later. The attacks were carried out by assailants on motorbikes wearing helmets with visors down to hide their faces. They threw acid into the faces of women who were out walking or in cars. In total, as many as twenty-five women may have been attacked.

The state-owned newspapers did not cover the story, but the news spread far and wide on social media. When the story broke, I thought perhaps that the attacks were a backlash against my page. I thought that I had misjudged the nastiness of the regime against women, and that it was time to close down the page. I didn't want to put anyone in danger.

But when I opened my in-box, the largest number of photos that day and for the rest of the week were from women in Isfahan. They were not going to back down, they told me. One woman wrote that whenever a motorbike passed by, her heart would skip a beat. She was scared but she was not going to give up. One woman wrote "Acid is not our right" on the palm of her hand. Another wrote "We don't deserve acid." Both were without hijab, but their open palms covered their faces.

Another wrote: "What sins have our daughters committed that you took away their sight and beauty?" Still another: "Where are my daughter's eyes?"

One of the victims was in full hijab and still had acid thrown in her face. In Isfahan, women didn't go out as much.

There was so much negative publicity that those behind the attacks may have been warned off privately. The government has never released its records of the attacks, and the only people arrested were four journalists and a photographer who covered the incidents.

At least one woman died as a result of an attack, and another lost the sight in one eye. The rest suffered severe burns to their hands and faces. Many in Iran blame religious zealots for the attacks.

I called the Friday prayer leader of Isfahan for comment. A year earlier, he had said that Islamic punishment, even whipping, should be meted out to ensure hijab compliance. Now, after the acid attacks, he had changed his tune: "I don't see whipping as a part of Islamic punishment," he told me. I broadcast the interview on my channels. After the interview, he was severely criticized by the news media close to the Revolutionary Guards. He never answered my calls again.

On October 20, thousands of demonstrators took to the streets of Isfahan. A smaller gathering was held in Tehran. I got up at 3:00 a.m. to monitor the events in Isfahan. I had worried that no one would turn out, but I needn't have. The demonstration did not get any television coverage in Iran, but the protesters were sending photos and videos filmed on their mobile phones to the My Stealthy Freedom page. We weren't a news organization, but people trusted us. More videos were sent to my page than to the established news media.

The police attacked some of the demonstrators to disperse the crowd—estimated at more than five thousand—but not before the many media organizations from outside Iran covered the event.

The women's responses showed that we were not going to be cowed. One woman sent a photo of herself without any head covering, with a piece of paper in her hand: "With acid you can wipe out our faces but not our thoughts."

A month or so after first contacting Sheryl Sandberg, I headed out to Menlo Park, California, to Facebook headquarters. The Islamic Republic views Facebook as a tool of regime changers, spies, and other deviant characters. Yet as I walked around the vast campus, I was surrounded by twenty-something men and women programmers and designers. It felt like being at a university rather than in a workplace. Everyone was very friendly. My guide left me in the middle of an open office, where everyone was working on laptops, to go and find Sheryl. I was expelled and driven away from mainstream publications, but through Facebook I had my own audience. Facebook was my home. I looked at the engineers and programmers in the room as if they were working for me personally. The Islamic Republic blocks access to Facebook, but that day, I felt I was among warriors whose work caused dread in power centers in Iran. Facebook and other social media were my allies and had enabled me to reach a massive audience.

I prayed that my brain wouldn't freeze and that I wouldn't start speaking Persian to Sheryl when it came time to meet her. Suddenly she and my guide materialized.

"Hi, you must be Masih," Sheryl said, smiling. She was dressed just like most of the young women in the room, in a black tee shirt and black pants, like a graduate student.

"Where is your office?" I said, groaning inwardly at my stupid comment. Why hadn't I thought of something more interesting to say?

"Right here," she said, waving to a small desk in the open space.

"Wow, you are even cooler than I imagined," I said. "I've seen your videos a number of times, but you look friendlier." I was really worried she might be stuffy and formal and official. "In Iran, managers are always really boring, but not you." I just couldn't stop talking.

Physically, she was even more delicate than I was, which I really liked since in almost every setting, I'm the smallest person in the room.

"You are one of my personal heroes because you have managed through your page to create a platform for Iranian women—for their voices to be heard and for the rest of us, the people around the world, to get a chance to learn about a different Iran."

I could feel tears pouring down my face.

She took me to a corner of the open space. "I want to give you something," she said, opening a drawer and handing me a tee shirt with LEAN IN printed on it.

She was interested in my private life—my journey from the village of Ghomikola to New York. I blurted out almost everything, the words coming in a rush.

"You should write a book," she said.

I had been scheduled to give a lunchtime address to some Facebook managers to round out my day. Before leaving me, Sheryl pulled me aside.

"Your campaign empowers women, and I want to help," she said.

"Let me think about it," I said. Besides the CIA and Mossad, I've also been accused of being in the pay of billionaire George Soros. But one of my weaknesses is that when people offer to do something for me, I freeze. I like to be self-sufficient.

Sheryl's lean-in idea was transformative for many women, even inside Iran. She believes in what she is doing, and she believed in My Stealthy Freedom. Her encouragement helped me and my volunteers plow on when critics were saying our movement had lost momentum.

Just over a year later, in January 2016, I was invited to be one of the speakers at Facebook's Women's Leadership Day event. Pouyan had come to visit, and so he and Kambiz and I flew to northern California. The two of them were my entourage, but on the day of my address, Pouyan opted to go to the movies instead of attending the conference. Teenagers will be teenagers. We arrived at a giant conference center and I sent Kambiz ahead to scout out the arena as I chatted with Sheryl and Marne Levine, Instagram's chief operating officer. Kambiz returned looking slightly pale.

"There must be about three thousand women in there. That's really scary."

"Thanks for the vote of confidence," I said.

The conference was designed to inspire Facebook women employees to be empowered, to be the next leaders. I couldn't tell them about technology or engineering. I had transformed my life and I told them about taking chances, believing in yourself, and not being afraid to fail. I talked about how often I had launched a campaign only to see it lose momentum and fade away. But I'm comfortable with failing. Somewhere in the audience I knew Kambiz was watching, urging me to focus on the positive, but it didn't matter—it was my story, and I felt compelled to tell it.

"Dare to fail. Be yourself and don't be afraid of failing or being judged."

Even as I spoke, I thought about making a short feature out of the event. After all, I was the first Iranian to address a Facebook event. But I needed something more.

Outside the auditorium, Sheryl, in an aqua-colored tee shirt, was pacing slowly, focusing on her own address coming up soon. I rushed up to her.

"I really need you to say a few words on camera to Iranian women," I said.

"Of course," she said with a smile, as if she had no other care in the world. She considered the camera without any hesitation and started talking.

"I want to say to all the amazing women on My Stealthy Freedom's page how much we all support you, how much women around the world are cheering for you, how much we all want to live in a world where every single woman has civil rights, civil liberties, opportunities to live as she wants to live, and the sisterhood that all of us have together around the world."

As she finished, there was a big crash of plates from the restaurant behind her.

"I've got to go," she said, and walked onto the stage. I followed her and stood in a corner near the front. Sheryl talked about losing her husband, Dave Goldberg, eight months earlier, and how she learned to cope with that loss. Many people in that room cried, and I was one of them.

CHAPTER TWENTY-FIVE

I hadn't realized how cold New York can be, and my first winter was one giant snowfall after another. I screamed in delight at every snowstorm, and like a small child would revel in seeing the streets and trees covered in pure untouched snow. I enjoyed stumbling around in knee-high drifts.

London was more temperate, but I loved New York's extremes—the 100-degree-plus days and the arctic conditions notwithstanding! Life moved faster in New York than in London, and though I was still waiting for my green card and work permit to be sorted out, I was busier than ever.

A knock on my door one wintry afternoon brought me face-to-face with Nazila Fathi, who could almost be my twin sister—she is petite, my height, with long curly hair. I vaguely knew her from Iran, where she worked for the *New York Times* when I was working for *Etemad Melli*. Although she was also an Iranian journalist, we didn't hang out, since her employer was an American media company and technically she was viewed as an American correspondent. I'm sure Nazila, like other foreign reporters, was watched by the security services. Now she was here to interview me for *Vogue* magazine.

To be honest, until a week before she walked in the door, I had never heard of *Vogue*.

"It's the bible of fashion," Kambiz said when *Vogue* first contacted me. "Lots of glossy photos of clothes and accessories." That didn't sound right to me.

"My Stealthy Freedom is not about fashion," I said. "It's about women's rights. Why would an American fashion magazine be interested in our struggle? Maybe I should turn them down."

"*Vogue* is not any fashion magazine. You'll get massive exposure with a group that you wouldn't normally reach."

Now, as I folded my legs beneath me in the armchair, ready to talk to Nazila, I still had my doubts. But an interview is always a bond of trust, and Nazila, being an Iranian woman who had also grown up in the Islamic Republic, knew all about the emotional and physical challenges women face in Iran.

Nazila had grown up in a middle-class family in Tehran, the child of professional parents, and was wide-eyed at my descriptions of rural poverty. Nazila had had an upbringing that was almost European. When I told her, "The scarf was so much a part of my body that I even slept with it on," she looked shocked.

"Unveiling was a long psychological process. For years I was told to be ashamed of my hair, but I think it's beautiful," I said as I twirled a stretch of my long curls around my fingers.

Nazila and I had both been raised in a culture that told us the veil protects you from corruption, shields you from bad people, and keeps you from sin. My family wholeheartedly bought into that propaganda, while hers only paid lip service to it. Hijab values become integral to your identity in the rural areas.

"You cannot deny your identity," I told Nazila as I warmed up. "That's the key message I want to deliver to Iranian women. Do not lose your identity. Don't let go of your identity. Just look at the pictures of Iran before the revolution and you see women with hijab and without hijab coexisting. That's what I want."

After she finished interviewing me, Nazila asked about my wardrobe and fashion choices.

"I don't know any brands. Banana Diplomatic? Pineapple Democratic?" I threw out some names.

"You mean Banana Republic?"

"Yes. I also wear lots of Zara," I said cheerfully.

Nazila looked thoughtful as she packed away her stuff and put her coat on. "They'll let you know about the photo shoot. Just a word of advice: It's a lot of work."

She was not wrong. On a crisp February morning, I walked into a chic restaurant in downtown Manhattan. I had never seen a fashion photo shoot, and it was intimidating to say the least. Along one wall was a long table full of breakfast food from bagels to scrambled eggs to fruit and large urns of coffee. Loud music blared as models tried on dresses and hairstylists and makeup artists milled around. A photographer shot dozens of pictures at a time as his assistant fiddled with the lighting. Another part of the room contained hundreds of items of clothing on racks. The scene was so alien to me that I nearly walked out, ready to abandon the whole project.

"Come on in. Let's see if your hair needs any work," a formidable-looking woman said as she took charge of me. She peered at my hair. "Your hair is great. We'll just make it more curly and blow it out, make it bigger."

It's funny; my hair in Iran was a source of embarrassment. Everyone there pitied me for having such unruly hair, but she loved it. Emboldened, I walked over to the clothes rack and began to rifle through the items.

"What are you doing?" a beautiful young woman in a white tee shirt and leather jacket asked me.

"I want to pick something nice to wear. I don't recognize these brand names. Do you have anything from Zara?"

She looked at me strangely. "*You* don't get to choose."

"Why not? It's *my* body," I protested.

"It's chosen for you," she said dismissively.

I was fuming. I was a women's rights activist fighting for women's right to choose, and I was being told I couldn't pick my outfit. I took a couple of deep breaths to calm down. I waited for an hour, observing different models come and go. Eventually a makeup artist worked her magic on me and I was presented with a long dress. "This is yours."

"Are you sure?" I asked the stylist.

She nodded.

I hurriedly put on the dress at the back and walked unsteadily on a pair of high heels to the assembled crew at the front. I stared at my reflection in the mirror. I didn't recognize the person I was seeing. An assistant came over and put a necklace on me and offered me a matching pair of earrings. The image was all wrong. The jewelry was the last straw.

"That's it. I quit. I'm not doing this." I stormed to the back to change into my own clothes. "I am a campaigner for women's rights, and I'm not going to wear something that is not me. This dress is just not me."

An assistant got on the phone to call the higher-ups. I could hear only bits and pieces of the conversation but kept hearing Anna Wintour's name. I took out my phone and called Kambiz.

"I am gonna walk out. I hate being a fashion celebrity. This was a big mistake," I said rapidly before he could respond. I then explained that I was back in my jeans and sweatshirt and ready to cancel the photo shoot.

Kambiz was silent for a long time. "The publicity would be good for the campaign," he said finally. "Are there no other dresses that are acceptable?"

"Who is Anna Wintour?" I asked him.

"You don't know?" He sounded annoyingly smug.

"I'm not American and I don't care about fashion."

"She's the grand ayatollah, the supreme leader of *Vogue,* and by definition sets the fashion trends."

"That settles it. I'm fighting ayatollahs all the time."

After some haggling, the stylist found me a simple shirt and a pair of patterned pants. "No dress and no jewelry," she said. "This is an Altuzarra top."

"Sure, I like Zara," I said, mishearing the designer's name. "I've got lots of Zara tops at home."

She shook her head in despair and walked off.

It took another three hours before I was finished, and I kept thinking, Why all the fuss? I did like the top and gave it back reluctantly. Later, I found the same top at a boutique, and it cost about ten times what I normally paid at Zara!

"I don't care about fashion. I want people to pay attention to what I say, not what I wear," I told Kambiz that evening as I packed for a trip to Geneva. "Being in *Vogue* keeps the campaign alive, but I don't want to become someone who is a fashion victim."

"Sometimes you have to look the part before people will be ready to listen to you," Kambiz said.

I next went to Geneva to pick up the Women's Rights Award at the Summit for Human Rights and Democracy, sponsored by twenty global human rights organizations. I had arranged for Pouyan to join me. I liked having him with me during international conferences. His presence gave me strength and comfort, and he could see his mother working.

The campaign was giving "a voice to the voiceless and stirring the conscience of humanity to support the struggle of Iranian women for basic rights, freedom, and equality," one of the organizers said by way of an introduction.

I hadn't prepared a formal address. I find it difficult to read from a prepared text, and I can't memorize long speeches, so instead I prepare a few key statements and build my narrative around them. I hopped up the steps to the podium and looked at the cameras, the TV lights, and the packed hall. I had wrapped a head scarf around my neck. Very deliberately, I lifted it up above my head, just like the hundreds of photographs of women on My Stealthy Freedom.

"This piece of cloth," I said, "in the hands of a regime that has made compulsory hijab into the law of the land, is an instrument of oppression against women. This piece of cloth, in the hands of politicians who do not believe in freedom, is a chain around the necks of Iranian women and over the past thirty-five years has choked their vitality and energy. Like the leaders of the American civil rights movement, like Martin Luther King, the women of my country also have a dream—we dream that one day our voice gets heard, the world stands up with us, and compulsory hijab leaves Iran forever."

Only a month earlier, Michelle Obama had declined to cover her hair during a visit to Saudi Arabia. I had a message for her, too.

"You may have seen pictures of Michelle Obama in Saudi Arabia with her hair uncovered," I said. "Now let me share a secret. If Michelle Obama goes to Iran, she better cover her hair or she won't be allowed to get through passport control. Because she is the First Lady, she will not end up in prison, but she will be deported. That is because no woman in Iran can be seen in public with her hair uncovered."

I always regarded myself as a journalist, a newspaper reporter. I didn't set out to be an activist. It was a gradual process. I never expected the My Stealthy Freedom campaign to be such a sensation, nor did I expect to overturn compulsory hijab rules overnight. I've always accepted that we have to change the misogynist culture pervading Iran; we have to prepare the ground. That's why campaign work meant coming up with fresh ideas every few months to keep our struggle in the news.

One of our campaign goals was to educate female politicians about compulsory hijab and ask them to join our protest. It was bad enough for Iranian women to be forced to wear the hijab, but the Iranian government also forced non-Iranian visitors to don head scarves. It was particularly galling when female politicians meekly obeyed this discriminatory law.

When I was a political journalist in Iran, the female journalists grumbled about the strict hijab laws, and in response officials would point to visiting delegations as an example for us to follow, saying, in effect, "Even non-Iranian politicians have accepted the culture of hijab when they visit our country, so you shouldn't make a big deal out of it."

I wanted to reach out to female politicians visiting Iran and ask them to join our protest. With Iran and the major powers inching their way toward a deal to resolve nuclear tensions, Western politicians and business leaders were eager to visit the country to get a better sense of developments. The Islamic Republic wanted to sell its vision of Iran. My role was to tell the truth about the oppression of women.

In January 2015, the vice president of the Bundestag, Claudia Roth, a member of the Green Party, headed to Tehran as part of a delegation of German parliamentarians. I wrote a public letter asking her to discuss the issue of compulsory hijab with Iran's leaders and join our protest by voicing her dissent publicly. I didn't truly expect Roth to go bareheaded, but I hoped she'd bring up the issue and create a discussion. I asked my followers to write to Roth directly to voice their concern. Hundreds did, bombarding her Facebook page with messages of protest.

As a campaigner, I was new to the world of politics and how to win over politicians. To this day, I don't know how. But in a Facebook post addressed to her I laid out my arguments.

> Dear Ms. Roth: You may have heard that Iranian officials say compulsory hijab is the law in Iran, and that foreigners should respect the laws of the host country. In that case, you'd expect Iran to also respect the laws of other countries. Case in point: France now requires women to submit photos without a hijab when they apply for a French visa, so that the applicant can be properly vetted. Iranian officials are not only not complying with this decision but have banned women from submitting such photos to Western embassies. In fact, Iranian authorities have allowed demonstrators to protest in front of the French embassy in Tehran to put pressure on the French.
>
> The irony is that Iran believes in freedom of choice for Iranian women as long as that choice is compulsory hijab. Please don't say one should not interfere in another country's

law; Iranian officials would protest loudly if countries like Germany or France or Italy or anywhere else were to ban Muslim women from wearing the hijab. So, I want you to protest the forced hijab on Iranian women.

If we keep silent in the face of unfair and bad laws, then slavery, which also used to be legal, would still be with us.

Claudia Roth issued a statement saying that she was in Iran to investigate the conditions of political prisoners and that discussion of the issue of compulsory hijab would jeopardize her mission. She had made previous visits to Iran, and each time, she had gone out of her way to appease the Islamic Republic.

I was livid. Iranian women risked their freedom by challenging the compulsory hijab laws, and here was a Green Party politician ignoring the voice of ordinary people so she could mingle with the Iranian leadership. Many women felt betrayed by Roth.

Our wave of protests was picked up by German media, putting Roth on the defensive. Roth said that her priority was seeing political prisoners, but her request to visit Narges Mohammadi, a prominent human rights activist, was denied. Mohammadi had received a sixteen-year prison sentence for campaigning against capital punishment. She was prominent among activists and was an opponent of compulsory hijab. Roth was silent about being denied a chance to visit Mohammadi.

Foreign politicians mainly interact with Iran's foreign ministry, which has no say over the condition of the country's political prisoners. It is rare for a foreign politician to be granted access to a political prisoner or to someone who has been jailed for human rights issues. At a time when European countries were grappling with their Muslim populations and dealing with the issue of hijab, I was introducing another element in the debate. If Muslim women in the West had a right to choose how they covered themselves, why couldn't Iranian women have the same right? Roth was the first politician that the campaign focused on, and we learned many valuable lessons.

Of course, I didn't expect to change hearts and minds overnight but I was quite delighted by the response from the Facebook community. And we were just starting.

In late March, just two months later, a number of Australian journalists reached out to me. The country's foreign minister, Julie Bishop, planned to visit Iran, and the journalists wanted to know my thoughts: To hijab or not to hijab? That was the question.

I gave a number of interviews to websites and Australian publications such as the *Melbourne Herald Sun* and the *Sydney Morning Herald* and waited. I kept repeating the same key message: "This is the time for Bishop to ask the Iranian government about compulsory hijab and human dignity."

This was the first visit by an Australian official in twelve years, and Bishop was not going to take any risks. As her arrival date approached, I told everyone that our first aim was to bring compulsory hijab from the margins into the mainstream political discussion, make our voices heard, and put our demands on the table. Eventually women would no longer be required by law to wear the hijab, but we had to fight long and hard to make that happen.

One of the challenges our campaign faced was from groups that said women's rights and compulsory hijab were important issues but this was not the right time. They claimed our issues would be resolved once poverty and homelessness had been eradicated, justice had prevailed, and a real democracy flourished in the country. I had no problems with those goals, but I wasn't going to sit around and wait. My cause is women's rights, and my first step is the removal of compulsory hijab laws. Putting it on the table as the centerpiece of our demands was a victory in itself.

Conservative newspapers and websites in Iran had said that Roth's refusal to help our campaign had delivered a deadly blow to My Stealthy Freedom. Now they were predicting another blow against us. Once again, My Stealthy Freedom campaigners flooded Bishop's Facebook page. If compulsory hijab was part of Iranian culture, the morality police would not need to detain 3.6 million women for showing a bit of hair on their head. The Iranian authorities stopped publishing the number of women who were being detained for not obeying compulsory hijab rules after we publicized it. Clearly they were embarrassed by it.

The stage was set. An Australian journalist called me from Tehran saying that Bishop had put a black shawl over her head during her meeting with Zarif and for the press conference after. The shawl covered only half her hair, allowing her some dignity, which she then threw away by insisting that she had chosen to wear the head covering. "As a matter of fact, I wear scarves and hats and headgear quite often as part of my everyday wear," she told the incredulous Australian traveling press.

It was infuriating to watch her spin her decision to acquiesce. Immediately, I searched the web and found at least twenty pictures of Bishop without a scarf or hat or any sort of headgear resembling what she wore in Tehran. I posted the pictures.

On the day of her departure from Iran, Bishop dropped the pretense. *Herald Sun* columnist Andrew Bolt captured the foreign minister's exit attire: "Just yesterday Bishop was pictured leaving her Tehran hotel room for Paris, wearing what looked like a diamante studded fedora circa Michael Jackson's *Smooth Criminal* days." Bishop wore a low-cut white tee shirt under a black dinner jacket. Under ordinary circumstances, any woman who dressed like that in Iran would end up in jail, but Bishop's convoy headed to the airport for Paris.

Bishop's political allies back in Australia praised her for showing sensitivity to Islam and respecting "Iran and their culture." But she took a hammering from her opponents and from feminists for not "empowering women." In a television report, Andrew Bolt said that she "looked ridiculous" and failed to "stand up for Western culture." Many Australians said that they were "quite disappointed" Bishop did not take a "stance for her fellow females."

The executive director of the Institute of Public Affairs, John Roskam, defended the foreign minister's choice as a necessary evil.

"Julie Bishop has gone to Iran to seek their cooperation," he told Bolt on Sunday. "That's the reality: We need a favor from them."

In Iran, the state-controlled media gloated over their victory. But our cause had received widespread publicity, especially in Australia. It didn't matter that Bishop hadn't taken her head covering off; it mattered that compulsory hijab was a topic of attention. Our aim was to thwart the Islamic Republic's propaganda that Iranian women had voluntarily chosen the hijab, and that this was, in any case, part of our culture. Of course, both arguments were false. My Stealthy Freedom fans were energized by the episode. For more than three decades, female politicians had traveled to Iran with little fuss over the issue of compulsory hijab, but now it had become a global conversation.

The next female politician to visit was Federica Mogherini, who had replaced Catherine Ashton as European Union foreign minister. Mogherini was focused on resolving the nuclear issue and didn't want to get involved with compulsory hijab. She ignored the issue completely.

She wrote an entry on her Facebook page about her visit. I wrote a long commentary, pointing out that I wished her all the success in removing sanctions against Iran but that I had a simple request. When Iranian officials like Zarif visited Italy, they wanted the European Union to respect their Islamic values—by not serving wine, for example. More often than not, the European Union respected those wishes. Yet the Islamic Republic insisted that non-Muslim visitors to Iran, including diplomats and politicians, don the hijab. Surely the Europeans had to stand up for the rights and values that are rooted in the freedom to choose.

For more than thirty years, I wrote to Mogherini, the issue of compulsory hijab has been a red line in the Islamic Republic. Compulsory hijab has been a taboo subject; like the chants of "Death to America" and "Death to Israel," it has become part of the foundation of the Islamic Republic. Yet many women in Iran want their voices to be heard. They should be free to choose what to wear. They do not want their freedoms to remain stealthy for the rest of their lives.

So, just as we are going to have a nuclear deal, it's time the Islamic Republic had a deal with Iranian women over compulsory hijab.

My comment under Mogherini's post received many times more "likes" than her own original post. But within an hour my words had disappeared. I complained about censorship in an article that ran in a number of publications, including *Bild* in Germany. A day or two later, Mogherini's office emailed to say that they had no idea how my comments had disappeared but that they'd welcomed my criticism. Once again, we had raised our profile.

In the meantime, I had been in touch with Marietje Schaake, a thirty-six-year-old member of the European Parliament from the Netherlands, who was interested in human rights issues in Iran. I asked her to press our case, but I needn't have worried. She certainly knew about our campaign, and she wrote to say that she intended to raise the issue when she visited in June 2015.

Her visit became the talk of Tehran. Tall, beautiful, and blond, Schaake stood out from the other six members of the diplomatic team as they met with Iran's high-ranking officials. For the first meeting, with top power broker Ali Larijani, the head of the Iranian Parliament, Schaake showed up with a scarf wrapped around her head like a woman from West Africa. It didn't completely cover her hair.

She wore a tight knee-length black dress with a zip-up front and a pair of leggings. Her neck and ears were uncovered. There was nothing revealing in her attire. But her exposed skin shocked Iranian politicians. Conservative and hard-line websites went ballistic, and a noted conservative said, "It's as if she's wearing underwear" or "going to a party." Iranian female officials wore traditional black chadors, covering everything apart from their faces and hands.

Without mentioning compulsory hijab, Schaake had made huge waves of her own in Iran and the West. European newspapers and the *New York Times* covered the uproar over her clothing, as did papers and websites in Tehran. "As a woman, a visit to a country where wearing a religious symbol is mandatory is difficult," Schaake wrote on her blog shortly after. More important for me, Schaake noted the impact of My Stealthy Freedom on the development of her views. "A serious discussion about what is and is not appropriate and respectful should not only be held over the heads of women." She added later, "The way we dress is not the only difference between us. Why not give people the choice to decide for themselves?"

Our campaign, after the earlier setbacks, was finally getting some traction among the political class. I'm convinced that if we don't lose hope we'll triumph in the end.

Sometime after her return, I contacted Schaake. "Compulsory hijab is not a small issue because as you saw for yourself, your diplomatic mission was dominated by questions over your improper hijab," I wrote.

"It's funny how they couldn't get past that one issue," Schaake said.

We met a couple of weeks after her return from Iran at the European Parliament in Brussels. It was the first time I'd been invited to meet a parliamentary lawmaker since being expelled from the Majlis a decade earlier. I had come a long way from my little village of Ghomikola, I thought, as I waited for Schaake's assistant to fetch me from the security gate.

"Going to Iran enabled me to witness personally how much women inside the country have been fighting to win their freedom to choose what they wear," she said. "On the way to Tehran, women on the airplane only wore the head scarves immediately after the plane landed in Iran. The women that I saw in the streets of Iran cover their hair very unwillingly."

Now that I was seeing her in person, she looked younger than her years and more beautiful, even, than in her pictures. As she took me through Parliament, she walked with obvious self-confidence, whereas in Iran she had looked ill at ease.

"They didn't like my outfits at all," she said.

I realized that she was still seething with anger over her treatment.

"They looked at me and saw a woman and dismissed everything I had to say. They looked at what I was wearing and how much hair I was showing and based on that decided that they didn't care what I was saying."

Until her visit, Schaake hadn't appreciated how oppressive compulsory hijab can be for those who are not in favor of it.

"People in Europe enjoy the liberty of wearing or not wearing the attire required by their religion," she said. "We are more used to protecting Muslim women from Islamophobes."

"I'd be curious [what would happen] if Islamic Republic officials, when they arrived in Europe, were forced to wear Christian symbols," I said.

Our campaign received validation from President Rouhani himself. Before embarking on his first major European visit to France and Italy, Rouhani agreed to an in-depth interview with French television.

Sitting in an ornate chair, the Iranian president was well prepared for the grilling by two veteran journalists, swatting away with ease questions on the nuclear program, Iran's economy, and relations with the West.

Then they surprised him. One of the journalists pulled out an eight-by-ten picture of a woman who had posed without her hijab on the My Stealthy Freedom campaign page and showed it to President Rouhani.

"Does that photo shock you? Are you offended by seeing an unveiled woman?"

I jumped up in my seat. Rouhani had officially been confronted for the first time with My Stealthy Freedom. Given the billions of dollars the regime was spending on countering and subverting our campaign, I was sure that he was fully aware of it. I held my breath, waiting for him to answer.

"We have so many issues, we don't have time for these things." Rouhani looked uncomfortable. He laughed nervously. He clearly hadn't expected to be confronted with our campaign. "Everyone in Iran is free to do whatever they like in their private lives."

"Really?" I screamed at my TV screen. Not that he could hear me.

"If I had a private party at my home, it'd be raided by the morality police."

The other journalist asked Rouhani whether he thought Iran could reform its views regarding the existing dress code for women. How likely was it that the women of Iran, just like those of Tunisia, Morocco, and Turkey, could have freedom of choice? Could Rouhani imagine that such a day could come?

He didn't give a straight answer. "Every country has rules and regulations, and we have to respect the law. It is up to the Parliament to amend such laws." He flashed a smile, laughing nervously.

As always, my mother's advice from long ago came back to me. I'd been expelled from Majlis and was exiled from Iran, but I had found a way to confront President Rouhani. The French journalists had kindly acted as my window.

Rouhani was one of the architects of Iran's compulsory hijab law, as he proudly wrote in his own memoirs.

"The point, President Rouhani, is that we must change bad laws to make them respectable," I said, addressing the TV screen.

In April 2016, I met another remarkable woman, Tina Brown, the founder of the Women in the World Summit, an annual summit that gathers together powerful women doing interesting things. Tina Brown had been editor in chief of *Tatler, Vanity Fair,* and *The New Yorker* and was the author of *The Diana Chronicles,* a biography of Princess Diana.

I was one of the headliners at the Women in the World Summit at Lincoln Center, but the night before my appearance, I sneaked in to watch Katie Couric, the American TV news presenter, interview Megyn Kelly, the Fox News presenter who had had a public row with then candidate Donald Trump. As I admired Kelly's poise and eloquence, I wondered if my story was going to be captivating for a New York audience.

"You're on," an assistant told me.

I carefully climbed the short set of steps to the stage, concentrating on not tripping. I strode to the center of the stage, where Tina Brown sat in a leather swivel chair. I took the other chair. I looked out at the audience. I could hear them, but the stage lights were aimed at me and I couldn't see them.

Tina introduced me as the "owner of a glorious head of hair that would be criminal to cover." Laughter spread throughout the audience, and that helped me relax and be myself. Tina led me through my life story—from my childhood to the campaign.

"I was enjoying the wind through my hair," I said in response to her question about why I had started the My Stealthy Freedom page. "Maybe it's nonsense to you, but to us it means a lot. And every time I feel the wind through my hair it reminds me of the time my hair was a hostage at the hands of the Iranian government."

And what about the dangers? That was a question I knew was coming.

"Do you fear sometimes these pictures are going to get the women into trouble when you post them on My Stealthy Freedom?" Tina asked, reading from her prepared questions.

"Being a woman in Iran means you live in a dangerous situation," I replied. "Women in Iran are breaking the law every day just to be themselves. You live with fear every day when you want to go out. According to the police of Iran, 3.6 million women were warned and stopped by morality police in the street within a year. And forty thousand cars were impounded. Why? Because the women drivers did not have a proper hijab. So these women didn't send their pictures to me, but they put themselves in danger by their actions because they say no to forced hijab. For me, just giving them a voice means a lot."

Then Tina asked about my parents. How did they feel when they learned that I no longer wear even a head scarf?

"My father would rather take me to heaven by force." I wasn't sure that made much sense in English, but in Persian everyone understood what it meant. "Thankfully, my mother, though she is both conservative and illiterate, is more understanding."

I wanted to finish with a flourish.

"While I enjoy my freedom, I still cannot forget about my people. Iranian women break the law if they don't cover their heads, if they are caught singing or dancing in public or attending a mixed party and much more." I took a deep breath.

"I'm a master criminal." I laughed. "The Iran government thinks I have too much hair, too much voice, and I am too much of a woman."

Increasingly, Iranian politicians faced tough questions on the issue of compulsory hijab. In July 2016, when Iranian foreign minister Javad Zarif visited Paris, he was challenged by a French female senator. She wanted to know why foreign tourists who were not Muslims had to abide by the compulsory hijab laws.

Zarif is a master of subterfuge. His job as Iran's top diplomat is to smile and hide the real crimes of the Islamic Republic. In the past, he has denied Iran's jailing of political dissidents and journalists. When he was asked about Jason Rezaian, the Iranian-American *Washington Post* journalist held in a cell in Evin prison, Zarif implied that he must have been a spy. In Paris, Zarif said that foreign visitors had no issue with the hijab because they respected Iran's culture.

When I heard his response, my mind almost exploded with outrage. Zarif's trickery knew no bounds. Compulsory hijab is not part of our culture, and my in-box was full of hundreds and hundreds of letters from women who said they loved visiting Iran but hated putting on the head scarf and wearing a long coat.

As I watched Zarif's performance over and over again, hoping to detect a sign of humanity, it occurred to me that as a man he had never had to suffer the humiliation of being told to wear the hijab, nor endured being scolded for wearing nail polish or berated for having a strand or two of hair sneak out from under his head scarf.

I hit upon an idea of Photoshopping a hijab onto a picture of Zarif. I posted a picture of Zarif looking grumpy wearing a blue head scarf and called on men to join the movement. I was taking a big risk. Zarif, the architect of Iran's nuclear deal, is a hero to many Iranians. He is fluent in English and has a ready smile when dealing with foreign dignitaries. After the chaotic Ahmadinejad foreign policy, which led to the country's isolation, Zarif was seen as Iran's Henry Kissinger. By picking on him, I risked the wrath of Iranians.

But there comes a time when you have to challenge even the toughest opponent.

"Mr. Zarif," I wrote in the Facebook post,

I have respect for your diplomatic skills. But take a look at this photo of yourself wearing the hijab. How do you feel? The picture is comical? Weird? Or do you see it as a personal insult?

That's exactly how the women who do not believe in compulsory hijab feel. For years, from childhood and the teenage period to womanhood, we've been forced to wear the compulsory head scarf and for years we have had to endure our loss of dignity.

Mr. Zarif, you and many other men have gotten used to seeing women in compulsory hijab every day and you think that is normal. But for millions of Iranian women, this compulsion is an insult to their dignity. We are not against hijab, but we are pro choice. We want to choose whether to wear the hijab or not.

But it is you and other Islamic Republic politicians who are denying our right to choose. You say everyone must obey the law. But bad laws should not be obeyed. Mr. Zarif, in the course of your diplomacy, you have often argued against unjust laws. For example, you said the UN sanctions against Iran were unjust and you did not accept them. That is exactly what we are trying to do in challenging the compulsory hijab law, which is unfair, so do not tell us law is law and we must respect the law.

Within hours, my in-box was exploding with photographs of men wearing the hijab in support of my campaign. The first ones were just individual men wearing head scarves, but later the photos were of men who had covered their heads standing next to wives or mothers or sisters who were bareheaded. The #Meninhijab campaign was born. And it showed that many Iranian men supported our campaign.

One man sent a picture of himself wearing a head scarf with his wife beside him without any hijab and wrote: "I sincerely want my wife to be able to live in an Iran where she is the one who can determine what she can wear. It is indeed extremely difficult for a woman in Iran to endure wearing these clothes in the midst of our sweltering-hot summers just because we want to avoid driving the ire of the officials in the country."

And it wasn't just Iranian men. Suddenly men from all over the world were sending their pictures with their heads covered in solidarity.

Zarif was furious. One of his aides called me, privately asking me to stop picking on Zarif. "You should be on our side. You were a reformist once—what happened? If only you knew the pressures we are under, you'd stop your activities," he said.

"When Zarif lies so brazenly, I cannot let it go," I told him. "I understand that Zarif has to stretch the truth when it comes to dealing with other governments, but on domestic matters, when he says we have no political prisoners or that compulsory hijab is our culture, I have to respond."

Time is on our side. Young people are not fans of compulsory hijab.

In the summer of 2016, a number of towns on the French Riviera banned the burkini, the full-body swimwear used by some Muslim women. Thierry Migoule, head of municipal services in Cannes, stated that the rule was about banning "ostentatious clothing which refers to an allegiance to terrorist movements which are at war with us." That decision became the focus of spirited global debates over women's rights, assimilation, and secularism. All across Europe and the United States, many women protested the ban.

I was totally against any such ban. The police in France were be-having just like the morality police in Iran. After all, both seem to have problems with choices made by women, and both acted as if women's bodies were the territory of lawmakers and law enforce-ment, who alone knew what was best.

In Iran, the authorities rejoiced over France's ban. Here was a chance for the Islamic Republic leaders to gloat over double stan-dards in Europe. The French preached human rights to other coun-tries but denied it to their Muslim population. Iranian leaders called on France to respect the human rights of Muslims who chose to dress in Islamic fashion. It was the supreme irony that Iran, which denied its own women the freedom to choose, was defending the right of Muslim women in France to have the choice to be covered up.

I am for freedom of choice. I support women's right to choose the hijab or not. In France and the United States, the pressure was on Muslim women not to wear clothing of their choice. I had to stand with the women. At least in France and the United States, there was freedom of speech, and the cause was receiving media coverage. In Iran, there is no such freedom.

As the debate raged over the merits of the burkini ban, a court in France overruled it, which did not pacify either side. A panel of Muslim activists was invited to discuss the ban before the European Parliament. As it happened, we were in the UK for a family vaca-tion. Kambiz had rented a houseboat in Cornwall but kept it a secret from Pouyan, Darya, and Bahman. The look on their faces when we entered our "hotel" on the water was priceless. As our vacation was coming to an end, Schaake sent me an email about the panel, due to meet in Brussels. Although it was last-minute, she asked if I could take part.

I couldn't have imagined in a million years that I'd be asked to address a European parliamentary panel in Brussels. But my excite-ment was tinged with anger. For more than thirty years, Iranian women had suffered under compulsory hijab laws and the European Parliament had looked the other way. Now, because some towns in

France wanted to ban the burkini, lawmakers wanted to learn more about the issue before passing legislation and making declarations. The more I thought about it, the angrier I became. In how many countries were women forced to wear the hijab? How come the European Union was silent on this issue but was now concerned about women not being allowed to wear a burkini? It was ridiculous and smacked of a double standard.

I wrote my speech on the drive back from Cornwall. Once we arrived, I paced around the house, talking to myself and practicing my address. Darya watched my every move and gesture.

"My mom always practices her speeches with me. I can be your teacher, too."

Children are so innocent and sweet. "Of course, darling. Kambiz is so critical," I said, and we both giggled. "I'm looking for a word that describes the double standards of these European lawmakers—they say something but act differently."

"Hypocrites. That's what you are looking for," Darya said confidently. She was almost fourteen but acted much wiser than her age, and I looked to her as a friend rather than a stepdaughter.

I hardly slept that night. Rising sometime after midnight, I killed time until the taxi arrived at 4:00 a.m. to take me to Heathrow for my flight to Brussels. Kambiz and the kids were heading to New York later in the day.

Check-in was a breeze, but when I looked at the display screen, I saw that my flight had been canceled. I was rebooked onto the next flight, at 8:00 a.m. It would still get me there in plenty of time for my panel at noon.

Catnapping on one of the more comfortable seats in the waiting room, I heard the word "Brussels" in an announcement, jumped up in a sleepy panic, and scanned the departures. My 8:00 a.m. flight had also been canceled. The airline was apologetic, but there was nothing that could be done. At this point I wondered if I could make my panel in time. I sat in Heathrow, drinking cups of coffee and fuming. To my utter disbelief, my next flight was also canceled.

Three flights in a row. I was practically in tears. I called the organizers to tell them of the situation. "Looks like you are not going to make the speeches, but come anyway," my contact told me.

If something keeps going wrong in Iran, we blame the invisible "powers"—anyone from the CIA to Iranian intelligence. I knew there was no plot, but three flights in a row had been canceled and I was going to miss my big occasion. Finally, I boarded a 10:00 a.m. flight, which would land at noon. Maybe I could make the second half of the panel, I thought. After waiting for so many hours in the airport and drinking about five coffees, my enthusiasm had evaporated, and I was jittery from being over-caffeinated.

I hardly use any makeup and rarely carry more than lipstick. That's enough for me. I use it to redden my lips and add color to my cheeks, and I also apply it gently around my eyes as an eye shadow. Now I realized that I had forgotten to take the lipstick with me.

In Brussels, I was the first one out the door and ran to the taxi line, dragging my carry-on luggage behind me. "Take me to the Parliament," I said to my driver. "Please, I'm in a big hurry. I'm supposed to be speaking there now. I'm the main speaker. Hurry."

"Usually the Parliament sends a car for their special guests." The driver turned around to get a better look at me. "You sure you don't have a car waiting for you?"

"My flight was canceled three times," I said, remembering just then that I didn't have any euros. "You take cards? Or can I pay you in dollars or pounds?"

"Only cash," he said, shaking his head. "Euros."

"Aaaagh! Wait here," I screamed as I ran back into the airport in search of an ATM to withdraw money. I raced back, hoping the car was still there.

"Are you sure you are a special guest at Parliament?" the driver asked dubiously.

"Just get me there."

To his credit, he sped to the center of the city, finding shortcuts and all the time promising to get me there in one piece. I called the organizers and told them I had arrived. The panel had already started, but maybe I could be part of the Q&A. It was better than nothing.

No sooner had I finished my call than we got stuck in an almighty traffic jam. It was like a car park that crawled forward in inches. Minutes ticked by with no movement. I was so close, and yet the Fates had conspired to stop me.

"It's easier if you walk or run from here," the driver said, pointing in some vague direction in the distance. "It's less than two kilometers. Maybe ten minutes or so."

I raced to the European Parliament, dragging my luggage behind me. Every few blocks, I'd stop and ask directions just to make sure I was still headed the right way.

"European Parliament? European Parliament?"

In ten minutes or so I reached the Place du Luxembourg. The Parliament is housed within the original Brussels-Luxembourg train station. I didn't have time to marvel at the historic or the modern architecture as I *click-clack*ed my way to my panel. Just outside, I dried the big beads of sweat rolling down my face and neck after my exertion, sprayed on some perfume, and stormed into the committee room.

Every head turned. The expressions on the faces of my fellow panelists told me that they were rather concerned about my sudden appearance.

"It was tough getting to Brussels, but I made it. My flight was canceled three times. The Islamic Republic probably had something to do with it, but I never give up."

As I sat down, I realized that the main panel discussion was over. But I wasn't going to be silenced. Instead of reading my address, I spoke from the heart.

All the females in my family, my mother, my sister, my aunties, they all wear the hijab. All the females that I know have worn the hijab from the age of seven, and I did, too. My dream is to be with my mother in France, in Belgium, walking shoulder to shoulder, without her getting bad looks or being judged because of her hijab. And to walk with my mother shoulder to shoulder in my own country without getting arrested. So, I want to be clear: When I talk about compulsory hijab, I am not talking as a Western woman but as an Iranian who grew up, was educated, and lived under the Islamic Republic. As the founder of the My Stealthy Freedom campaign, which has more than one million followers, I'm in touch with thousands and thousands of women in Iran. I was a journalist in Iran for more than ten years.

Here, all I'm hearing, as a reaction to terrorist attacks, as a reaction to Donald Trump's campaign, all people want to talk about is Muslim people and their rights in the West....

Why was the burkini ban in France suspended in less than a month, but hijab has remained compulsory for more than thirty-eight years?

When it comes to compulsory hijab, the female politicians use one of four arguments, and I wanted to challenge them.

First, they say compulsory hijab is required by law inside Iran. Each country has its own laws, and we must respect their laws. But slavery was also the law. If no one objected to slavery, we'd still have African Americans as slaves. They say the law must be respected. No. We should not respect bad laws but fight to make the laws respectable. Remember: Women didn't have the right to vote but protested against bad laws to win the right to vote.

Some people say that hijab is a cultural issue, and we wear it to respect Iran's culture. But compulsory hijab is not part of Iran's culture. When you force a seven-year-old girl to wear the hijab, how can it be a cultural issue? During the apartheid era in South Africa, did you also claim that racism was a cultural issue?

More cowardly is the argument that compulsory hijab is a domestic issue, an internal matter, and foreigners should not intervene. But if you are a female tourist from Europe or America and visit Iran, you have to don the hijab. It is no longer a domestic issue. Curiously, no one claimed that the burkini ban was an internal matter in France.

The final argument is that there are bigger issues tormenting Iran than the issue of compulsory hijab. I know there is corruption and political repression. Fighting compulsory hijab is fighting for human dignity, and what can be greater than that? We are fighting for human dignity.

I say that most female politicians are hypocrites. They stand up with French Muslim women and condemn the burkini ban because they think compulsion is bad, but when it happens in Iran, they look the other way.

Compulsory hijab is the most visible symbol of oppression against women, and we have to stand together and bring this wall down.

I received a rousing round of applause, but I was famished—I had not eaten all day. A video of my address was uploaded to YouTube, and I got a lot of positive feedback. But when I watched the video, all I could see was my pale face, which made me look malnourished, and my curly hair, frizzy and out of control.

I had laid out our campaign's objections to compulsory hijab at one of the most important political venues in Europe. Within a week, the video of my address was seen by more than one million people on YouTube alone. We were putting female politicians on notice.

CHAPTER TWENTY-SIX

Throughout 2016, even as I was campaigning against the Islamic Republic, the rising specter of populism materialized in the guise of Donald Trump. His message struck a chord. The old rules didn't seem to apply to him. He said outrageous things that added to his popularity. His misogynist comments, his anti-Islam rants, and his talk of a wall along the Mexican border did not hurt his prospects as he crushed the old order of the Republican Party. Although my focus was Iran, I could not ignore the Trump phenomenon. For my weekly VOA show, *Tablet*, I created a number of programs devoted to Trump.

The more Trump attacked the Muslims, the more jittery the liberals, the Democrats, and anti-Trump forces became in challenging human rights abuses in Islamic countries, especially in the Islamic Republic of Iran.

The My Stealthy Freedom movement celebrated women's freedoms, and as Trump gained in the polls, it became a challenge to get active endorsements. People were afraid to be too vocal because they didn't want to appear anti-Islamic in the era of Trump. I realized, I told a *Washington Post* reporter, that I was fighting both Trump's Islamophobia and the Islamic Republic of Iran's misogynist policies. "The atmosphere that [Trump has] created in the United States puts us in trouble as well when we want to talk against Islamic restrictive laws. Because people now don't want to touch the sensitive issue of compulsory hijab because they think it's a cultural issue and they don't want to be seen to be aligned with Donald Trump."

"A Barbie wearing a head scarf can make news," I told her. "In the U.S., it shows you're tolerant, you're open-minded, and you're not like Donald Trump."

It was a big challenge. "If we talk loud against Islamic restrictive laws, then people think we're supporting Islamophobia. But if we keep silent, then we have to forget about our own identity and obey all the discriminatory laws."

In November 2016, I went with Kambiz and stood patiently in a long line that snaked around the running track of an indoor gym in Brooklyn as he waited to vote in the presidential election.

"I wonder if there are any Trump supporters here," I said, looking at the diverse crowd.

"Not likely. This is the Socialist Republic of Brooklyn," he joked.

But Donald Trump won and became the forty-fifth president of the United States. And almost immediately, women's groups led the protests against him.

Just as Trump took the oath of office the protests started. And women were on the front lines. On Saturday, January 21, I jumped onto the subway and headed to Manhattan for the Women's March against Trump. I had never participated in a demonstration in the West before. I had always lived the life of an exile, more concerned with daily events in Iran, but now Trump had made me appreciate my life in America. I was only a green card holder, but I enjoyed the same freedoms as a citizen.

I got stuck near the United Nations building, which was packed with women of all nationalities, old and young, mothers and grandmothers, walking and chanting. I'd never witnessed anything like this. In Iran such demonstrations, unless officially organized, are not allowed.

Here was a civics lesson for me. Thousands and thousands of women were protesting the president of the United States, the most powerful man in the world. I looked around wide-eyed with amazement. In Iran, the only permissible demonstrations are against the United States and Israel.

I expected the security forces to appear from the tall buildings and arrest everyone. I looked for sharpshooters hiding on rooftops and undercover agents ready to pounce. It took me a while to join the chanting of the crowd.

I even took a photo of myself holding a sign that read: WE'RE ALL IMMIGRANTS. BUILD BRIDGES NOT WALLS.

That evening, I put the photo on my Instagram page with a message:

Why am I opposed to a wall? Because I come from a country where I have experienced walls all around me. I come from a country where the government forces hijab on Christians, Jews, and other minorities, and if they say NO, they will face a wall, too. That is why the idea of a wall in the United States makes me shudder. I know very well that ordinary citizens on the other side of the wall will be suffering immensely. Often politicians and celebrities find a way of minimizing the damage from these policies while ordinary citizens on the other side of the wall are the ones that suffer the most

In one of his first moves, on January 27, Trump signed an executive order to halt visas for citizens of Iran, Iraq, Libya, Somalia, Sudan, Syria, and Yemen for at least ninety days, a ban against seven Muslim-majority countries—the so-called Muslim ban. In one stroke, he had stopped Pouyan from traveling to see me, and I couldn't leave to visit him because there was no guarantee that I'd be allowed back. I was baffled and, quite frankly, enraged. Here I was, a campaigner against Islamic extremism who was forced to flee Iran with my teenage son, but now I dared not leave the United States, my new home. I was a double victim here. In Iran, I faced one wall, and in the United States, I faced another. Iran has built a wall around my family, preventing them from leaving the country. I have not been able to see them for eight years and may never see them again.

When the ban was announced, I sat on the steps outside the house, smoking cigarettes as if they were a life-enhancing drug as I tried to figure out how I was going to see Pouyan. I had called him to complain about the unfairness of it all, but he wouldn't have any of it.

"Maman, the Syrians have it much worse," he said.

I wasn't expecting that. "But this is not—" He wouldn't let me finish.

"Compared to what Syrian refugees have to endure, I feel guilty talking about a visa problem. I'll wait till this is resolved."

He was growing up fast and I missed holding him, and yet I knew I had to let him be his own man. Lost in my thoughts, I left the stoop for a walk to clear my head. Cody, a giant chocolate-colored Newfoundland dog, ran up to me and, perhaps sensing my mood, quietly sat down, blocking my path. His owner, my neighbor Stephanie, ambled over with a concerned expression. Normally, Cody jumps up and slobbers all over me, something that makes me very uncomfortable. Today, Cody sensed there was something wrong and limited himself to just sniffing my sneakers.

"How are you coping?" Stephanie said. "I have been thinking about you and your son. I don't know my country anymore. I don't recognize my people who now want to ban foreigners. We are a nation of immigrants." I was so touched that I burst into tears. My neighbor gave me belief in the goodness of the American people, hope that there are other Americans who will speak out on behalf of refugees and people in exile like me.

Donald Trump's victory made life more challenging. In response to his election, Sweden claimed to have the first feminist government in the world. You only had to refer to the Swedish government website to find the meaning: "Gender equality is central to the Government's priorities—in decision-making and resource allocation. A feminist government ensures that a gender equality perspective is brought into policy-making on a broad front, both nationally and internationally. Women and men must have the same power to shape society and their own lives. This is a human right and a matter of democracy and justice."

And then the Swedes sent a delegation to Iran. I thought, well, here at last was the first feminist government to visit the Islamic Republic, and after the furor over the burkini ban and all the fuss about women's right to choose what to wear, the empowered women in the feminist government would have the power to shape their own choice of what to wear and not put on the hijab. When I saw the pictures from Iran, it was like getting kicked in the stomach. For a ceremonial walk past Iranian president Rouhani, the women put on head scarves, long coats, and clothing that even Iranian women themselves would not wear. Apparently the Swedes act as feminists when faced with Western men and when making cheap political points at the expense of Trump. When faced with patriarchal societies that subjugate and oppress women as a matter of government policy, they wilted.

Isabella Lövin, Sweden's deputy prime minister, gained worldwide fame after she posted a picture of herself surrounded by other women mocking a picture of President Trump signing an anti-abortion order surrounded by male aides and advisers. Lövin had explained to the world that Trump represented a threat to female rights.

The Swedish delegation's parade past President Rouhani quickly became known as the "Walk of Shame" after I wrote an article for My Stealthy Freedom. I posted two photos next to each other: Lövin's feminist government and the Walk of Shame. It went viral.

By actually complying with the directives of the Islamic Republic, Western women legitimize the compulsory hijab law. This is a discriminatory law and it's not an internal matter when the Islamic Republic forces all non-Iranian women to wear hijab as well. Trump's words on women are worthy of condemnation; so are the discriminatory laws in Iran. If you are a feminist, then you care about women's rights all over the world and not just where it is safe.

Ann Linde, the Swedish trade minister, a women's rights campaigner, defended her action and said that she had not wanted to wear a head scarf. "But it is law in Iran that women must wear the veil. One can hardly come here and break the laws," she explained.

It probably would not have received so much attention had it not been for the Swedish government's insistence that they were feminist. Other Swedish politicians were more critical. Jan Björklund, leader of the opposition Liberal Party, said that the head scarf is "a symbol of oppression for women in Iran," and that the Swedish government should have demanded that Linde and other female members of the delegation be exempted from wearing it.

Magdalena Andersson, the Swedish finance minister, posted a picture of herself with two female colleagues wearing a hat. The message was clear: It was not a big deal. A hat and a head scarf are one and the same.

When I was growing up, I had to have my hair all covered up. I had no choice. A hat was not an option then, and it's not an option now. I had expected more from the Swedish feminists and felt greatly disappointed. After I wrote an open letter, Andersson had the decency to apologize. Soon afterward, I received an invitation from Sweden's Liberal Party to address a conference in Uppsala, north of Stockholm. Pouyan was having trouble getting a visa to the United States, but we could meet in Sweden. Who knew when I would be able to see him again? I called him and then booked flights to Stockholm for both of us.

I had never addressed a political conference, and this was a huge deal for me. The night before I flew to Sweden, I talked in my sleep, so much so that I woke Kambiz. He shook me awake.

"You were talking in your sleep."

"What did I say?"

"Something about 'They came for the Muslims but they always come for women,'" Kambiz said. "You kept repeating it."

Perhaps it makes sense, perhaps it doesn't, but my best lines percolate in my brain during the day, and clarity comes when I'm asleep.

I wrote part of my speech in the car as Kambiz drove me to JFK.

There is a famous quotation from an opponent of Adolf Hitler who said:

First, they came for the Socialists, and I did not speak out—

Because I was not a Socialist.
Then they came for the Trade Unionists, and I did not speak out—
Because I was not a Trade Unionist.
Then they came for the Jews, and I did not speak out—
Because I was not a Jew.
Then they came for me—and there was no one left to speak for me.

In the United States after the Trump ban, the words were changed to: "First, they came for the Muslims, and I didn't speak out...." But in all religions and in all societies, first they come for the women. I told Kambiz that I was thinking of beginning my speech with that. "What do you think?" I asked, looking to him expectantly.

"Love it, but you need more."

"Of course I need more, but the rest is easy."

Except that when I tried my speech on Pouyan in the hotel room an hour before the event was to begin, it all went wrong.

"Mom, it doesn't make any sense," he said, waving the pipe he now smoked. "If you don't improve your English, you'll sound as if you are speaking nonsense."

Pouyan was correcting my English, my grammar, and now my ideas. I knew he loved me and wanted me to succeed. He wanted me to be perfect, but I like my imperfect self.

"I don't care if it doesn't make any sense. I want to talk nonsense." I was getting loud. "In fact, there is too much sense in the world and not enough nonsense. I'm getting up on that stage and talking nonsense."

Pouyan, ever sensitive to my moods, didn't want me to walk on-stage full of stress. "I've changed my mind," he told me. "I love it. Your nonsense is better than other people's sense."

I had survived war.

I had survived sanctions.

I had been forced into exile.

I was not afraid of war.

I was not afraid of sanctions.

And I certainly wasn't afraid of Donald Trump.

CHAPTER TWENTY-SEVEN

I came to know Shahnaz Akmali after her son, Mostafa, was shot in the head.

Shahnaz was from a poor family, and she toiled for long hours for little pay and had no interest in politics. Like many women, she had been raised to stay on the periphery, to be part of the background. Her life changed in 2009 after the security services killed her only son during the nationwide protests following the election of Ahmadinejad.

Shahnaz was so grief-stricken that for months she wore Mostafa's shoes to walk around the streets of Tehran. That came later. At first, she could barely leave the house. But when she was stronger, Shahnaz would go to the spot where Mostafa's body had been found and stare hard at the ground as if she were searching for clues that would explain his death. By then, of course, nothing remained. Even his blood had been washed away. Shahnaz spoke to shopkeepers, to the families that lived in the neighborhood, but no one could supply any details that would help her.

"Those were chaotic days," Shahnaz told me. "Lots of people running back and forth, shots being fired, tear gas canisters..."

During visits to Mostafa's grave at Behesht-e Zahra, the biggest cemetery in Iran, on the outskirts of Tehran, Shahnaz came to meet other families who, just like her, had lost their loved ones during the protests. They came from different backgrounds and neighborhoods, but death had brought them together. Shahnaz visited the other families and set up regular meetings where they all could get together. Not everyone could attend, so Shahnaz bought a camera and started making videos of her visits to the other families.

I first came across Shahnaz when I compiled a list of the victims of the political crackdown. Later, the story of Mostafa's death became part of *The Victims of 88*. We don't know for sure how many people were killed during the 2009 protests, but I wanted to preserve their memory in a television documentary. Filming families talking about the lives and deaths of their loved ones wasn't easy. When Mostafa died, Shahnaz didn't even have an email account or a Facebook page, but she had become tech savvy by the time I reached out to her in 2014. I explained my project and told her that I hoped the families would benefit from the media attention.

"I want to keep my son's name alive," Shahnaz said. "Everyone has forgotten, but I can't."

Although I had many volunteers who helped, Shahnaz was a devoted and sensitive filmmaker. In a scene I'll never forget, Shahnaz struggled to push a young man named Bijan in a wheelchair up a steep hill on outskirts of Tehran. He was paralyzed after being shot by security forces. At the top of the hill, she is out of breath and he is overwhelmed with emotion. Neither can speak.

Shahnaz had no concept of the eight-and-a-half-hour time difference between Tehran and New York and took to calling me at all hours, sometimes in the middle of the night. She wanted to unburden herself. "I can't cry for Mostafa and I'm going crazy," she said. "I haven't cried since they forced us to bury him in the middle of the night. I need to cry but I can't."

She called often, and we spoke for hours about her son—what he was like, what he liked to do—and about my challenges living in New York. One night she called to say that she expected to be fired from her job and we talked till dawn. We both knew she ran the risk of getting arrested once the documentary was released.

In June 2016, my two-hour documentary was broadcast on Manoto TV. I had never abandoned the families of those who were killed in the 2009 protests. The brutality had fractured countless families. My focus had shifted to the issue of compulsory hijab and other human rights issues, but I hadn't forgotten those families. The documentary, which ran to two hours, was my response.

"If they arrest me, be my voice," Shahnaz pleaded. "Make sure the world knows about me. Don't forget me."

In the immediate aftermath of its airing, the authorities did not arrest any of the families who had participated in the film. But in January 2017, Shahnaz was arrested and taken to Evin prison. I was ready to hit back. The moment I heard of her arrest, I reached out to human rights organizations and urged them to call for her release. I had never met Shahnaz, but she had become my friend and I wasn't going to abandon her. I publicized her case on international media and launched a Twitterstorm for her release. After three weeks of constant media attention, the authorities released Shahnaz on bail.

My interactions with Shahnaz helped me toward another of my goals. I've said it many times: I wanted to help the Iranian people, especially women, find their voices. I wanted to move people to be the storytellers of their own lives, control their own narratives, I wanted everyone to be a leader.

People have not shied away from criticizing the My Stealthy Freedom campaign. I've addressed most, if not all, of the complaints in the past four years. It can get tiresome to explain to critics that, yes, it is true that I live in New York, but the photographs, videos, and messages of support are all from inside Iran. If the opposition to compulsory hijab were not so strong, the campaign would have withered years ago.

As My Stealthy Freedom entered its fourth year, it was time to raise the level of our activities. I held long discussions with other women's groups about holding weekly protests against compulsory hijab. I was determined to push ahead with the idea, but the timing had to be right.

Iranian environmentalists had started a campaign called "Tuesdays without cars," to encourage greater use of bicycles in order to cut down on Tehran's horrendous air pollution. On some days, schools are shut because of pollution levels. I hit upon the idea of "Wednesdays without compulsory hijab." But I hesitated. Riding a bicycle to reduce pollution was one thing; protesting the compulsory hijab laws, a regime red line, was another.

"Do you think the movement is ready?" Kambiz wondered.

"We are already in the streets," I replied. "Now we need to be more visible—to show our presence. We are not going away. The more visible we are, the more powerful we become."

Still I hesitated.

On May 19, 2017, Rouhani won reelection in a landslide by promising greater social freedoms. Quite frankly, I thought it was time to see if he could deliver on his promises. And I got my chance sooner than expected. All across Iran, there was an explosion of street parties to celebrate Rouhani's victory. The joy lasted only for one day, as security forces prevented Rouhani supporters from getting too carried away.

The next day, a group of women clad in long black chadors held a demonstration in Tehran. One carried a sign that read, in reference to the celebrations: PROTEST AGAINST UNVEILING AND INDECENCY. This unknown woman, a member of one of the conservative factions, called women who supported Rouhani and joined in the parties immoral.

I knew how to respond. Wearing a white dress, I launched the new campaign on my *Tablet* show on VOA.

Choosing not to wear the hijab is not an insult. It's a choice. It's a lifestyle. Just like your choice to wear a black veil. Black and white need to coexist in peace, not through aggression and insults. I am not against you. You shouldn't be against me.

Instead of calling on the morality police to suppress us with violence, let's stand together. We, too, have the right to live freely, not with fear, anxiety, and in secret.

Then I asked everyone to take to the streets every Wednesday, either without the hijab or wearing a white scarf or shawl. The men could wear white shirts or a white wristband.

"Our issue is not just a piece of cloth. It's about human dignity."

I was extremely nervous. For the first time, I had called on my supporters to come out in the open, on the streets, in shopping malls, in parks, and to be visible by wearing something white as a sign of protest against compulsory hijab. Wearing the white shawl was a powerful symbol of resistance. White was our color of resistance.

I chose #WhiteWednesdays for our new campaign. I discussed the idea with groups of feminists, and most warned that it was too dangerous. My instincts told me otherwise. My conversations with hundreds and hundreds of young Iranian women had convinced me that there was a great deal of passion and energy ready to be tapped.

As Tuesday night in Brooklyn edged closer to midnight, I made myself a pot of strong tea and planned to stay up all night to monitor developments in Iran, which is eight and a half hours ahead of New York. I had asked women to send photos and videos of themselves without veil and with their white shawls. My stomach was in knots. I fidgeted around the house, wondering what would happen if no one heeded my call for the new campaign.

Just after midnight, the first video arrived, followed by a photograph, followed by another, followed by another. Before long I had more than a hundred. I posted dozens of videos and photos. The women walked in the major streets of Tehran and other cities, quite unafraid, either without hijab or wearing a white shawl. In one video, one young woman excitedly talked to the camera as she walked down a main street: "I'm so pumped up to be in this campaign. I want to talk to you of my imprisonment. They've imposed hijab on me since I was seven," she said as she shook her head scarf loose. "I never felt committed to it and I won't be."

The following Tuesday night, again I was up monitoring the arrival of fresh videos of White Wednesday protests. Our movement had gone from social media pages to the streets of Iran. After the second week, the backlash started. The conservative factions called for Black Wednesdays, urging supporters to wear black head scarves and chadors on the same day that we were wearing white. Hardly anyone turned up. Another idea was to call for Red Wednesdays to defend compulsory hijab. Again, no takers. In the end, the various counterprotests against White Wednesday did not get off the ground.

Next came threats. Shadowy groups promoted by the Revolutionary Guards began issuing warnings of acid attacks on those wearing white. At universities, guards detained students wearing white head coverings. And still the protests continued unabated.

The Iranian authorities once again resorted to fake news. The story of my fake rape that had been discredited three years earlier was spread across social media accounts, from Instagram to Twitter to Telegram. I had dealt with the issue already, but it didn't matter. The attackers wanted to scare young women away from the campaign by hurting my reputation. The funny thing is that the attacks made us realize how desperate our enemies must be. We are more determined to continue. They are waging a war on our collective memory. By sullying my reputation, they hope to damage, besmirch, and nullify my message.

I'm not someone who is going to back down from threats. Not because I'm brave, but because Iranian women are brave. I am fighting not for myself but for the millions who want the freedom to choose. I had been attacked mercilessly and developed a thick skin. I had to protect other women.

Bahar, a beautiful twenty-something from a small town outside Tehran, sent me a short video that shows her walking around without a head scarf for the #WhiteWednesday campaign. I posted it the second week of the campaign. A few hours later, she sent me an urgent message asking me to take the video down. I didn't see her message till four hours later. Quickly, I called her.

"I was getting married soon, but my fiancé saw my video. He comes from a conservative family and insisted that I take it down to save his reputation. He said he would cancel the wedding if I didn't take the video down, because he didn't want to marry a woman who didn't wear the hijab. That's when I called you to save my marriage."

"I'm so sorry. I'll take it down now," I said at once. I didn't want to ruin her life.

"When I didn't hear back from you, I went to see my mother," she continued, as if I hadn't spoken. "I'd never talked to my mother about my feelings about hijab, but I had to tell her what I had done and how my fiancé was threatening to cancel the wedding. I was very nervous."

Bahar burst into tears as she spoke.

"'If your fiancé won't respect your choice now,'" my mother said, "'he's not going to respect it later, either. Don't ruin your life. Call off the wedding.' And that's what I did. And I want you to keep posting my video."

"Are you sure? I can easily remove it," I said, offering her another chance to change her mind. "With one video, you've canceled your wedding."

"I just changed the course of my life, but I'm a lot happier."

And there is Nafas, a young woman from Tehran. She sent me a video of herself in a white shawl, addressing the camera. She said she was wearing white every Wednesday to protest compulsory hijab. Her father told her that he had seen the video, and he asked her not to make new ones.

"How did your father see the video?"

"Everyone I know has seen the video. The White Wednesday videos are more popular than you think."

Then Nafas called me the following week.

"My father is not going to work on Wednesdays," she said, "to stop me from going out and making videos. 'If they arrest you, they'll throw you in cells full of spiders and all kind of bugs. How can you cope there when you are afraid of a little beetle?' he asked, and I told him, 'If your generation had put up with spending a few days in jail, then maybe we wouldn't have had to endure compulsory hijab.'"

Nafas was ecstatic.

I am not the first campaigner against compulsory hijab, but I hope to be the last one. My journey has seen me leave my village and my country because I want the freedom to determine my own identity and to be myself rather than assume a role that I don't believe in.

The story of Nafas and her father transports me back to when I clashed regularly with AghaJan in Ghomikola over my hijab. I wanted to climb trees and run in the fields and ride a bicycle. All were forbidden to me. As I grew older, I had to rebel to find myself.

The truth is that we need to create a free Iran. A country where people can freely choose. The future of Iran will be determined by rebels like Nafas, Bahar, and others. And me. I want an Iran that is democratic—where women have equal rights.

Iran today is like a battlefield.

On one hand, the enforcers of compulsory hijab have access to guns and batons, unlimited cash, and a pliant, subservient media. In 2016, the government allocated 6 trillion tomans ($1.7 billion) for the protection of hijab—compared to 174 million tomans ($49 million) for the protection of the environment.

On the other hand, we have women and men whose weapons are computers, mobile phones, and social media: Twitter, Facebook, Instagram, and more.

I'm a child of an Iran that carries many scars—the scar of the revolution, the wounds of an eight-year war, the lacerations of mass executions, the daily nicks and slashes of discrimination that women face daily. I now carry the scar of exile. By themselves each of these is enough to knock you out for good. There are periods when darkness prevails and threatens to swallow you whole. To overcome the despair and the country's dark era, I think about my mother's words and open my eyes as wide as I can and stare out into the darkness. The human rights situation in Iran, and the situation with respect to women's rights, is dark and gloomy. But I'm sure that young Iranian women are as brave as previous generations of young women, and that they have opened their eyes wider than ever before to win over the darkness.

I don't know when I will return to Iran. Living in exile has been painful. I've been thrown out of my house. I've managed to sneak back in via social media and satellite television. I'm out of Iran, but it's as if I never left the country.

When I was growing up, I used to watch the clerics, the Friday prayer leaders, and other officials of the Islamic Republic on our fourteen-inch black-and-white television. Now the same clerics hear my voice from satellite TV and on Facebook. They know my name. It is not only my voice they are hearing. It is the voice of millions of Iranian women who are no longer willing to be silent. The women of Iran want to be free to make their own choices.

That's why the struggle will continue…until we all feel the wind in our hair.

EPILOGUE

On December 27, 2017, a Wednesday, Vida Movahed, a thirty-one-year-old mother dressed in all black, calmly climbed a five-foot-tall utility box in Enqelab Street (Revolution Street), one of Tehran's busiest, removed her head scarf, tied it to a stick, and waved it for all to see. Three different witnesses filmed her short protest against compulsory hijab and sent it to me. She was arrested, but the video of her act of defiance, her resistance, spread through social media with unparalleled speed.

The next day, small street protests in the city of Mashhad over high prices and corruption quickly spilled over into some eighty-five other cities and towns. A police crackdown on protestors and social media ended the unrest, leaving 25 dead and 3,700 arrested. But throughout the protests and for days after, Movahed's single act of defiance captured the attention of many activists.

The protests over the economy ended, but Movahed's fate concerned us. I contacted many organizations and media outlets to publicize her case. At the time, we didn't even know Movahed's name. I created a hashtag in Persian "Where is the girl of Revolution Street?" which was retweeted more than 19,000 times. One of my key supporters, Shahparak Shajarizadeh, said we should all emulate Movahed's act of defiance, and that prompted other women from the #WhiteWednesdays campaign to stage similar protests in different towns and cities across Iran. On January 24, 2018, Amnesty International, the London-based rights group, called on Iranian authorities to "immediately and unconditionally" release Movahed, who had been "protesting peacefully against the country's mandatory Islamic dress code."

In their statement, Amnesty called on the Rouhani government to "end the persecution of women who speak out against compulsory veiling, and abolish this discriminatory and humiliating practice." United Nations special rapporteur on Iran Asma Jahangir had called on Iran six months earlier to end its compulsory hijab laws. The momentum was building against compulsory hijab.

Two days after Amnesty's statement, Movahed was quietly released.

Then other women took her protest further. On January 29, six women in different parts of Tehran, some carrying white scarves, others green and red, also made the symbolic gesture, removing their head scarves and waving them for all to see. One protester said, "I took my scarf off because I'm tired of our government telling me what to do with my body."

More and more women took to the streets to remove their head scarves in public—on busy street corners, standing tall on utility boxes, platforms, anything that elevated them so they could be seen. The issue of compulsory hijab, a topic that had been taboo for almost forty years, had burst into the open. Everyone was now talking about compulsory hijab, newspaper columns were devoted to the issue; even politicians entered the debate. It was no longer a trivial issue. The law wasn't going to change overnight, but women were not giving up.

The security forces were not as enlightened as the rest of the population. At least thirty anti-hijab activists, including twenty-two-year-old Shima Babaei, were arrested. Some women protesters were roughed up; at least three suffered broken bones. Shahparak was followed for two weeks before she too was arrested as she took off her head scarf on a busy sidewalk. She was released when her family posted bail.

Every morning, I face the day proud of my sisters who are bravely challenging the antiquated and discriminatory compulsory hijab laws, and at the same time I fear for their safety as I remember my own prison days. And yet the fight goes on, because Iranian women want the freedom to choose. After the arrests, I received a selfie video from a young woman who stood outside the local Basij offices in Tehran and defiantly took off her white head scarf. As she stared into the camera, she loudly said: "Our weapon is a white scarf, and today I'm here to ask why have Shima Babaei and others been arrested. Even if you arrest me, be assured that there will be many more who will come out to protest.

"I'm ready to pay the price if it will bring a free Iran."

ACKNOWLEDGMENTS

This book is about my journey from a village in northern Iran to the metropolis that is New York City, a journey of self-discovery in which I forged my identity after I learned to say NO. It is a tale that may be familiar to many women.

I owe a special debt to many people who helped me on this path, picked me up when I fell, and encouraged me to go on. It is now nine years since I boarded a flight out of Iran, but I've never forgotten how it is to be Iranian. Today, I'm in more contact with people from my country than I ever was when I actually lived there.

The idea for this book came from Sheryl Sandberg, who in our first meeting at Facebook encouraged me to write my memoirs. I had written three semi-autobiographical books in Persian when I was in Iran, dealing with my divorce and expulsion from the Parliament and the disputed 2009 presidential elections, but I wasn't convinced that my story would appeal to a Western audience. I'm grateful to Sheryl for her support and belief in me.

In Iran, in addition to my newspaper columns, I maintained a number of blogs in which I wrote personal stories about growing up in my village and life in Tehran. Parts of this book are based on my newspaper articles, columns, and blogs.

I have changed the names of my high school friends to make sure they don't face any repercussions.

This book would not be possible without the help of friends and colleagues in Iran who helped me to get to this stage. Soudabeh Q. and Nargess A. deserve special thanks for being towers of strength that I could count on as I started my journalism.

Acknowledgments

Warm and heartfelt thanks to imprisoned women's rights activist Atena Daemi, who never wavered in her support for our campaign against compulsory hijab, even from inside prison, where she was sent for defending human rights.

I owe an enormous debt to gratitude to the many friends and supporters who still reside in Iran; I hope they know who they are and how deeply they are appreciated.

I cannot do justice to those who listened at length to my tales and encouraged me to go on, especially during of periods when I was under constant attack from Iranian government proxies and cyber trolls: Mon T., Karim Sadjadpour, Mina and Evan Siegel, Neda Shahidyazdani.

My campaign against compulsory hijab benefited from the support of many thinkers, academics, lawyers, and activists. I learned a lot from the indefatigable lawyer Nasrin Sotoudeh, and from women's rights activists Mehrangiz Kar, Shadi Sadr, Tahmineh Milani, Shadi Amin, and Shirin Ebadi.

Special thanks to some of the best and brightest of the women and men who have been indispensable in their support, constructive criticism, and good cheer. I am grateful to Parvaneh Hosseini, Leila Alikarami, Saghar Qyasi, Fariba Davoodi Mohajer, Nasim Sahra, Azadeh Davainchi, Naeime Doustdar, Monireh Kazemi, Shahla Shafiq, Marmar Moshfeghi, Moniro Ravanipour, Leili Nikounazar, Parvaneh Vahidmanesh, Nasrin Afzali, Reza Haghighatnejad, Sepideh Jodeyri, Aida Ghajar, Azadeh Assadi, Vahid Yücesoy, Pouria Zerati, Saman Arbabi, Mostafa Azizi, Hamed R., and Sharagim Zand.

I feel extremely lucky to have landed at Little, Brown, where my editor, Judy Clain, provided enormous support with her clear vision and enthusiasm, and guided me to make this book better. Thanks to Craig Young, Reagan Arthur, and the amazing team at Little, Brown: the publicist and marketing geniuses Katharine Myers and Lauren Velasquez, the wonderful Mario Pulice for his art direction, Deborah Feingold for her extraordinary photographs. Words cannot describe what a pleasure it was to work with Betsy Uhrig and Janet Byrne, who patiently helped me finish the book even as I was consumed with running my various campaigns.

I want to thank Jennifer Walsh and my brilliant agent, Claudia Ballard, of William Morris Entertainment, who shepherded this book to publication

Special thanks to Naireh Tohidi for catching errors and historical inaccuracies, and helping the book reach another level.

I'm indebted to my parents: my mother, Zarrin Khanom, and AghaJan, who love me dearly even though they cannot leave the country to visit me. I owe boundless thanks to my brothers, Ali and Mohsen, who recounted our family history and have always backed my campaigns even at huge personal cost to themselves; and to my sister, Mina, who accepted our differences.

To my son, Pouyan: you made me laugh, made me cry, but always made me proud. I spent so little time with you, but now you've grown into a fine young man. My love and thanks to my family in exile, Parvin Foroohar, who has been like a second mother to me, and my stepchildren, Darya and Bahman, for giving me positive energy, making me laugh, and letting me be a kid again.

Last and not least, my cowriter, Kambiz Foroohar, my love and the rock in my life, who heard many of my stories again and again without complaint and has kept me going with his sense of humor and ceaseless encouragement.